THE ARDEN SHAKESPEARE

THIRD SERIES

General Editors: Richard Proudfoot, Ann Thompson
and David Scott Kastan

SHAKESPEARE'S SONNETS

THE ARDEN SHAKESPEARE

*Second Series

THE ARDEN SHAKESPEARE

SHAKESPEARE'S SONNETS

Edited by
KATHERINE DUNCAN-JONES

For my mother and my daughters

The Arden website is at
http://www.ardenshakespeare.com

The general editors of the Arden Shakespeare have been
W. J. Craig and R. H. Case (first series 1899-1944)
Una Ellis-Fermor, Harold F. Brooks, Harold Jenkins and
Brian Morris (second series 1946-82)

Present general editors (third series)
Richard Proudfoot, Ann Thompson and David Scott Kastan

This edition of *Shakespeare's Sonnets*, by Katherine Duncan-Jones
first published in 1997 by Thomas Nelson and Sons Ltd

Published by The Arden Shakespeare
Reprinted 2004

Editorial matter © 1997 Katherine Duncan-Jones

Arden Shakespeare is an imprint of Thomson Learning

Thomson Learning
High Holborn House
50-51 Bedford Row
London WC1R 4LR

Printed in Croatia

British Library Cataloguing in Publication Data
A catalogue record for this book is available from the British Library
Library of Congress Cataloguing in Publication Data
A catalogue record has been requested

ISBN 1-903436-56-7 (hbk)
NPN 9 8 7 6 5 4
ISBN 1-903436-57-5 (pbk)
NPN 9 8 7 6

CONTENTS

The Editor

Katherine Duncan-Jones has published well over forty articles on Elizabethan and Jacobean literature. Her biography *Sir Philip Sidney: Courtier Poet* appeared in 1991, and her *Ungentle Shakespeare: Scenes from his Life* was published by the Arden Shakespeare in 2001. She is a Tutorial Fellow in English at Somerville College, Oxford, and a Fellow of the Royal Society of Literature.

ILLUSTRATIONS

GENERAL EDITORS' PREFACE

The Arden Shakespeare is now nearly one hundred years old. The earliest volume in the first series, Edward Dowden's *Hamlet*, was published in 1899. Since then the Arden Shakespeare has become internationally recognized and respected. It is now widely acknowledged as the pre-eminent Shakespeare series, valued by scholars, students, actors, and 'the great variety of readers' alike for its readable and reliable texts, its full annotation and its richly informative introductions.

We have aimed in the third Arden edition to maintain the quality and general character of its predecessors, preserving the commitment to presenting the work as it has been shaped in history. While each individual volume will necessarily have its own emphasis in the light of the unique possibilities and problems posed by the work, the edition as a whole, like the earlier Ardens, insists upon the highest standards of scholarship and upon attractive and accessible presentation.

Newly edited from the original quarto and folio editions, the texts are presented in fully modernized form, with a textual apparatus that records all substantial divergences from those early printings. The notes and introductions focus on the conditions and possibilities of meaning that editors and critics have discovered in the work. While building upon the rich history of scholarly activity that has long shaped our understanding of Shakespeare's texts, this third series of the Arden Shakespeare is made necessary and possible by a new generation's encounter with Shakespeare, engaging with the works and their complex relation to the culture in which they were – and continue to be – produced.

THE TEXT

On each page of the work itself, readers will find a passage of text supported by commentary and textual notes. In the text itself, unfamiliar typographic conventions have been avoided in order to minimize obstacles to the reader. Elided forms in the early texts are spelt out in full wherever they indicate a usual late-twentieth-century pronunciation that requires no special indication. Marks of elision are retained where they are necessary guides to the scansion and pronunciation of the line. Final -ed in past tense and participial forms of verbs is always printed as -ed, without accent, never as -'d, but wherever the required pronunciation diverges from modern usage a note in the commentary draws attention to the fact. Where the final -ed should be given syllabic value contrary to modern usage, e.g.

> Lest my bewailed guilt should do thee shame,
>
> *(Son* 36.10)

the note will take the form

> 10 **bewailed** bewailèd

COMMENTARY AND TEXTUAL NOTES

Notes in the commentary, for which a major source will be the *Oxford English Dictionary*, offer glossarial and other explication of verbal difficulties; they may also include discussion of points of interpretation and, in relevant cases, substantial extracts from Shakespeare's source material. Editors will not usually offer glossarial notes for words adequately defined in the *Concise Oxford Dictionary* or *Webster's Ninth New Collegiate Dictionary*, but in cases of doubt they will include notes. Attention, however, will be drawn to places where more than one likely interpretation can be proposed and to significant verbal and syntactic complexity. Notes preceded by * involve discussion of textual variants or readings emended from the early edition(s) on which the text is based.

The textual notes are designed to let readers know when the edited text diverges from the early edition(s) on which it is based. Wherever this happens the note will record the rejected reading of the early edition(s), in original spelling, and the source of the reading adopted in this edition. Other forms from the early edition(s) recorded in these notes will include some spellings of particular interest or significance. The textual notes take a form that has been in use since the nineteenth century. This comprises, first: line reference, reading adopted in the text and closing square bracket; then: abbreviated reference, in italic, to the earliest edition to adopt the accepted reading, italic semicolon and noteworthy alternative reading(s), each with abbreviated italic reference to its source. Distinctive spellings of the basic text follow the square bracket without indication of source. Names enclosed in brackets indicate originators of conjectural emendations when these did not originate in an edition of the text, or when this edition records a conjecture not accepted into its text.

PREFACE

Pope's exclamation at the beginning of *The Rape of the Lock*, 'What mighty contests rise from trivial things', applies supremely to *Shakespeare's Sonnets*. Any and every detail of these poems may be the occasion of angry dispute, and many have been so, though I have tried not to get too much involved in such controversies. With reference to the text of individual sonnets, the minutest features of spelling, punctuation and format have momentous consequences for resonance and meaning. I have never felt more strongly than when working on this text the force of Oscar Wilde's account of a writer's hard labours: spending the whole morning putting in a comma, and the whole afternoon taking it out. In the belief not only that such matters are immensely important, but also that the 1609 Quarto printing reflects the minutiae, as well as the substance, of a copy manuscript certainly authorized, and perhaps also penned, by Shakespeare himself, I have attempted to represent the details of this text as faithfully as the requirements of modernization will allow. This is, for instance, the first edited text of *Sonnets* to include the two pairs of empty parentheses which follow the six-couplet poem numbered 126. While previous editors have suggested that these were inserted by the printers, who noticed that the poem was composed only of twelve lines, not fourteen, I think this an unlikely intervention. We know that George Eld's compositors were accustomed to working for such meticulously niggling writers as Ben Jonson, and a detailed analysis of their 1607–8 publications by Peter Murray suggests that they habitually reproduced the characteristic spelling forms they encountered, rather than imposing 'house style'.[1]

---

1   Murray, *passim.*

Contextually, also, matters which may not seem immediately of vital interest or importance here are so. Paramount is the question of date. The weight of tradition has favoured an early date, placing *Sonnets* close in time to the two narrative poems, in 1593–4, and bracketing all three non-dramatic works together as probably connected with the patronage of the young Henry Wriothesley, Earl of Southampton. Biographically, for many Victorian and Edwardian critics, this dating made it possible to sideline *Sonnets* as an uncharacteristic, and perhaps in some respects compromising or even disgraceful, product of Shakespeare's youth. The writing of them could be seen as a brilliant but embarrassing folly which he left behind him as his career as a dramatist developed, rather as he had left behind him his (supposed) early exploits as a poacher of Sir Thomas Lucy's deer. In the present edition it is proposed that, on the contrary, though we may never discover how early some individual sonnets or versions of sonnets were composed, there is good reason to believe that the whole sequence as published in 1609 was put into its final shape after 1603, and possibly quite close to its printing. It is for this reason that so much space is given, in the Introduction, to the issue of dating, for the evidence and arguments presented here represent a radical departure from previous study. And as for the compromising or 'disgraceful' elements of the sonnets: their homoeroticism is here confronted positively, and is newly contextualized within the powerfully 'homosocial' world of James I's court. The case for their association with Southampton largely collapses, but the case for their connection with William Herbert, Earl of Pembroke, becomes newly plausible. The 'Pembrokian' hypothesis is re-examined, with the citation of some new supportive evidence. As a whole, the sequence can be seen, not as a youthful folly, but as the mature and considered work of a successful professional writer.

Some of what is done here was anticipated in John Kerrigan's excellent Penguin edition (1986). For instance, he too included *A Lover's Complaint*, and argued for its place as a structural component of the published sequence. However, there appears still to be strong resistance to this poem, which is rarely included in discussion of *Sonnets*, or, indeed, of any of Shakespeare's work. The decision of the New Cambridge editors to place *A Lover's Complaint* with the narrative poems, and to exclude it altogether from Blakemore Evans's 1996 edition of *Sonnets*, suggests that the case for its authenticity and integrity needs to be reaffirmed. It is for this reason that its formal and thematic place in the sequence is discussed in some detail in the penultimate section of the Introduction. A matter which Kerrigan did not address is the form of the sequence's title, *Shakespeare's Sonnets*. Though some other editors, most notably Stephen Booth, have used this form of title, its authority and meaning have never before been fully examined.

Because so much of the contextualization of *Shakespeare's Sonnets* here is essentially new, priority has been given to matters of date and context, rather than to a full chronicle of the work's critical history. But if the present text commands acceptance, there will be much fresh work for critics to do in the next millennium, as they come to terms with the exciting complexities of this extraordinary work of the Jacobean Shakespeare.

In preparing this edition, my first debt is to previous editors of *Shakespeare's Sonnets*, and above all to the great Edmond Malone, whose 1780 edition was the first to take this text seriously and to undo the harm done to it by the publisher John Benson in 1640. H.E. Rollins's wonderfully encyclopaedic two-volume variorum has been my daily resource for more than three years. I have also derived much illumination from Ingram and Redpath and from Stephen Booth. John Kerrigan's 1986 Penguin edition is so close in time, and so excellent in its subtlety and scholarship, that I have avoided consulting it as often as I would have liked, for fear of relying on it excessively. Several people have helped me by perusing sugared sections of the notes or the Introduction or both. First and foremost among these private friends is my mother, Mrs E.E. Duncan-Jones; others include Dr Henry Woudhuysen, Professor Steve May and Dr Julia Griffin. Constant and generous communications on the vexed matter of dating from Professor Kent Hieatt have ensured that I could never succumb to the temptation to shelve it. I have also derived enormous help and inspiration from glimpses of Professor Helen Vendler's work in progress, and from a conversation with her in Los Angeles, during which among other things she showed me how to deal with those 'rebel powers' in sonnet 146. Kevin Billington lent me videos of the readings from *Shakespeare's Sonnets* made for Channel Four under his direction in 1983: if the 'performance history' of these non-dramatic texts ever comes to be written, these deserve pride of place. Others who have given me specialist help include John Carey, Jeremy Catto, Martin Dodsworth, Barbara Harvey, Ernst Honigmann, John Kerrigan, Don McKenzie, Paul Morgan, Jan Piggott, Judith Priestman, Christopher Ricks, Geraldo de Sousa, Fiona Stafford, Brian Vickers, George Walton Williams, Michael Webb, Bee Wilson and Emily Wilson. Gryszina Cooper, at the Centre for Computing in the Humanities, has twice come to my rescue at moments of electronic collapse compounded by human fallibility. Libraries and archives where I have worked happily include, in addition to my regular haunt, the Bodleian Library in Oxford, the British Library, the Public Record Office, the Stratford Records Office, the Shakespeare Institute, Westminster Abbey, the Henry E. Huntington Library, Trinity College, Cambridge, Dulwich College Library and Balliol College, Oxford. At the stage of near-completion this text benefited enormously from the keen eyes and diverse perceptions of Richard Proudfoot and Ann Thompson, and at a later stage still from the meticulous scrutiny of the copy-editor, Roger Fallon. My own stubbornness should be blamed for those errors and deficiencies that survive their labours. I owe my college, Somerville, grateful thanks for support and friendship, and in particular for a term of sabbatical leave in the spring of 1996. Many Somerville students over the years have opened my eyes to readings I hadn't thought of – so many that it would be invidious even to attempt to record all their names.

Katherine Duncan-Jones
Oxford

INTRODUCTION

DATE

External evidence

The public story of *Shakespeare's Sonnets* began late in 1598, with Francis Meres's mouthwatering account in *Palladis Tamia* (which had been entered in the Stationers' Register on 7th September):

> As the soule of *Euphorbus* was thought to live in *Pythagoras*: so the sweete wittie soule of *Ouid* liues in mellifluous & hony-tongued *Shakespeare*, witnes his *Venus* and *Adonis*, his *Lucrece,* his sugred Sonnets among his private friends, &c.[1]

For enthusiastic book-buyers, it might appear that in the following year, 1599, it had become possible to join the fortunate ranks of Shakespeare's 'private friends', for William Jaggard published a small octavo volume called *THE PASSIONATE PILGRIME. By W. Shakespeare*, to which were appended six further lyrics introduced by a separate title-page, *SONNETS. To sundry notes of Musicke*. Only the three sonnets which open *The Passionate Pilgrim*, and one further sonnet and lyric, can be confidently claimed as Shakespeare's. The two opening poems were later to appear in the 1609 Quarto (Q) as sonnets 138 and 144, and the other three were taken from the 1598 Quarto of *Love's Labour's Lost*. However, most early readers must quite naturally have assumed that all twenty poems in *The Passionate Pilgrim* (PP) were Shakespeare's, and that they corresponded with the sonnets to which Meres referred. Evidently the little volume sold well, for

---

1 Francis Meres, *Palladis Tamia. Wits Treasury. Being the Second Part of Wits Commonwealth* (1598), fols 281ᵛ–2ʳ.

two editions seem to have been published in close succession, the first surviving only as a fragment.[1] But for discerning readers of contemporary poetry, many of whom, like Francis Meres and John Weever,[2] must have also been admirers of Shakespeare's plays, *The Passionate Pilgrim* was surely disappointing, in both quality and quantity. Such readers may naturally have concluded that Meres had over-praised Shakespeare's 'sugred Sonnets', which were not, after all, such delicate sweetmeats. Slight, quirky, occasionally sententious and frequently obscene, Jaggard's miscellany did the fast-rising playwright no great credit. Indeed, *PP* 2 and 9 (one an authentic Shakespeare poem, the other probably not), with their unattractive allusions to the female genitalia either as 'hell' or as a 'wound', might have caused readers alert to such nuance to wonder whether Meres's '&c.' concealed another such allusion,[3] and characterized Shakespeare – who was, according to Meres, a reanimated Ovid – as a writer who specialized in making ingeniously unpleasant allusions to that part of the body.

According to the later testimony of Thomas Heywood, Shakespeare had been 'much offended' with William Jaggard, 'that altogether unknowne to him presumed to make so bold with his name'[4]. In 1612 Jaggard had compounded his offence by bringing out a third edition of *The Passionate Pilgrim*, which was now plumped out with the addition of two epistles and other material from Thomas Heywood's *Troia Britannica* (1608). It was this which provoked Heywood's public remonstrance in *An Apology for Actors*. Heywood was evidently afraid that Shakespeare might blame him for this latest piracy and misattribution, since Jaggard had been his publisher for the authorized *Troia Britannica*, and was stung into making a public attack on Jaggard by the need to clear his own name. It should not be assumed, simply because there is little documentary evidence

1   Cf. *TxC*, 455.
2   John Weever, *Epigrammes* (1599) sig. E6ʳ.
3   Cf. *RJ* (First Quarto) 2.1.37–8, 'O that she were / An open *Et Cetera*'; *2H4* 2.4.181, 'And are etceteras nothings?'; Partridge, *Bawdy*, 109.
4   Thomas Heywood, *An Apology for Actors* (1612), sig. G4.

2

close in time to their publication, that Shakespeare did not care about the two 1599 publications of *The Passionate Pilgrim*. Heywood, one of the earliest admirers and closest imitators of Shakespeare's first published poem, *Venus and Adonis*,[1] was most likely well placed to know for certain both that Shakespeare had been angry with Jaggard in 1599, and that he was even more so when he repeated the offence in 1612. Jaggard's 1612 piracy was all the more brazen in its audacity because, as Heywood said, 'he [Shakespeare] since, to do himself right, hath published them in his own name'. That is, in 1609 Shakespeare had assumed control of his own text of his *Sonnets*, by selling the collection to Thorpe and giving it the title *Shakespeare's Sonnets*. Judging by the extreme scarcity of surviving copies of *The Passionate Pilgrim*, Jaggard's little venture had done vexingly well, and it may have seemed for the time being to have spoiled the market for authentic 'sugred Sonnets' by Shakespeare. Indeed, it probably contributed importantly to the eleven-year gap between Meres's succulent reference in 1598 and the eventual publication of Q in 1609 – although, as I shall argue in more detail, the 1609 sonnets may correspond only partially with those 'sugred' ones referred to by Meres.

One piece of evidence has been oddly neglected. It may be that Shakespeare in fact took immediate measures to put right the wrong done to him by Jaggard in 1599, if we suppose that he is the 'W.S.' in the following Stationers' Register entry for 3 January 1599/1600:

Eleazar Edgar. Entred for his copye under the handes of the Wardens.

> A booke called *Amours* by J.D. with certain *other sonnetes* by W.S.

As H.E. Rollins records, Sir Sidney Lee did not believe that this 'W.S.' could possibly be Shakespeare. Lee argued, with characteristic

1 Duncan-Jones, 'Red and white', 495–7.

3

vehemence but without any evidence, for William Smith. J.Q. Adams, on the other hand, felt that this 'W.S.' could perfectly well be our man. Fence-sitting, Rollins asked 'Who shall decide, when doctors disagree?'[1] However, it seems to be Lee's dismissal that has held the field in the later twentieth century. Schoenbaum, for instance, failed even to include this entry among surviving documents possibly referring to Shakespeare. Yet it does seem perfectly believable both that Shakespeare may have prepared a collection of his sonnets late in 1599, provoked by Jaggard's piratical and mediocre *Passionate Pilgrim*, and that at one time he planned to publish it. His collaborator in the enterprise could have been John Davies (later 'Sir'), John Davies of Hereford, John Dickenson, John Donne (most excitingly) – or some other J.D. If he was acting in conjunction with Sir John Davies, the volume might have been connected in some way with the somewhat mysterious ?1599 publication *EPIGRAMMES and ELEGIES. By I.D. and C.M.*, which consisted of the dead Marlowe's translation of Ovid's *Elegies* accompanied by Sir John Davies's *Epigrams*. A connection with Davies is suggested by the Huntington Library copy of *The Passionate Pilgrim*, which is bound up, in an apparently contemporary vellum binding, both with the 1599 octavo *Venus and Adonis* and with Davies's *Epigrammes*. The *Epigrammes* excited official disapproval, being included among other scurrilous and libellous works ordered to be burned, by order of the Bishop of London, in June 1599.[2] If the 'J.D.' of '*Amours*' was Sir John Davies, he could well have decided not to jeopardize his reputation with further print publication of his own epigrams, but to limit his poems, such as the 'cobwebb of my invention' which he seems to have composed for Robert Cecil in January 1599/1600,[3] to manuscript circulation within a coterie. In that case, the title '*Amours*' would refer most readily to Ovid's *Amores*, suggesting a renewed attempt by Davies to get Marlowe's translations into

1   Rollins, 2.55
2   Millar MacLure in Marlowe, *Poems*, xxxi–xxxii; Robert Krueger in Davies, 379.
3   Krueger in Davies, xxxviii; BL MS Lansdowne 88, fol. 4ʳ.

print, this time with a perhaps less controversial accompaniment. Given the number of publications of popular works that have disappeared altogether in this period, there is even a remote possibility that J.D.'s '*Amours*' along with W.S.'s '*sonnetes*' actually did reach print, but has left no surviving exemplars. If this were the case, and the author of the sonnets Shakespeare, the title-page description of *Shakespeare's Sonnets* in Q as 'Neuer before Imprinted' might serve to assert the independence of (most of?) this sequence from the J.D./W.S. collection, as well as from *The Passionate Pilgrim*. Eleazar Edgar, who entered the double work in the Register, emerged in the early Jacobean period as an up-market bookseller and publisher, whose earliest recorded publications were editions of the newly acceded monarch's *Daemonologie* and *The True Lawe of Free Monarchies* (*STC*, 14365, 14410). Other publications by Edgar indicate connections with the theatre. They include Dekker's *The Double PP* (1605); Marston's *Sophonisba: The Wonder of Women* (1606); Francis Beaumont's *The Woman Hater* (1607); Middleton's *A Mad World My Masters* (1608); and Cyril Tourneur's *A Funerall Poem . . . Upon Sir Francis Vere* (1609). The 1600 Stationers' Register entry offers at least a possibility that Shakespeare prepared some sonnets for publication early in 1600, motivated by a desire to put right Jaggard's damaging misappropriation and misidentification of his work. There may or may not have been a serious intention to publish. The 'staying entry' of 'as you lyke yt / a booke' on 4 August of the same year may be analogous. The chief purpose of the entry in the Register of '*sonnetes* by W.S.' could have been to prohibit further piracy by Jaggard. Indeed, the fact that twelve years elapsed between the two profitable *PP* printings of 1599 and Jaggard's expanded edition of 1612 offers some evidence that Jaggard was indeed in some way restrained during the intervening years, and obliquely supports the identification of this 'W.S.' with Shakespeare.

If the 'certain *other sonnetes* by W.S.' entered for publication in January 1600 are taken to be Shakespeare's, it is possible to speculate a little further on which particular sonnets these may have been. Of course, they could have been poems of which we have no knowledge because they never saw the light. But if the publication, or staying entry, was intended above all to set right the wrong done by Jaggard, it seems a fair presumption that the collection included 'When my love swears that she is made of truth' (*PP* 1; *Son* 138) and 'Two loves I have, of comfort and despair' (*PP* 2; *Son* 144), the two authentic sonnets with which *The Passionate Pilgrim* opened. Both poems, but especially the second, seem to call for a fuller poetic and narrative context in which the speaker's treacherous lust and triangular passion are more fully analysed. It is unlikely that the group included the *Love's Labour's Lost* poems, since these had already seen print in the 1598 Quarto of the play, and presumably also in the lost 'Bad' Quarto in 1597. Perhaps, then, these 'certain *other sonnetes*' included or comprised the 'dark lady' sequence, later to appear as *Sonnets* 127–54: a sequence of twenty-eight darkly satirical heterosexual poems whose moral and artistic instability seems to reflect a male disgust with the lunar, menstrual, cycle alluded to in their number. Labelling this group of sonnets, unpoetically, 'Zone 4', Kent Hieatt and his collaborators have found in it 'a high proportion of early rare words', and 'no late ones'.[1] Both external and internal evidence suggest that this sequence may have corresponded with the 'sugred Sonnets' referred to by Meres, and that it was essentially complete in 1599, undergoing no more than a little stylistic tinkering before publication in 1609. The other part of the sequence most probably belonging to a period before 1600 is the opening 1–17, but the arguments for this belong to a later section.

There is no dispute about the volume to which the Stationers' Register entry of 20 May 1609 refers –

1   Hieatt, 'When?', 91.

20 May

Tho. Thorpe. Entred for his copie under the handes of m*aste*r Wilson and m*aste*r Lownes Wardenes a booke called Shakespeares sonnettes vjd.[1]

Not only is Shakespeare's surname here given in full; the title corresponds with that on the title-page of Q, 'SHAKE-SPEARES SONNETS'. Exactly when in 1609 the volume was published cannot be established, because of the resounding silence into which it fell. A note on the back of a letter to Edward Alleyn, dated 19 June [1609], records under the heading 'Howshold stuff' the purchase of 'a book. Shaksper sonetts 5d'[2]. But this is almost certainly a forgery by John Payne Collier, inserted by him in a convenient space on an authentic document, as was his habitual practice.[3] Collier himself never published this reference, and Rollins records it as Alleyn's,[4] but it is nevertheless highly suspect.

'Howshold stuff' would be a curious heading under which to record the purchase of such a book, and it is a phrase rather suspiciously corresponding with *The Taming of the Shrew*, Induction.2.140.[5] In his account books Alleyn frequently refers to expenditure under the heading 'Howshold' or 'Howshold charges', but not, elsewhere, 'Howshold stuff'[6] – and to write out such a heading for a single fivepenny purchase would be rather odd. Some of the letter forms, especially 's' and 'k', differ somewhat from those in the other accounts written above. Collier and his assistant Peter Cunningham were accomplished and intelligent forgers and fabricators, and seem here to have provided after-comers with what would, if authentic, be most

---

1 Reproduced in Schoenbaum, *Records*, 219.
2 Reproduced in *Henslowe Papers*, vol. 2, item 12.
3 See Race's article in *N&Q*; note also the succession of further studies of Collier's activities by the same scholar in the same journal.
4 Rollins, 2.54.
5 See Race.
6 Cf. Dulwich College Alleyn Papers MS VIII (1594–1616) and IX (1617–22).

precious: testimony to the precise date of publication of Q, the price at which it was sold, and its eager acquisition by one of Shakespeare's theatrical associates. Sadly, however, it cannot be trusted, and if this document is discounted, we are left with little evidence of the price at which it was sold, though an early owner of the Huntington (formerly Steevens) copy has written on the title-page 'pretium – 1ˢ – N: L: S:'. If a shilling was indeed the original selling price, this was a rather expensive quarto. The survival of thirteen copies, most in good condition, suggests that the volume did not undergo the kind of enthusiastic thumbing that destroyed hundreds of early copies of Shakespeare's earliest published poem, *Venus and Adonis*. Also, whereas *Venus and Adonis* went through at least sixteen editions in Shakespeare's lifetime, *Shakespeare's Sonnets* was not reprinted even once – and this despite the fame of the Jacobean Shakespeare. We might also compare the fate of another 1609 publication, *Troilus and Cressida*, whose quarto was printed early in the year, and of which only four copies survive. Assuming that the size of the print-runs was the same, the evidence of survival-rates suggests that *Troilus and Cressida* was three times as popular among readers as *Shakespeare's Sonnets*.

The reason for the popularity of *Troilus and Cressida*, along with the numerous other play texts published in 1608–10, may lie in a further area of external evidence that provides an important context for the dating of *Shakespeare's Sonnets*. This is the incidence of plague outbreaks, which has been surprisingly neglected by previous scholars. Both of Shakespeare's narrative poems, *Venus and Adonis*, 1593, and *Lucrece*, 1594, had been published during plague outbreaks which were severe enough to cause civic orders for the public theatres to be closed. A consequent loss of income, and a decision to turn, instead, to print publication, looking to a reward from a courtly patron, readily explains the place of these two poems in the chronology of Shakespeare's works. By the period of Jaggard's *Passionate Pilgrim* Shakespeare's economic dependence on, and investment

in, the public theatre was very much greater, following his mem-
bership of the Globe Theatre syndicate set up in February
1599.[1] If Jaggard's piracy detracted from the value of those
highly praised 'sugred Sonnets' that were, perhaps, being saved
up against a plague-ridden day, it is not surprising that
Shakespeare was angry with him. By 1609, when *Shakespeare's
Sonnets* finally saw the light, his investment in the theatre was
greater still, after the King's Men's acquisition of the Blackfriars
building in August 1608.[2] Notoriously, the death of Elizabeth
and the peaceful accession of James I in March 1603 heralded an
exceptionally severe and prolonged plague outbreak, which
caused those theatres under civic control to be closed for nearly
thirteen months, from May 1603 to September 1604, with only
short intermissions.[3] Thomas Dekker's *The Wonderfull Yeare.
1603* celebrated the curious concatenation of James's peaceful
accession and his arrival in London with the onset of the worst
plague outbreak in living memory. For Shakespeare's company,
too, this 'wonderful' year – both splendid and terrifying – was to
be greeted

> With mirth in funeral and with dirge in marriage,
> In equal scale weighing delight and dole.
>
> (*Ham* 1.2.12–13)

On the one hand, they were swiftly elevated to the status of
'King's servants' (on 17 May 1603), and the King offered them
some economic and artistic protection from the consequences of
the plague orders, both through cash gifts and through requests
for private performances at Hampton Court and elsewhere. But
on the other hand, the Globe stood bleakly empty, and as Barroll
points out, this above all was 'where the big money was to be
made'[4]. Since the epidemic was also widespread outside London,

1   Schoenbaum, *Life*, 154–5.
2   Ibid., 213–16.
3   Barroll, 173, 99–115.
4   Barroll, 115.

a provincial tour was not the solution. During this phase of theatre closure it seems probable that Shakespeare turned once more to his sonnets, revising poems he had already written, and expanding and redesigning his sequence in a manner which suited the new culture heralded by the new reign. Recent stylometric studies (discussed below) point to 1603–4 as a plausible time for the composition or completion of most of the 'fair youth' sonnets after 1–17, as well as *A Lover's Complaint*, despite the fact that neither sonnet sequences nor love complaints were conspicuously fashionable genres by this date.[1] But as I shall suggest later, both are radical refashionings of genre. Perhaps it was only because of the fitful suspension of closure orders during August and September 1604, followed by six months during which the theatres were open, that a version of the *Sonnets* did not see print in that year.

As Barroll has shown, London's public theatres were paralysed once again by closure orders from July 1606 onwards. Apart from a brief interlude of playing during the summer of 1606, 'plague continued off and on for three years, until December 1610'[2]. Yet again, Thomas Dekker was quick to chronicle the effects of this prolonged epidemic on the City of London, first in *The Dead Tearme*, 1608, and then in *The Ravens Almanacke*, published early in 1609, in which he prophesied further plagues to descend on sinful Londoners during that year. In the opening passage of *Worke for Armorours*, 1609, written in 'this present Summer', he specifically described the effect of plague on playwrights, actors and poets:

> *Play-houses*, stand (like *Tavernes* that have cast out their Maisters) the dores locked up, the *Flagges* (like their *Bushes*) taken down, or rather like *Houses* lately infected, from whence the affrighted dwellers are fled, in hope to live better in the *Country*. The *Players* themselves did

---

1   Cf. Nosworthy; Hieatt, 'When?'; Jackson '*Complaint*'.
2   Barroll, 174.

> never worke till now, there *Comedies* are all turned to
> *Tragedies*, there *Tragedies* to *Nocturnals*, and the best of
> them all are weary of playing in those *Nocturnal Tragedies*.
> *Proh Dolor!* their *Muses* are more sullen then old *Monkeys*:
> now that mony is not stirring . . . O *Pittifull Poetry*, what
> a lamentable prentiship hast thou served, and (which is
> the greatest spite) canst not yet be made *Free!*[1]

For some reason the authorities still permitted bear- and bull-
baiting: as Dekker went on to say, 'The company of *Beares* hold
together still, they play their Tragi-Comedies as lively as ever they
did'. So Edward Alleyn, as Master of the Bear Garden, was still in
business, and would theoretically have been in a position to buy a
copy of *Shakespeare's Sonnets* from one of its two London booksellers, had he so wished. Not many others of his class and
economic status remained in London that summer. By the end of
May 1609, when Q was entered in the Stationers' Register, plague
deaths had reached an alarmingly high level. In some weeks of
April and May deaths from plague in the City of London
approached a hundred a week, and it was feared that the total
might rise even further, though in fact this was to be its peak. As
soon as the Easter Law Term ended the City was swiftly deserted
by the professional classes, gentry and courtiers, whose business
for the time being was done.[2] 'Shakespeares sonnettes' was entered
in the Register a few days before Ascension Day, which marked the
end of the Easter Law Term.[3] Perhaps something of a last-minute
rush attended Shakespeare's sale of the copy manuscript to
Thorpe. He may well have been anxious to complete the transaction as quickly as possible before retreating from plague-ridden
London for the summer, presumably to Stratford, where there was
other business to be dealt with. The hasty departure of the author,

---

1   Thomas Dekker, *Worke for Armorours* (1609), sig. B1ʳ.
2   Wilson, 120–1; Barroll, 180–1. John Bell, *Londons Rembrancer* (1665), gives weekly
    figures for plague deaths in the City from 1606–10.
3   Cf. Cheney, 68–9; and Table 16, showing years, including 1609, when Easter Day
    was on 16 April.

rather than any kind of conspiracy, most probably accounts for Thorpe's being the signatory of the dedication.

Shakespeare seems not to have been in Stratford since the death of his widowed mother the previous September. His considerable holdings in tithe income, land and commodities all needed to be seen to, and there was at least one outstanding piece of litigation in Warwickshire. This was his recovery of a debt of £6, with 24s interest, from John Addenbrooke, which was concluded at the Stratford Court of Record on 7 June 1609.[1] The description of Shakespeare as '*nuper in curia domini Jacobi*' ('recently at the Court of King James') could suggest that he had lately arrived back in Stratford, and now enjoyed an elevated status in his home town as a 'King's servant',[2] who frequently performed at court. As E.A.J. Honigmann has shown, this was 'a particularly busy period of Shakespeare's career, when he accepted new responsibilities in London, but also had to take hold of the reins in Stratford, and was detained there against his will'[3]. Such a sequence of events would help to account for the mediocre printing of the text and the apparent absence of authorial proof-correction. Indeed, this may have been a repetition of an old pattern, for both *Venus and Adonis* and *Lucrece* had been entered in the Register in late spring, during plague outbreaks, after which summer journeys to Stratford are probable. Neither seems to have been authorially press-corrected.[4]

External evidence, in conclusion, suggests four probable phases of composition, of which the second and third are highly conjectural.

1   Schoenbaum, *Life*, 183, 192.
2   For the documents relating to the Addenbrooke case, see Chambers, *Shakespeare*, 2.114–16. Curiously, the Addenbrooke affair, for which seven documents survive, is not discussed at all in Bearman, rating only a passing reference on p. 31. Schoenbaum, too, describes it as 'leaving a trail of records more numerous than interesting'. (*Life*, 184).
3   Honigmann, 45.
4   Plague may also account for the uniquely bad state of Jonson's *The Case is Alterd*, also belonging to the summer of 1609. After intervening to correct the title-page, Jonson, too, may have left London, either for the country residence of Sir Robert Cotton or for that of one of his aristocratic patrons (cf. Jonson, 3.96).

(1) ?–1598. Some sonnets, at least, must have been written by the time of Meres's allusion in *Palladis Tamia*. Though it is theoretically possible that none of the 'sugred Sonnets' referred to by Meres correspond with those eventually published in 1609, it is rather unlikely, in view of the appearance of 138 and 144 in *The Passionate Pilgrim*. Some would also argue that the circulation from 1620 or so of manuscript texts of sonnet 2 may derive from an earlier version.[1]

(2) 1599–1600. In the aftermath of *The Passionate Pilgrim* Shakespeare may have prepared a collection of sonnets which was entered in the Stationers' Register on 3 January 1600. Even if this was merely a 'staying entry', not denoting any firm intention to publish, the Wardens of the Stationers' Company would need to see and verify the manuscript.

(3) 1603–4. Severe plague outbreak and consequent loss of income from the theatre make this a plausible time for Shakespeare to have turned once more to non-dramatic poetry. *A Lover's Complaint* and some of the 'dating' sonnets, such as 107 and 125, appear to belong to this time, which may have been the period in which the sequence began to take its final shape.

(4) August 1608 – May 1609. An even more severe and prolonged plague outbreak again deprived Shakespeare of income from the theatre. He may have finished work on *Shakespeare's Sonnets* during this period before selling the manuscript to Thorpe.

Internal evidence: the likelihood of revision

Before I examine the two traditional areas of internal evidence for the date of Shakespeare's sonnets, style and topical allusions, something should be said about the general characteristics of sonnets and sonnet sequences in Shakespeare's period. It is fairly obvious that the sonnet, an almost uniquely contained, delimited form of versification, is peculiarly susceptible to tinkering. It does

---

1   Taylor, 'Some MSS'; Kerrigan, 441ff. For a discussion of this claim, see Appendix, pp. 453–7.

not take long to copy out a single sonnet, and in copying it out, whether for a 'private friend' or for other purposes, a poet of a self-critical bent, or one who is sensitive to criticism or changing circumstances, is extremely likely to introduce changes, whether of single words or of whole lines or quatrains. A sonnet sequence, still more, is almost bound to be the product of several second thoughts and rearrangements. It is remarkably easy to reorder sonnets, either, as Robert Sidney did in his poetical manuscript, by inscribing different numbers or directions, such as 'This should be first', beside them;[1] or, if individual sonnets or small groups are written on loose sheets of paper, by reshuffling them like a pack of cards. Those sixteenth-century sonneteers who published sonnet sequences, and became involved in later printings, seem almost always to have revised. Where manuscript evidence survives, that, too, generally points to revision. The pre-eminent sonneteer of Renaissance France, for instance, Pierre de Ronsard, transformed his 1578 *Sonnets pour Hélène* into what was in effect 'a new sonnet cycle' in the augmented and revised edition of 1584.[2] Likewise, the earliest English 'sonneteer', Thomas Watson, produced one version of *Hekatompathia* in manuscript for personal presentation to his patron, the Earl of Oxford, and another, longer, annotated one for print publication a year or so later.[3] Fulke Greville revised his sequence *Caelica* several times, over a period of years, at one time shortening it, and at another reinstating previously rejected sonnets, as the Warwick Castle manuscript shows.[4]

The most extreme example of repeated revision of a sonnet sequence is offered by Shakespeare's Warwickshire neighbour Michael Drayton. Out of the early *Ideas Mirrour*, 1594, Drayton eventually generated the final version of *Idea*, 1619, through the process of at least five revisions. Only twenty of the original

1   BL MS Add. 58435 Robert Sidney, *Poems* 124 and *passim*.
2   Stone, 228–43.
3   BL MS Harley 3277; Thomas Watson, *Hekatompathia* (1582).
4   Cf. Farmer.

fifty-three sonnets included in *Ideas Mirrour* survived in the 1619 sequence. As well as writing new sonnets, Drayton made continual verbal and stylistic changes to old ones. He was notoriously sensitive to mockery, such as that of Sir John Davies in his 'Gullinge Sonnets',[1] or Marston in his *Scourge of Villanie;* and he was anxious to adjust his poems to the changing requirements of fashion. Indeed, Shakespeare may allude defensively to Drayton's celebrated versatility in his own sonnet 76, opening with the question:

> Why is my verse so barren of new pride,
> So far from variation or quick change?

In the course of a quarter of a century Drayton transformed a sequence of soft, 'golden', conventionally self-pitying love sonnets into something much more tough, colloquial and unpredictable – as he himself boasted, 'in all Humors sportively I range'[2]. His later-written, Jacobean sonnets, from the 1605 version onwards, include strong elements of satire and misogyny. As Kathleen Tillotson put it, writing of the 'sternness and finality' of these poems, 'They are the sonnets of a satirist; even the traditional promise of immortality must open with a jeer at the "paltry, foolish, painted things".'[3] Daniel, too, was a compulsive reviser of his own sonnets, though not on the same grand scale as Drayton. His *Delia* went through at least eleven editions from the original *Delia and Rosamund* in 1592 to the text included in his *Whole Workes* in 1623, with verbal changes, additions, and some rearrangement, but mostly confined to the period 1601–2.

With so much evidence available that other, better-documented sonneteers continually rewrote and reordered their work, it becomes a near-certainty that Shakespeare must have done so too, given that at least a decade elapsed between the

---

1 Davies, 163–7.
2 Drayton, 2.310.
3 Drayton, 5.139. For a detailed analysis of Drayton's revisions, see Drayton, 5.137–44; note also the useful 'Finding-List' on pp. 326–8.

'sugred Sonnets' alluded to by Meres and the eventual emergence of Q. Whatever the order of their original composition may have been, it is most unlikely that it bears much relation to the order of the sonnets as finally arranged in Q, although some scholars, strangely, have assumed that Shakespeare did begin to write at 1 and simply carried straight through to 154.[1] Numerological finesses, such as the play, on the human body in 20, on '[h]our minutes' in 60, the grand climacteric in 63, and a double climacteric in 126, suggest either that sonnets already written were subsequently carefully located, or that some were specially written or revised for particular positions in the sequence. (For discussion of individual examples, see commentary.) Any individual sonnet, unless topical allusion can be shown to peg it to a particular date, may have undergone revision over a period of days, weeks, years or decades. Indeed, even an apparently topical sonnet, such as 107, may, for all we know, be the product of revision, incorporating or adapting topical elements in a sonnet written earlier.

Drayton, as Kathleen Tillotson has shown,[2] was still labouring to impose logic and forcefulness on the 'vague conceits' of his early sonnets nearly thirty years later. If the only version of his sequence that survived were the 1619 one, some of Drayton's sonnets would doubtless pose just the sort of stylistic puzzles that some of Shakespeare's do, with perplexing occurrences of both 'early rare words' and 'late rare words'[3]. The fact that scholars attempting to date *Shakespeare's Sonnets* on stylistic evidence have ranged from as early as 1582 to as late as 1609[4] may not simply reflect the well-known capacity of these poems to provoke extreme disagreement. It may also testify to the genuinely multi-layered character of the sonnets, some of which may have been worked over and tinkered with on different

1 This assumption mars Graziani's otherwise excellent article.
2 Drayton, 5.139.
3 Cf. Hieatt, 'When?', 96–7.
4 Rollins, 2.53–77.

occasions at widely spaced intervals. Though Heminge and Condell could not recall finding many blots in the autograph texts of Shakespeare's plays, it is unlikely that his working papers for *Sonnets* were so immaculate.

Internal evidence: style

The pursuit of individual stylistic or verbal links between *Sonnets* and Shakespeare's other works leads in many directions. Even a trail which at first looks straightforward can quickly prove to lead into a thorny wood. This can be illustrated with reference to one example which apparently points to an early date, and another which seems strongly to suggest a late one. To start with the 'early' one: the only line in *Shakespeare's Sonnets* that is an exact quotation, 'Lilies that fester smell far worse than weeds' (94.14), derives from *The Reign of King Edward the Third*. This play was printed in 1596, but may have been written as early as 1591, for the short-lived company of Pembroke's Men.[1] Whether or not Shakespeare had a hand in the writing of the play, as many have thought, there is no doubt that he was very familiar with it, and echoed parts of its action in *Henry V* and *Measure for Measure*.[2] This being so, his quotation of an aphoristic line from it can scarcely be taken as reliable evidence that sonnet 94 was written close in time to the period of the composition, performance or publication of *Edward the Third*, 1591–6, since he evidently went on remembering and thinking about the play in the Jacobean period. Indeed, for all we know, Shakespeare may have quoted the line in the expectation that it would be recognized by readers of the second edition of *Edward the Third* in 1599, and/or it may have been in this second edition that he himself read the play with closest attention.

The quotation may also be evidence against Shakespeare's authorship of the play, rather than in favour of it, since, as Lee maintained forcefully, 'It was contrary to Shakespeare's practice

1   Cf. Proudfoot, 181–2.
2   Cf. Muir, chs 2–3.

literally to plagiarize himself.'[1] One of Shakespeare's few other exact quotations, again a single aphoristic verse line, 'Who ever loved, that loved not at first sight?' (*AYL* 3.5.82), was included as an acknowledged tribute to its author, the 'dead shepherd' Marlowe, who had been murdered six or seven years before *As You Like It* was written. On this analogy, it cannot be safely assumed that close verbal reminiscence necessarily implies proximity in time to the work recalled, whether a work by Shakespeare himself or another writer.

Looking to the other end of the chronological spectrum, Kent Hieatt has suggested cogently that *A Lover's Complaint* is strongly linked with one of the 'last plays', *Cymbeline,* with reference to the occurrence of fifteen 'very rare words' in both works.[2] He also points out that the first quatrain of sonnet 73, 'That time of year thou mayst in me behold', with its 'bough–leaves–shake–bear complex', is closely analogous both to a passage in another mature play, *Timon of Athens* (4.3.265–8), and, even more, to a speech by Belarius in *Cymbeline* (3.3.60–4):

> then was I as a tree
> Whose boughs did bend with fruit. But in one night,
> A storm, or robbery (call it what you will)
> Shook down my mellow hangings, nay, my leaves,
> And left me bare to weather.

In combination with the presentation of the speaker, in all three passages, as a visibly old and dying man, the parallels with *Timon* and *Cymbeline* might appear to point to sonnet 73 as written close in time to the two plays. Indeed, a period between 1603 and 1609 is what I would personally favour. But again, it is only honest to acknowledge that Shakespeare's verbal and metaphoric memory was both acute and retentive. Writing speeches for traumatized old men in *Timon* and *Cymbeline* could have caused him to recall

---

1 Quoted in Rollins, 2.234.
2 Hieatt, '*LC, Cym* and *Son*'.

words and images he had deployed in a sonnet some years earlier. And as suggested above, we can never be certain, in default of any early manuscript evidence, that this, or any, sonnet is not the product of a complex process of revision, being a rewritten version of one first composed at an unknown earlier date.

More sophisticated stylistic studies, of course, do not rely on single examples or parallels, but on large collections of words, images or phrases, which are then connected with other, more clearly datable, parts of Shakespeare's work, or with that of his contemporaries. Such work was initiated in the late nineteenth century, being undertaken particularly systematically by such German scholars as Hermann Conrad and Gregor Sarrazin, among many others.[1] Their final conclusions were extremely diverse, as Rollins observed: 'the result has often been for men and women of presumably equal intelligence to attain diametrically opposed results'. Such diversity has continued undiminished in the later twentieth century. For instance, T.W. Baldwin, a learned Southamptonite, plumped for an initial group of sonnets (or quire of paper) completed in 1594, and five or six further batches presented to Southampton annually up to 1598 or 1599.[2] Claes Schaar, in 1962, first assembled a useful collection of parallels with other Elizabethan sonneteers, and then trawled links between *Sonnets* and the rest of Shakespeare's oeuvre. This led him to date one group of sonnets to 1592–3, and another to 1594–5. Verbal parallels with Shakespeare's later work are, he suggested, instances of his later development of a 'germ' whose original site was in *Sonnets*, but which 'may long have continued to echo in the poet's mind'.[3] In 1975, however, Eliot Slater, setting up a more scientific statistical method for analysing the incidence of rare words in Shakespeare's work, came to the threefold conclusion that *A Lover's Complaint* is authentically Shakespearean (a view then disputed); that *Sonnets*

1   Rollins 2.63–5.
2   Baldwin, 340–4.
3   Schaar, 183–94.

belongs to the 'second quarter' of Shakespeare's work; and that *A Lover's Complaint* belongs to its 'third quarter'.[1]

Despite the widely diverse conclusions reached in the past, there does seem a chance that computer-aided stylometric analysis, such as that undertaken by Kent Hieatt and his collaborators, will one day come up with results that prove more generally compelling than those assembled by all previous searchers. The interim suggestions offered by Hieatt in 1991, on the basis of some painstaking and wide-ranging analysis, seem to offer a good working hypothesis, especially if the phrase 'a number' is treated as elastic:

> *Sonnets* is like Daniel's *Delia* and Drayton's *Idea* in containing a core of sonnets written in the first half of the fifteen-nineties, but in part revised on into the seventeenth century, and a number of new sonnets added to this core.[2]

However, given the strong probability that any or every sonnet may be the product of revision, combined with the likelihood that the whole sequence was revised and rearranged during the period immediately before its publication, it seems unlikely that stylometric analysis can ever produce the whole answer. Also, the absolute generic difference between sonnets and plays needs to be borne in mind. Shakespeare may have drawn on a range of vocabulary and literary reference when he was writing sonnets that was wholly distinct from what he used when writing plays. This may have led him on occasion to deploy a 'late rare word' in a sonnet written early, or an 'early rare word' in a sonnet written late. For instance, working on sonnet-writing or sonnet-revision towards the end of the possible period of composition could occasionally have prompted recollections of words or images from the narrative poems, which he then redeployed many years later. Though some individual parallels between passages in *Shakespeare's*

1   Slater, *passim.*
2   Hieatt , 'When?', 98.

Sonnets and Shakespeare's other works are very striking (many, but of course not all, are pointed out in notes to individual sonnets), such parallels cannot be taken in isolation as secure evidence of the date of composition of *Sonnets* or of its component parts. To command general support, stylometric analysis needs to be considered in conjunction with other kinds of evidence.

Internal evidence: topical allusions

Two sonnets, more than any others, have been investigated for the light they appear to shed on the date of composition. One alludes to personal history, the other to public events. Sonnet 104, 'To me, fair friend, you never can be old', chronicles the passage of three whole years 'Since first I saw you fresh', and congratulates the youth for looking no older than he did three years ago. If this is taken as referring literally to the period of the speaker's friendship with the fair youth, it might seem that if we could only discover when this began, it would be possible to date this sonnet (and presumably many of its companions) to a time three years later. However, many other sonneteers had used a fictionalized three-year time-scheme. These included Desportes, Vausquelin de la Fresnaie, Ronsard and – one of Shakespeare's most immediate models – Daniel.[1] It is also remarkable, though perhaps coincidental, that Tennyson, whose *In Memoriam* has *Shakespeare's Sonnets* as its model, imposed a fictional three-year scheme, with three Christmases and springs, on a collection of lyrics actually written in the course of nearly seventeen years. Though the possibility of a literal and personal three-year reference cannot be entirely excluded, we are unlikely to encounter solid documentation of the exact calendar of Shakespeare's relationship with his 'fair friend' anywhere outside the sonnets themselves.

The other much-discussed 'dating' sonnet, 107 ('Not mine own fears, nor the prophetic soul') offers more promising material for investigation. Its account of a peaceful and 'balmy' time

1 Rollins, 1.225–6.

which defeats the false prophecies that preceded it clearly alludes to large external events, sufficiently momentous to be well documented. In an article confidently entitled 'Shakespeare's sonnets dated', Leslie Hotson linked it with the year 1589. He took line 5, 'The mortal moon hath her eclipse endured', to allude to the crescent-shaped formation of the Spanish Armada, defeated in 1588; and he reinforced this dating with reference to sonnet 123, linking line 2's 'pyramids, built up with newer might' to Pope Sixtus V's erection of Egyptian obelisks in Rome.[1] Though impressively documented, Hotson's theory has commanded little support. It would require us to believe not only in a Shakespeare who took an active interest in cultural events in Rome, but also in one who had mastered the art of writing densely allusive and complex sonnets at the very beginning of his literary career.

Many intermediate dates have been suggested,[2] but the only really convincing one is also the most obvious. The 'wonderful year', 1603, saw the eclipse, or death, of the 'mortal moon' Elizabeth, and the peaceful accession of James I, with the release from prison and reception into favour of several leading courtiers. Shakespeare's early patron, the Earl of Southampton, who had been committed to the Tower for his part in Essex's rebellion in 1600/1 was immediately released – 'the King's first act of his accession to the crown of England was to set Southampton free (10 April 1603)'[3]. Shakespeare's later patron, William Herbert, Third Earl of Pembroke, had jeopardized his position at Elizabeth's court by his affair with Mary Fitton and underwent a short spell of imprisonment in 1601. He too enjoyed immediate blessings at the hand of the new monarch, being installed as a Knight of the Garter on 25 June 1603. The 'balmy time' of 107.9 can be most obviously construed as referring to the miraculously peaceful period initiated by James's

1   Hotson, 1–36.
2   Summarized in Rollins, 1.263–70.
3   Sidney Lee, *DNB* entry on Southampton.

accession in March 1603, which culminated in his City progress in March 1604 and his subsequent coronation. Elsewhere Shakespeare frequently identifies kingship above all with sacramental 'balm' or chrism. A king's crown may be taken off, but divine unction can never be undone:

> Not all the water in the rough rude sea
> Can wash the balm off from an anointed King . . .
> (*R2* 3.2.54–5)

John Kerrigan has shown how closely the diction and imagery of 107 are connected with the rhetoric of works celebrating James's accession, such as Joseph Hall's *The Kings Prophecie. OR, Weeping Ioy* (1603), as well as with works, such as a 1617 sermon by Donne, which look back to this time.[1] However, he fails to point out that James's ceremonial entry into London was postponed to the early spring of 1604, because of the severe plague outbreak. Though the coronation took place quietly on 25th July 1603, it was not until a year after Elizabeth's death that the 'balmy time' of James's reign was publicly celebrated. Sonnet 107 belongs most probably to the summer of 1604.

An even closer analogy to 107 is to be found in sonnet 51 of the 1605 edition of Drayton's *Idea*, which exactly mirrors its account of public events turning out, contrary to expectation, peaceful and harmonious, yet even in their peacefulness demonstrating an instability which contrasts with the single-minded love of the speaker:

> Calling to mind since first my Love begun,
> Th'incertaine Times oft varying in their Course,
> How Things still unexpectedly have runne,
> As't please the fates, by their resistlesse force:
> Lastly, mine Eyes amazedly have seene
> ESSEX great fall, TYRONE his Peace to gaine,
> The quiet end of that Long-living Queene,

---

1 Kerrigan, 313–18.

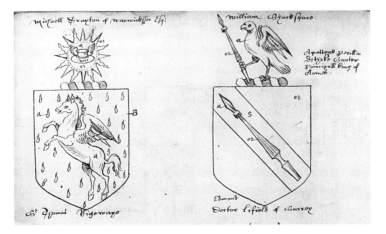

1 Michael Drayton's coat of arms beside Shakespeare's. From BL MS Harley 6140, fol. 46ᵛ

> This King's faire Entrance, and our peace with *Spaine*.
> We and the *Dutch* at length our selves to sever;
> Thus the World doth, and evermore shall Reele:
> Yet to my Goddesse am I constant ever.[1]

Drayton's editors suggest 'that Drayton had seen Shakespeare's sonnet and had it in mind'.[2] This is indeed very probable, especially since Drayton's sonnet must have been written in 1604–5, after the treaty with Spain in August 1604, while Shakespeare's, in which 'Uncertainties now crown themselves assured', seems to belong to the summer of that year, immediately after James's City progress and coronation. Perhaps Drayton wrote his 1605 sonnet in emulation of Shakespeare's. The two shared a tactless negligence in failing to write an elegy for Elizabeth, for which both were rebuked by Henry Chettle in adjacent stanzas of *Englands Mourning Garment*.[3] Some further association between them, as

---

1 Drayton, 2.336.
2 Ibid., 5.141.
3 Henry Chettle, *Englands Mourning Garment* (1603), sig. D3ᵛ.

2 Triumphal arch with pyramids, 'The new Arabia felix', erected above the Cheapside conduit, March 1603/4. From Stephen Harrison, *The Arch's of Triumph* (1604), sig. F (Bodleian Gough London 145)

two Warwickshire men who were professional writers, may be indicated by the placing of their arms side by side in an early-seventeenth-century heraldic manuscript (See Fig. 1). Whoever Shakespeare's 'private friends' may have been in the late 1590s, after 1603 Drayton was probably among their number. There may have been an element of friendly emulation in their respective sonneteering activities.

Other sonnets which appear to include topical reference, especially the group 123–5, are also best construed with reference to events after 1600. All three may be read as addressed defiantly to 'Time', who appears to be the 'suborned informer' whom the speaker sends packing in 125.13. The 'pyramids, built up with newer might' of 123 may correspond with the elaborate obelisks and triumphal arches erected for James's procession through the City of London on 15 March 1603/4, in particular the huge one in the Strand (of which, unfortunately, no visual record survives) in which a vast rainbow was supported by 'two magnificent *Pyramid's*, of 70. foot in height, on which were drawne his Maiesties seuerall pedigrees *Eng.* and *Scot*'.[1]

Shakespeare's speaker's refusal to be impressed by extraordinary pyramidical structures (see Fig. 2), which 'To me are nothing novel, nothing strange', is entirely consistent with the fact that Shakespeare played no part in devising shows or speeches for this occasion. Many other leading dramatists were actively involved in designing James's City progress, most prominently Dekker, Jonson and Chettle; Shakespeare was not. In 124, 'If my dear love were but the child of state', the constancy of the speaker's 'love' is contrasted with the unstable fortunes of those who depend on political favour. The final couplet –

> To this I witness call the fools of time,
> Which die for goodness, who have lived for crime.

1 Jonson, 7.106.

– has been linked with a wide variety of victims of execution or martyrdom, from as early as Edmund Campion in 1582 to as late as Essex in 1601. But readers of *Shakespeare's Sonnets* in 1609 would most naturally understand the lines as alluding to the Gunpowder Plot of November 1605, followed by the execution of the chief plotters in January 1605/6, and it may be these that Shakespeare's speaker chiefly invokes. The conspirators, most of them veterans of Essex's rising, can aptly be described as 'fools of time', on whom 'Time', as in 125.13, has 'informed', betraying them to a criminal's end which may nevertheless be viewed by their Catholic supporters as martyrdom, a death encompassed 'for goodness'.

Sonnet 125, 'Were't ought to me I bore the canopy', again distinguishes the pure constancy of private love, this time defined explicitly as the love of two people – 'mutual render, only me for thee' – from the dangerous complexities of court favour. The 'canopy' of the opening line may refer once more to James's ceremonial passage through the City on 15 March 1603/4, 'hauing a *Canopie* borne ouer him by 8. knights'[1]. Once again the speaker's personal detachment from such pageantry is distinguished from the role of others – most naturally construed as other writers – who have participated in it. Jonson's career as a writer of court masques burgeoned during the years 1604–9; Shakespeare enjoyed no such career, and may have felt rather defiantly defensive about this. In the second quatrain of 125 the speaker casts his mind back to fallen favourites whom he has 'seen' 'spent', or destroyed. The image of 'compound sweet', though so far as I know this has never been pointed out before, could be applied most naturally to Elizabeth's favourite the Earl of Essex, who had been rewarded in 1590 with the 'farm of sweet wines' – the right to charge tax on imported sweet wines.[2]

---

1   Stephen Harrison, *The Arch's of Triumph* (1604), sig. K1. Cf. also Gilbert Dugdale, *The Time Triumphant* (1604).
2   Strictly speaking, what Essex lost was the renewal of this grant, which had expired in 1598; cf. Lacey, 241–3, 257–67. For Rowland Whyte's account of Essex's arrival in the Queen's bedchamber, see HMC *De L'Isle and Dudley*, 2.395–6.

He lost it spectacularly in September 1599 after his unlicensed return from Ireland, when he rushed unannounced into Elizabeth's bedchamber at Nonsuch, still booted and muddy, with his face dirty. He could be very aptly described as a 'pitiful gazer', for his sight of her, grey-haired and without her make-up, initiated the sequence of events that led first to his fall from favour, then to his rebellion, and finally to his execution in February 1600/1. As well as suggesting a sweet food or medicine, the phrase 'compound sweet' may suggest a beguiling or attractive financial agreement, for as a verb 'compound' could denote 'to bargain' or 'to make a pecuniary arrangement' (*OED* 10, 14).

Shakespeare's Sonnets may incorporate some material written very early. The earliest poem of all may be the short-lined 145, 'Those lips that love's own hand did make', if Andrew Gurr's suggestion that it puns on the surname 'Hathaway' is accepted, together with his proposed dating of it to 1582 (see notes). But if we start from the premiss that Q is authorized – the evidence for which is explored further below – it follows that Shakespeare is likely to have put the sequence into its final shape close in time to 1609. In including topical allusions, he would want to refer above all to events readily recognized by readers in that year. We should not be surprised, therefore, if the four sonnets which offer the most explicit 'dating' references all seem to point to a period of about seven years before Q's publication, from Essex's fall in 1599–1600 to the execution of the Gunpowder Plotters in 1606. To readers in 1609 these allusions to public events may have served to make the whole sequence appear topical, even if, as seems probable, it also incorporates a good deal of material written much earlier. Like internal evidence, external reference points to 1603–4 as initiating an intense period of writing (and perhaps revising) which may have continued, off and on, until shortly before publication.

PUBLISHING HISTORY

The authenticity of the 1609 Quarto

As published in 1609, *Shakespeare's Sonnets* was by no means so aberrant and mistimed as those who attempt to pigeon-hole the entire sequence as early work have often maintained. It is true that the great Elizabethan vogue for sonneteering, in the wake of Sidney's *Astrophil and Stella,* had spent its force by the end of the 1590s. But James's accession in 1603 stimulated a second wave. From the viewpoint of Jacobean readers, Q could be received as part of this small but vigorous movement to provide the new court culture with its own refashioned sonnet sequences and lyric collections. These were no longer idealistically Petrarchan or Sidneian, but characterized by sportiveness, satirical and epigrammatic touches, and abrupt reversals of mood. Drayton's 1605 redaction of *Idea*, in which he positively boasted of the 'Wilde, madding, jocund, and irregular' style of his verse, has already been mentioned. John Davies of Hereford's *Wittes Pilgrimage*, bearing the title-page motto *Iucunda vicissitudo rerum* ('the joyful changefulness of things'), which may also belong to 1605,[1] expresses a conscious delight in variety and contradiction. It is one of the few sequences to match Shakespeare's in length, consisting of 152 sonnets, followed by a long section of commendatory and miscellaneous poems. Here, 104 playfully amorous sonnets are set in antithesis to a further 48 which are religious and soberly philosophical. The volume is dedicated to Philip Herbert, Earl of Montgomery, and to 'his most honorable other halfe', James Hay. Most of the other sonneteers of the early Jacobean period were Scottish. William Alexander's *Aurora*, for instance, was published by Shakespeare's Stratford schoolfellow Richard Field in 1604. Another Scottish gentleman,

---

1 John Davies of Herford, *Wittes Pilgrimage, through a world of amorous sonnets* (no date, but entered in the Stationers' Register on 27 September 1605).The sonnet sequence is followed by an extensive collection of miscellaneous lyrics, many of them associated with the Herbert family.

Alexander Craig, produced three lyric collections between 1603 and 1609, of which the middle one, his *Amorose Songes, Sonets and Elegies* (1606), is a highly unusual sonnet sequence. Craig distributes his sonnets between eight ladies, chief among them 'Idea' (presumably in emulation of Drayton), and includes also such contrasted love-objects as the 'grave' and stony-hearted Lithocardia and the excitingly promiscuous Lais. Like Drayton and Davies, Craig positively glories in the labyrinthine variety of 'His wandring verse'[2]. His previous volume, *The Poeticall Essayes* (1603), is even more remarkable for its variety of tone and subject-matter, celebrating both the Stuart royal family and his own lady, left behind in Banff. Craig takes Jacobean grotesqueness to unusual lengths, as when he drinks his absent lady's health in tobacco as well as wine:

> for thy health once I carouse each day:
> From pype of Loame and for thy saike I souke,
> The flegm-attractive far-fett *Indian* smoake.

His self-contradictions and wild changes of mood are appropriate for that 'wonderful year', in which Scottish gentry newly arrived in London encountered both a splendid new court and a plague-infected City:

> Here where the Pest approacheth us so narre,
> To smoother breath before we be aware:
> For at the gates of our most royall King,
> Corrupted Carrions lie: O fearfull thing.[2]

A more immediate analogy to *Shakespeare's Sonnets* is provided by a sonnet in the same collection in which Craig expresses his double rage at being betrayed simultaneously by a male friend and a female mistress:

---

1   Alexander Craig, *The Amorose Songes, Sonets and Elegies* (1606), sig. I8ᵛ.
2   Alexander Craig, *Poeticall Essayes* (1603), sig. F1ʳ.

> Deceitfull shee, and most unconstant hee:
> Thus for each lyne I gave my selfe a lye,
> That heretofore into their praise I pend.[1]

Though this collection is not technically a sonnet sequence, its self-consciously hectic energy, in which the poet seems frequently to feel betrayed by the suppleness of his own art, does offer some analogies to Shakespeare's, especially to such sonnets as 147 – in which

> My thoughts and my discourse as madmen's are,
> At random from the truth vainly expressed

– or the closing 152, which concludes

> . . . I have sworn thee fair: more perjured eye,
> To swear against the truth so foul a lie.

The years 1603–9 also saw a proliferation of satirical and epigrammatic poetry, which the salty, 'humorous' character of most of the Jacobean sonnet sequences seems to match. Epigrammatists and satirists include John Owen, Henry Peacham, Richard West (published by Thorpe), and the prolific Samuel Rowlands.[2] Two further Jacobean sonnet-sequences, however, represent a throwback to the more 'golden', and Petrarchan, style of the 1590s: David Murray's *Caelia: containing certaine Sonets* was appended to his *Sophonisba*, 1611, dedicated to Prince Henry; and William Drummond's dignified two-part sequence was included in his ?1614 *Poems*. Though it is with the more salty, self-contradictory sequences of 1603–6 that *Shakespeare's Sonnets* has most in common, these late examples testify to the persistence of the sonnet-sequence genre in the first decade of James's reign.

---

1 Ibid., sig. E2ᵛ.
2 John Owen, *Epigrammatum libri tres* (1606); Henry Peacham, *The More the Merrier, containing three-score and odde head-lesse epigrams* (1608); Richard West, *Wits a.b.c., or A Century of Epigrams* (1608); Samuel Rowlands, *Looke To It: for Ile Stabbe Ye* (1604), *Hell's Broke Loose* (1605), *Humors Looking Glasse* (1608). Cf. also William Percy's 'one singuler Booke of Epigrammes', dated 1610, in Huntington MS HM4, fols 195–217.

The traditional twentieth-century view has been that Q was published in some surreptitious or piratical manner. This notion is sometimes reinforced by a further assertion that it was 'suppressed' soon after publication,[1] though there is no evidence for either claim. The origins of the widespread belief that Q is unauthorized lie, probably, in deep anxieties felt by British scholars who worked in the aftermath of the infamous 'Labouchère amendment' of 1885, which criminalized homosexual acts between consenting adult males, and the subsequent trial of Oscar Wilde in 1895. Wilde had repeatedly associated himself with *Shakespeare's Sonnets*, first by writing 'The Portrait of Master W.H.'[2] and then in his determined defence of his famous letter to Lord Alfred Douglas, beginning 'My Own Boy', which he described as being 'like a little sonnet of Shakespeare'.[3] As such, claimed Wilde, the letter was as far beyond the powers of ordinary human analysis as *King Lear* or *Sonnets*. Wilde's conviction and sentence to two years' imprisonment with hard labour must have made it a matter of some urgency for ambitious Shakespeare scholars, whose own social standing depended to a large extent on the character of the material they studied, utterly to expunge the association that Wilde had set up between *Shakespeare's Sonnets* and his own friendships with numerous young men. That England's – Europe's? – greatest poet should have both composed and published highly personal poems which explored a passionate relationship with a 'lovely boy', evidently, like Oscar Wilde's 'Bosie', a young aristocrat, must have appeared totally unacceptable.[4] Shakespeare's works were

---

1   Cf. J. Dover Wilson, Cam², xlii.
2   First published in *Blackwood's Edinburgh Magazine* (July 1889).
3   H.Montgomery Hyde, *The Trials of Oscar Wilde* (NY 1962) 245 (Third Trial); cf. also First Trial, 115.
4   Sidney Lee's friend and Balliol contemporary H.C. Beeching, whose career was as a churchman, continued to maintain that the sonnets were personal documents; cf. H.C.Beeching, ed., *The Sonnets of Shakespeare* (1904), viiff., in which he explicitly rebuts Lee's purely literary reading, asking, for instance, 'Did any Elizabethan client . . . speak of his love for his patron as keeping him awake at night?' It may be significant that Beeching's *DNB* biography includes no mention of this edition.

increasingly taught in schools and universities: how could he possibly have nourished – and have publicly articulated – passions of the sort that led to Wilde's being condemned to two years' imprisonment with hard labour?

After his initial rashness in supporting first Pembroke, then Southampton, as candidates for Shakespeare's 'fair friend', Sidney Lee made a speedy about-turn, in 1897–8, altering his *DNB* article on Shakespeare for the benefit of American readers.[1] To exonerate Shakespeare thoroughly, Lee adopted a belt-and-braces approach: the text was not made public by Shakespeare himself, but neither was it personally compromising. According to Lee, the text had been criminally appropriated by the unscrupulous and piratical Thomas Thorpe, for whom no language of abuse was too strong. But in any case, as he proceeded to demonstrate over the next few years, with special reference to an extensive investigation of French Renaissance poetry, the poems could be seen to lie comfortably within the boundaries of literary tradition – so the text was by no means so compromising as it might at first appear. By 1905 he was prepared to assert that 'Hundreds of sonneteers had celebrated, in the language of love, the charms of young men.'[2] As Schoenbaum would have said, 'They had not.' But because of Lee's undoubted diligence and scholarship, such claims, though often wholly unsupported by evidence, seem to have been accepted without challenge. Also, according to Lee, most of the sonnets had been completed by 1594, so by the time Thorpe published them, and, 'With characteristic insolence', tacked on a love complaint by another writer, Shakespeare must have pretty much forgotten about them. Should any residue of a 'personal' interpretation survive Lee's account of the sonnets' 'borrowed conceits', at least the whole collection could be conveniently sidelined, biographically, as partaking of the folly of a great

---

1   Schoenbaum, *Lives*, 370–1.
2   Sidney Lee, ed., *Shakespeare's Sonnets* (1905), 10.

man's youth, rather than being regarded as the considered product of Shakespeare's maturity. Why it should be more acceptable to view Shakespeare as fascinated by a male love-object during the first decade of his married life than in his Jacobean maturity is not clear. But certainly in literary-historical terms there might appear to be some neatness in bracketing *Sonnets* with *Venus and Adonis* and *Lucrece* as three products of the early 1590s, after which Shakespeare could be viewed as devoting his writing energies entirely to the theatre. Many late-twentieth-century critics have clung tenaciously to this neat and tidy chronology.[1]

Contrary to what most previous editors have maintained, there is every reason to believe that the 1609 Quarto publication of *Sonnets* was authorized by Shakespeare himself. A powerful internal argument lies in his repeated deployment of the theme of immortalization through verse.[2] Though this traditional motif has precedents in Horace and in the French Pléiade poets, it is hard to see how a writer so aware of practicalities as Shakespeare could claim to immortalize his friend in 'black lines' (63.13) unless he either allowed the sequence to achieve wide circulation in manuscript, which he clearly did not, or ensured that it was printed. Daniel and Drayton, the other two Elizabethan sonneteers who made prominent use of the theme of the immortalizing power of poetry, undoubtedly did use and control print publication of their sequences.[3] In addition, three external witnesses testify to Shakespeare's own involvement. The first and most powerful, Thomas Heywood, has already been quoted. According to Heywood, Shakespeare eventually published his sonnets 'in his owne name' – presumably a reference to the genitive title, *SHAKE-SPEARES SONNETS* – in order to put right the wrong done to him by the piratical Jaggard in 1599. Since Shakespeare was still alive in 1612, and Heywood was a

---

1   This scenario is vigorously explored by Schmidgall; cf. also Bloom, 3, where Bloom states that *Sonnets* belongs to '1592 to 1596 or so'.
2   As in 18, 19, 32, 55, 60, 63, 65, 100 and 101.
3   For a contextualization of the theme of poetic immortality, see Leishman, 69–91.

devoted admirer of Shakespeare's work, it seems unlikely that Heywood would make such a claim in print unless he was quite sure of his ground.

William Drummond, possibly also writing in Shakespeare's lifetime, *circa* 1614, just at the time when he published his own sonnets, made some notes on various English poets. Listing those who had written 'on the Subject of Love', he cited Wyatt, Surrey, Sidney, Daniel, Drayton and Spenser. He noted that although Ralegh and Dyer had been praised by Puttenham, 'their Works are so few that are come to my Hands, I cannot well say any thing of them. The last we have are Sir *William Alexander* and *Shakspear*, who have lately published their Works.'[1] Sir William Alexander's youthful sonnet sequence *Aurora*, already mentioned, had been published in 1605, by Shakespeare's Stratford school-fellow Richard Field. Shakespeare's 'Works' on the topic of 'Love' must presumably denote the 1609 Q, and the plural form of reference may indicate that Drummond accepted *A Lover's Complaint* as an integral part of the collection. It is noteworthy also that Drummond's phrase 'The last we have' chronicles the reception of *Shakespeare's Sonnets* as a Jacobean text, not as a late appearance of a sequence originally written much earlier – but not much can be made of this.

The third witness is the most dubious. The entrepreneurial publisher John Benson, in his Epistle prefaced to *Poems: Written by Wil. Shake-speare. Gent* (1640), referred to: 'some excellent and swetely composed Poems, of Master *William Shakespeare*, which in themselves appear of the same purity, the Authour himselfe then living avouched'. While it may at first seem that Benson is claiming to know from personal experience that Shakespeare habitually 'avouched' the integrity and authenticity of Q, it is more probable that he simply alludes to Q's title-page, which describes the sonnets both as 'SHAKE-SPEARES', and

---

1   William Drummond of Hawthornden, *Works* (1711), 226.

as 'Neuer before Imprinted'. Though Benson had in fact drawn on the 1612 *Passionate Pilgrim*, as well as altering and rearranging the authentic sonnets, his point may have been to advertise his own text as based on work publicly acknowledged by Shakespeare, in contrast to *The Passionate Pilgrim*.

The manner in which Q was entered in the Stationers' Register on 20 May 1609 by Thomas Thorpe as 'a Booke called SHAKESPEARES sonnettes' appears to have been perfectly regular and businesslike. It is quite consistent with Thorpe's practice in publishing other texts which we know to have been authorized. Among his other recent publications were Jonson's *Sejanus his Fall* (1605), *Hymenaei* (1696), *Volpone* (1607), *Masques of Blackness and of Beautie* (1608); Chapman, Jonson and Marston's *Eastward Ho!* (1605); Marston's *What You Will* (1607); and Chapman's *Conspiracie and Tragedie of Byron* (1608). These seem in each case to have been authorized texts, and in many cases to have been authorially corrected while at press.[1] The majority were printed by George Eld, the printer of Q. Sidney Lee's oft-repeated assertion that Thorpe's line of business was as a 'procurer of neglected "copy"'[2] is completely unsupported by evidence. Indeed, it seems that during the period of his publication of *Shakespeare's Sonnets* Thorpe had built up a powerful reputation as a publisher of authorized texts by leading dramatists. But we may wonder why, if Shakespeare himself sold *Sonnets*, he did not turn once more to Richard Field, his Stratford school-fellow, who had published his narrative poems in 1593 and 1594, and, more recently, Alexander's sonnet sequence *Aurora*.

The answer may lie in Thorpe's theatrical associations. Though non-dramatic poetry did not figure much in Thorpe's 'list', his work for Shakespeare's fellow dramatists must

---

1 For a full list of Thorpe's publications, see Katharine F. Pantzer, *STC*, 3.168; for a detailed account of his publishing career, see Duncan-Jones, '*Sonnets* unauthorized?'.

2 Lee, 94.

inevitably have drawn him to his attention. After all, Shakespeare had been one of the 'leading Tragedians' in Jonson's *Sejanus his Fall* (Tiberius or Sejanus, perhaps?), and it has even been suggested that he had a hand in writing it.[1] He could scarcely have failed to notice the up-market print publication of this play, which had been a flop in the theatre, and to observe also that it was published by Thorpe and printed by Eld, 'who discharged his difficult task with a high degree of accuracy'[2]. Having noticed that, Shakespeare surely also took note of Thorpe's 1607 publication of *Volpone*. It may reasonably be supposed that Thorpe gave a good price for literary texts by dramatists, for Jonson, to name but one, is most unlikely to have settled for anything else. For Shakespeare too, in a severe plague year, the price must have been an important consideration, even if he ended up feeling that he had 'sold cheap what is most dear' (110.3).

The division of copies between two booksellers, William Aspley and John Wright, indicates that Thorpe was determined to maximize his return on his adventurous 'setting forth' of Shakespeare's sonnets, and may suggest also that a larger than normal print-run had been produced.[3] William Aspley's shop was in St Paul's Churchyard, at the sign of 'the Parrot'; John Wright's was a little to the north, at the door of Christ Church nearest to Newgate.[4] Whether the moneyed classes returned to the City after the plague-ridden summer of 1609 by way of the Strand or of Holborn, they would pass near one of the shops at which *Shakespeare's Sonnets* was on sale. If title-pages were posted up as publicity, the large-size capitalized 'SHAKE-SPEARES' in the top line was bound to be attractive, at this

1   Barton, 94.
2   Jonson, 4.330.
3   The suggestion recorded by Kerrigan (427) 'that Thorpe diverted copies to avoid the suppression of his volume by Shakespeare' is absurd. Aspley had worked for Thorpe on many other publications; John Wright may have been chosen as the secondary bookseller precisely because his shop was in a conspicuous position.
4   *STC*, 3.6, 190.

period when his reputation was at its lifetime zenith.

Needless to say, given the widespread view of Q as a surreptitious publication, many scholars have also regarded the text itself as exceptionally badly printed, though the text has also had some enthusiastic champions.[1] Lee, as ever, was the most outspoken of Q's critics, claiming not only that there was at least one 'defect' every ten lines, but also that 'the compositors followed an unintelligent transcript'. For Lee, nothing at all about Q could be praised – he saw it as a slovenly version of a stolen manuscript itself of poor quality. However, through a painstaking analysis of supposed 'misprints' H.E. Rollins demonstrated that a high proportion of the word-forms so identified by Lee and others were no more than either variant spellings, perfectly acceptable in the period, or slight orthographical oddities. He reduced the list of eighty-four 'misprints' assembled by Lee and others to a mere thirty-six. The present edition, in which some previously emended words are retained, reduces the list yet further. Some of the oddities labelled 'defects' by Lee may reflect a dogged attempt by Eld's compositors – who were accustomed, after all, to working for the exceptionally pernickety Jonson – to be faithful to the peculiarities of their copy. For instance, the fourteen occurrences of 'their' for 'thy' seem to testify to the literalness with which they replicated what they thought they read in their copy, even when it made poor sense.

Admittedly, unlike those of Jonson's texts which had undergone careful proof-correction, Q could not be described as especially well printed, and *A Lover's Complaint*, especially, shows signs of haste and carelessness – unless, which is possible, that part of the manuscript copy was markedly worse written. But some of the features that give a bad impression visually have no bearing on textual accuracy. For instance, there seems to have been a severe shortage of good-quality titling type, needed for the initial letter of of each sonnet, and this problem was

1 Rollins 2.6–11.

exacerbated by Shakespeare's habit of opening sonnets with questions or exclamations. Twenty-three sonnets open with the letter W, which appears in four different founts: large 'VV' (three times), smaller 'vv' (eleven times), small 'w' (seven times) and italic '*w*' (twice). Other large capitals that appear in varying sizes include H, S and O. Yet the compositors may have done their best to be faithful in printing from manuscript copy that was at times hard to read. Indeed, some of the peculiarities of spelling that Lee called 'defects' may reflect Shakespeare's own characteristic spelling patterns. Though MacD. P. Jackson has distinguished compositors 'A' and 'B', partly with reference to differences in the spelling of some frequently occurring words, such as 'O'/'Oh', 'ritch'/'rich', 'dost'/'doost', some of the oddly spelt words that occur only once, such as 'miter' (metre, 17.12) or 'sugiest' (suggest, 144.2), may reflect the spelling of the copy. Compositorial habit is less likely to operate in the case of less common words. Also, one of the compositors may have been more faithful to the forms he found in his copy than the other was, his spelling practice being closer to the copy than that of his colleague.[1]

Whether the copy manuscript itself was autograph, as Chambers and others have suggested, or a scribal transcript, perhaps with authorial corrections, Lee's account of it as 'unintelligent' is simply abusive. For instance, care is consistently given to the elision or inclusion of medial 'e' in relation to metre, and this is something that appears to have been characteristic also of Shakespeare's orthography.[2] There are very few instances of metrically necessary soundings or elisions which have not been marked visually. In order to make this clear, Q's elisions are recorded among the textual collations. Q's care for metrical correctness is consonant with careful reading of authorial copy.

---

1 For strong evidence that Eld's printers at this period were normally faithful to the accidentals they found in their copy, see Murray.
2 Partridge, *Orthography*, 70.

Since we know next to nothing about Shakespeare's scribal habits, especially with reference to non-dramatic poetry, it is difficult to estimate the extent to which other features of Q may reflect them. For instance, thirty-three words are italicized. These may well have been italicized in the copy. Setting up in italic required compositors to turn to another case of type, and there seems no great reason why Eld's men should have gone to this extra trouble unless they believed that the change of fount was required of them by their copy. As George Wyndham pointed out in 1898,[1] many of the italicized words are either proper nouns, such as '*Adonis*' (53.5), '*Mars*' (55.7), '*Eaues*' (93.13) or '*Philomell*' (102.7), or words of Greek or Latin origin, such as '*Autumne*' (104.5), '*Abisme*' (112.9), or '*Hereticke*' (124.9). But some of the italicized proper names cannot be adequately explained with reference to normal printing-house practice.[2] The most complex example is 135, with its seven italicized occurrences of '*Will*', which are subtly and precisely distinguished from six unitalicized, and uncapitalized, occurrences of 'will'. It is hard to envisage that anyone other than the poet could differentiate these thirteen instances of '*Will*' / 'will' in such a careful manner. Also, it is hard to imagine why anyone except the poet should have gone to the trouble of italicizing various words that do not fall into the normal categories, such as '*Rose*' (1.2), '*Hews*' (20.7), '*Informer*' (125.13) or '*Alloes*' (*LC* 273). Lee's suggestion[3] that Shakespeare never learned to write italic script seems quite unconvincing, given his chosen profession, and the high standards of Stratford Grammar School.

The manuscript on which Q was based may indeed have been 'formally distinctive, if not eccentric', as Kerrigan suggests, but that is surely no argument for its being also 'non-authorial'[4]. Were a literary autograph certainly by Shakespeare ever to turn

1 Rollins, 2.7.
2 Cf. McKerrow, 251.
3 Lee, 294.
4 Kerrigan, 431.

40

up, it could well prove to be 'formally distinctive'. After all, Jonson was to praise Shakespeare's writing for its uniquely characteristic nature:

> Look how the fathers face
> Liues in his issue, euen so, the race
> Of *Shakespeares* minde, and manners brightly shines
> In his well torned, and true-filed lines
> In each of which, he seemes to shake a Lance,
> As brandish't at the eyes of Ignorance.[1]

Though he was no doubt alluding chiefly to Shakespeare's literary style, Jonson may have been familiar also with his spear-shakingly recognizable penmanship. If the orthography of Q is eccentric, its eccentricity may be to some extent authorial. According to A.C. Partridge, 'Shakespeare's spelling was old-fashioned in its attachment to full-spellings and its curious blend of Tudor, individual and pseudo-phonetic representations.'[2] He sees Shakespeare as learning better habits, after 1600, from Ben Jonson, but it is unlikely that his habits were wholly transformed. Indeed, in a later study Partridge has suggested that the 'numerous idiosyncratic spellings' in Q may be Shakespeare's own.[3] The 'book' sold to Thorpe may have taken the form either of an autograph manuscript or of an authorially corrected scribal transcript.

Benson and beyond

The still popular practice of rearranging *Shakespeare's Sonnets* to produce the appearance of a different overall meaning or bearing began with the bookseller John Benson's edition in 1640.[4] Though boldly entitled *Poems: Written by Wil. Shake-speare. Gent*,

---

1 Jonson, 8.392
2 Partridge, *Orthography*, 79.
3 Partridge, *Grammar*, 111.
4 *Poems: Written by Wil. Shake-speare. Gent . . .*, to be sold by John Benson, dwelling in St. Dunstans Church-yard (1640).

Benson's edition was even more outrageously piratical and misleading than Jaggard's 1612 *Passionate Pilgrim*, whose material it
incorporated. About thirty of the poems it attributes to
Shakespeare are by other writers.[1] The later parts of the volume
are particularly confusing, with *A Lover's Complaint* surrounded
by poems of Heywood's, and *The Phoenix and the Turtle* placed
after the song (perhaps by Fletcher) 'Take, O take those lips away'
and before Orlando's mawkish verses beginning 'Why should this
a desert be?', from *As You Like It* (3.2.121ff.). These last, when
forced into a context which makes them appear to be amorous
verses of Shakespeare's own, seem particularly feeble. There is
little doubt that Benson set out at once to ingratiate and to mislead his readers. There is a visible attempt, though not an entirely
efficient one, to suggest that the addressee throughout is a woman.
The 'he' pronoun is often, though not quite always, altered to
'she', and changes such as 'sweet love' for 'sweet boy' (108.5), or
the entitling of 122 'Vpon the receit of a Table Book from his
Mistris', reinforce the suggestion that these are conventional, heterosexual love sonnets. But Benson's adaptation was unsystematic
and incomplete. Though 126 ('O thou my lovely Boy . . .') is
among eight sonnets omitted from his collection, the even more
compromising 20 ('A woman's face . . . ') is retained, with a title,
'The Exchange', which will surely not prevent attentive readers of
the last six lines from noticing that the addressee must be anatom-
ically male. In his prefatory epistle, Benson had the impudence to
praise Shakespeare's sonnets for their lucidity:

> in your perusall you shall finde them *Seren*, cleere and eli-
> gantly plaine, such gentle straines as shall recreate and
> not perplexe your braine, no intricate or cloudy stuffe to
> puzzell intellect, but perfect eloquence.

He must have been well aware that his own rearrangement and

---

1   The figure is imprecise because of the Shakespearean dubia included in *The
    Passionate Pilgrim.*

titling of the sonnets, his habitual running together of two or more sonnets to give the appearance of a longer poem, together with his mingling of Shakespearean with non-Shakespearean poems throughout the volume, was extremely misleading. His epistle may be taken as cogent evidence that the very difficult and original 1609 sonnets had indeed acquired a reputation, over the previous thirty years, for being 'intricate or cloudy'. Though he makes no explicit allusion to the sex of Shakespeare's addressee, Benson's use of the word '*Seren*' may have been intended to offer vague reassurance on this score to readers who had picked up a notion that *Shakespeare's Sonnets* was in some way abnormal, as well as puzzling.

For well over a century, Benson succeeded in muddying the textual waters. It was his edition that was read and edited, almost exclusively, until the superb work of Malone in 1780. Even the publisher Bernard Lintott (perhaps aided by the dramatist Congreve), though he presented a text based on Q, seems to have shared Benson's determination to heterosexualize the sequence, at least superficially. Sonnets 1–154 are described as '*One Hundred and Fifty Sonnets, all of them in Praise of his Mistress*' (note the assertiveness of that '*all*'); and very oddly, *A Lover's Complaint* is called '*A Lover's Complaint of his Angry Mistress*', thus identifying a male narrator, rather than a female complainer, as the 'Lover' of the title.[1] Neither of these descriptions, one would have thought, could long survive a close perusal of the poems themselves, which the editor transmits rather carefully. Possibly the unknown editor wanted to be faithful to Q, but Lintott felt that these titles should be added to reassure book-buyers that all the poems they were about to read were dedicated to the praise of Shakespeare's mistress, leaving them to discover the unlikelihood of this only when they got the volumes back home.

---

1   *A Collection of Poems, in Two Volumes: Being all the Miscellanies of Mr. William Shakespeare, which were Publish'd by himself in the year 1609, and now correctly printed from those Editions*, Printed for Bernard Lintott (?1711).

Though George Steevens included (without any comment or annotation) a version of Q in his 1766 edition of *Twenty of the Plays of Shakespeare*,[1] neither this nor the Lintott text seems to have excited much interest. Edward Capell prepared a further edition, based on 'Lintott', but it never reached print.[2] It was not until 1780 that the 1609 text was properly instated as the sole authoritative text of Shakespeare's sonnets, when Edmond Malone brought out his two-volume *Supplement* to the 1778 Johnson–Steevens edition of the plays. Malone, apparently unruffled, observed that 'one hundred and twenty [*sic*] of the following poems' are addressed to a man, and claimed that parallels with the plays 'leave not the smallest doubt of their authenticity'[3]. But the harm had been done. Benson's edition had successfully introduced doubts about whether or how often the speaker addressed a man, and implicitly suggested that, if rearranged, the sonnets might yield up a more conventional, accessible and socially acceptable message.

Even Malone, while observing wisely that 'Daniel's sonnets, which were published in 1592', appear to be Shakespeare's chief model, apparently failed to notice the structural parallel between Daniel's *Delia* plus *The Complaint of Rosamond,* and *Shakespeare's Sonnets* plus *A Lover's Complaint*. He relegated *A Lover's Complaint* to the very end of the volume, interposing *The Passionate Pilgrim* and *The Phoenix and the Turtle* before it. Though he did not explicitly challenge the authenticity of *A Lover's Complaint*, Malone's low-key remark that 'This poem was printed in 1609, with our author's name, at the end of the quarto edition of his *Sonnets*',[4] combined with his relegation of it to the very end of the volume, suggests that he had some doubts about it. Although a few later editors, such as Pooler,

---

1   George Steevens, ed., *Twenty of the Plays of Shakespeare* (1766), iv.
2   The copy of Lintott's edition marked up by Capell is in the library of Trinity College, Cambridge.
3   Malone, 1.579–81.
4   Ibid., 1.732.

have included *A Lover's Complaint* in editions of *Sonnets* despite such doubts – Pooler conceded no more than that 'it contains lines that might have been written by Shakespeare'[1] – it is only with Kerrigan's edition in 1986 that the *Complaint* has been confidently restored to its original position as an integral component of the sequence. Benson's disintegration of Q did lasting damage.

CONTEXT AND ALLUSION

How do we reconcile Shakespeare's consistently scornful allusions to sonnets and sonneteering in his plays with the fact of his having composed one of the longest sonnet sequences of the period? Sonnet-writing, in the early comedies, is presented either as a trite and cynical aid to wooing – Proteus advises the lovesick Thurio

> You must lay lime, to tangle her desires
> By wailful sonnets, whose composed rhymes
> Should be full-fraught with serviceable vows
> (*TGV* 3.2.69–71)

– or as a sign of the mentally debilitating effect of love. Each of the four young men in *Love's Labour's Lost* in turn betrays his collapse into passion by the penning of a (bad) sonnet – or, in one case, lyric – prompted by the new experience. Their composition of a sonnet apiece is the clinching proof, in *Much Ado,* that Beatrice and Benedick have fallen in love (*LLL* 4.3; *MA* 5.4.86–90). In *All's Well* Parolles uses a part-sonnet to warn Diana against Bertram, to which Bertram responds, 'He shall be whipp'd through the army, with this rhyme in's forehead' (*AW* 4.3.203–25). Certainly sonnets and soldiery do not mix. When the Dauphin, in *Henry V,* proposes to compose a sonnet in praise of his horse, it is quite clear from his companions' comments that this reveals his narcissism and weakness of character, and not

1   Ard[1], xl.

merely because sonnet-writing is an inappropriate ploy for a commander on the eve of fighting a major battle (*H5* 3.7.42ff.). A taste for reading collections of sonnets, likewise, is associated by Shakespeare with feeble-mindedness, as when the hopelessly weedy Master Slender, in *The Merry Wives of Windsor*, declares 'I had rather than forty shillings I had my book of songs and sonnets here' (*MW* 1.1.179–80). Two of Shakespeare's most intelligent lovers, Orlando and Hamlet, deliver themselves when in love of puerile verses (though not in sonnet form) which suggest mental and aesthetic collapse. In the theatre, it seems, Shakespeare almost invariably presents the writing of love poetry in general, and sonnets in particular, as ridiculous.

The answer may lie in the radical difference between *Shakespeare's Sonnets* and all its Elizabethan and Continental predecessors. These poems have none of the tediously predictable quality of the love sonnets mocked in the plays. They are not merely non-Petrarchan and non-Sidneian, but in important respects both anti-Petrarchan and anti-Sidneian. Though Sidney ostensibly distinguished Astrophil's heartfelt utterances from 'poor Petrarch's long deceased woes'[1], he did, nevertheless, write within the elastic boundaries of Petrarchanism, as redrawn by sixteenth-century French and Italian imitators. At a technical level, Sidney's sonnets are all written in the exacting 'Italian' form. The inclusion of songs within the sequence is also a broadly Petrarchan feature. But most conspicuously, the poems as a whole are, like Petrarch's, addressed to a single fictionalized and idealized female love-object, 'Stella', who proves, in the face of all of Astrophil's rhetorical endeavours, to be unattainable. Like Petrarch's Laura and Sidney's Stella, the addressees of Sidney's many English imitators, such as Lodge, Drayton, Daniel, Barnes and Fletcher, are also female.

Despite Sidney Lee's bold claim, quoted above (p. 33), that 'Hundreds of sonneteers had celebrated . . . the charms of

---

1   *AS*, 15.7.

young men', there is actually only one other Elizabethan sonnet sequence with a young male addressee, Richard Barnfield's mini-sequence of twenty 'Sonnets' included in his *Cynthia* (1595).[1] Indeed, there appears to be some as yet unexplained connection between Shakespeare and Barnfield. Two poems by Barnfield were included alongside Shakespeare's in *The Passionate Pilgrim;* Francis Meres, when he revealed to the world the existence of Shakespeare's 'sugred Sonnets', also gave particular praise to 'my friend master Richard Barnefielde'; and most teasingly, Barnfield's *Cynthia* is prefaced by a floridly over-written commendatory poem by one 'T.T.', whose tone of cryptic knowingness is somewhat analogous to that of Thomas Thorpe's dedication to Q. It ends:

> So those rare Sonnets, where wits ripe doth lie,
> With Troian Nimph, doe soare thy fame to skie,
>> And those, and these, contend thy Muse to raise
>> (Larke mounting Muse) with more then common praise.

Like Barnfield's twenty sonnets to 'Ganymede', but unlike every other Elizabethan sequence, Shakespeare's sonnets 1–126 celebrate a young male love-object; and so in a sense does *A Lover's Complaint*, much of which consists of a nameless maiden's anatomy of the irresistible charms and wiles of her young seducer. In making a young man's beauty and worth his central focus, Shakespeare may be seen as overturning the conventions of more than two hundred years of 'Petrarchanism', broadly interpreted.

Despite a widespread notion, promoted by such Victorian and Edwardian critics as Gerald Massey and Thomas Tyler, that the major question prompted by *Shakespeare's Sonnets* is the identity of the 'dark lady', only just over a sixth of the sonnets in the volume are unambiguously associated with a woman. Even those which are so associated can be seen as brutally defiant of Petrarchanism. Instead of exploring the subtle and complex

---

1   Richard Barnfield, *Cynthia. With Certaine Sonnets, and the Legend of Cassandra* (1595).

effect on the speaker of an obsession with a chaste and high-born lady who can never be possessed physically, 127–52 offer backhanded praise of a manifestly non-aristocratic woman who is neither young, beautiful, intelligent nor chaste, but, like Touchstone's Audrey, provides a perfectly adequate outlet for male desire. In the famous 130 ('My mistress' eyes are nothing like the sun') the poet issues an explicit challenge to all those other poets by whom mistresses have hitherto been 'belied with false compare'. Though Shakespeare's celebration of 'black' beauty has often been linked with Sidney, whose 'Stella' has black eyes, it is really horribly different, for this woman also has a muddy complexion, bad breath and a clumsy walk. With utter cynicism, the speaker praises her as 'a poor thing, but mine own' (compare *AYL* 5.4.58), celebrating her in swaggering terms which are ingeniously offensive both to her and to women in general. While Sidney's Astrophil wished that 'Pleasure might cause her read' his sonnets,[1] there could surely be no question of the woman described in *Sonnets* either reading or understanding what is said about her, let alone receiving any pleasure from it. Shakespeare's speaker seems, like Touchstone, to brag to other men in his audience that he can make satisfactory sexual use of a woman too stupid to realize that she is also being set up as the butt of his wit.

A strongly misogynistic bias is hinted at early on in the sequence. The youth may be celebrated in sonnet 18 as 'more temperate' in beauty than other poets' love-objects partly because, unlike them, he does not menstruate, so his beauty is not continually diminished by 'nature's changing course' (menstrual bleeding was known as 'monthly courses', *OED* 27). In 20 the youth is praised for possessing female beauty without female instability – 'An eye more bright than theirs, less false in rolling' – nor is he 'acquainted / With shifting change, as is false women's fashion' (see notes). He is anatomized as physiologi-

1   *AS*, 1.3.

cally, as well as morally, superior to the female love-objects so over-praised by those poets who have been 'Stirred by a painted beauty' (21.2). A suspicion of some preoccupation with the negative connotations of menstruation is confirmed when the reader reaches the woman-focused 127–54 if it is observed that the total of these 'dark lady' sonnets is twenty-eight, corresponding with the lunar month or menstrual cycle.

In 1–126, which constitute what is in every sense the greater part of *Shakespeare's Sonnets*, Shakespeare seems rarely to refer to Petrarchanism, except by means of the implicit challenge or redefinition that he offers to it throughout in eulogizing a young male friend, rather than a distant, idealized woman, and in making almost no claims to spiritual enlightenment. An early annotator wrote at the end of his copy of Q 'What a heap of wretched Infidel Stuff'[1]. Although the exclusion of Petrarch's treatment of secular love as a route to religious transcendence characterizes many English responses to Petrarchanism, it is unusually marked in the case of Shakespeare. Indeed, in some sonnets he seems to push his idolatrous substitution of friend-worship for Christian worship to flamboyantly blasphemous extremes, as in the mock-Trinitarian rhetoric of 105, 'Let not my love be called idolatry', culminating in:

> Three themes in one, which wondrous scope affords.
> Fair, kind and true have often lived alone,
> Which three, till now, never kept seat in one.

One answer, then, to the question of why Shakespeare composed a sonnet sequence might be literary. He sought to appropriate and redefine the genre, rejecting the stale conceits of mistress-worship, and to create a sonnet sequence so different from all its predecessors that the form could never be the same again. The title, 'SHAKE-SPEARES SONNETS', can be read as suggesting this. Shakespeare presents the paramount sonnet sequence, which

---

1   The copy in the Rosenbach Collection; cf. Rollins, 2.348.

both continues and conclusively redefines that 'excellence of sweet poesie' which had been demonstrated nearly twenty years earlier in Sidney's *Astrophil and Stella*. The homoerotic thrust of 1–126, combined with the outrageous misogyny of 127–54, may also be construed as designed to gratify the literary culture of James's court, rather than (necessarily) to reflect or express any personal preference on the part of Shakespeare 'the man'.

However, an alternative or additional approach to answering the question I have asked – why did Shakespeare write a sonnet sequence, since he seems to have despised traditional love poetry? – lies in recourse to biography, or biographical speculation. Romantic critics have liked to view Shakespeare as surprised into sonneteering by some real-life experience. Ever since the edition of *Sonnets* in 1837 by James Boaden, the first Pembrokian, scholars have pursued possible personal allusions. A popular view, especially among those who have not studied the whole sequence thoroughly, singles out the identity of the 'dark lady' as the chief question to be addressed. Frank Harris went to the length of suggesting that Shakespeare was stung into dramatic, as well as poetic, creativity by an unhappy affair with Mary Fitton, and owed her 'the greater part of his renown'[1]. This notion has been passionately endorsed by A.L. Rowse, who, on lighting on Emilia Lanier, exclaimed to his friends 'This is she! This is the Lady!' He gave one of the books in which he chronicled his 'discovery' the confident title *Shakespeare's Sonnets: The Problems Solved* (1973).

The search for 'the Lady' appears to have been driven by two motives. The first is a post-Romantic determination to conventionalize and familiarize *Shakespeare's Sonnets*, to attach the poems to that very courtly love tradition which, I have just suggested, Shakespeare was explicitly rejecting and debunking. Once identified, Shakespeare's *femme fatale* could supposedly join the ranks of other such ladies, from Petrarch's Laura to

1   Harris, 231.

Keats's Fanny Brawne or W.B. Yeats's Maud Gonne, and as a consequence Shakespeare, as a love poet, could be comfortably assimilated into a great European tradition. Some Victorian and Edwardian scholars, such as Gerald Massey and Thomas Tyler, devoted large parts of their lonely lives to the quest for 'the lady', and Frank Harris and Bernard Shaw competed to dramatize the story of Shakespeare's 'tragic love'. Working before the twentieth-century critical cult of ambiguity and word-play, these writers seem to have been oblivious to the sheer nastiness of many of the 'dark lady' sonnets, which can now be seen to encompass not so much passionate devotion to a distantly cruel mistress as elaborate mockery of a woman who is no more than a sexual convenience.

The second, and possibly most powerful, driving force behind the quest for 'the Lady' has been its power of *suggestio falsi*. The foregrounding of 'the Lady' strongly implies that the predominant thrust of *Shakespeare's Sonnets* is heterosexual. Devotees of an idealized, domesticated, image of Shakespeare the man may be a little uncomfortable at a suspicion of adultery, but this is nothing like so alarming as a suspicion of pederasty. The awkward fact that more than four-fifths of the sequence is devoted to celebrating a fair youth and to exploring the speaker's relationship with him can be bypassed if readers' attention is firmly enough directed towards 'her'. In the case of Rowse, this motive has been delightfully transparent. While happy to categorize Marlowe as 'a raving homo', Rowse has been equally outspoken in his identification of 'the Bard' as a 'red-blooded heterosexual', instinctively thrilled by 'the frou-frou of skirts'.[1] To his credit, he does take full account of 1–126, but offers splendidly idiosyncratic readings of these sonnets. Stupid people may have thought the notorious 20 a little compromising, for instance, but according to Rowse, 'the boot is quite on the other leg . . . it was not Shakespeare who was homosexual, but the

---

1   Personal conversation with K.D.-J. at All Souls, *c*. 1984.

young peer who would not have minded. This is indisputable.'[1]

Despite such attempts to foreground 'the Lady', 'Mr. W.H.' (Dedication 3) has of course also been the subject of much speculation, as has the 'rival poet' apparently alluded to in 78–86. Rollins offers a very full account of biographical interpretation up to 1944, and Schoenbaum continues the story brilliantly up to 1991 in his revised *Shakespeare's Lives*, concluding that 'this author fearlessly predicts that, whether or not there will be an end of human foolery, we have not heard the last of W.H.'[2] Schoenbaum's remark was prompted in part by a more recent attempt to put a woman at the centre of *Shakespeare's Sonnets*, Barbara Everett's 1986 article on 'Mrs. Shakespeare'. She suggested that Anne Hathaway, 'a powerful, even attractively masculine woman', identified herself as the master-mistress of the poet's passion, and that the valuable text was appropriated and sold to Thorpe by her presumed brother William Hathaway. In its bold creativity and defiance of documentary evidence this article merits comparison with Rowse at his most imaginative.

No doubt Schoenbaum's general proposition is correct, and the present edition is no more likely to put an end to biographical speculation than previous studies have done.[3] Nevertheless, the contextualization suggested here for *Shakespeare's Sonnets*, as a sequence in part written after 1600, and put into its final shape close in time to its authorized publication in 1609, carries with it some further implications for the identification of 'Mr. W. H.' The case for Southampton, one of the two strongest candidates, effectively collapses if this dating is accepted. Not only are Henry Wriothesley's initials the wrong way round; he was over 35 in 1609, and recollections of the time when he was a 'lovely boy' were rather distant. Also, as Chambers pointed out, if Southampton were the poet's 'fair friend', 'one would

1   Rowse, xxv.
2   Schoenbaum, *Lives*, 566.
3   For another attempt to put an end to further speculation, see Foster, who claims that 'W.H.' is a misprint for 'W.SH.'

expect to find some hints . . . of the major interests of Southampton's early life; his military ambitions, his comradeship with Essex, the romance of his marriage. There are none.'[1]

Chambers also declared himself 'rather struck by the fact that, although Southampton was still alive, it was not to him, but to Herbert and his brother that [the First Folio] was dedicated'. He felt that the case for William Herbert (1580–1630), Third Earl of Pembroke (see Fig. 3), had been 'mishandled' by previous scholars, such as Tyler, because of their preoccupation with Mary Fitton, the supposed 'dark lady'. She continued to attract strong devotees despite evidence for her fair complexion; despite the fact that she was unmarried at the time of her affair with Herbert, not tied by a 'bed-vow', like the woman of sonnet 152; and despite the fact that, as a Maid of Honour, she was a well-guarded court lady not very likely to consort with a middle-aged actor. Even now there is some danger that Mary Fitton's candidature for the role of 'dark lady' may confuse the case for Herbert, so it requires to be disposed of. The monstrously sexist assumption that a woman who is sufficiently attracted to one man to consummate her love without marriage would have been prepared to have sex with anyone has coloured a surprising number even of later-twentieth-century interpretations of *Shakespeare's Sonnets*.[2] This assumption also crucially underpins Rowse's support for Emilia Lanier, which seems to depend on a belief that a woman who was Lord Hunsdon's mistress would be willing to have sex with anyone, including, therefore, Shakespeare. Yet in reality, the mistress of such an eminent nobleman as either young William Herbert or old Lord Hunsdon would be most unlikely (even if so inclined) to jeopardize her own position and the status of her future or actual

1 Chambers, *Shakespeare*, 1.565–7.
2 For an extended challenge to another instance of the persistence of this view, see Lindley.

3 Simon van de Passe, engraved portrait of William Herbert, Third Earl of
Pembroke (1580–1630). From Henry Holland, *Bazilωlogia: A Booke of Kings*
(1618), fol. 89ʳ (Bodleian 4° Rawl. 170)

child by promiscuity. If the 'dark lady' is still to be sought in literal terms, it should be borne in mind not only that Mary Fitton was light-complexioned and unmarried, but also that though a nobleman might readily visit taverns and stews, as do Shakespeare's Prince Hal in *1* and *2 Henry IV*, and Lysimachus in *Pericles*, it would be virtually impossible for a common player, even a member of the King's Men, to penetrate the chambers of the Maids of Honour.

The chief bearing of Mary Fitton on the case for William Herbert as 'W.H.' lies in the fact that she was at least the fourth well-born girl whom Herbert resolutely refused to marry. In 1595 an attempt to betroth Herbert to Elizabeth Carey, daughter and sole heir of Sir George Carey, had to be abandoned because of the young man's 'not liking'. (Her subsequent marriage to Sir Thomas Berkeley has often been identified, most recently by David Wiles,[1] as the likely occasion for *A Midsummer Night's Dream*). Two years later, in the summer of 1597, a further attempt was made to match him suitably, this time to Bridget Vere, Lord Burghley's grand-daughter, and daughter of the Earl of Oxford. This, too, collapsed after some months of negotiation. Herbert's father was by now a sick man, and desperate to see his elder son suitably matched before he succeeded to the earldom. Yet another marriage, to a niece of Charles Howard, Earl of Nottingham, was attempted, and failed, in the summer of 1599. Robert Sidney's agent Rowland Whyte reported that 'I do not find any disposition at all in this gallant young Lord to marry'[2]. It was not that Herbert was lacking in sexual passion: indeed, according to Clarendon's later testimony, 'he was immoderately given up to women'. It was to marriage, specifically, that he was strongly averse. Early in 1600–1 he had made Mary Fitton pregnant, 'but utterly renounceth all marriage', despite a spell in the Fleet Prison followed by banishment from

1 Wiles, *passim*.
2 HMC *De L'Isle and Dudley*, 2.478; Brennan, 101.

court. In the light of Herbert's well-documented reluctance to marry, Dover Wilson's speculations are attractive. He suggested that the Countess of Pembroke 'asked [Shakespeare] to meet the young lord at Wilton, on his 17th birthday', and commissioned him to compose an appropriate number of pro-marriage sonnets for the occasion.[1] This would locate sonnets 1–17 in April 1597, and suggest that Meres, in referring to Shakespeare's 'private friends', could be alluding to the Herbert family. Wilson's notion that young Herbert's tutor, Samuel Daniel, might have introduced Shakespeare to the family is also quite plausible. But in default of any supporting evidence, these can be no more than wild conjectures.

In any case, William Herbert's reluctance to marry, though certainly extremely apt to sonnets 1–17, constitutes only one of many arguments for his identity both with the dedicatee 'Mr. W.H.' and with the poet-speaker's 'fair friend'. That Thorpe's dedicatee is the same man as the addressee of 1–126 has often been doubted. Yet most first-time readers will naturally conflate the two. In wishing the dedicatee 'THAT. ETERNITY. / PROMISED. / BY. / OUR. EVER-LIVING. POET.' Thorpe seems to add his own support to the poet's 'ENSUING.' claims to immortalize his friend in 'black lines' (63.13). Though some have strained to interpret 'BEGETTER.' as 'procurer', the word's most obvious connotation is 'inspirer'. The poet's brain is the womb made fertile by his noble subject–matter, which brings forth sonnets as the subject's babies. An analogous application of this fairly common metaphor occurs in Sidney's *Astrophil and Stella*, 50, where Astrophil is in painful labour with 'thoughts' of Stella, to which he gives birth as lines of verse, 'poor babes', which he is tempted to kill for their inadequacy. Shakespeare's own Richard II, more solipsistically, attempted to identify his brain as a womb in which his own soul begets 'A generation of still-breeding thoughts' (*R2* 5.5.6–9).

---

1   Cam², c.

But even more directly applicable to the dedication of *Sonnets* is Sidney's dedication of the *Old Arcadia* to the Countess of Pembroke. He calls the *Arcadia* 'this child which I am loath to father'. His sister has inspired the work, by 'desiring' him to write it, so that his 'young head', womb-like, has had 'many fancies begotten in it'[1]. If Herbert, the Countess of Pembroke's son, born just at the time when the *Old Arcadia*, too, was coming to fruition,[2] was 'Mr. W.H.', he would have readily picked up the allusion to his uncle's celebrated dedication, lately published anew in the 1605 *Arcadia* – as well as many verbal and metaphoric echoes of Sidney within the sonnets themselves (see notes). For readers proceeding into the first seventeen or eighteen sonnets, focused on the addressee's failure to become a father, there emerges an elaborate paradox. W.H. is proclaimed by Thorpe as the sonnets' 'ONLY. BEGETTER.' – but it seems that he has begotten only sonnets, not the living children who would immortalize him 'a mightier way', 'With means more blessed than my barren rhyme' (16.1–4). In what follows, therefore, I shall assume that 'Mr. W.H.' is the same individual as the original of the young man addressed and celebrated within the sonnets, and shall set out the case for his being based on William Herbert.

The financial aspect of patronage, in this period, should never be overlooked. After three years in which London's public theatres had been closed because of plague, Shakespeare must have been looking for the best reward possible for his precious sonnets. It is most improbable that he would have wished the book to be dedicated, sentimentally, to some obscure actor or sea-cook (the mythical 'Willie Hughes'), or a penniless kinsman (his infant nephew William Hart, or his presumed brother-in-law William Hathaway) – least of all to 'William Himself' or 'William [S]h[akespeare]'. None of these could offer him prestige

---

1   *OA*, 3.
2   See Duncan-Jones, *Sidney*, 168ff.

and protection, or, most crucially, a substantial cash reward. His well-documented generosity to writers makes William Herbert, Earl of Pembroke, a powerful candidate. Clarendon described him as so lavish in rewarding talented men that neither his own very large fortune nor that of his wife matched up to the exceptional liberality of his habits: rather than jockeying for favour or reward on his own behalf, he 'was still ready to promote the pretences of worthy men'[1]. And according to Aubrey,

> He was the greatest Maecenas to learned Men of any Peer of his time: or since . . . He was a good Scholar, and delighted in Poetrie; and did sometimes (for his Diversion) write some Sonnets and Epigrammes.

As an exceptionally generous and intelligent patron of letters, and even something of a poet, Herbert was a worthy heir to his uncle Philip Sidney. Unlike Sidney, he had the resources, or at least the credit-rating, to support his lavishness. For instance, during the very year of Q, 1609, he gave a hundred pounds for the purchase of books to the newly founded Bodleian Library in Oxford.[2] He was already living and giving considerably beyond his means. Two letters to Sir Michael Hicks, one in May 1609, one in November, show him appealing for renewal of Hicks's loan to him of £1,800.[3] Hicks seems to have been quite happy to do this, for this was the year in which Pembroke's public career, initially slow to develop, really took off. On 27 May 1609 he was incorporated as a member of the King's Virginia Company of London.[4] By 1618 he was the largest individual investor in the company, with a stake of £400.[5] A response to news of this high-profile commitment, in the very week of Q's registration with the Stationers' Company, may be discerned in Thorpe's image of himself as 'THE. WELL-WISHING. /

---

1   Quoted in Cam², cxxi.
2   Bodleian Benefactors' Register.
3   BL MS Lansdowne 91, fols 45, 143.
4   *CSP Dom. 1603–10*, 515.
5   Brennan, 149.

ADVENTURER. IN. / SETTING. / FORTH.' While Thorpe was an 'adventurer in setting forth' in the sense that he made an investment, and took a risk, in 'setting forth', or publishing, 'THESE. ENSUING. SONNETS.', Herbert was now committed to a much more exciting kind of 'setting forth' – expeditions to explore and colonize the New World. While Thorpe was an 'adventurer', or investor, in books, Herbert was an 'adventurer' in ships, men and commodities. And while the name 'Virginia' alluded to the colony's origins in the previous reign, that of the Virgin Queen, the form of Herbert's own name, 'Mr. W.H.', alluded to the period before his father's death in January 1600/1, as the time when, not yet either an earl, or of age, or married, the youthful Herbert had 'begotten' the ensuing sonnets, in particular 1–17.

Much has been made of the supposed impropriety of an earl's being addressed as 'Mr.', though Chambers did not feel that 'in such a document there would be anything very out of the way . . . in the suppression of an actual or courtesy title'.[1] If 'W.H.' denotes William Herbert, one obvious function of the 'Mr.' would be to indicate that the sonnets dedicated to him had their origin, or 'begetting', in the period before his inheritance of the Earldom of Pembroke. Rather as William Alexander had stressed on the title-page the fact that his sonnet sequence *Aurora* (1604) contained 'the first fancies of the *Authors youth*', the 'Mr.' may have indicated the pre-1601 conception of *Shakespeare's Sonnets*. My conjecture is that when Shakespeare left London for Stratford in some haste at the end of May 1609 he left instructions with Thorpe to use this form of address to Herbert, and to set out the dedication in pointed capitals. Though the initials of 'T.T.' are at the bottom, and the over-rhetorical wording is evidently Thorpe's, the dedication, like the text itself, had Shakespeare's authority.

Both Shakespeare and Thorpe might reasonably have looked to Pembroke's generosity to make their venture worthwhile. If

1   Chambers, *Shakespeare*, 1.566.

Nashe, as we now know, was given a reward of £5 for dedicating *Christs Teares over Jerusalem* (1593) to Lady Carey,[1] it seems unlikely that Pembroke would have paid any less for the dedication of *Shakespeare's Sonnets*. Indeed, given Pembroke's well-attested munificence, he may have paid more. Something between £5 and £10 might be a reasonable guess. The effort expended by Shakespeare and Thorpe in gaining a reward of this magnitude should be compared with the rather different effort that Shakespeare was also investing, at just this time, in recovering the sum of £6, with 24s interest, from his debtor John Addenbrooke (see above, p. 12).

The dedication of the First Folio plays to Pembroke and his brother by Shakespeare's 'fellows' Heminge and Condell in 1623 alludes to the Herbert brothers as having 'prosequuted both them, and their Author living, with so much fauour'. No doubt they too hoped for, and gained, good rewards from Pembroke and his brother. If they were aware that *Sonnets* had not only been authorized by Shakespeare himself – no 'stolne, and surreptitious copy', this – but that it had also been dedicated to Herbert, their momentous decision, whose long-term consequence has been the marginalization of all Shakespeare's non-dramatic work, to gather up plays only, would be fully explained. Pembroke did not need to have the sonnets presented to him if they were his already. Heminge and Condell's account of Shakespeare as 'parent' of the plays which are now 'Orphanes' may echo T.T.'s imagery of W.H. as 'begetter' of the sonnets.

The mock-lapidary form of the dedication, centred, and set out in capitals with a stop after each word, but in English (see Fig. 4), may allude to two recent works by Ben Jonson. Both had been published by Thorpe. The 1607 'BEN: IONSON his / VOLPONE' (note the genitive form of title, analogous to 'SHAKE-SPEARES SONNETS') has on the title-page verso a centred, capitalized dedication to 'THE TWO FAMOVS

---

1   Duncan-Jones, 'Nashe'.

VNIVERSITIES' by 'BEN. IONSON / THE GRATEFVLL ACKNOWLEDGER' (see Fig. 5) – a phrase mimicked in Thorpe's description of himself as 'THE. WELL-WISHING. / ADVENTURER.' For the Latinate device of placing a point after each capitalized word, but with an English text, the model was perhaps the consuls' proclamation in Act 5 of *Sejanus his Fall*, not centred, but capitalized and pointed. Since Jonson's learned tragedy *Sejanus* appears to have been written partly in response to Shakespeare's less learned *Julius Caesar*, Shakespeare may in turn have looked closely at it, echoing and appropriating some of its most portentously learned-seeming accoutrements. And Jonson, in turn, may have responded to the dedication of *Shakespeare's Sonnets*. As Dowden and others have observed, Jonson's 1616 dedication of his *Epigrammes* to the Earl of Pembroke opens rather oddly. After a centred and capitalized dedication 'TO . . . WILLIAM / EARLE OF PEMBROKE, / L. CHAMBERLAYNE, &c.', his epistle begins:

> MY LORD. While you cannot change your merit, I dare not change your title: It was that made it, and not I. Vnder which name, I here offer to your Lo: the ripest of my studies, my Epigrammes; which though they carry danger in the sound, doe not therefore seeke your shelter: For, when I made them, I had nothing in my conscience, to expressing of which I did need a cypher.[1]

Jonson's stress on his adoption of a correct and unalterable 'title' – 'MY LORD' – under which to address Pembroke certainly sounds like a side-swipe at some other writer who has had the temerity to change it; and his assertion that the ensuing poems, though epigrams, a genre often regarded as dangerously personal or satirical, are in fact not so, may also allude to some other, more compromising or 'dangerous' form of poetry, which had indeed required the use of 'a cypher'. If this passage does indeed refer to

---

1   Jonson, 8.25.

TO.THE.ONLIE.BEGETTER.OF.
THESE.INSVING.SONNETS.
Mʳ.W.H. ALL.HAPPINESSE.
AND.THAT.ETERNITIE.
PROMISED.

BY.

OVR.EVER-LIVING.POET.

WISHETH.

THE.WELL-WISHING.
ADVENTVRER.IN.
SETTING.
FORTH.

T. T.

4 Dedication leaf of the 1609 Quarto (Bodleian Malone 34, title-page verso)

15

TO THE MOST NOBLE
AND MOST ÆQVALL
SISTERS

THE TWO FAMOVS VNIVERSITIES,

FOR THEIR LOVE
AND
ACCEPTANCE

SHEWN TO HIS. POEME
IN THE PRESENTATION:

BEN JONSON

THE GRATEFVLL ACKNOWLEDGER

D······
BOTH ···········

There followes an *Epistle*, if
yourdare venture on
thelength,

5 Dedication leaf of Ben Jonson's *Volpone* (1607) (Bodleian Malone 225[4])

Shakespeare's Sonnets and its dedication, the phrase 'nothing in my conscience' also suggests that Jonson may have been one of the first of many readers to feel that Shakespeare's sonnets are morally compromising, and that the 'public manners' (111.4) that prompted him to publish his devotion to a young nobleman as a 'lovely boy' deserved rebuke. Shakespeare had committed a *faux pas* comparable with that of his own Falstaff when he addresses King Henry as 'my sweet boy' in front of the assembled court and echoes Daniel's *Rosamond* in appealing to him as 'My King! My Jove!' (*2H4* 5.5.42, 46).

If Shakespeare's patron and friend was Pembroke, Shakespeare was not alone in celebrating his beauty as well as his high birth and munificence. Francis Davison prefaced his courtly miscellany *A Poetical Rhapsody*, originally printed in 1602 but augmented and reprinted in 1608, with a sonnet praising Pembroke's 'lovely' 'shape' as well as his Sidneian ancestry. I quote the slightly revised 1608 text, since this immediately precedes the publication of *Sonnets*:

> Great Earle, whose brave Heroicke minde is higher
> And nobler, then thy noble high Degree:
> Whose outward shape, though it most lovely be
> Doth in faire Robes a fairer Soule attier:
> Who rich in fading wealth, in endlesse Treasure
> Of Vertue, Valour, Learning, richer art:
> Whose present greatnes, men esteeme but part
> Of what by line of future Hope they measure.
> Thou worthy Sonne unto a peerelesse Mother,
> Or Nephew to great *Sidney* of renowne,
> Who has deserv'd thy *Coronet*, to crowne
> With Lawrel crowne: a crown excelling th'other
> I Consecrate these Rimes to thy great Name,
> Which if thou like, they seeke no other fame.[1]

---

1 Francis Davison, *A Poetical Rapsodie* (1608), sig. A2ʳ. Cf. also John Davies of Hereford, *Wittes Pilgrimage* (?1605), sig. Q2ʳ⁻ᵛ.

Henry Brown, the only scholar to have proposed Francis Davison as a candidate for the 'rival poet', has been dismissed with utter contempt and disbelief.[1] Yet in certain respects Davison seems a distinct possibility. *A Poetical Rhapsody* is partly composed of poems by himself, his brother Walter and a friend veiled under the label 'Anomos': these two fellow poets could possibly be alluded to as 'his compeers by night' (86.7). The subtext of the miscellany, both in 1602 and in 1608, was its passionate plea on behalf of Francis Davison's father, William, briefly Secretary of State to Queen Elizabeth, but cast into disgrace after his delivery of the warrant for the execution of Mary, Queen of Scots. As the son of an eminent statesman, even a fallen one, Francis Davison enjoyed a far higher social status than Shakespeare, and in the latter's eyes may have appeared 'a better spirit' (80.2). William Davison, who had been a distinguished agent in Scotland and the Netherlands, was still alive in 1608,[2] and still banished from court: he could possibly have been alluded to as his eldest son's 'affable familiar ghost' who – a retired spy of Walsingham's – 'nightly gulls him with intelligence' (86.9–10).

Yet it must be acknowledged that John Davies of Hereford, Samuel Daniel, George Chapman and Ben Jonson are all also plausible candidates for the role of 'rival poet'. All were protégés of Pembroke, and any or all might have been viewed by Shakespeare as offering a threat or competition to him in the pursuit of Pembroke's favour. Davies, for instance, included a poem to Pembroke in *Wittes Pilgrimage*, in which he is addressed as 'Faire featurd Soule! well-shapen Spright!'[3] Also, as suggested above, some individual sonnets appear to reflect friendly competition between Shakespeare and Drayton, who seems not to have numbered Pembroke among his patrons. Perhaps, indeed, the 'rival poet' is a composite figure, and the mini-sequence 76–86 should be seen as exploring the theme of the speaker-poet's

1   Rollins, 1.284.
2   He died in his house in Stepney about 21 December 1608.
3   John Davies of Hereford, *Wittes Pilgrimage*, sig. Q2[r-v].

sense of being threatened by other poets through a fictionally amalgamated writer, drawing on several individuals, rather than as embodying any single thread of allusion.

Conclusive evidence for a particular friendship between Shakespeare and Pembroke is lacking. No reliance can be placed, unfortunately, on W.J.Cory's account of a letter from the Countess of Pembroke (his mother) containing the sentence 'We have the man Shakespeare with us'.[1] Yet the circumstantial evidence is plentiful. There is no doubt that Pembroke favoured plays and players; he is documented as giving frequent and generous help to Ben Jonson, whose career was in so many ways parallel to Shakespeare's; he was rising high, and a conspicuous target for those seeking patronage, in 1609; his personal initials were W.H.; Thomas Thorpe openly dedicated a further work to him in 1610, applying to him the unusually intimate epithets 'gracefull' and 'sweete';[2] and he was to be the prime dedicatee of the First Folio.

Two further documents, while not clinching the case, suggest strongly that some degree of unconventional intimacy between Pembroke and a celebrated playwright and actor is at least within the bounds of possibility. On 6 August 1604 Giovanni Scaramelli, Venetian Secretary in England, sent the Doge and Senate a detailed eyewitness account of James I's coronation. He describes the coronation procession; the King's arrival at the Abbey, under a canopy supported by four rods with silver bells hanging from them; the disrobing and anointing; the coronation itself; and then the oaths of allegiance made by the peers. Each earl in turn advanced, knelt before the King, and kissed his hand, and in some cases also the crown. Then, in an account which singles out very few individuals by name, Scaramelli comes out with a startling anecdote:

---

1 Brennan 224.
2 J.H., trans., *St. Augustine of the City of God* (entered in the Stationers' Register in 1608), printed by George Eld (1610), sig. A3; cf. also the second edition of John Healey's *Epictetus his Manuell* (1616), floridly dedicated to Pembroke by Thorpe.

The Earl of Pembroke, a handsome youth, who is always with the King, and always joking with him, actually kissed his Majesty's face, whereupon the King laughed and gave him a little cuff.[1]

Scaramelli's word, *schiaffetto*, is a diminutive of *schiaffo*, defined by John Florio as 'a cuffe, a buffet, a box, a whirret or clap with a hand on the cheeke'.[2] Pembroke's extraordinary boldness in making such a public display of his personal intimacy with the King suggests a remarkable degree of social and physical self-confidence. Like the youth of sonnet 20, whose epicene beauty 'steals men's eyes and women's souls amazeth', Pembroke seems to have combined a career as a determined womanizer with an enthusiastic participation in the homosocial familiarities of James and his minions. This may have enabled him also to move easily and affably among the King's players.

A further document testifies to the depth of his affection for one of these in particular, Richard Burbage, who surely qualifies for the status of 'best friend' to Shakespeare. On 20 May 1619 Pembroke wrote a letter to Viscount Doncaster, then ambassador to Germany, who had 'Mr. Doctor Dunn' among his companions. The occasion for the letter's being written at all lay in the recent death of Burbage. The Duke of Lennox was entertaining the departing French ambassador to 'a great supper',

> & even now all the company are at the play, which I being tender harted could not endure to see so soone after the loss of my old acquaintance Burbadg.[3]

Burbage had died on 9 March, so Pembroke's grief was sustained for well over two months. He may indeed have felt more devastated by Burbage's death than by that of Queen Anne, which had

1   *CSP Venetian 1603–7*, 77. The original reads: 'Et fra questi il Conte di Pemruch, giovane gratioso et che sta sempre col Rè e su i scherzi, basciò anco la faccia a Sua Maesta, che si pose a rider a gli diede un schiaffetto.'
2   John Florio, *Queen Anna's New World of Words* (1611).
3   BL MS Egerton 2592, fols. 81–2.

occurred a few days earlier. Like the coronation incident, this autograph letter reveals Pembroke as a man quite ready to step out of line at grand court occasions for the sake of particular affections and allegiances. Just as his full-frontal kiss of James sounds to have been a public display of a particularly close relationship, so Pembroke's absence from the play in the Great Chamber at Whitehall appears to have been a deliberate signal of his special personal affection for the leading actor of the age. It was a public display of a private loss: otherwise why would he tell Doncaster about it? No doubt he also made it clear to his court companions that grief was the reason for his refusal to watch the play, thus underlining the fact that he knew Burbage better than they did. Rather strikingly, the play performed that night was *Pericles*.[1] Pembroke's 'tender harted' recollection of the dead Burbage may also have encompassed sad memories of this play's chief author, Shakespeare, dead three years earlier.

For the purposes of *Shakespeare's Sonnets*, however, the important point here is that Pembroke was prepared to receive and express affection in an individual and somewhat unconventional way. It is by no means unthinkable that he had been on terms of some intimacy with Burbage's colleague Shakespeare. Though Jonson may have liked to think that Shakespeare and Thorpe's address to him as 'Mr.' was a solecism, this could in truth have reflected their awareness that Pembroke was a man who positively enjoyed breaching protocol in the cause of friendship.

Finally, it appears that Pembroke perused and responded to *Shakespeare's Sonnets*. One of his own poems, the lyric initiating his debate about love with Benjamin Rudyerd, opens with a verbal and thematic elaboration of Shakespeare's sonnet 116, 'Let me not to the marriage of true minds', and incorporates the phrase 'love is not love':

---

1   Bentley, 7.31.

> If her disdaine least change in yow can move
> yow doe not love
> for while your hope, giue fuell to your fyer,
> yow feel desire
> Love is not love, but given free,
> And soe is mine, soe should yours bee.[1]

Once it is accepted that the publication of Q was authorized by Shakespeare, and that it was in the Jacobean period that he put the sequence into its final form, an identification of Pembroke as the dedicatee and addressee of *Sonnets* becomes overwhelmingly attractive. If some of the 'fair youth' sonnets, or versions of them, were written as early as 1592–5, these may indeed have been originally associated with Southampton, dedicatee of the narrative poems in 1593 and 1594. But as completed and published in 1609 the sequence strongly invites a reference to Pembroke.

RECEPTION AND CRITICISM

Reception

The early history of *Shakespeare's Sonnets* is not quite 'a blank' (*TN* 2.4.110), but nearly so. Whereas the early narrative poems were received with immediate enthusiasm, prompting dozens of early allusions, citations and imitations, the 1609 Q seems to have been greeted largely in silence – a silence the more surprising given Shakespeare's literary celebrity in 1609, in contrast to his relative obscurity in 1593–4. A few tiny pieces of evidence suggest that this silence may have been stunned or disappointed. Early readers, like later ones, may have found the collection disconcerting, disappointing or even shocking. What may be an oblique disparagement by Ben Jonson has already been quoted (see above, p. 61). The annotator of the Rosenbach copy, whose comment after the final sonnet, 154, was 'What a heap of wretched Infidel Stuff', has also been cited. Likewise, an early-seventeenth-century reader of the

---

1 Huntington MS HM 198, fol. 138ʳ.

Steevens-Huntington copy has made many marks which look vaguely hostile or critical, and one which clearly is: 129, the sonnet on the compulsive force of lust, has been entirely scored out.

Young Jacobean writers whom we might expect to have responded with eager excitement to the long-awaited appearance of a sonnet sequence by Shakespeare seem not to have done so. John Donne, for instance, must surely have studied *Sonnets* closely, yet there are very few verbal links to demonstrate that he did so. Though Milton contributed a commendatory poem to the Second Folio edition of the plays in 1632, there is no clear evidence that he ever read *Shakespeare's Sonnets*, unless his dismissal of 'a star-ypointing pyramid' as an adequate monument carries some reference to the speaker's dismissal of 'pyramids' in 123; but this seems rather tenuous. Indeed, some of *Sonnets*'s influence may have been negative, provoking a younger generation of poets to turn to the devotional themes that Shakespeare had so conspicuously neglected.

It is striking that George Herbert's New Year letter to his mother, incorporating two sonnets in which he asks why contemporary poets celebrate none but secular love-objects, belongs to the winter of 1609–10. Young George Herbert – a cousin, if the Pembrokian hypothesis is correct, of 'Mr. W.H.' – may have been shocked to find the leading dramatist of the age giving his name to a collection of poems part homoerotic, part cynically heterosexual in their preoccupations, and virtually never spiritual, and addressing them under a thin disguise to his noble kinsman. Herbert's two sonnets make good sense as a shocked response to Q by the pious and ambitious 17-year-old:

> My God, where is that ancient heat towards thee,
>   Wherewith whole shoals of Martyrs once did burn,
>   Besides their other flames? Doth Poetry
> Wear *Venus* livery? only serve her turn?
> Why are not *Sonnets* made of thee?[1]

---

1 Herbert, 206.

The second sonnet seems to offer rewritings of specific images in *Shakespeare's Sonnets*. For Shakespeare's repeated image of human procreation as 'distillation' (5) Herbert has

> Each Cloud distils thy praise, and doth forbid
> *Poets* to turn it to another use.

For Shakespeare's image of the 'crystal eyes' of those who seek to look into his heart (46.6), Herbert has

> Why should I *Women's eyes* for Chrystal take?

And in the three lines which follow he may be responding to Shakespeare's repeated references to his own poor or 'blunt' 'invention' (38.8; 59.3; 76.6; 103.7; 105.11):

> Such poor invention burns in their low mind
> Whose fire is wild, and doth not upward go
> To praise, and on thee, Lord, some *Ink* bestow.

Possibly the publication of *Shakespeare's Sonnets* was one of the factors that provoked George Herbert to embark on the programme of reclamation of secular poetic rhetoric that was to emerge as *The Temple*.

When Herbert wrote those two sonnets to his mother he was in his first year as a Cambridge undergraduate. Students at Oxford and Cambridge and the Inns of Court had been just the category of readers who had responded most warmly to *Venus and Adonis* – so much so as to be mocked for their enthusiasm in the Parnassus Plays and elsewhere. Yet responses to *Sonnets* seem to have been more muted. One recent Oxford graduate, Leonard Digges, appears to have been a would-be devotee. He inscribed the flyleaf of a copy of Lope de Vega's *Rimas* (Madrid, 1613) with a commendation of 'this Booke of Sonets, which with Spaniards here is accounted of their Lope de Vega as in Englande we sholde of our Will Shakespeare'.[1] The volume itself

1   Morgan, 118.

was a gift from James Mabbe, a Hispanist, and Fellow of Magdalen College, Oxford, to one 'Will Baker'. Mabbe and Digges were both to contribute commendatory verses to the First Folio. Paul Morgan has taken Digges's note as evidence 'that in 1613 or 1614 men interested in literature regarded Shakespeare's poems as the supreme achievement in contemporary poetry'.[1] Yet it can be construed in just the opposite way. Digges's phrase 'as in Englande we sholde of our Will Shakespeare' – note 'we sholde', not 'we do' – could indicate that in Digges's view Englishmen ought to be as proud of the dramatist Shakespeare's sonnets as Spaniards are of those of the dramatist Lope de Vega, but that, regrettably, they are not.

As stepson to Shakespeare's Stratford friend Thomas Russell, Digges was probably acquainted with Shakespeare, and may have felt especially bound to champion all his works, including *Sonnets*. Yet it is noticeable that neither in his commendatory poem prefixed to the First Folio, nor in the longer one, possibly composed for a later Folio, but appropriated by Benson for his 1640 *Poems*, does Digges make any allusion to Shakespeare's non-dramatic work. The evidence for Shakespeare's power as 'a Poet', Digges claims in the second poem, lies in the continued enthusiasm of theatre audiences, and specifically in their preference for revivals of Shakespeare's plays rather than Jonson's. Indeed, in comparing the esteem in which Lope de Vega's sonnets are held with that of 'our Will Shakespeare', Digges may be including himself in a large class of English readers who ought to think highly of *Shakespeare's Sonnets* but find it difficult to do so, however much, out of both personal and national loyalty, they may want to champion their merits.

The only early-seventeenth-century writer who can be shown to have read Q attentively and appreciatively is Sir John Suckling. He incorporated half a dozen verbal reminiscences in

1   Ibid., 119–20.

his tragedy *Brennoralt* (written about 1640). Some are sensuous images, like the phrase 'buds of marjoram' (99.7) which he includes in a catalogue of the irresistible beauties of 'a sprightly girle about fifteen'.[1] Other passages appropriate more elaborate conceits, like the dying Iphigene's lines to Almerin, the man she loves –

> For I like testie sickmen at their death,
> Would know no newes but health from the Physitian[2]

– adapted from 140.7–8:

> As testy sick men, when their deaths be near,
> No news but health from their physicians know . . .

It is rather striking that virtually all of the reminiscences of *Sonnets* occur in speeches by Iphigene, a woman disguised – not transiently, but throughout her life – as a man. Early in the play, in an echo not noted either by Rollins or by Suckling's editors, Iphigene echoes the old man in *A Lover's Complaint*, 'Sometime a blusterer, that the ruffle knew / Of court, of city'; compare Iphigene's

> O *Almerin;* would we had never knowne
> The ruffle of the world![3]

She continues with a lament for those youthful joys which

> Like glorious Mornings, are retir'd into
> Darke sullen clouds

echoing Shakespeare's 33.1,

> Full many a glorious morning have I seen . . .

The death of her female friend Francelia, supposed her mistress, is marked with the lines

---

1   Suckling, *Plays*, 222.
2   Ibid., 230; not noted by Beaurline as a Shakespearean reminiscence.
3   Ibid., 194.

> Shee's gone. Life like a Dials hand hath stolne
> From the faire figur e're it was perceiv'd[1]

echoing two of Shakespeare's tenderest lines about the fair youth (104.9–10):

> Ah, yet doth beauty, like a dial hand,
> Steal from his figure, and no pace perceived . . .

Suckling's ascription of so many lines and images from *Sonnets* to a transvestite character suggests that, like other early readers, he took full note of the sequence's sexual ambivalence – of the male addressee of 1–126, the 'master mistress' of the speaker's 'passion' – but that, unlike most readers, he enjoyed its unconventionality and gender confusion, making an inventive application of it in his play. There is little evidence that *Brennoralt* achieved any fame before the closing of the theatres in 1642, but it was performed six or seven times in the Restoration period, and was seen several times by Pepys. In 1661 he declared that 'It seemed a good play, but ill acted', and in 1667 he called it 'a good tragedy that I like well'[2]. But it is unlikely that Pepys, or any members of Restoration audiences, recognized some of the most touching lines in the play as quotations from *Shakespeare's Sonnets*.

Strangely, Benson's 1640 edition had far more literary influence than Thorpe's quarto. Perhaps because it was itself a 'miscellany', it was drawn on heavily by other anthologists and compilers of poetical miscellanies, such as Joshua Poole and Milton's nephew Edward Phillips.[3] Like Benson, these writers heterosexualized the poems. Phillips, for instance, cobbled together a series of final couplets from the 'fair youth' sonnets under the title 'A Perswasive Letter to his Mistress.'[4] Such unacknowledged pillagings did little for Shakespeare's reputation

---

1   Ibid., 231.
2   Bentley, 5.1207–9.
3   Joshua Poole, *Englands Parnassus* (1657); Edward Phillips, *The Mysteries of Love and Eloquence* (1658); for a fuller account, see Rollins, 2.329ff.
4   Phillips, op. cit., 138–9.

as a non-dramatic poet, and may have contributed to the steady decline of interest in or appreciation of *Sonnets* during the eighteenth century. In the case of the Shakespeare scholar George Steevens, neglect was compounded by positive hostility. To Edmond Malone's admirable *Supplement* to Johnson's Shakespeare, Steevens appended savage annotations in which he reviled the sonnet form in general, and the 'labour'd perplexities' of Shakespeare's sonnets in particular.[1] Hostility to Shakespeare became tangled up with jealousy of Malone, undoubtedly the better scholar, and in his 1793 edition of the *Plays* Steevens roundly declared:

> We have not reprinted the Sonnets, &c. of Shakspeare, because the strongest act of Parliament that could be framed, would fail to compel readers into their service; notwithstanding these miscellaneous Poems have derived every possible advantage from the literature and judgement of their only intelligent editor, Mr. Malone . . . Had Shakspeare produced no other works than these, his name would have reached us with as little celebrity as time has conferred on . . . that of Thomas Watson, an older and much more elegant sonnetteer.[2]

Though the vehemence with which Steevens attacked both sonnets and *Sonnets* was exceptional, a degree of neglect and hostility was commonplace. Indeed, Malone himself, though calmly scholarly in his printed remarks, evidently found *Shakespeare's Sonnets* extremely baffling, as is revealed by an amusing drawing (see Fig. 6). The paucity of Malone's comments on *Sonnets* appears also to reflect this puzzlement.

In succeeding decades distaste and confusion were widespread. Wordsworth eventually changed his mind. In 1806 he

1 Malone, 1.606 and *passim*.
2 Quoted in Rollins, 2.337–8. For a fuller account of Malone's differences with Steevens over Shakespeare's non-dramatic poems, see Martin, 44–7.

Mr Steevens borrowed this volume from me in 1779, to peruse the Rape of Lucrece, in the original edition, of which he was not possessed. When he returned it, he made ~~the~~ this drawing. — I was then confined by a sore throat, and attended by Mr Atkinson the Apothecary, of whom the above figure whom Shakspeare addresses, is a caricature.

E.M.

wrote contemptuously of 'the Sonnet's scanty plot of ground', but in a sonnet published in 1827 he implored critics to 'Scorn not the Sonnet' with which 'Shakespeare unlocked his heart'. Coleridge, however, remained uncomfortable, despite continuing to deploy the sonnet form himself. In his fourth Shakespeare lecture (28 November 1811) he discussed the narrative poems, but made no reference whatsoever to *Sonnets*. In 1818 he remarked in passing, in the course of a lecture on Donne, that Shakespeare 'is never positively bad, even in his Sonnets'. Near the end of his life, in May 1833, he had apparently moderated his hostility a little, in a defence that sheds light on his previous distaste. He acknowledged that

> I believe it possible that a man may, under certain states
> of the moral feeling, entertain something deserving the
> name of love towards a male object – an affection beyond
> friendship, and wholly aloof from appetite.

But he went on to exonerate Shakespeare from any such 'love', claiming that

> It seems to me that the sonnets could only have come
> from a man deeply in love, and in love with a woman; and
> there is one sonnet which, from its incongruity, I take to
> be a purposed blind.[1]

---

1   Coleridge, 2.355–6.

---

6   Drawings by George Steevens and Edmond Malone inscribed on the verso of the first flyleaf of *SHAKE-SPEARES SONNETS* (1609). Steevens borrowed the book from Malone in 1779, and returned it to Malone with the roundel portrait of Shakespeare added on a tipped-in strip of paper. Malone, then ill with a sore throat, added a caricature of Mr Atkinson, his apothecary, startled at the words that Malone has caused to issue from Shakespeare's mouth: 'If thou could'st, Doctor, cast the water of my sonnets, find their diseas[e,] or purge my editor till he understood them I would applaud thee &c' (Bodleian Arch. Gd. 41)

Why Shakespeare, if deeply in love with a woman, should have misled readers by including 'a purposed blind' (presumably 20, 'A woman's face . . . '), Coleridge does not explain. In her screenplay of Jane Austen's *Sense and Sensibility* (1995) Emma Thompson shows Willoughby and Marianne as each equipped with a little volume of *Shakespeare's Sonnets*.[1] Though this scene works well as a visual signal of the natural erotic and literary sympathy between the young people, it is wholly anachronistic, for in 1811 no such dainty edition existed, nor was relish for *Sonnets* at all usual in the early nineteenth century.

Coleridge's rather confused suggestion that, though 'love towards a male object' could on occasion be acceptable, no such love lay behind *Sonnets*, found little support. Severer critics, like Henry Hallam in 1839, perceived that they were indeed emotionally abnormal, and condemned them as such:

> There is a weakness and folly in all excessive and misplaced affection, which is not redeemed by the touches of nobler sentiments that abound in this long series of sonnets . . . so many frigid conceits are scattered around, that we might almost fancy the poet to have written without genuine emotion, did not a host of other passages attest the contrary.[2]

Though Tennyson undoubtedly modelled his sequence of elegies for Henry Hallam's son Arthur, *In Memoriam* (1850), closely on *Sonnets*, both he and his friends were determined, in later years, to play down this connection. Benjamin Jowett, for instance, presented Tennyson's devotion to *Shakespeare's Sonnets* as an immature error of judgement, brought on by the shock of Arthur Hallam's death:

> in his weaker moments, [Tennyson] . . . used to think Shakespeare greater in his sonnets than in his plays. But

---

1 Emma Thompson, *Sense and Sensibility: The Screenplay* (1995), 61–2, 82.
2 Quoted in Rollins, 2.359.

he soon returned to the thought which is indeed the thought of all the world. He would have seemed to me to be reverting for a moment to the great sorrow of his own mind. It would not have been manly or natural to have lived in it always . . . The love of the sonnets which he so strikingly expressed was a sort of sympathy with Hellenism.[1]

Jowett's final allusion to 'Hellenism' – here an unconvincing euphemism for 'Greek love', or homoeroticism – shows that he was unable to pretend to himself, as Coleridge had done, that the whole sequence was inspired by love for a woman.

Thanks to such careful propaganda, the Poet Laureate's aberrant devotion to *Sonnets* could be both condoned and explained. No such reclamation could be achieved in the case of Oscar Wilde. His charmed fascination with them, and his invocation of them in his own defence on the final day of his third trial, in May 1895, had a lasting, and deeply inhibiting, effect on their subsequent reception. Indeed, Wilde himself, in the penultimate year of his life, showed some awareness of this. He wrote to a schoolboy in March 1899:

My dear Boy . . . So you love Shakespeare's Sonnets: I have loved them, as one should love all things, not wisely but too well. In an old *Blackwood* – of I fancy 1889 – you will find a story of mine called 'The Portrait of Mr. W.H.', in which I have expressed a new theory about the wonderful lad whom Shakespeare so deeply loved. I think it was the boy who acted in his plays.[2]

Contrary to Emma Thompson's fantasy in which shared appreciation of *Shakespeare's Sonnets* serves to reinforce heterosexual attraction, Wilde's letter makes it clear that a taste for this work was in his eyes a promising trait in an attractive young man. In the

1   Quoted in Tennyson, 2.313.
2   Wilde, *Letters*, 789.

year of this letter, 1899, the explicit association of *Sonnets* with pederasty was compounded further by Samuel Butler, who for Wilde's boy actor Willie Hews substituted an old sea-cook of the same name,[1] thus helping to make such readings ridiculous, as well as (according to the values of the time) morally compromising. Many of those who have tried to integrate *Sonnets* into Shakespeare's biography in the twentieth century have followed Coleridge in energetically promoting a myth of a woman – the 'dark lady' – as the chief inspirer of Shakespeare's work. Sometimes contemporaries detected the element of obfuscation or humbug in this. Max Beerbohm, for instance, drew an outrageous caricature of the diminutive womanizer Frank Harris deviating from the habits of a lifetime in order to respond to advances from his great hero Shakespeare – 'Had Shakespeare asked me . . .', though in another (see Fig. 7) he showed 'William Shakespeare writing a sonnet' while gazing knock-kneed at a young courtier embracing a lady.

A final example may illustrate the complex manner in which interpretation of *Shakespeare's Sonnets* almost always becomes entwined with the personality (and sexuality) of the critic, as well as his or her cultural location. This is the case of W.H. Auden. Though anyone with a knowledge of Auden's biography might expect him to celebrate and endorse the homoerotic character of 1–126, he was absolutely determined not to do so, at least publicly. In his 1964 Signet edition Auden claimed – as G. Wilson Knight had done[2] – that the primary experience explored in *Sonnets* was 'mystical', and he was extremely scathing about putative readers of homosexual inclinations who might be 'determined to secure our Top-Bard as a patron saint of the Homintern'. Yet his public adoption of this position seems to have been a characteristic instance of Auden's cowardice, for later in 1964 he confessed to friends that a public account of

1   Rollins, 2.182–3.
2   Knight, *passim*.

7   Drawing by Max Beerbohm of 'William Shakespeare writing a sonnet' (1907)
(courtesy of Mrs Reichmann)

Shakespeare (evidently equated by Auden with the speaker in
Sonnets) as homosexual 'won't do just yet'[1]. Perhaps Auden was
referring to the changes in legislation then under discussion:
Parliament finally decriminalized homosexual acts between consenting adults in July 1967.[2] Consequent changes in attitude have
also been slow to take effect. Not until the American Joseph
Pequigney's *Such Is My Love* in 1985 was a homoerotic reading
of *Shakespeare's Sonnets* positively and systematically champi-
oned.[3]

1   Pequigney, 79–80.
2   For a concise account of the reform of legislation relating to homosexuality in
    Britain, see Hyde, *Other Love*, 255–97.
3   But see also S. C. Campbell's *Only Begotten Sonnets*, a homoerotic interpretation
    (2 vols, 1979)

Criticism

Though not all twentieth-century critics may have been fully conscious of this, a fear that a personal interpretation of the 'young man' sonnets might link Shakespeare, or even the love of Shakespeare – as in the case of Wilde – with criminalized activity seems to have operated as a powerful disincentive. Most serious critics and scholars have studiously resisted, or side-stepped, the temptation to connect *Sonnets* with Shakespeare's own life and personality. All three of the most distinguished post-war editors have dodged the issue. Ingram and Redpath were the most daring, in their brief comment on

> our general impression, which is that the relationship was
> one of profound and at times agitated friendship, which
> involved a certain physical and quasi-sexual fascination
> emanating from the young friend and enveloping the
> older poet, but did not necessarily include paederasty in
> any lurid sense.[1]

Stephen Booth, in spite of his preoccupation with bawdy puns, was determined not to get involved: 'William Shakespeare was almost certainly homosexual, bisexual or heterosexual. The sonnets provide no evidence on the matter.'[2] Though working as recently as the mid-1980s, John Kerrigan also side-stepped the possibility that *Sonnets* could offer any reflection of Shakespeare's own predilections. He speaks of the 'sonnets to the youth' as arising 'out of comradely affection in the literature of friendship' (Sidney Lee lives!). He goes on to refer dismissively to 'innumerable crackpot theories about the poet's life and love-life – fantasies in which the Sonnets have played a large part'.[3] Earlier twentieth-century scholars tended to concentrate, instead, on such matters as Shakespeare's adaptations of classical myth, verbal links between *Sonnets* and the plays, or

1 IR, xi.
2 Booth, 548.
3 Kerrigan, 55, 74.

his debt to Continental sonneteers. Pooler's 1918 Arden edition is a good specimen of this tradition of scholarship, and J.B. Leishman's *Themes and Variations in Shakespeare's Sonnets* (1961) represents one of its major achievements, offering a richly learned contextualization of such images and tropes as immortalization through verse and 'Love as the Defier of Time'.

The emergence of New Criticism in the 1930s was fortunate for admirers of *Shakespeare's Sonnets*, for it opened up techniques of 'close reading' which were on principle decontextualized, thus prohibiting biographical reference. This approach, too, has been illuminating, especially in the hands of William Empson[1] and his followers. Indeed, this has been the dominant mode of criticism up to the present day, with Anthony Hecht's introduction to Blakemore Evans's New Cambridge edition (1996), which consists of a detailed discussion of half a dozen individual sonnets, a testimony to its robust survival.

Not one of the fifty-three editions collated by Rollins in 1944 was prepared by a woman, and of twenty-two further editions listed but not collated, only two were by women.[2] Yet a noticeable feature of work on *Sonnets* in the later twentieth century has been the high incidence of distinguished and original studies by women. Perhaps there is something particularly attractive to women readers about the enclosed space of 'the sonnet's narrow room', and its predominantly reflective, introspective subject-matter. Possibly, also, women readers are able to remain at once calmly observant of, yet emotionally receptive to, the masculine homoerotic thrust of 1–126 that has caused such upset to generations of male readers. Indeed, the place of *Shakespeare's Sonnets* in 'gender studies' has also been explored as much by women as by men, as in the pioneering work of Eve Sedgwick and a bold survey by Marjorie Garber. Kate Chedgzoy has explored the

---

1 Empson, 50–6, 133–8.
2 Rollins, 1.xi–xiv; the editions are those of C.C. Stopes (1904) and Charlotte Porter (1912).

8   Jane Lapotaire in the Channel 4 series of readings from *Sonnets*, 1983

vital part played by the *Sonnets* in Oscar Wilde's 'act of self-fashioning'. Whatever the underlying reasons, female predominance is striking. Specialized studies by Molly Mahood, Winifred Nowottny and Rosalie Colie opened up all sorts of new techniques for analysis, semantic, linguistic and generic. More recent critics of great originality have included Anne Ferry and Heather Dubrow. The ongoing work of Helen Vendler is sure to produce one of the most profoundly sensitive readings of the century.[1]

SHAKESPEARE'S SONNETS

The title

The title of Shakespeare's sonnets is *Shakespeare's Sonnets*. On this point, the Stationers' Register entry and Q are quite consistent; and the appearance of 'SHAKE-SPEARES / SONNETS' as a running title in every single opening of Q also ensures that, however far a reader proceeds into the sequence, the labelling of the poems being read both as sonnets and as Shakespeare's can never get forgotten. (See Fig. 12, p. 104.) This 'genitive' title is the first of many features that wholly distinguish *Shakespeare's Sonnets* from other sonnet collections of the period.[2] The only other sequence to include the author's name in the possessive as part of the title is *Syr. P.S. his Astrophel and Stella* (1591), a posthumous publication, whose title, probably devised by the piratical publisher Thomas Newman, no doubt emphasizes Sidney's authorship for the purpose of publicity. However, since *Astrophil and Stella* was one of Shakespeare's most important models, and probably the sequence he most wished to 'overgo', this wording may have had some influence on the title of *Sonnets*, especially if its dedicatee was Sidney's nephew and male heir, William Herbert. There were plenty of other models for 'genitive' titles – there are well over fifty such titles for printed books in the

---

1   Commentary on *Sonnets* to be published by Harvard University Press.
2   For a useful list of these, see Roche, Appendix A.

period 1558–1640. But the application of such a title to a literary, poetic, text by a living writer is distinctly unusual.[1] Its purpose may be to draw attention to Shakespeare's fame and status. As followed by the phrase 'Neuer before Imprinted', the suggestion may be, 'Here are those sonnets of the celebrated Shakespeare for which you book-buyers have been waiting for so long.' But as repeated throughout the volume, a detail half noticed as we read on and on in this extraordinarily cryptic, yet personal-seeming, sequence of poems, the title inevitably hints that these sonnets may be about Shakespeare, as well as by him. As *Coryates Crudities* (1611) described the adventurous travels of Thomas Coryate, so *Shakespeare's Sonnets* – a first-time reader suspects – may chronicle the emotional and poetic journeyings of William Shakespeare. A literal identification of the 'I' of *Sonnets* with Shakespeare himself has been actively repudiated by most late-twentieth-century critics. Yet it should be acknowledged that this form of title, provided that we believe the work to be authorized, positively invites such an identification. Indeed, in referring to Shakespeare as publishing his sonnets 'in his owne name' Thomas Heywood may have been alluding to the spear-shaking wording of the title.

The second work in Q also has a title defined by a possessive, but one that is interestingly different from, and complementary to, *Shakespeare's Sonnets*. *A Lover's Complaint* is heralded by its own distinct label and declaration of authorship: 'A Louers complaint. / *BY* / WILLIAM SHAKE-SPEARE.' (See Fig. 10). Here, a first-time reader may naturally anticipate that the 'Lover' will be male, and so perhaps close kin to 'William Shakespeare'. Although the word could be applied to women in this period (see headnote to *A Lover's Complaint*), such an application was extremely uncommon. Just as such a reader may have been startled to discover that the majority of the sonnets are addressed, not to a chaste lady, but to a fair youth, they will be

---

1 For a more detailed discussion of 'genitive' titles and their implications, see Duncan-Jones, 'Sonnets called?'

9 Ben Kingsley in the Channel 4 series of readings from *Sonnets*, 1983

startled afresh, probably, to learn that the complaining 'Lover' of this second title is female. Though Shakespeare is credited with the authorship of the poem, his fictionalized role within it, if we identify him with the 'I' of lines 3–4 –

> My spirits t'attend this double voice accorded,
> And down I laid to list the sad tuned tale

– appears to be as a listener, not a speaker. Also, since the maid is still speaking at the end, there is no indication that the poet-speaker has mediated to interpret or 'reword' her complaint. The poet's distance from the complaint is also increased by the fact that the maid's interlocutor is not the 'I' of the opening stanza, but 'A reverend man, that grazed his cattle nigh' (57). The title declares Shakespeare to be the author, yet the poem itself relegates him to the position of a mere reporter or eavesdropper, whose personal interest in the nameless maid's narrative is left open to conjecture.

The relevance of A Lover's Complaint

Some contrast and/or complementarity between a male-voiced sonnet sequence and an appended female-voiced 'complaint' was a normal feature of the two-part form. To put it crudely, the sonnet sequence explores the frustrated desire of a male lover, the ensuing complaint, in a kind of echo effect, voices the misery of a woman who is the victim of male desire. The sense of a sexual balance being redressed is particularly strong in *Sonnets*, where misogynistic images of a 'dark lady' in Sonnets 127–52 are immediately followed by the sympathetic presentation of a nameless maid. As Malone observed, the earliest Elizabethan archetype for this two-part structure was Samuel Daniel's *Delia . . . with the Complaint of Rosamund*, first published in 1592.[1] The male voice of the *Delia* sonnets seems to develop in gentle stages from

---

1 According to Roche, 343, this form 'undoubtedly' derives from the publication of Petrarch's *Canzoniere* with *Trionfi*. However, given Daniel's particular devotion to the more recent poets of the French Pléiade movement, it seems possible that he found models there.

Daniel's own voice, in his dedicatory epistle to the Countess of Pembroke, to the heightened and various voice of the sonnets, with their heading 'TO DELIA'. Though Daniel's own name is not associated with his sonnets in the explicit way that Shakespeare's is with his, we should notice that 'Delia' is an anagram of 'Daniel', if the nasal 'n' of his name is represented, as it might be in manuscript, with the tilde. The close coincidence of the poet's name with that of the addressee suggests an element of narcissistic self-projection. Shakespeare may have imitated this, in so far as he introduces no named figure into his sonnets except – at the head of the page – himself, and, in 135–6, one, two or more men called 'Will'. After fifty sonnets, Daniel's *Delia* is rounded off with an 'Ode' in which the erotic joys of animals and hills are contrasted with the cruelty of Delia to her lover. *The Complaint of Rosamund* is prefaced with its own decorative, architectural titlepage. Like the speakers in *The Mirror for Magistrates*, Rosamund appears as a ghost, who begs to have her sad tale told by Daniel's 'Muse', so that

> *Delia* may happe to deyne to read our story,
> And offer up her sigh among the rest

– thus forging an explicit link between sonnets and 'complaint': the addressee of the sonnets is to be the audience of the complaint. Unlike Shakespeare, Daniel resumes his own voice in the final stanza:

> So vanisht shee, and left me to returne,
> To prosecute the tenor of my woes.

He creates a complex and subtle relationship between the chastely unreceptive Delia and the scrupulous, though technically unchaste, Rosamund, over-swayed by the high rank of her lover, Henry II.

In the years immediately following the publication of *Delia . . . with . . . Rosamund*, many other poets developed the motif of a young person seduced or sexually threatened by a man of high rank. Shakespeare himself explored it in *Lucrece* (1594), a major

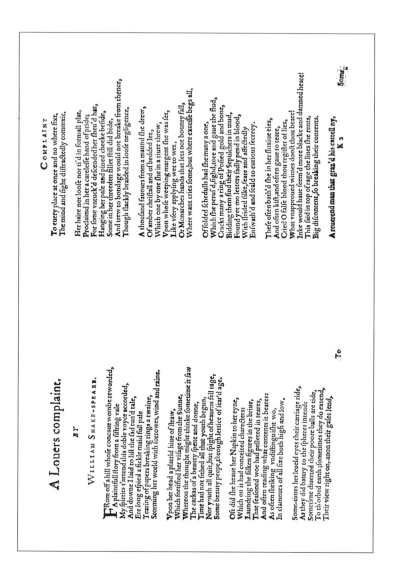

10 Opening of *A Lover's Complaint* in the 1609 Quarto (Bodleian Malone 34, sigs K1ᵛ–K2ʳ)

component of which is Lucrece's 'complaint' in lines 764–1036. Drayton developed it – with no apparent embarrassment about this story's homoeroticism – in *Peirs Gaveston* (1593), and also in *Matilda* (1594), his English counterpart to *Lucrece*. And as a component of a published sonnet collection, the form of complaint by a victim of sexual harassment was adopted by (among others) Thomas Lodge in his *Elstred*, voiced by the cast-off mistress of the Ancient British king Locrine: this is appended to his sonnet sequence *Phillis* (1593). Richard Barnfield adopted a three-part structure in his *Cynthia. With Certaine Sonnets and the Legend of Cassandra* (1595). *Cynthia* is a tribute to the Queen, in Spenserian stanzas; twenty sonnets explore the love of Daphnis for Ganymede (previously celebrated by Barnfield in *The Affectionate Shepheard*, 1594); and *Cassandra*, in sixains, explores the grief of the Trojan prophetess, seduced by Agamemnon, but unable to warn him of his doom.

Though rather lightweight, Barnfield's volume shares three important features with *Shakespeare's Sonnets*. The first is the most remarkable. Despite Sir Sidney Lee's protestations to the contrary, Barnfield is the only other Renaissance poet to address a sequence of sonnets to a 'lovely Boy'. Second, *Cynthia*, like *Sonnets*, has a male dedicatee, William Stanley, Earl of Derby. Though not unique, this is slightly unusual. Daniel's *Delia*, for instance, is dedicated to the Countess of Pembroke, and Lodge's *Phillis* to the Countess of Shrewsbury. The third, and most puzzling, link between *Cynthia* and *Sonnets* lies in its inclusion of a poem by 'T.T. in commendation of the Authour his worke'. This writer's fondness for contorted word-order and somewhat awkward compound epithets, such as 'PEGASE foote-sprung fountain', 'ILLIONS foorth-telling SYBILLIST', 'Larke mounting Muse', makes it tempting to wonder whether this could be that same T.T. who was to describe himself as 'the well-wishing adventurer' in commending a later male-on-male sonnet sequence.[1]

---

1   Thomas Thorpe was aged about 25 at this time. Another florid poem by 'T.T.' commends John Trussell's *Raptus I. Helenae* (1595).

Be that as it may, a formal connection between sonnet sequence and complaint was thoroughly established by the time *Shakespeare's Sonnets* was published. Scholars have been puzzled by stylistic evidence that *A Lover's Complaint* is a late poem, written after 1600. But if it was after 1600, and perhaps even after 1603, that Shakespeare began to marshal his sonnets, some written recently, some much longer ago, into the large-scale structure to be published in 1609, it would make perfect sense that *A Lover's Complaint* should have been written then as a carefully designed component of the whole. What is less immediately apparent is that *A Lover's Complaint* is not merely a formal pendant to the sonnets, but a carefully balanced thematic counterpart to them. What first strike the eye are the formal and stylistic contrasts between the two sections. After 153 numbered sonnets, and one six-couplet intermediate 'envoi' (126), come forty-seven unnumbered rime-royal stanzas. After the grand philosophical abstractions of the sonnets, especially those concerned with time and poetry, *A Lover's Complaint* appears disconcertingly detailed, concrete and inward-looking. Indeed, it is unusual among all Shakespeare's poems in its minute focus on small material objects, such as the 'plaited hive of straw' worn by the maiden on her head (8); the jewels and letters that she takes out of her handbag and throws into a stream (Fig. 11); the 'grained bat' on which her interlocutor leans (64); or the translucent 'crystal' tears that run down the young wooer's rosy cheeks (285–6). And after the single, though complex, 'I' whom we encounter in the preceding sonnets, this short poem offers dizzyingly complex layers of reported speech. The maid is overheard reporting to an old man both her own experiences, and, in fifteen stanzas, the wooing speech of her seducer, which in turn incorporates wooing stratagems of many other women.

However, the youth himself constitutes one of the strongest thematic links between *A Lover's Complaint* and the sonnets. Apparently a wealthy and promiscuous young courtier, he seems to be as universally admired and sought after as the fair youth of sonnets 1–126. Compare, for instance, 31.1–4:

11 The Cheapside Hoard, a collection of Elizabethan jewels (Museum of London)

> Thy bosom is endeared with all hearts
> Which I, by lacking, have supposed dead;
> And there reigns love, and all love's loving parts,
> And all those friends which I thought buried.

with *Complaint* 127–30:

> That he did in the general bosom reign
> Of young, of old, and sexes both enchanted
> To dwell with him in thoughts, or to remain
> In personal duty, following where he haunted . . .

Like the addressee of sonnets 1–126, the maiden's seducer is fascinatingly unreliable, and his unreliability is conveyed in terms of spring weather. Compare 34.1–2:

> Why didst thou promise such a beauteous day
> And make me travail forth without my cloak . . . ?

and *Complaint* 101–3:

> Yet if men moved him, was he such a storm
> As oft 'twixt May and April is to see,
> When winds breathe sweet, unruly though they be.

Also, the woman, who seems initially little more than an animated version of one of those 'many maiden gardens' which would delight in procreation with the fair youth in sonnets 1–17, turns out as the poem proceeds to have much in common with the poet-speaker of the sonnets. Not only is she, like him, in the grip of an obsessive devotion to a fair youth; like him, she is betrayed by the very words she uses. The *Sonnets*-speaker finds himself ultimately trapped in a web of his own poetic fabrication. In setting himself, in defiance of tradition, the paradoxical task of celebrating a dark-complexioned and unfaithful mistress, he has committed both artistic and moral treachery, as he acknowledges in 152.13–14:

> For I have sworn thee fair: more perjured eye,
> To swear against the truth so foul a lie.

The maid, analogously, in attempting both to justify her sexual fault and to purge herself of the weakness that led to it, discovers that in rewording the youth's wooing speeches she is captivated by them all over again. The seducer's rhetoric – not words alone, but also love-gifts and body language – is so dangerously persuasive that even in repeating it she succumbs to it once more (327–9):

> O, all that borrowed motion, seeming owed,
> Would yet again betray the fore-betrayed,
> And new pervert a reconciled maid.

It is in this paradoxical sense that the maid of *A Lover's Complaint* is 'fickle'. Like the *Sonnets*-speaker, she is compulsively faithful to an unfaithful love-object: she knows all about that love which does not 'alter when it alteration finds' (116.3). At first she is viewed in the process of weaning herself from her seducer by breaking and throwing away all his love tokens – objects which, we later learn, were merely 'borrowed', being bestowed on him by his female admirers. But her attempt at self-purgation turns instead into reinfection. In

94

the course of expounding the youth's treachery, which extends even to his body fluids – letters written in blood can lie, and so can tears, sighs and saliva ('that sad breath his spongy lungs bestowed', 326) – she is trapped by it once more. She proves, indeed, to be just as powerfully driven by negative and self-destructive desire as the lust-mad 'men' of sonnet 129. If we take sonnets and 'complaint' together, we can see that this book of sonnets turns out to be a book of lies and lying. It explores that negative equation according to which love is blind and poets are liars: love poets, therefore, can tell nothing but lies. Yet there is no escape from these lies.

A Lover's Complaint gathers up and complements the two negative conclusions of the sonnets. The 'lovely Boy' of sonnet 126, though temporarily triumphing over time, as the poet has claimed to do, must eventually be rendered up to age and death; and in sonnets 152–4 the poet-lover is both morally compromised and physically infected. Likewise, the 'fickle maid' is already touched by 'seared age' (14), and finds that she is unable to free herself from emotional dependence on the betraying words of her lover. Though little in the main body of *Shakespeare's Sonnets* appears to allude to the time of severe plague during which it was published, the 1608–9 plague may have some bearing on the images of infection both in sonnets 153–4 and in the final stanza of the *Complaint,* in each case alluding to an 'eye' – possibly figuring a less visible orifice – as a locus for 'infected moisture' (*LC* 323). Neither emotionally nor physically, it seems, can human desire be escaped. And though poetic language may beautify, promote or redefine desire, in the process of so doing it, too, becomes infected.

Sonnet structure, Sonnets *structure*

The building blocks of *Shakespeare's Sonnets* are units of fourteen pentameter lines rhyming according to the 'English', or 'Surreyan', form of the sonnet, as defined by Gascoigne in 1575:

> some thinke that all Poemes (being short) may be called
> Sonets, as indeede it is a diminutive worde derived of

Sonare, but yet I can best allowe to call those Sonets which are of fourtene lynes, every line conteyning tenne syllables. The first twelve do ryme in staves of foure lines by crosse metre, and the last twoo ryming together do conclude the whole.[1]

This correctly describes the rhyme-scheme Shakespeare uses: abab, cdcd, efef, gg. Despite deploying the 'English' form of sonnet, however, Shakespeare shows himself fully aware of the Italian form, with its pause, or *volta*, between the first eight lines (the octave) and the last six (the sestet). Much more often than not, some 'turn', fresh field of imagery or fresh direction is adopted in line 9, and line 8 is only rarely run on into line 9. Of the first eighteen sonnets in Q, for instance, five have a full stop at the end of line 8, nine have a colon, two end with a question mark and only two (5 and 6) end with a comma. There are three substantial deviations from the basic sonnet form, perhaps significantly located. Sonnet 99 has fifteen lines, and is followed by a poem in which the speaker rebukes his Muse for time-wasting and triviality. Sonnet 126, which marks off the end of the 'fair youth' sequence, is composed of six couplets, followed by two pairs of empty parentheses; and 145, slight and quibbling in subject-matter, but perhaps punning on the name 'Hathaway', is written in four-foot lines. For detailed discussion of all these, see the notes.

Though formally conventional, the sonnets are of course in most other ways unusual. Stylistically and semantically they are exceptionally complex, as Stephen Booth has shown: 'words, lines, and clauses often give a multitude of meanings – of which none fits a single "basic" statement to which the others can be called auxiliary'.[2] Though Booth explores an unprecedentedly

---

1 George Gascoigne, *Certayne Notes of Instruction* (1573) (Gascoigne, 1.471–2). Shakespeare may have been influenced also by a passage earlier in Gascoigne's 'Notes': 'If I should undertake to wryte in praise of a gentlewoman, I would neither praise her christal eye, nor her cherrie lippe, &c. For these things are *trita & obvia* . . . I would undertake to aunswere for any imperfection that shee hath, and thereupon to rayse the prayse of hir commendacion' (ibid., 1.425–6).
2 Booth, xii.

wide range of coexistent semantic readings in his 'analytic commentary', he does not by any means exhaust these possibilities, which are, in truth, inexhaustible. Indeed, this is one of the joys of *Sonnets* for modern readers. Here, even more than in the rest of Shakespeare's work, it is open to each and every reader to arrive at an individual and original response. The notorious truism that no two people ever concur in interpreting *Sonnets* is not cause for despair, but for rejoicing. In addition to the slippery syntax which Booth opens up so revealingly, there are many individual words, often simple in themselves, with multiple and contradictory connotations, such as 'lines' in 18.12. This can be construed as referring to 'lines of verse', 'lines of descent' or 'lines (wrinkles) on a face'. Inevitably, many further layers of suggestion are lost through modernization. The word appearing in Q as 'fild', for instance, could in at least two of its four occurrences be modernized either as 'filed' (= polished, rhetorically smooth) or as 'filled'.[1] In other cases 'inclusive' spelling forms have to be narrowed down, such as 'trauaile', which in Q's spelling in 27.2 ('trauaill tired') and 34.2 ('make me trauaile forth') encompasses both 'travel' and 'travail': if the word is modernized to 'travel', the second sense will disappear from view. It is partly for this reason that many of Q's spelling forms are recorded in the textual apparatus. But the explanatory notes are deliberately kept brief, so that readers can explore further for themselves.

As for the structure of the sequence as a whole, T.P. Roche has observed very wisely that 'Our main difficulty as readers of sonnet-sequences is that we have not yet learned the rules of the game, have not learned to read beyond the plangent voices of the poet-lovers.'[2] This caveat applies most of all, perhaps, to the kind of structural and numerological analysis that Roche himself, among others, has developed. Yet since the pioneering analysis of

---

1   Cf. Duncan-Jones, 'Modernizing'.
2   Roche, 461.

Sonnets's pyramidal structure by Alastair Fowler, which has the unusual merit of incorporating *A Lover's Complaint*, it has been widely agreed that there is indeed some principle of overall arrangement at work, though scholars are divided on its nature and significance. Both Fowler and Roche, for instance, discover 'Trinitarian' imagery in the structure, but Roche makes far stronger claims than Fowler does for an explicit and un-parodic Christian reference. Also, by counting 153 and 154 as a single sonnet, Roche discovers that the total number of sonnets tallies with the 'miraculous draught of fishes' in St John's Gospel: 'Simon Peter went up, & drewe the net to land full of great fishes, an hundred and fiftie and three: and for all there were so many, yet was not the net broken' (John, 21.11). This is indeed a remarkable correspondence, though a more convincing way of arriving at 153, rather than 154, as the total number of sonnets, would be to omit from count the non-sonnet 126. Analogously, Barnabe Barnes's *Parthenophil and Parthenope* (1593) reaches a total of 154 poems and sonnets in its first two sections, and John Davies's *Wittes Pilgrimage* (?1605) totals 152.[1] But the allusion to the 'draught of fishes' need not necessarily point – as Roche claims – to a religious or spiritual frame of reference underpinning these sequences, all three of which are explicitly and insistently secular. The symbolic suggestion may be, rather, of containment within a measured structure. The sequences are composed of many and various units, yet a 'net' of ordered structure encloses them securely within the same space. The biblical analogy may point to 153 as defining the largest number of separate units that can be held together without disintegration, rather as the biblical 'threescore and ten' is taken as a figure defining the normal limit of the human life-span. In neither case need a poet's deployment of a biblically-derived number identify the work in which it occurs as specifically religious.

The arrangement of *Shakespeare's Sonnets* appears to allude

---

1   The Davies example is missed by Roche.

to many other number systems in addition to those based on biblical allusion. For instance, Sidney's *Astrophil and Stella* consists of 108 sonnets. The exact significance of this figure has been much discussed, and never satisfactorily explained. Yet it cannot be doubted that Sidney's closest friends and admirers believed it to be significant, since Sidney's friend Greville imitated it, as did several other poets in the Sidney circle.[1] If, once more, the non-sonnet 126 is left out of count, we can discover the figure of 108 sonnets contained also in *Sonnets*. Sonnets 1–17 all take the form of persuasions to marriage and procreation; a new and wider perspective is opened up in 18, in which the speaker for the first time expresses his own devotion to the youth, and determination to immortalize his beauty in 'eternal lines'. Sonnets 18–125 may then be seen to constitute, on the Sidneian model, a great central sequence of 108 sonnets. The reason why the persuasions to marriage add up to seventeen is open to conjecture, but it may possibly relate to the fact that eighteen was the age at which young men were believed to be ready for consummated marriage. Human physiology may also account for the length of the 'dark lady' sequence, 127–54. Though no one has pointed this out before, the figure 28 most probably alludes to the length of the lunar month, which is also that of the female menstrual cycle. In enclosing the great central, Sidneian, sequence of 108 sonnets, between the two shorter units of 17 and 28 sonnets, Shakespeare may have designed a contrast between the steadfast growth to physical perfection of the young man and the emotional and moral turbulence of the 'dark lady' cycle, with its images of sex-crazed lunacy:

> Past cure I am, now reason is past care,
> And frantic mad with ever more unrest;
> My thoughts and my discourse as madmen's are,
> At random from the truth vainly expressed . . .
>
> (147.9–12)

1 Fowler, 175–6.

The 'temperate' beauty of the 'fair youth', which transcends seasonal and cyclical change, is contrasted with the unstable and corrupting power of the 'dark lady'. Her association with devilish temptation and venereal infection, in contrast to the beauty and loveableness of the youth, is nastily spelled out in 144, 'Two loves I have, of comfort and despair'.

It is probably not by chance that this unpleasant dichotomization of the angelic 'man right fair' and the grossly carnal 'woman coloured ill' occurs under the figure 144 (12 × 12), this number being popularly known as a 'gross'. It is one of many placings of individual sonnets which appear to be numerologically significant. Some of these have temporal references, such as 12, 'When I do count the clock that tells the time', alluding to the number of hours in a day, as in John, 11.9, 'Jesus answered, Are there not twelve houres in the day?' Sonnet 60, opening

> Like as the waves make towards the pebbled shore,
> So do our minutes hasten to their end

puns on 'hour minutes', the sixty minutes which compose each of 'our' hours. Sonnet 52, with its allusion to annual 'feasts', and their 'seldom coming, in the long year set', alludes to the fifty-two weeks of a calendar year. Other numbers relate to the human lifespan. For instance, the figure 70, or 'threescore and ten', is strongly associated with the limit of a human life: it is noticeable that in 71, 'No longer mourn for me when I am dead', the speaker anticipates the aftermath of his own death. The number 63, the 'grand climacteric' 7 × 9, is traditionally associated with change and mortality. In sonnet 63 the speaker stresses his own senility and anticipates that of the youth; and in the envoi 126 (63 × 2), marking the completion of two grand climacterics, the death of the young man, also, is seen as imminent. The two pairs of empty parentheses can be viewed as graves gaping open in readiness for the two corpses of poet and beloved.

Many more numerological finesses may be discerned. For

instance, the embarrassingly anatomical sonnet 20, 'A woman's face with nature's own hand painted', probably draws on primitive associations of the figure with the human body, whose digits, fingers and toes, add up to twenty.[1] More specifically literary allusions and responses may be present in sonnets whose location corresponds with comparable positions in Sidney's *Astrophil and Stella*. For these, and for more detailed discussion of all these examples, see the commentary. As Roche suggests, much remains to be discovered about the principles, or 'rules of the game', according to which sonnet sequences are organized. But that there are sophisticated principles of organization at work cannot be seriously doubted. Indeed, it seems that Shakespeare was unusually inventive and ingenious both in his deployment of numerological structure and in his symbolic use of numerical allusion. The popular practice of rearranging the sonnets as set out in Q to produce a different overall meaning or drift is wholly unwarranted.

Put into its final shape early in the Jacobean period, *Shakespeare's Sonnets* takes its place alongside the many collections of satires, epigrams and playfully self-contradictory poems of the first decade of the seventeenth century. Explosively witty, emotionally complex, and sometimes breath-takingly cynical, the 1609 *Sonnets* does not, viewed as a whole, seem to constitute the 'sugred' collection that Meres's 1598 allusion might have led readers to expect. Indeed, it is in the company of satirical epigrams that the single sonnet 2 is often found in seventeenth-century miscellanies.[2] Charles Gildon in 1710 labelled Shakespeare's sonnets 'epigrams'.[3] Though this classification may have been partly defensive, since love sonnets were deeply unfashionable in the Augustan period, it was not altogether inappropriate. Rosalie Colie has written brilliantly on the

1 Cf. Hopper, ix, 9.
2 See, for instance, MS Folger V.a.345, which includes many of the epigrams of Harington and Bastard.
3 Rollins, 2.332–3.

convergence, in *Shakespeare's Sonnets*, of salty epigram with sugary sonnet, which achieves a unique blend of styles and genres:

> I would suggest that, although Shakespeare trusted the sonnet-distillations to preserve his passion, for him both the banquet of *agape* and the sensual feast were heightened and refined by a pinch of salt. Or, to alter the metaphor slightly, with honey and salt, the styles and attitudes of sonneteer and epigrammatist, he could preserve the mixed bitter and sweet experience of loving, in a solution entirely his own.[1]

Colie's metaphors are apt, for there is a sense throughout *Sonnets* that the process of metamorphosing the raw materiality of human experience into the verbal constructs of poetry is analogous to domestic methods of preservation and distillation. Even as roses, or 'beauty's rose' (1.2), are boiled with sugar to produce a distilled essence of rose-water, so beautiful human bodies, and the love they provoke, are 'sugred' with rhetoric to produce such lucid affirmations of human and poetic perfection as sonnets 18 and 55. But as the sequence proceeds, both the raw human material and its rhetorical adjuncts seem to deteriorate, or fester, leading to poetic effects whose complexity is deeply disturbing. From the sweet fragrance of the 'rose distilled' of 1–17 we come to taste 'Potions of eisell' (111.10), 'siren tears' (119.1) and 'infected moisture' (*LC* 323). Some of Shakespeare's Elizabethan sonnets may indeed have been, as Meres called them, 'sugred'. But his Jacobean sequence, consumed in its totality, is salt, satiric and bitter, taking its place thematically, as well as chronologically, alongside such painfully adult, sexually cynical, works as *All's Well*, *Lear*, *Antony and Cleopatra*, *Troilus* and *Timon*.

---

1   Colie, *Resources*, 75.

THIS EDITION

In wording, format and punctuation, Q has been followed more closely than in any previous modernized edition. This may be illustrated with reference to the poems whose Q versions are shown in Fig. 9. In 123, for instance, the exclamation mark after the opening word 'No' has been retained, as has the colon at the end of line 4, the comma after 'brief' in line 5, and the colon at the end of line 8. In 124, the colon at the end of line 8 has been retained - many recent editors, such as Booth and Kerrigan, substitute a full stop; and in 125 the comma after 'all' in line 6 has been retained. In the twelve-line envoi 126, Q's capitalization of 'Boy' has been retained; and even more notably, this is the first modernized text ever to reproduce the two pairs of empty italic parentheses at the end. For a detailed discussion of these, see the notes on this poem. Though Q's italicizations, such as *Heriticke*, *Informer*, *Audite* and *Quietus*, are not preserved, they are recorded in the textual notes.

In collating textual variants the chief object has been to note the present edition's few deviations from Q, and precedents for such deviance; and to record those accidentals of Q lost in modernization, such as the elision of unsounded 'e', the use of italics, parentheses and hyphens, and unusual and/or possibly significant spellings, which may reflect the character of the copy manuscript. Neither Q's punctuation, nor the present text's deviations from its punctuation, are recorded in the textual notes except in the few instances where it appears to have major consequences for sense. When modernization is universal, as in 3.2, 'another' for Q's 'an other', or 30.7, 'afresh' for Q's 'a fresh', no precedent is cited. In a divergence from normal Ard[3] practice, of the early editions, only those of Malone and Capell have been collated, so the originator of an emendation or conjectural reading (e.g. Theobald, Steevens, Sewell) is not necessarily credited. *Malone*, for instance, denotes a reading adopted, but not in every

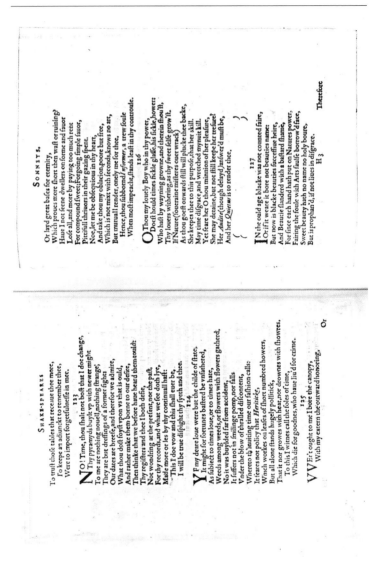

12   Page opening from the 1609 Quarto (Bodleian Malone 34, sigs H2ᵛ–H3ʳ)

case originated, by Edmond Malone. However, the most notorious cruxes, such as 12.4, 25.9-11, 34.12, 44.13, 46.9, 51.11, 69.14, 126.2, 146.2 and 152.13, are discussed in some detail in the notes. For *LC*, only Capell, Ard[1], Riv, Oxf and Kerrigan have been collated.

For a full historical collation of early editions, H.E. Rollins's variorum *Sonnets* should be consulted, or, for *LC*, Rollins's 1938 variorum *Poems* (Philadelphia and London, 1938).

SHAKE-SPEARES

SONNETS.

Neuer before Imprinted.

AT LONDON
By G. Eld for T. T. and are
to be solde by William Aspley.
1609.

TITLE-PAGE (Fig. 13) facsimile of the 1609 Quarto (Bodleian Malone 34) title-page. The double emphasis on Shakespeare's authorship of the sonnets (see Introduction, pp. 35–6) and on this as their first public appearance was no doubt a marketing strategy.

DEDICATION At its simplest, this much-discussed preliminary appears to indicate that *T*[homas]. *T*[horpe]., the publisher of *Shakespeare's Sonnets,* endorses the poet's desire to praise and immortalize his friend, *Mr. W.H.*, who is the *begetter*, or inspirer, of the poems which follow. The durability (*eternity*) of the wishes, and, it is implied, of what is wished for, is emphasized by the capitalization of each word and division by points, suggesting that this is a quasi-Roman inscription, written as if on stone. T.T. shows that he has read the sonnets he is publishing, or at least the first seventeen, and understands that the poet's young friend is dilatory in begetting children; he has, however, 'fathered' this volume of poems, which offers him a different kind of immortality.

1 ONLY. like so many words in the sonnets themselves, double-edged: primarily it suggests that *Mr. W.H.* is supreme or paramount (cf. 1.10 and n.) but there may be a secondary suggestion that he has only begotten sonnets, not children.

10 ADVENTURER. *OED* (sense 4) cites this example, with the definition 'One who undertakes or shares in commercial adventures or enterprises'.

11–12 SETTING. FORTH. synonymous with 'publishing', and a phrase commonly used in this sense; cf. *OED* set 144e, with an example from Robert Greene: 'I have . . . set forth many pamphlets, full of much love and little scholarism' (*Greene's Mourning Garment* [1590]).

TO. THE. ONLY. BEGETTER. OF.
THESE. ENSUING. SONNETS.
Mr. W.H. ALL. HAPPINESS.
AND. THAT. ETERNITY.
PROMISED.   5
BY.
OUR. EVER-LIVING. POET.
WISHETH.
THE. WELL-WISHING.
ADVENTURER. IN.   10
SETTING.
FORTH.

T.T.

SHAKESPEARE'S
SONNETS

1   The sonnet sets out a eugenic propo-
    sition: the most excellent examples of
    natural beings are under an obligation
    to reproduce themselves. But the
    addressee, to whom this rule applies,
    is narcissistically dedicated to self-
    love, allowing his beauty to go to waste
    by hoarding it up.

1   **creatures** created things, whether
    animal or vegetable

2   **beauty's rose** The rose was often
    associated with female beauty and,
    more specifically, female genitalia; cf.
    The Romance of the Rose, or Chaucer's
    Wife of Bath's Prologue, 447–8. But
    the capitalization and italicization of
    the word in Q may signal a wider field
    of reference, encompassing both gen-
    ders and, possibly, a metaphysical
    ideal of beauty. Since the Tudor
    emblem was a rose, there may also be
    a reminiscence of the widespread
    desire, in the first half of her reign,
    that Elizabeth I should marry and
    reproduce. The memory of the dead
    queen and dead dynasty was fresh at
    the time of Q's publication.

3   **riper** suggests fruit rather than flow-
    ers, indicating the speedy process of
    growth. Cf. also the proverb 'Soon
    ripe, soon rotten' (Tilley, R133),
    echoed in *R2* 2.1.153.

4   **His tender heir** The possessive pro-
    noun is the first indication that the
    addressee is male. A *tender heir* is, pri-
    marily, a young heir (cf. Lat. *tener*);
    but there is probably also an allusion
    to a false etymology of *mulier* (Lat.
    woman, wife) from *mollis aer* (Lat. soft
    air), which was attributed to Cicero,
    and occurs in one of the earliest
    English printed books, William
    Caxton, trans., *Jacobus de Cessolis: The
    Game of Chess* (*c.* 1483) Scolar Press,
    1976, sig. G8: 'the women ben
    lykened unto softe waxe or softe ayer,
    and therefore she is callyd Mulier
    whiche is as moche to saye in latyn as
    mollis aer'. Shakespeare used this pun
    as a crucial narrative element in *Cym*
    5.5.448–9. For those who pick up this
    allusion, l. 4 suggests both (i) his
    memory may be sustained by his

    child; and (ii) his wife (*mulier*) may
    give birth to (*bear*) the child which
    replicates him. The internal rhyme
    heir . . . bear reinforces the notion of
    replication.

5   **contracted** He is pledged to himself,
    as in a contract of marriage; but he is
    also diminished (*contracted*) to the
    self-reflexive scope of his *own bright
    eyes*.

6   Like a candle, the young man sustains
    his beauty (*flame*) with fuel made from
    his own body (substance): cf. *3H6*
    2.6.1, where Clifford, mortally woun-
    ded, says 'Here burns my candle out'.

8   suggests the polarization of the young
    man's being, one half a cruel *foe* to the
    other, which is *sweet*: the insertion of
    sweet before the second *self* hints at the
    speaker's affection.

10 **only . . . spring** There may be a sug-
    gestion that the young man shows
    great promise as a courtier: cf. *R2*
    5.2.46–7, in which the Duchess of
    York asks her son Aumerle 'who are
    the violets now / That strew the green
    lap of the new-come spring?' – that is,
    who promise to be favourites with the
    new King? The word *only* carries a
    positive sense of 'supreme', 'out-
    standing', as in Robert Greene's
    description of Shakespeare as 'the
    onely Shake-scene in a countrey'
    (*Groat's-worth of wit* [1592], printed
    in Schoenbaum, *Life,* 115–16); or, on
    the previous leaf of Q (Dedication, ll.
    1–3), Thomas Thorpe's description of
    'Mr. W.H.' as 'only begetter' of *Son.*
    In his beauty, the young man is a *her-
    ald,* or precursor, to a spring full of
    'gauds', or rich ornaments: *gaudy* does
    not necessarily carry connotations of
    vulgarity or excess; cf. *LLL* 5.2.812.

11 **bud** a common image for a promising
    young man: cf. Henry Gifford's poem
    For Soldiers (*c.* 1580), 1, 'Ye buds of
    Brutus' land' (Jones, 324).
    content happiness, but also 'con-
    tents', that which is contained: the
    innermost wealth of his beauty and
    manhood is 'buried', instead of being
    unfolded, as the *bud* image suggests it
    should.

1

From fairest creatures we desire increase,
That thereby beauty's rose might never die,
But as the riper should by time decease
His tender heir might bear his memory:
But thou, contracted to thine own bright eyes,   5
Feed'st thy light's flame with self-substantial fuel,
Making a famine where abundance lies,
Thyself thy foe, to thy sweet self too cruel.
Thou that art now the world's fresh ornament,
And only herald to the gaudy spring,   10
Within thine own bud buriest thy content,
And, tender churl, mak'st waste in niggarding.
   Pity the world, or else this glutton be,
   To eat the world's due, by the grave and thee.

---

12 **tender churl** *Tender* is repeated, in the same position, from l. 4; but whereas a *tender heir* would replicate the young man's beauty, the young man himself, youthful but inept or clumsy, squanders his beauty even as he tries to preserve it. That the word *churl*, with normal connotations of miserliness and lack of breeding, could occasionally be used with affection, is suggested by Juliet's reproach to the dead Romeo, 'O churl! Drunk all, and left no friendly drop' (*RJ* 5.3.163).
mak'st waste suggests both 'wastes' = throws away, and 'lays waste': the potentially fruitful world will be left desolate by the youth's failure to procreate.
niggarding acting in a mean, stingy fashion

13 **this glutton** demonstrative: the following line defines the kind of glutton he will be.

14 awkwardly expressed: what is owed to the world, the young man's wealth of beauty, is instead consumed by himself, first, and will be finally devoured by the grave. Dying is commonly referred to as 'paying one's debt to nature' (Tilley, D168). For the sterile body as itself a grave, cf. *VA* 757–60.

1] *Malone;* SHAKE-SPEARES, *SONNETS. Q* 2 rose] *Rose* 6 self-substantial] *Malone;* selfe substantiall *Q*

2   When the young man has lost his beauty, he can guard against reproach by pointing to offspring in whom it is renewed. This is a traditional argument for procreation, though one more commonly used in poems in which a male speaker attempts to seduce a female addressee. (Perhaps it was because of the ease with which it could be accommodated to the heterosexual convention that this poem acquired great popularity in the 1620s and 1630s, from when a dozen MS texts survive, eleven of which represent a different, probably inauthentic, version (see Appendix, p. 453).)

1   **forty winters** The number is formulaic for 'many', as in the 'forty years' during which the Israelites fed on manna in the wilderness (Exodus, 16.35). The citation of *winters*, rather than summers, stresses the withering, blighting aspect of time.

2–3 **thy . . . Thy** If stress is placed on *thy*, it is implied that the speaker's brow is already wrinkled.

3   **proud livery** splendid clothes, imaging the young man's physical attractions, but also suggesting that they are impermanent

4   **tattered weed** torn garment

6   **treasure** continues the image in 1.11–12, in which the youth is miserly in hoarding up his beauty, adding to it an allusion to the parable of the talents (Matthew, 25.14–30), in which a lord, figuring God, after some years' absence asks his servants to account for the talents (coins) he had left in their keeping

7   **deep-sunken eyes** contrasted with *bright eyes* in 1.5

8   **all-eating shame** recalls the image of gluttony at the end of the previous sonnet. Traditionally, it is time that devours all (*tempus edax rerum*: cf. 19.1 and n.); the attribution of this process to *shame* makes ageing seem disgraceful.
    thriftless unprofitable; praise that is no praise

9   **deserved** would merit

11 **sum . . . excuse** enumerate my assets, and make reparation (*excuse*) for my own (*old*) age. Alternatively, *my old excuse* could refer to the arguments used previously, in sonnet 1, by the poet: i.e. 'justify yourself on the basis established earlier by me'.

12 **Proving** demonstrating, or discovering, or both
    by succession *beauty* inherited legally, by inherited right (*OED* succession 4b)

14 **And . . . cold** The (no longer) young man will perceive the renewal of his blood-line and beauty when his own body has undergone the wintry process of ageing.

2

When forty winters shall besiege thy brow,
And dig deep trenches in thy beauty's field,
Thy youth's proud livery, so gazed on now,
Will be a tattered weed of small worth held:
Then being asked, where all thy beauty lies,   5
Where all the treasure of thy lusty days,
To say, within thine own deep-sunken eyes,
Were an all-eating shame and thriftless praise.
How much more praise deserved thy beauty's use
If thou couldst answer, 'This fair child of mine   10
Shall sum my count, and make my old excuse',
Proving his beauty by succession thine:
    This were to be new made when thou art old,
    And see thy blood warm when thou feel'st it cold.

4 tattered] totter'd *Q*, *1R*   *For a MS version see Appendix, p. 463.*

3   The sight of his own face reflected in a mirror should warn the youth of the need to father children, so that his beauty may be renewed in offspring, even as his mother's has been renewed in himself. More explicitly than the two preceding sonnets, this one indicates that the addressee is male. The poet begins by reinforcing the young man's narcissism, but finds within it an argument for procreation.

1–2 **Look . . . Now** The stress on these opening words lends emphasis to the command.

3   **fresh repair** the youthful condition of your face, which is currently in 'good repair'

4   **beguile the world** trick, betray the world; the stress on the youth's obligation to *the world* recalls 1.14.
    unbless some mother deny some (potential) mother her happiness (bliss, or blessing); the verb is apparently Shakespeare's coinage.

5   **uneared** unsown, as with ears of corn; i.e. a virgin womb

6   Human procreation was often described in terms of agriculture; cf. Agrippa's account of Julius Caesar's affair with Cleopatra: 'He plough'd her, and she cropped' (*AC* 2.2.228; cf. also *MM* 1.4.44). There is a further play on the association of *husbandry* with marriage – being a husband – as well as practising *husbandry*, i.e. farming, with additional connotations of 'husbanding' precious resources .

7   **fond** foolish, silly; but also *fond* = loving

7–8 **the . . . self-love** a stronger reminiscence than in 1.14 of *VA* 757–60

9   **Thou . . . glass** The literal *glass* of l.1 here becomes metaphorical. A 'glass' or 'mirror' often stood for an exemplary image, rather than an exact simulacrum; cf. George Gascoigne,

The Steele Glas (1576); and *The Mirrour for Magistrates* (1559 onwards). Suggests 'you see your mother's youth imaged in you', and 'your mother sees herself imaged in you', and 'others, seeing you, receive an image of your mother when she was young'. The selection of mother, rather than father, to exemplify the continuation of family traits may suggest a reference to a well-known mother; for instance, for those who identify the youth with William Herbert, the 'subject of all verse', Mary Sidney, Countess of Pembroke. It is consistent with this sonnet's preoccupation with engaging the youth's interest in the feminine; it hints also that the youth is still so young as to have a freshness of complexion which is as much feminine as masculine, as in 20.1.

10 **lovely April** her bloom of youth; cf. *AYL* 4.1.147.

11 **windows of thine age** The implicit suggestion is that the *glass* gazed on in youth will become a translucent 'window' in maturity, recalling St Paul's famous account of the prospect of spiritual vision in maturity: 'For now we see through a glass darkly; but then face to face' (1 Corinthians, 13.12).

12 In spite of his own wrinkles, he will, in his child, view his own earliest youth. Within the cycle of man's life, youth is the Golden Age; cf. 'the golden prime of this sweet prince', *R3* 1.2.252; or Andrew Marvell's 'The Picture of little T.C. in a Prospect of Flowers', 1–2: 'See with what simplicity / This Nimph begins her golden daies!' (Marvell, 1.40–1).

13 **remembered not to be** without a desire to be remembered; or with a desire not to be remembered

3

Look in thy glass, and tell the face thou viewest
Now is the time that face should form another,
Whose fresh repair if now thou not renewest
Thou dost beguile the world, unbless some mother.
For where is she so fair whose uneared womb   5
Disdains the tillage of thy husbandry?
Or who is he so fond will be the tomb
Of his self-love, to stop posterity?
Thou art thy mother's glass, and she in thee
Calls back the lovely April of her prime: 10
So thou through windows of thine age shalt see,
Despite of wrinkles, this thy golden time.
   But if thou live remembered not to be,
   Die single, and thine image dies with thee.

5 uneared] vn-eard   8 self-love] selfe loue   13 live] love *Capell*   14 image] Image

4 This sonnet extends the metaphor of beauty and sexuality as money initiated in 1 and 2, adding to it the idea of wills and inheritance. The young man is wasting this *legacy* on himself, and as a result has nothing to leave to the next generation; nor will there be a next generation.

1–2 **spend / Upon thyself** The primary image is of self-contemplation and a failure to turn to women as the 'other', as in 3.1–6; but there is subsidiary allusion to masturbation. That Shakespeare, like Pepys, used 'spend' for 'discharge semen' is shown in *AW* 2.3.284.

2 **beauty's legacy** both the beauty that has been bequeathed to him by nature, and the beauty that he should bequeath to his children

3 **but doth lend** perhaps an echo of ll. 31–5 of Wyatt's famous lyric beginning 'My lute awake': 'And then may chance thee to repent / The time that thou hast lost and spent / To cause thy lovers sigh and swoon, / Then shalt thou know beauty but lent / And wish and want as I have done' (Wyatt, 145).

4 **frank** generous
free generous, open-handed, with some connotations of nobility; cf. *Oth* 1.3.405, 3.3.199.

5 **niggard** miser
abuse misuse; with a possible sexual innuendo (cf. *OED* abuse 6, 'To violate, ravish, defile')

6 The abundant beauty which was given you so that you would give it to others.

7 **usurer . . . use** exploits two opposite senses of *use* (*OED* 8a, 'To employ or make use of for a profitable end'; and

12, 'To expend or consume')

8 **sum of sums** puns on 'some': many 'somes' make a huge *sum;* cf. *MV* 3.2.157–8.
live make a living; live in posterity

9 **traffic** trade, negotiation; sexual commerce; cf. Partridge, *Bawdy*, 208.

10 If the emphasis is placed on *of,* this means 'you trick yourself out of possession of the sweetest, most intimate, part of yourself'.

11 **how** The word seems redundant, but underlines the searching nature of the question.

12 An audit, or examination of (financial) accounts, would normally be something to 'give' rather than to *leave*. The suggestion here is that the young man will both *leave* (depart from) the mortal world, and *leave* (as in *legacy*, l. 2) an empty balance sheet to posterity. *Audit*, capitalized and italicized in Q, is repeated in this form at the very end of the 'fair youth' sequence, sonnet 126, in which 'Nature' threatens imminently to summon him to her '*Audite* (though delayd)'. 'Acceptàble' must be stressed thus.

13 **unused beauty** not used in renewing itself through procreation; with a secondary sense of 'unprecedented, exceptional' beauty. His beauty is unique and, if not reproduced, will die with him.

14 **used** usèd
th'executor In a literal sense, if the young man has a child, that child can act as his executor; figuratively, a child can 'execute', or manifest, the father's beauty to a future age.

4

Unthrifty loveliness, why dost thou spend
Upon thyself thy beauty's legacy?
Nature's bequest gives nothing, but doth lend,
And being frank, she lends to those are free:
Then, beauteous niggard, why dost thou abuse   5
The bounteous largesse given thee to give?
Profitless usurer, why dost thou use
So great a sum of sums, yet canst not live?
For having traffic with thyself alone,
Thou of thyself thy sweet self dost deceive;   10
Then how, when nature calls thee to be gone,
What acceptable audit canst thou leave?
    Thy unused beauty must be tombed with thee,
    Which used, lives th'executor to be.

12 audit] *Audit*   13 unused] vnus'd   14 used] vsed

119

5   The process which has brought the young man to his present physical perfection will in the same manner bring him to decay. However, deploying a metaphor which readers of Sidney's *New Arcadia* will recognize as symbolizing marriage, the speaker tells him that he can preserve the essence of his beauty, even as Elizabethan housewives preserve roses by distilling rose-water.

1   **hours** pronounced as two syllables, and spelt 'howers' in Q
    frame create

4   **unfair** 'to deprive of fairness or beauty' (*OED*, with this example); suggests also 'treat unfairly', the second sense being appropriate to the activity of *tyrants*

6   **hideous** in its original sense, 'causing dread or horror' (*OED* 1)

7   Vital 'humours' in the human body were seen as equivalent to sap in nature, maturity producing a chilling and drying comparable with the effect of autumn on vegetation; cf. Burrow, 12. *Checked* is used in *OED*'s sense

II. 3, 'to arrest, stop or retard'.

8   **Beauty o'er-snowed** suggests both a once verdant landscape now covered with snow, and white hair on a human head

9   **summer's distillation** rose-water, much used in Elizabethan cookery and medicine; cf. *Fettiplace*, 147–8. The central issue is still the preservation of *beauty's rose* (1.2). The source of the image is a passage in Sidney's *Arcadia* in which 'crystalline marriage' is compared to 'a pure rose-water kept in a crystal glass' (*NA*, 333).
    left in retrospect, gives *leaves* in l. 7 some of the character of a verb

12 Some such word as 'survive' is implied: the omission of a main verb enacts the incompleteness that is evoked.

14 **Leese** archaic form of 'lose', perhaps adopted here to assonate with *meet* and *sweet*.
    still always, for ever; perhaps with a pun on the *still* in which flowers are transmuted into a liquid essence

5

Those hours that with gentle work did frame
The lovely gaze where every eye doth dwell
Will play the tyrants to the very same,
And that unfair which fairly doth excel.
For never-resting time leads summer on   5
To hideous winter, and confounds him there,
Sap checked with frost and lusty leaves quite gone,
Beauty o'er-snowed and bareness everywhere;
Then were not summer's distillation left,
A liquid prisoner pent in walls of glass,   10
Beauty's effect with beauty were bereft,
Nor it, nor no remembrance what it was.
    But flowers distilled, though they with winter meet,
    Leese but their show; their substance still lives
        sweet.

1 hours] howers   7 leaves] leau's   13 distilled] distil'd

6   This follows on immediately from the
    preceding sonnet: the youth must dis-
    til his beauty's rose – that is, marry. In
    so doing he will make some woman
    happy and will multiply images of
    himself, thus defying death.

1   **ragged** a transferred epithet: winter's
    hand tears nature's beauty, causing it
    to be *ragged;* and an allegorical figure
    of winter might wear a *ragged* cos-
    tume.
    deface despoil; and, more specifically,
    obliterate the young man's facial fea-
    tures

3   **vial** a flask or container, symbolizing a
    womb

3–4 **treasure . . . treasure** The young
    man is to enrich a woman by bestow-
    ing his beauty on her; his *treasure* is
    also the due of a female 'beauty'. That
    treasure could refer to semen is indi-
    cated by *Oth* 4.3.89; *place* could also
    have sexual undertones (*Oth* 4.1.261
    and *passim*).

5   That way of causing treasures to

increase is not the kind of usury (Q's
spelling suggests also 'usage') which is
forbidden. To 'use' could denote sexual fruition; cf. *Oth* 5.2.70. Usury, i.e.
lending out money or goods on interest, was officially regarded as sinful
and contrary to Scripture, though in
practice widespread.

6   **happies** makes happy
    those . . . loan those who, by having
    children, lend their wealth freely to
    the world

8   **ten for one** i.e. if he increases himself
    tenfold by begetting ten children

10 **refigured** replicated your 'figure', or
    face or appearance; but also added
    numbers to the figure one by produc-
    ing a hundred grandchildren, each of
    ten children generating ten more

13 **self-willed** echoes *self-killed* in l. 4;
    suggests, as well as 'wilful, selfish',
    'making a will of his possessions only
    to himself'; and directing his sexual
    desire ('will') only towards himself
    fair beautiful; but also well-judging

6

Then let not winter's ragged hand deface
In thee thy summer, ere thou be distilled:
Make sweet some vial, treasure thou some place
With beauty's treasure, ere it be self-killed.
That use is not forbidden usury   5
Which happies those that pay the willing loan;
That's for thyself to breed another thee,
Or ten times happier, be it ten for one:
Ten times thyself were happier than thou art,
If ten of thine ten times refigured thee;   10
Then what could death do if thou shouldst depart,
Leaving thee living in posterity?
   Be not self-willed, for thou art much too fair
   To be death's conquest and make worms thine heir.

---

1 ragged] wragged *Q;* rugged *Capell*   4 beauty's] *Malone;* beautits *Q;* beauties *Benson*   5 usury] usery

7 Even as the sun is gazed on and admired as it rises to its height, but neglected in its setting, so the young man will lose the admiration he now enjoys unless he begets a child. The point is clinched by the postponement of the word 'sun' until the end, when it converges with *son*.

1 **gracious** full of grace, like a monarch

2 **under eye** The sun is itself like an eye (cf. 18.5), which is in every sense 'above' human eyes.

4 Human beings gaze downwards to avoid being dazzled by the midday sun, just as subjects bow before a monarch. Lear swears 'by the sacred radiance of the sun' (*KL* 1.1.109).

5 **And having** The implied subject of the verb is still *the gracious light*, i.e. the sun.
   steep-up precipitous; perpendicular; cf. *LLL* 4.1.2.

6 **strong . . . age** Aristotle in his *Rhetoric* (2.12–14) divided human life into three ages, giving supremacy to the middle one. That *middle age* for Shakespeare suggested flourishing prime, rather than being, as now, a euphemism for incipient decay, is suggested by *WT* 4.4.107–8. Cf. also Burrow, 8–11.

7 places a double emphasis on the durability of the sun's sway over humankind; however, the phrase *beauty still*, at the half-way point of the sonnet, also suggests 'motionless beauty', a delusive fixity.
   adore conceals a play on 'ore', the source of gold

8 **Attending on** waiting on, as courtiers wait on a monarch; but also paying attention to

9 **high-most pitch** topmost point
   weary car The sun was viewed in

classical mythology as a horse-drawn chariot.

10 **reeleth** staggers; a word often associated with drunkenness (cf. *OED* reel 7)

11 **fore-duteous** often presented in modern editions as ' 'fore duteous'; but 'fore' as a prefix suggests 'previous', and need not be short for 'before'. Either way, the meaning is clear: eyes pay tribute to the sun in the forenoon (morning), not later.

12 **low tract** low trajectory, path
   look another way alludes to the proverb, 'The rising, not the setting, sun is worshipped by most men' (Tilley, S979). This was often given a political application, as in Sidney's citation of the Queen herself in his widely circulated 'Letter to Queen Elizabeth' (*Prose*, 54, 184). There is an implication not only that the young man will age, but that his current popularity will not last.

13 **thyself . . . noon** In his prime of life the young man is outlasting himself; he is as if on the point of death (cf. *depart* in 6.11); and he is expending his energy (semen) in fruitless masturbation: 'noon' was a recognized metaphor for male sexual excitement; cf. Sidney, *AS*, 76.9; *RJ* 2.4.119.

14 **diest** pronounced as one syllable. The young man will 'die' *Unlooked on* in the sense that his image will no longer be seen; and he will experience orgasm in private, instead of directing his sexuality to procreation with its public consequences.
   get beget; acquire. In the second sense, he will recover the 'sun/son', thus counteracting the cycle of decline.

7

Lo, in the Orient when the gracious light
Lifts up his burning head, each under eye
Doth homage to his new appearing sight,
Serving with looks his sacred majesty;
And having climbed the steep-up heavenly hill,   5
Resembling strong youth in his middle age,
Yet mortal looks adore his beauty still,
Attending on his golden pilgrimage:
But when from high-most pitch with weary car
Like feeble age he reeleth from the day,   10
The eyes, fore-duteous, now converted are
From his low tract, and look another way:
    So thou, thyself out-going in thy noon,
    Unlooked on diest, unless thou get a son.

---

3 new appearing] new-appearing *Malone*   5 steep-up] *Malone;* steepe vp *Q*   11 fore-duteous] (fore dutious) *Q, Benson;* ('fore duteous) *IR, Booth, Cam³;* 'fore duteous *Malone, Ard¹, Oxf, Kerrigan*

8   A new field of imagery is introduced, that of music. The young man is made melancholy by hearing music; this is because its harmony and concord prompts him to confront his obligation to marry.

1   **Music to hear** Probably a vocative address: 'you, the sound of whom is like music'. Shakespeare refers quite frequently to music as provoking pensiveness or melancholy; cf. Jessica's remark, 'I am never merry when I hear sweet music', *MV* 5.1.69; cf. also *TN* 1.1.

2   **Sweets** things which are sweet, or delightful

4   **annoy** pain, irksomeness

5   **well-tuned** well-tunèd

6   **unions** chords, which unite notes in harmony. There is probably another echo of Cecropia's speech on marriage in Sidney's *NA*, 333, already alluded to in 5.9–12: 'And is a solitary life as good as this? Then can one string make as good music as a consort'.

7–8 **confounds . . . bear** Instead of distributing and multiplying his talents, the young man confines all his potential multiplicity within himself, so 'confounding', or destroying, it: *parts* suggests both the separate musical parts assigned to singers or instruments in a consort of music, and the *parts*, or excellent attributes, that he should transmit to others; cf. 17.4 and 69.1.

9   **one string . . . another** The idea of the 'male' string as the one essential to harmony is suggested also in Marlowe's *Hero and Leander*, 229–30: 'Like untun'd golden strings all women are, / Which long time lie untun'd, will harshly jar' (Marlowe, *Poems*, 16).

10 **Strikes each in each** suggests sexual union; cf. *Tit* 2.1.117–18.

13 **speechless song** The music is imagined as instrumental rather than vocal: its message to the youth is not conveyed by words, but by its innate harmony in blended notes.

14 **'Thou . . . none'** Without marriage, the young man, though greeted as *Music* in the opening line, will have no harmony; there is also an allusion to the ancient mathematical truism, derived from Aristotle's *Metaphysics*, 1080a, 'one is no number' (Tilley, O54); and perhaps specifically to its use as a wooing strategy in Marlowe's *Hero and Leander*, 255–6: 'One is no number; maids are nothing then, / Without the sweet society of men' (Marlowe, *Poems*, 17). He will also be *none* in the sense of 'a nonentity' if he fails to transmit his inherited aristocratic identity. The chiming of *single* with *sing* (12) and *Sings* (14) reinforces the effect of *one pleasing note* (12).

8

Music to hear, why hear'st thou music sadly?
Sweets with sweets war not, joy delights in joy;
Why lov'st thou that which thou receiv'st not gladly,
Or else receiv'st with pleasure thine annoy?
If the true concord of well-tuned sounds   5
By unions married, do offend thine ear,
They do but sweetly chide thee, who confounds
In singleness the parts that thou shouldst bear:
Mark how one string, sweet husband to another,
Strikes each in each by mutual ordering,   10
Resembling sire, and child, and happy mother,
Who all in one, one pleasing note do sing:
    Whose speechless song being many, seeming one,
    Sings this to thee: 'Thou single wilt prove none.'

5 well-tuned] *Malone;* well tuned *Q*   *For a MS version see Appendix, p.464*

9   This sonnet redeploys the 'public good' argument invoked in 1 and 4. If the youth remains unmarried for fear of dying suddenly and leaving a desolate widow, he should remember that the whole *world* will be his *widow* if he dies without issue, and he will have allowed his own beauty to be destroyed. The weakness of the sonnet lies in its opening proposition: if fear of leaving a widow is *not* the motive for not marrying, none of what follows applies.

2   **consum'st** suggests eating (auto-cannibalism); burning (as in a self-consuming candle); and economic consumption

3   **hap** chance, happen

4   **makeless** mateless ('make' = mate, peer); but with a secondary layer of *OED*'s sense 1, 'Without an equal; matchless; peerless', implying that only the youth would be an adequate match for *The world*

5   **world . . . widow . . . weep** The alliteration has a somewhat theatrical effect of emphasis.

7   **private widow** *widow* in the normal, human sense – individual whose husband has died

8   **By children's eyes** by looking at the beauty of her children's eyes, recalling those of their dead father; but also through the vision of the children themselves, who remember their father and look forward to renewing him in their own progeny

9   **Look what** whatever, that which (cf. *OED* look 4b). However, there is a also a continuation of the image of 'looking' from the previous line – 'Look out for what a prodigal spends'.

10 Though the prodigal (*unthrift*) has parted with his treasure, it is still around somewhere in the world.

11 **beauty's waste** the waste, or consumption, of physical beauty; with some suggestion also of its 'wasting', or natural decay through ageing

12 Beauty which is so preserved (*kept unused*) is destroyed in the process; cf. *consum'st* in l. 2. There may be another subsidiary reference to masturbation (cf. *Son* 4, 7.13), in which the youth 'uses', or sexually enjoys, his own beauty, and in the process erodes it, especially since each sexual emission was believed to shorten life.

14 **himself** The subject is either *bosom*, as a metonym for the young man; or the young man himself.

    murd'rous shame shameful act which is murderous in its effect

9

Is it for fear to wet a widow's eye
That thou consum'st thyself in single life?
Ah, if thou issueless shalt hap to die,
The world will wail thee like a makeless wife;
The world will be thy widow, and still weep   5
That thou no form of thee hast left behind,
When every private widow well may keep,
By children's eyes, her husband's shape in mind:
Look what an unthrift in the world doth spend,
Shifts but his place, for still the world enjoys it;   10
But beauty's waste hath in the world an end,
And kept unused the user so destroys it:
   No love toward others in that bosom sits
   That on himself such murd'rous shame commits.

1 Is it] It is *Benson*

10 This is the earliest sonnet in the sequence in which the poet indicates his own devotion to the young man, and uses it as a bargaining counter. The youth's self-hatred is indicated by his refusal to sustain his own family line; if the other, more public, arguments fail, he should at least procreate for the sake of his friend the poet.

1 **shame** picks up the penultimate word of the preceding sonnet: its use here is both exclamatory – 'For shame!' – and argumentative: 'Your sense of shame should impel you . . .'.

  bear'st Shakespeare often associates the 'bearing' of love with shame or sin; cf. *Oth* 5.2.240, 'Think on thy sins. – They are loves I bear to you'.

3 **beloved of many** Cf. 31.1.

5 **murd'rous hate** develops the *murd'rous shame* of 9.14

6 **stick'st not** do not hesitate to (*OED* stick 15)

7 **that beauteous roof** the house, or aristocratic family, to which the youth belongs. It may be for the sake of association with *ruinate* and *repair* that *roof* is used as a synecdoche for the whole house.

8 A contemporary application of the image of continuing the family line as house-building is offered by Charles Blount (1563–1606); he 'chose to be drawne with a Trowell in his hand, and this Mot: *Ad reaedificandam antiquam domum*, to rebuild the ancient

House: For this noble and ancient Barrony was decaied' (Fynes Moryson, *An Itinerary* (1617; Glasgow, 1907), 2.260–1).

9 **thought** intention, outlook

  my mind my opinion of you

10 **fairer lodged** contained in a more beautiful exterior

11 **presence** visible demeanour, appearance; what is perceived when one is in your *presence*, a word with royal and aristocratic connotations (*OED* 2b)

  gracious full of grace, or bounty; another word suggesting the aristocratic status of the addressee

12 **kind-hearted** amiable in intention; but also with some suggestion of *kind* = natural, according to 'kind', supporting the idea of the youth's present behaviour as unnaturally unfeeling

13 **for . . . me** a new and at this point unforeseen argument: it is not merely for the sake of the *world* that the youth should replicate himself, but as a gesture of affection to the speaker.

14 **in . . . thee** in your children or in yourself. We might expect the final emphasis to fall on *thine*, rather than on the youth's own continuance, and it would have been easy for Shakespeare to have written 'love of mine . . . thee or thine'. That he did not do so may prepare for a movement away from the theme of procreation towards that of loving friendship.

10

For shame deny that thou bear'st love to any,
Who for thyself art so unprovident;
Grant, if thou wilt, thou art beloved of many,
But that thou none lov'st is most evident:
For thou art so possessed with murd'rous hate   5
That 'gainst thyself thou stick'st not to conspire,
Seeking that beauteous roof to ruinate
Which to repair should be thy chief desire:
O change thy thought, that I may change my mind;
Shall hate be fairer lodged than gentle love?   10
Be as thy presence is, gracious and kind;
Or to thyself at least kind-hearted prove,
   Make thee another self for love of me,
   That beauty still may live in thine or thee.

12 kind-hearted] *Malone;* kind harted *Q*

11 The young man's fast-fading youth will be compensated for in the rapid development of a child. 'The world must be peopled' (*MA* 2.3.251), and the addressee's excellence particularly obliges him to reproduce himself. A resumption of the argument of sonnet 1.

1 **fast . . . fast** speedily; steadfastly
   grow'st will grow

2 **thine** your offspring (picked up from 10.14); or 'a wife of thine', whose swelling womb compensates for her husband's loss of semen
   from . . . departest The child will grow out of, and will manifest, what the young man bestows or is separated from: he will 'part' or distribute himself in offspring.

3 **fresh blood** Inheritance was commonly seen as the transmission of blood.
   youngly thou bestow'st You give your blood (semen) to a wife while you are young, and, perhaps, in a youthful manner.

4 **convertest** turn away; are transformed: Elizabethan pronunciation made this an acceptable rhyme with *departest;* cf. the rhyme of 'convert' with 'heart/art' in *Luc* 592.

5 **Herein** in marriage and procreation

7 **minded so** held the same opinion as you
   the times the human era

8 **threescore . . . away** The world would be depopulated within sixty years; *make away* = 'put an end to, destroy' (*Glossary*).

9 **for store** for increase, as well as for preservation

10 **Harsh . . . rude** rough in appearance, lacking beauty or 'feature', and unpolished or lower-class. The triple adjectives recall the complementary triads in ll. 5–6, but do not precisely match them.

11 **Look whom** whomsoever; cf. *Look what* in 9.9.
   gave the more gave her gifts abundantly. Somewhere behind this is Christ's assertion 'For he that hath, to him shall be given' (Mark, 4.25).

13 **seal** the stamp or image which represents nature's authority, with a possible echo of the Song of Solomon 8.6, 'Set me as a seal upon thine heart, as a seal upon thine arm: for love is strong as death'.

14 **print more** reproduce your image in children. For fathering a child as printing, cf. *WT* 2.3.98, 'Although the print be little, the whole matter / And copy of the father'. However, 'print' need not refer to the written word, and may here suggest rather a seal of authority marked in wax.
   that copy that exemplar of nature's excellence, with a subsidiary play on 'copy' as Lat. *copia* = abundance, picking up the idea of *store* (l. 9)

11

As fast as thou shalt wane, so fast thou grow'st
In one of thine, from that which thou departest;
And that fresh blood which youngly thou bestow'st
Thou mayst call thine, when thou from youth
       convertest;
Herein lives wisdom, beauty and increase;   5
Without this, folly, age and cold decay.
If all were minded so, the times should cease,
And threescore year would make the world away:
Let those whom nature hath not made for store,
Harsh, featureless and rude, barrenly perish;   10
Look whom she best endowed, she gave the more,
Which bounteous gift thou shouldst in bounty cherish:
    She carved thee for her seal, and meant thereby
    Thou shouldst print more, not let that copy die.

6 this,] *Malone;* this *Q*

12 Evidence of the passage of time
throughout the natural world prompts
the poet to consider that his friend is
subject to the same process, against
which there is no defence except procreation. However, the effect is almost
self-cancelling, for the poetic evoca-
tion of time's all-inclusive operation
is so persuasive as to leave the remedy
in doubt. The sonnet's number
alludes to the number of hours in a
day; see Introduction, p. 100.

1   **count the clock** hear, and count, the
chimes made by the clock

2   **brave** splendid, brilliant, showy
hideous two syllables; cf. 5.6 and n.
There may also be an association with
'hidden'.

3   **the . . . prime** the violet after its peak
of perfection: *prime* was originally
associated with the first hour of the
day (*OED* 1, 2), and then, by extension, with youth or early spring.
Shakespeare often linked violets
(which symbolized faithfulness) with
the vulnerability of early youth; cf.
especially *Ham* 1.3.7–8, 4.5.181–3,
5.1.233–4.

4   *****sable . . . white** black hair turned
white. Q's 'or siluer'd ore' has occasioned much editorial debate, with a
preference among eighteenth-century
editors for Charles Gildon's emendation to 'are silvered o'er', and some
late nineteenth-century supporters of
Brinsley Nicholson's suggestion 'o'er
silvered all' (Rollins, 1.32–3), which is
tightened up by Ingram and Redpath
as 'o'er-silver'd all'. The association of
both 'or' (in heraldry) and 'ore' (in
mining) with gold has also generated
some unhelpful speculation: it is
unlikely that Shakespeare meant to
imply that with the passage of time
human hair turned gold as well as silver, like that of the widow in Oscar
Wilde 'whose hair has gone quite gold
with grief'. Booth, adopting Malone's
emendation of 'or' to 'all', points out
sensibly that 'Shakespeare's contemporaries probably emended the line as
they read'. Sisson's objection to 'all
silvered o'er' as too similar to 'all

girded up' in l. 7 is in fact a point in its
favour, since the repetition of similar
words and phrases within a sonnet is a
habitual finesse (cf. Sisson, 2.209–10).

6   **erst** once, formerly
canopy the herd give shade to sheep
and cattle as if with a canopy

7–8 **summer's . . . beard** a richly inclusive image of crops which have been
cut and harvested, with an implicit
personification of the trussed-up and
white-bearded corn (formerly green)
as an old man being carried to his
grave. Though a *bier* could be any
kind of barrow or litter for carrying
heavy goods, its strongest association
was with the porterage of dead bodies,
as in Ophelia's 'They bare him bare-
faced on the bier' (*Ham* 4.5.164). In
harvesting rituals, the cutting of the
corn was often seen as the ritual
slaughter of an old man, as in the folk-
song 'John Barleycorn'. Q's capitalization of 'Sommers' may point also to a
recollection of Nashe's play *Summers
Last Will and Testament* (written
1592/3, published 1600), in which
Summer is represented as an old man
on the point of death: 'Harvest and
age have whit'ned my greene head'
(Nashe, 3.237). The phrase *girded up*,
or tied round with strings or straps,
applies equally well either to sheaves
of corn being carried into a barn or to
dead bodies being carried into a
church.

9   **question make** enquire, speculate:
implies a question about both the
future of the friend's beauty and its
nature. Since in the octave all other
mortal beauties have been revealed as
unstable, perhaps this beauty, too, is
already beginning to fade.

10   **thou . . . go** Ageing is seen as a journey, with future time as a desolate
land. It is also hinted that the young
man will 'waste' time, occupying himself well or, more probably, badly; cf.
beauty's waste, 9.11.

11   **sweets . . . forsake** Things which are
sweet and beautiful cease to be so.

12   **die . . . grow** picks up the opening
line of the preceding sonnet, but with

12

When I do count the clock that tells the time,
And see the brave day sunk in hideous night;
When I behold the violet past prime,
And sable curls all silvered o'er with white:
When lofty trees I see barren of leaves,   5
Which erst from heat did canopy the herd,
And summer's green all girded up in sheaves
Borne on the bier with white and bristly beard:
Then of thy beauty do I question make,
That thou among the wastes of time must go,   10
Since sweets and beauties do themselves forsake,
And die as fast as they see others grow,
    And nothing 'gainst time's scythe can make defence
    Save breed to brave him, when he takes thee hence.

---

reversed emphasis: that stressed the speedy growth of a child, this the speedy decay of everyone and everything.

13 **And nothing** Unusually, the catalogue of loss extends to the penultimate line, making the remedy seem frail. However, sexual innuendo furnishes a more positive reading. The *nothing* which lies between women's legs (cf. *Ham* 3.2.115–17) can *save*, or preserve, the *breed*, or offspring,

which will counteract the destructive force of *time's scythe*.

time's scythe a conventional image of death-as-reaper which recalls the harvest-as-death metaphors of lines 7–8

14 **breed . . . him** children, to defy the unstoppable advance of time: the loss of what was *brave* in l. 2 is here countered by the defiant or splendid confrontation of loss.

4 all silvered] *Malone;* or siluer'd *Q;* o'er-silver'd *IR;* ensilvered *Oxf* o'er] *Malone;* ore *Q;* all *IR*
7 summer's] Sommers 8 bier] beare 11 themselves] them-selues 13 time's scythe] Times sieth

13 This poem develops the theme of personal affection between poet and youth, introduced in sonnet 10. Adopting an intimate mode of address, the poet warns him that his present identity will be lost if he does not renew it in children.

1 ***Yourself!** But Q places only a comma between 'selfe' and 'but', leaving the phrase 'but loue you are' susceptible of being read as 'you are love incarnate'; but *dear my love* in l. 13 suggests that here, too, *love* is vocative. The first sentence could be paraphrased as 'O that your identity were absolute and permanent.'

2 **yours** sustaining your own identity; for a comparable (though different) analysis of the instability of identity, cf. *AC* 4.14.1–14.
here live live here, in the world; with possible play on 'heir'

3 **Against** in anticipation of; in defence against
this coming end the end of your life

4 **sweet semblance** beautiful appearance; but the word *semblance*, with its connotations of 'seeming', suggests something fragile and provisional about this beauty
some other a child; with subsidiary sense of a wife, to whom the young man's beauty would be 'given' in a different sense

5 **hold in lease** hold by leasehold, i.e.

possess only on a temporary basis; there may also be a pun on 'leese', archaic form of 'lose'; cf. 5.14.

6 **determination** end, with connotations of the end of a legal agreement; cf. *OED* 1b, 'The cessation of an estate or interest of any kind'.
were subjunctive: would be

9 **so . . . house** such a beautiful exterior as the young man's body; and such an aristocratic lineage, as in *beauteous roof,* 10.7

10 **husbandry** frugal management; and being a husband, as in marriage
might has the power to

11–12 **the . . . cold** continues the seasonal imagery of the preceding sonnet, with the ageing process seen as the assault of a single *winter's day*, leading to the empty anguish of *death's eternal cold. Barren rage* suggests posthumous frustration: after death the youth may remember, too late, that he has left no issue.

13 **unthrifts** foolish prodigals; cf. 9.9.
dear . . . know refers both forward and back: 'only unthrifts would neglect their inheritance, as I have already told you'; and 'as you well know, you had a father'. There is a further suggestion that 'you know my love to be dear (valuable)', thus distinguishing the poet and youth, in their *dear,* or valuable, friendship, from *unthrifts.*

13

O that you were yourself! But, love, you are
No longer yours, than you yourself here live;
Against this coming end you should prepare,
And your sweet semblance to some other give:
So should that beauty which you hold in lease   5
Find no determination; then you were
Yourself again after yourself's decease,
When your sweet issue your sweet form should bear.
Who lets so fair a house fall to decay,
Which husbandry in honour might uphold   10
Against the stormy gusts of winter's day
And barren rage of death's eternal cold?
   O none but unthrifts, dear my love you know:
   You had a father; let your son say so.

7 Yourself] You selfe *Q;* Your self *Benson, Cam²*   14 father] Father   son] Son

14 The poet claims that he has knowledge of the stars, but not of superstitious astrology, being directed by his friend's eyes, which tell him that in him alone lies responsibility for the future survival of truth and beauty. The identification of the beloved's eyes with stars is Petrarchan, but Shakespeare may have been specifically responding to Sidney's *AS*, 26, in which the speaker defends his own brand of 'astrology', governed by 'those two stars in Stella's face'.

1 **pluck** pull out, extract, with a slightly comic tone; cf. *R3* 1.1.55.

2 **I have astronomy** I have knowledge of astronomy.

5 **fortune . . . tell** predict the future with reference to precise (and fleeting) moments

6 forecasting weather by assigning particular conditions to precise (and fleeting) moments

7 **with. . . well** whether it will go well with princes: phrases inverted, perhaps for the sake of rhyme, or perhaps to suggest the ponderousness of a conventional astrologer

8 ***aught predict** Though Q's 'oft predict' has been defended by previous editors, as suggesting 'frequent predictions', as Booth points out, '*oft* is almost never used as an adjective, and this is the only recorded use of *predict* as a noun'. In addition, 'frequent predictions' suggests something facile

and easy, rather than discerning. Charles Gildon's suggestion of *aught predict* = 'anything that I find predicted' (Rollins, 1.39) makes good sense. A compositor could easily hear or misread 'ought' as 'oft', and in some speech it is possible that 'ought' had a vocalized 'f'; cf. Dobson, 2.946–7.

10 **constant . . . art** Your eyes are steadfast guides (*constant stars*), in which I discern such skill in divination, or matter for divination.

11 **As** demonstrative: as; that

12 continues the previous sonnet's focus on the youth's self, or individual characteristics, which, if transformed (converted) *to store* – to increase, multiplicity (cf. 11.9 and n.) – will ensure the flourishing continuance of truth and beauty. For the *art . . . convert* rhyme, cf. 11.4n.

14 When you are dead, truth and beauty will also come to an end. For *date*, cf. *OED* 5, 'The limit, term or end of a period of time'. Cf. Ralegh's reply to Marlowe's 'Passionate Shepherd': 'Had joyes no date, nor age no need' (see Ralegh, 15–17, for both poems). Shakespeare used the conceit of all beauty being encompassed in the love object frequently in *VA*, as at 11–12, or 1019–20; cf. also *PT* 62–4: 'Truth may seem, but cannot be; / Beauty brag, but 'tis not she; / Truth and beauty buried be.'

14

Not from the stars do I my judgement pluck;
And yet, methinks, I have astronomy,
But not to tell of good or evil luck,
Of plagues, of dearths, or seasons' quality;
Nor can I fortune to brief minutes tell,   5
Pointing to each his thunder, rain and wind;
Or say with princes if it shall go well
By aught predict that I in heaven find;
But from thine eyes my knowledge I derive,
And, constant stars, in them I read such art   10
As truth and beauty shall together thrive
If from thyself, to store thou wouldst convert:
    Or else of thee this I prognosticate,
    Thy end is truth's and beauty's doom and date.

---

5 minutes] mynuits   7 princes] Princes   8 aught] *this edn;* oft *Q*   13] *not indented in Q*   14 truth's]
Truthes   beauty's] *Malone;* Beauties *Q*

15 Viewing the instability of all mortal things (as in sonnet 12), the poet sees that youth, too, is subject to age and decay. He attempts to renew his friend's beauty by means of verbal wit.

1 **consider everything** consider that everything

3 **this . . . shows** The idea of the whole world as a theatre was commonplace in the Renaissance, and was given local definition for Shakespeare by the opening of the Globe Theatre in 1599. Cf. *AYL* 2.7.137–65. The implication is that human activities are no more than (empty) *shows*, superficial and delusory.

4 **the . . . comment** reverting to the idea of astronomy in the preceding sonnet; suggests that the stars, as audience to the theatre of the world, comment on and guide human life, but in ways that are undiscernible to us (*secret*)

6 **Cheered** cheerèd; = encouraged, heartened
checked Cf. 'sap checked with frost', 5.7 and n.

7 **Vaunt** exult, rejoice

8 **wear . . . memory** disappear until their glory is no longer remembered; cf. *KL* 4.6.13, 'This great world / Shall so wear out to naught'. *Brave state* = splendid condition; cf. 12.2 and n.

9 **the . . . stay** the perception of this unstable condition of the world

10 **you . . . youth** another play on the friend's self or quintessence: *you . . . youth* makes *youth*, a temporary attribute, seem integral to the addressee – part of his 'you-ness'.

11 **Where** in his mind's eye (*sight*), where the youth himself is subject of a 'show', or miniature drama
wasteful . . . decay *Wasteful time –*

time that lays things waste, and is itself wasted – and *decay* are two aspects of the same process, and there is no real doubt that the youth will be subjected to their operation: so perhaps they 'debate' only in the sense of engaging in discussion; or time and decay contend or compete, as in *all in war* in l. 13. Alternatively, *with decay* may be attached to *To change*, = 'time deliberates how to change you by making you decay'.

12 **sullied night** implies not only that age (*night*) will succeed youth (*day*), but that the young man will become morally corrupted

13 **all in war** The subject is presumably the *I* of the following line, who has declared all-out war on time for the sake of his friend.

14 Another image of the simultaneous processes of decay and growth; cf. 11.1 and 12.12. This time the stress is on regeneration. The primary image, building on *men as plants* in l. 5, is from horticulture, in which, by means of 'grafting', a cutting from one plant is made to grow on another: this is analogous to what the poet does in making the youth's 'parts' live afresh in his sonnets, as well as in persuading him to join himself to a wife. But there is also an ingenious pun, not noticed before. The poet engages in a continuous process of writing, or engraving, so that the repeated 'you' sounds (*you . . . youth . . . youth . . . you . . . you . . . you*) in ll. 10–14 are converted, by the addition of an 'n', into the sound *new*. The effect is of a word-game, in which time's removal of *-th* from *youth*, leaving a bare *you*, is outsmarted by the poet's conversion of the word into *new*.

15

When I consider everything that grows
Holds in perfection but a little moment;
That this huge stage presenteth naught but shows
Whereon the stars in secret influence comment;
When I perceive that men as plants increase,   5
Cheered and checked even by the self-same sky,
Vaunt in their youthful sap, at height decrease,
And wear their brave state out of memory:
Then the conceit of this inconstant stay
Sets you, most rich in youth, before my sight,   10
Where wasteful time debateth with decay
To change your day of youth to sullied night:
   And all in war with time for love of you
   As he takes from you, I engraft you new.

3 stage] state *Malone*   4 stars] Stars   8 wear] *Malone;* were *Q* , *Benson*   13 time] Time   14 engraft]
Malone; ingraft *Q*

16 Continuing from the end of the preceding sonnet, the poet suggests that procreation will renew the young man's image more accurately and powerfully than verbal artistry. Discussed in great detail by Booth, xi–xvii.

1 **a mightier way** more powerfully than through the poet's 'grafting', 15.14

3 **fortify** strengthen

4 **means . . . rhyme** Marriage is a more *blessed* form of renewal than writing partly because it offers 'bliss', or happiness, in addition to the 'blessing' of children. The poet's verse is *barren* not necessarily because it is uninventive (though cf. 26.5. and 76.1), so much as because it can generate only verbal images of the youth, not living children.

5 At present you are at the peak of your capacity for giving and receiving pleasure; yet *hours* have already been shown to be treacherous: cf. 5.1.

6–7 **many . . . flowers** continues the image of *men as plants* from the preceding sonnet: many virtuous young women, as yet unmarried and childless (to 'set' = to sow and germinate seeds), would gladly bear your children. Gardening was a conventional image for fathering children, even in aristocratic circles: cf., e.g., a 1596 letter from the Spanish agent Antonio Perez to Penelope Rich, then pregnant, with greetings to her pregnant sister and sister-in-law: 'she gave yow not those delicate shapes to kepe them ydle, but rather that you shoulde pushe fourthe unto us here many buddes of those dyvine bewties. To those Gardners [the three husbands] I wysshe all happines for so good tyllage of their grounds' (Ungerer, 1.90–2). It should also be remembered that

Priapus was the tutelary deity of gardens.

8 Your children will resemble you more closely than an artificial image, whether a painted portrait or a verbal (flattering?) description; also 'with greater liking'.

9 **lines of life** the outlines or features of your living children; lines of descent: for a perhaps over-elaborate glossing of the phrase, see Empson, 54–5.

that life repair restore; renew; replicate you to the life

10 **this** appears to be defined by the phrases in the rest of the line, placed in parentheses in Q; but also, as in 18.14, 'this sonnet which you are reading now'

time's . . . pen A 'pencil' was a bunch of hairs used as a paintbrush; figuratively, it could be 'transferred to word-painting or descriptive skill' (*OED* 1a and b). Time has *painted* the youth in bringing him to his present state of perfection; the poet, in writing, can hope to copy this creation only partially, and in this sense is his *pupil*. It is disconcerting, after the declaration of war on time in ll. 1–2, to find the poet acknowledging subservience to *this bloody tyrant*, especially since *time's pencil* will deface the beauty it has created.

11 **fair** fairness, beauty

12 Cf. 13.1. Neither time nor the poet can transmit the true living essence of the young man to (future) men.

13 If he 'gives' himself in marriage to a woman, he will sustain his identity in a stable condition. *Still* suggests both 'yet' and 'motionless' – the fluidity of his identity will be counteracted.

14 **drawn . . . skill** (if you are) delineated by your own ability; he will make war on time by making love.

16

But wherefore do not you a mightier way
Make war upon this bloody tyrant, time,
And fortify yourself in your decay
With means more blessed than my barren rhyme?
Now stand you on the top of happy hours,   5
And many maiden gardens, yet unset,
With virtuous wish would bear your living flowers,
Much liker than your painted counterfeit:
So should the lines of life that life repair,
Which this, time's pencil or my pupil pen,   10
Neither in inward worth nor outward fair,
Can make you live yourself in eyes of men:
    To give away yourself keeps yourself still,
    And you must live drawn by your own sweet skill.

---

10 this, time's . . . pen,] this (Times . . . pen)

17 The last of the sonnets explicitly rec-
ommending procreation: living
descendants of the addressee will
demonstrate to future ages the truth
of the claims made for him by the
poet.

2 **If** has here some of the force of
'though': it is implied that the youth's
merits transcend what can be shown
in art; yet even if they were fully
shown, they would not be credited.
filled Q's 'fild' has been modernized
as *filled*, but the possibility of a play
on 'filed', = polished, rhetorically
refined, cannot be excluded; cf.
Introduction, p.97.

3 **it . . . tomb** There has been an interesting shift from the suggestion of
4.13 that the young man is self-
tombed to the notion that the poet is
constructing a tomb for him.
Collections of verse were often
described as 'monuments', following
Horace; cf. Spenser's description of
his *Epithalamion* (1595) as 'for short
time an endlesse moniment' (*Epithalamion*, 433: *Shorter Poems*, 679).

4 **your life** your living essence
parts 'abilities, capacities, talents'
(*OED* 12). The poet's verse not only
gives an incomplete image of the
youth, it fails to do justice to his true
merits, even as a funeral monument
would offer only a partial image of the
deceased.

5 **write** express in written words; but
also write the words 'the beauty of
your eyes'

6 **in . . . number** enumerate in new
verses: *numbers* = metrical feet or, by
extension, verses; cf. *LLL* 4.3.57,
'These numbers will I tear, and write
in prose'. *Fresh numbers* also suggests
'in currently fashionable verse forms,
such as the sonnet'; and the sonnets
we are reading are themselves 'numbered'.

8 **heavenly touches** celestial brush-
strokes or artistically rendered features: cf. *AYL* 5.4.27, 'Some lively

touches of my daughter's favour'; and
strained touches, 82.10. 'Touches' can
also denote sexual contact.

9 **my papers** metonym for the poet's
verses, identified with specific pieces
of paper on which he has written
them. No accommodation is made for
fresh transcriptions or printings. We
should remember Meres's phrase
about Shakespeare's 'sugred Sonnets
among his private friends' (see
Introduction, p. 1). Whatever the date
of the sequence in its 1609 Q form,
Shakespeare must have been aware of
working copies of some of his sonnets
that were already over ten years old.

10 **old . . . tongue** The loquaciousness of
old men was a commonplace; cf.
Aristotle, *Rhetoric*, 2.13; or Sidney's
elderly Kalander: 'nature loves to
exercise that part most which is least
decayed – and that is our tongue' (*NA*,
23). The suggestion is both that the
verses' 'yellowed papers' have aged
and lost authority, and that they
are the work of an old and/or old-
fashioned poet.

11 **true rights** what is truly your due;
with a possible pun on 'rites', or
appropriate ceremonies
a poet's rage *furor poeticus*, the product of a (suspect) state of poetic inspiration

12 **stretched . . . song**. The strained, or
false, measures of an out-of-date
poem; cf. *OED* stretched 4a, with this
example. *Antique* suggests both 'old'
and, as in 'antic', 'grotesque or eccentric'; cf. Hamlet's 'antic disposition',
Ham 1.5.172.
stretched stretchèd

14 ***twice . . . rhyme** Q's punctuation,
with no break after *twice*, but a comma
after *it*, suggests that the young man
may live a second life in his child, *and*
a second (or third) life in the poet's
numbers. Though Booth defends this
reading, it seems to the present editor
confusing rather than convincing.

17

Who will believe my verse in time to come,
If it were filled with your most high deserts?
Though yet, heaven knows, it is but as a tomb,
Which hides your life, and shows not half your parts:
If I could write the beauty of your eyes,   5
And in fresh numbers number all your graces,
The age to come would say, 'This poet lies;
Such heavenly touches ne'er touched earthly faces.'
So should my papers (yellowed with their age)
Be scorned, like old men of less truth than tongue,   10
And your true rights be termed a poet's rage,
And stretched metre of an antique song;
    But were some child of yours alive that time,
    You should live twice: in it, and in my rhyme.

---

2 filled] fild   7 poet] Poet   11 poet's] Poets   12 metre] miter   antique] Antique   14 twice:] twise

18 Despite the claim in the preceding sonnet that the poetic affirmation of the youth's beauty and virtue will not be believed in future ages without the confirming evidence of progeny, the poet now proceeds to affirm these excellences in terms which refer more explicitly to poetry than to progeny.

2 **temperate** well tempered or moderated, steering a middle course between extremes

3 **darling . . . May** The image of often-spoiled spring blossom hints at early death or young love blighted: cf. *TGV* 1.1.42–5; or Imogen's lines in *Cym* 1.4.35–7: 'comes in my father, / And like the tyrannous breathing of the north, / Shakes all our buds from growing'.

4 **summer's . . . date** Summer has only a temporary and too brief tenancy (leasehold) on nature.

5 **the . . . heaven** the sun

6 **his** may represent either 'its' or 'his'; but, given the comparison with the fair youth, a conception of the sun as also a beautiful male (Phoebus Apollo) seems apt.

7 **every . . . declines** Everything and everyone that is beautiful eventually becomes less so, or ceases to be beautiful at all: *sometime* suggests either occasional deviation – a beautiful person who has an 'off day' – or a moment after which a process of irreversible deterioration sets in. The first *fair* may allude particularly to fair

women; see note on the next line. For the second *fair*, = fairness, beauty, cf. 16.11. The word *declines* suggests the sun's declension, or setting.

8 encompasses both accidental and cyclical decay, *untrimmed* suggesting both 'stripped of ornaments, or trimmings' and 'set off balance'; for the second, cf. *OED* trim 13a, 'to distribute the load of (a ship or boat) so that she floats on an even keel'. There may also be an allusion to menstruation, or 'monthly courses' (*OED* 27), in *nature's changing course*, implying that the youth transcends the physiological variability of female love-objects.

10 **fair** fairness, as in *from fair* at l. 7
ow'st own, possess; but with a subsidiary implication of owe = are obliged to pay, as in the concept of death as a debt to nature

11 **his shade** the darkness of death, as in 'the valley of the shadow of death', Psalm 23.4

12 **in . . . grow'st** The primary suggestion is of *lines* of verse which, *pace* 17.1–12, will endure until the end of time. The word *growest* may seem inapplicable to poetry, suggesting, rather, 'lines of descent', with 'growing' children; yet the final couplet does not support this. *Lines* has also been associated with the threads of life spun by the Fates (Booth *et al.*).

14 **this** this sonnet; or, more broadly, this work of art, *Shakespeare's Sonnets*

18

Shall I compare thee to a summer's day?
Thou art more lovely and more temperate:
Rough winds do shake the darling buds of May,
And summer's lease hath all too short a date:
Sometime too hot the eye of heaven shines,   5
And often is his gold complexion dimmed;
And every fair from fair sometime declines,
By chance, or nature's changing course, untrimmed:
But thy eternal summer shall not fade,
Nor lose possession of that fair thou ow'st,   10
Nor shall death brag thou wander'st in his shade
When in eternal lines to time thou grow'st:
    So long as men can breathe or eyes can see,
    So long lives this, and this gives life to thee.

---

1 summer's] Summers   4 summer's] Sommers   7 sometime] some-time   9 summer] Sommer
11 wander'st] wandr'st

19 Contending with time, as in 15.13–14, the poet gives him permission to erode and destroy everything in nature except his young friend; however, as he claims in the couplet, even when destroyed by time his love will *live young* in art.

1–7 The injunction to time is analogous to *Luc* 936–59.

1 **Devouring time** 'Time devours all things' (Tilley, T326); from the much-quoted Latin phrase *tempus edax rerum* (Ovid, *Met.*, 15.234); cf. also *Per* 2.3.45–8.

2 **make . . . brood** The earth's consumption of her own children was also a commonplace.

4 The Phoenix was believed to live for half a millennium, then burn itself on a fire ignited by the sun, from which it was born anew to start the cycle afresh (cf. Lactantius's poem *De Ave Phoenice*). The implication here may be that time has this poet's permission to burn the Phoenix for ever, without self-renewal.

5 **Make . . . seasons** While positive and negative aspects of time's work alternated in lines 1–4, there is now a sense of its operation speeding up, with 'glad and sorry seasons' coming in quick succession.

7 **sweets** pleasures, sweet things; cf. 12.11

9 **carve . . . hours** do not, with the passage of time, put lines on my friend's face; there may also be a suggestion of wrinkles forming divisions on the face, like lines marking hours on a clock face.

10 **no lines** Time's unwelcome *lines* are in contrast to the poet's *eternal lines* in 18.12.

antique pen an old pen, but also one that produces grotesque or fanciful effects; cf. 17.12 and n.

11 **course** either 'natural progress', or 'pursuit', as in hunting

untainted unsullied, untouched; but also uninjured; cf. *OED* 2a, and *TN* 3.4.56, 'sure the man is tainted in's wits'.

allow license, permit

13 **old Time** both descriptive and familiar: the poet acknowledges time's antiquity, with capitalization that may be authorial, but also, as he approaches his solution to the problem of time's power, feels able to address him colloquially as an 'old fellow'.

14 **My love** primarily 'him whom I love', as in l. 9; but with a subsidiary suggestion of 'the love I feel'

19

Devouring time, blunt thou the lion's paws,
And make the earth devour her own sweet brood;
Pluck the keen teeth from the fierce tiger's jaws,
And burn the long-lived Phoenix in her blood;
Make glad and sorry seasons as thou fleet'st,   5
And do whate'er thou wilt, swift-footed time,
To the wide world and all her fading sweets:
But I forbid thee one most heinous crime,
O carve not with thy hours my love's fair brow,
Nor draw no lines there with thine antique pen;   10
Him in thy course untainted do allow
For beauty's pattern to succeeding men.
    Yet do thy worst, old Time, despite thy wrong,
    My love shall in my verse ever live young.

1 lion's] Lyons   3 tiger's jaws] Tygers yawes   9 hours] howers   13 despite] dispight

20 You look more beautiful than a woman, but you are superior to a woman both in constancy and in allure; Nature fell in love with you, giving you male genitals which equip you to give pleasure to women, but your primary devotion must still be to me. A famously puzzling sonnet, which has often been taken to exonerate Shakespeare from any imputation of homoerotic passion. However, it can be read as suggesting the exact opposite, both because its naivety is too simple to be believed ('because we are both men we can have no physical congress'), and because its language is slippery and self-subverting; cf. note on l. 12. The placement of this anatomical sonnet at 20 may allude to a traditional association of this figure with the human body, equipped with twenty digits; see Introduction, p. 101.

1 **with . . . hand** created by nature herself; but the word *painted* bears connotations of false or superficial beauty, as in 21.2 or 83.1–4, which are not completely purged by the succeeding lines. The handiwork of nature, who uses her *own hand*, is implicitly contrasted with that of time, who uses such implements as a *scythe* (12.13), a *pencil* (16.10) or an *antique pen* (19.10).

2 **master mistress** suggests both double gender and double allegiance, as in feudal loyalty and/or courtly love; cf. 'Lord of my love', 26.1. The young man may also 'master mistresses', i.e. inspire devotion superior to that bestowed on women.

3–4 **not . . . change** refers to the misogynist commonplace that all women are fickle: cf. 'Women are as wavering as the wind' (Tilley, W698). There is also a pun concealed in *not acquainted*, = 'not equipped with a "quaint" (cunt)' (the word was used in this form by Florio as late as 1598); and a possible one in *shifting change*, for to shift, *OED* 9, means to change clothes, especially undercloches, and women, because of menstruation, have a special familiarity with 'changing shifts'.
false women's fashion the manner

of women, who are all false. It would be pleasanter to take this as applying only to 'those women who are false', not women in general; but the context will hardly allow it.

5 **less . . . rolling** Though the primary suggestion is that the youth's eyes do not roll at all, are not untrustworthy, there could also be an implication that even his eyes are to some extent *false in rolling*, only not so much so as if he were a woman. For an example of male eyes rolling in a suspect manner, cf. *Oth* 5.2.38, 'you are fatal then / When your eyes roll so'.

6 **Gilding** Making everything seem gold, the eye being imagined as emitting light, like the sun. Like *painted* in l. 1, *Gilding* introduces some associations with false or deceptive appearance; cf. *Mac* 2.2.56: 'If he do bleed, / I'll gild the faces of the grooms withal / That it may seem their guilt.'

7 At this time 'hue' denoted either 'form, aspect', or 'external appearance of the face' (*OED* 1a and 2). Given the opening image of *A woman's face*, the second seems most applicable; the sestet then opens with a *correctio* of ll. 1–2: 'A man in facial appearance, who has all the varieties of appearance under his control'. *Controlling* may have some of the connotations of 'controller', *OED* 1 and 2, a steward or household officer; cf. the distinction made in 94.7–8 between those who are 'Lords and owners of their faces' and those who are merely 'stewards' of them. He 'controls' *all hues* both by exemplifying them and – anticipating the following line – by causing the *hues* of those who see him to be transformed by love and amazement. There may be a pun on 'hews'/ 'whose'; and possibly some further pun is signalled by Q's italicization of '*Hews*', though the suggestion of Oscar Wilde and others that it alludes to an actor or other person called William Hughes (Rollins, 2.183–4) lacks supporting evidence.

8 **Which** refers either to the *man* or to his *hue* or both

20

A woman's face with nature's own hand painted
Hast thou, the master mistress of my passion;
A woman's gentle heart, but not acquainted
With shifting change, as is false women's fashion;
An eye more bright than theirs, less false in rolling,   5
Gilding the object whereupon it gazeth;
A man in hue, all hues in his controlling,
Which steals men's eyes and women's souls amazeth;
And for a woman wert thou first created,
Till nature as she wrought thee fell a–doting,   10
And by addition me of thee defeated,
By adding one thing to my purpose nothing:
  But since she pricked thee out for women's pleasure,
  Mine be thy love, and thy love's use their treasure.

---

10 **nature . . . a-doting** The conceit has an Ovidian flavour, recalling such stories as that of Pygmalion falling in love with an image of his own making (*Met.*, 10.260–92), but also Shakespeare's own narrative of *VA*.

11 **by . . . defeated** deprived me of you by adding male genitals

12 **one . . . nothing** The primary suggestion is that the added feature is of no value to the loving poet. But since *nothing* also referred to female genitalia (cf. 12.13 and n.) the line could yield a paradox that supports a homo-erotic reading: 'the one thing that nature added is, for my purposes, equivalent to a woman's sexual parts'.

13 **she . . . out** she chose you (cf. *2H4* 3.2.110ff., in which Falstaff selects his military recruits by 'pricking' their names on a list); and 'she equipped you with a prick (penis)'

14 Put your love for me first, but let women enjoy sexual relations with you (and bear you children). For the sexual connotations of *use*, cf. 4.13–14; for *treasure*, 6. 3–4.

---

2 master mistress] *Cam²;* Master Mistris *Q*, *Benson;* master-mistress *Malone*   6 whereupon] wherevpon   7 hue] hew   hues] *Hews*   10 a-doting] a dotinge   13 pricked] prickt

21 This poem is equivalent to Sidney's *AS*, sonnets 3, 6 and 15, in which wrong ways of writing love sonnets are dismissed. The speaker rejects the conceits of poets who habitually make extravagant comparisons with stars, jewels and flowers, in favour of truthful (and private?) cogency.

1 **that Muse** metonym for 'the poet inspired by *that Muse*': but with a lingering suggestion that *that Muse* might, unconventionally, be male

2 **Stirred** moved
a painted beauty presumably contrasted with the face 'by nature's own hand painted' of the preceding sonnet; suggests a falsely adorned (female) mistress, who is both *painted* with cosmetics and *painted* with poetic metaphors

3 **Who** The subject is *that Muse.*

4 **every . . . rehearse** mentions or describes *every* beautiful thing in the world alongside his own beautiful (love object)

5 **a . . . compare** a linking, or coupling, made out of extravagant or exalted similes: *compare* = comparison; cf. *TN* 2.4.101. For *couplement*, cf. *LLL* 5.2.532 (RP).

6 **sea's rich gems** The sea was thought to conceal many precious jewels; cf. *R3* 1.4.26–32.

7 **first-born** Q's 'borne' permits a suggestion both of new-born flowers, and of the earliest ones 'borne' by plants in spring.
rare special, choice, exceptional

7–8 **rare . . . air** The internal rhyme, reinforced by the rhyme on *are* in lines 5, 7, 10 and 12, suggests the triteness of the other poet.

8 **this huge rondure** this great sphere of earth and heaven, from Fr. *rondeur*; a pretentious-sounding word, not used by Shakespeare elsewhere, which mimics the other poet's inflated diction

9 **True in love** can apply either to the poet or to his subject-matter: 'I, who am true in love . . .'; or 'let me write truly about what is true in love'.

11 **any mother's child** any human being; cf. *MND* 1.2.80, 3.1.75. The colloquial, humdrum character of the phrase contrasts with such grandiose words as *couplement* and *rondure*. It also, disconcertingly, undercuts the preceding sonnet's claim that the object of the poet's love has a beauty which is paramount and exceptional.

12 **those gold candles** the stars, with a possible allusion to Sidney's identification of the subject of his sonnet sequence as 'Stella', or Star. The rejection of conventional comparisons anticipates sonnet 130.
heaven's air The repetition of the phrase from l. 8 reflects the sonnet's concern with *couplement;* there may also be a buried pun on 'heaven's heir'.

13 **hearsay** second-hand gossip; what is heard but not seen

14 proverbial: cf. Tilley, P546. Presumably the suggestion is that the poet does not wish to vulgarize his love-object by larding him with public compliment, or to risk losing him.

21

So is it not with me as with that Muse,
Stirred by a painted beauty to his verse,
Who heaven itself for ornament doth use,
And every fair with his fair doth rehearse,
Making a couplement of proud compare   5
With sun and moon, with earth and sea's rich gems;
With April's first-born flowers and all things rare
That heaven's air in this huge rondure hems;
O let me true in love but truly write,
And then believe me: my love is as fair   10
As any mother's child, though not so bright
As those gold candles fixed in heaven's air:
    Let them say more that like of hearsay well,
    I will not praise, that purpose not to sell.

2 Stirred] Stird   5 couplement] *Malone;* coopelment *Q*   6 sun] Sunne   moon] Moone
7 first-born] *Malone;* first borne *Q*   13 hearsay] heare-say

22 This sonnet celebrates the loving dependence of the speaker on his friend and his appropriation of his friend's youthful beauty.

2 **youth and thou** Since the speaker has vacillated between addressing his friend as *you* and *thou*, there may be a pun here on *youth* = 'you-ness'; cf. 15.12 and n.

of one date of the same age

3 **behold** shall behold

4 **look I** I anticipate

expiate extinguish, bring to a close (*OED* 7)

5–7 Despite the disclaimers in 21, Shakespeare here uses a familiar poetic conceit, that of the exchange of hearts; cf. Sidney's lyric 'My true love hath my heart and I have his', which was already very popular in the late 1580s (*OA*, 45: Sidney, *Poems*, 75–6 and 406–7). Because the poet's heart is lodged inside his friend, he adopts

his friend's beauty as his own *seemly raiment*.

9 **wary** cautious, careful, with perhaps a shade of *OED* 4, 'Careful in expenditure, thrifty, prudent'

9–10 **be . . . will** Be as careful of yourself as I shall be, or as I desire (*will*) to be on your own behalf, not on my own.

11 **chary** charily, carefully: *chary* and *wary* are here almost indistinguishable in sense, though the first is adjectival, the second adverbial.

12 He will keep his friend's heart as tenderly from harm as a nurse does her baby. The epithet *tender,* though directly applied to the nurse, seems partly reflected from the heart as a 'tender babe', and partly also suggests that the poet 'tenders', or treats, his friend's heart lovingly.

13 **Presume not on** do not expect to get back (your heart)

22

My glass shall not persuade me I am old
So long as youth and thou are of one date;
But when in thee time's furrows I behold,
Then look I death my days should expiate:
For all that beauty that doth cover thee   5
Is but the seemly raiment of my heart,
Which in thy breast doth live, as thine in me;
How can I then be elder than thou art?
O therefore love be of thyself so wary
As I not for myself, but for thee will,   10
Bearing thy heart, which I will keep so chary
As tender nurse her babe from faring ill:
    Presume not on thy heart when mine is slain;
    Thou gav'st me thine not to give back again.

---

3 furrows] *Malone;* forrwes *Q*

23 The poet cannot adequately express his love in speech, because of the intensity of his passion; he therefore implores his friend to read and respond to his written expressions of love.

1 **an unperfect actor** an actor who is not 'word perfect', does not know his lines correctly

2 **is . . . part** forgets his lines, loses his mastery of his role: 'part' was the technical term for the lines and cues to be learned by an actor.

3–4 **some . . . heart** some savage beast or a fiercely passionate human being, whose excess of passion collapses on itself

5 **for . . . trust** not able to trust myself; or nervous of the responsibility (position of trust) I am in

6 picks up *unperfect* from l. 1: 'the ceremony to which love is entitled' or 'the correct words that are required for the fulfilment of love's ritual', Q's *right* suggesting both 'right' and 'rite'

8 **O'ercharged with** weighed down with; and crushed with the 'charge' or responsibility

mine . . . might the strength of the

love I feel; the strength of my beloved

9 **my books** my writings, alluding either to *Son*, or more widely to other papers and writings; 'book' was also the normal term for the prompt-book from which a play was acted

10 **dumb presagers** silent indicators: to 'presage' normally carries connotations of foretelling the future, but in *VA* (457) Shakespeare applied it to Adonis' silent blush, an 'ill presage' of the words he is about to speak.

11 **look for recompense** look for an equal return of love

12 The subject is still *my books,* which look eagerly for a fuller return of love than might be yielded to a ready speaker who has spoken more fully and eloquently.

13 **silent love** Cf. Sidney, *AS,* 54.13–14: 'Dumb swans, not chattering pies, do lovers prove; / They love indeed, who quake to say they love.'

14 **To . . . eyes** negates the commonplace assertion that 'love is blind' (Tilley, L506): instead, love is claimed to read or to discern with sharpened insight (*fine wit*)

23

As an unperfect actor on the stage,
Who with his fear is put besides his part;
Or some fierce thing, replete with too much rage,
Whose strength's abundance weakens his own heart;
So I, for fear of trust, forget to say   5
The perfect ceremony of love's right,
And in mine own love's strength seem to decay,
O'ercharged with burden of mine own love's might:
O let my books be then the eloquence
And dumb presagers of my speaking breast,   10
Who plead for love, and look for recompense,
More than that tongue that more hath more expressed:
   O learn to read what silent love hath writ!
   To hear with eyes belongs to love's fine wit.

14 with] wit   wit] wiht

24 This is an elaboration of the idea of lovers 'looking babies' in each other's eyes (cf. *OED* baby 3). By looking closely into the speaker's eye, the young man can see a perfect image of himself, his own eyes being like a glass window; but he cannot see how much the poet loves him.

1 **steeled** formed a permanent image as if fashioned with or in steel: Capell's popular emendation to 'stell'd', though supported by the description of Hecuba in *Luc* 1444, 'a face where all distress is stell'd', seems unnecessary, and loses the association of steel with mirrors (cf. Gascoigne's *The Steele Glas* (1576)) and, possibly, with 'styled' = wrote or inscribed, a sense supported by Ingram and Redpath in IR. There may be a further play on 'stilled' = frozen, motionless; cf. *still* in l. 7.

2 **table** a writing tablet or flat surface on which a picture can be painted: for a comparable use, cf. 'our heart's table', *AW* 1.1.95. There may be an implication that the image is fixed in a 'table of steel'.

3 **the frame** probably not a decorative frame, but a supportive structure or framework, such as an easel

4 **perspective . . . art** The skill of the finest painter lies in his ability to suggest effects of distance. Though *OED*'s earliest example of 'perspective' as 'showing the effect of distance' (II 3a.) is 1606, it appears to be the application here, with associations also of the commoner 'perspective glass' = an optical instrument for seeing things not accessible to normal view. The word *perspective* must be accented twice: pèrspectíve.

5 **through the painter** both by means

of the painter and, more literally, *through* the painter-poet, whose eye is transparent

7 **my bosom's shop** a surprising image, coming so soon after the assertion at the end of sonnet 21, but the point of *shop* here seems to be not so much that the friend's image is offered for sale, but that it is stored and displayed; cf. *OED* 3c, 'a place where something is produced or elaborated . . . often said of the heart, liver or other internal bodily organs'. Cf. also the poem in G. Gascoigne's *The Adventures of Master F.J.* (1573) beginning 'Beautie shut up thy shop' (Gascoigne, 1.414).
still always

8 Your eyes are the glass windows through which my bosom is seen; probably with some play on 'glazing' and 'gazing', especially since 'glaze' could mean 'stare', as in *JC* 1.3.21
glazed glazèd

9 **good turns** Q's hyphenation draws attention to this as a familiar phrase. It could have sexual connotations, as in *AC* 2.5.58; but a more immediate parallel is offered by 47.1–2, where, again, *good turns* are associated with fashioning images of the beloved.

10 **drawn** delineated; extracted

11–12 **the . . . peep** The sun, in love with the young man, enjoys gazing out of his eyes and into those of the poet, in order to see the youth's reflected image. Behind the conceit lies the notion that the speaker loves the young man so much that 'the sun shines out of his eyes'; there may also be a side glance at the youth's role as son, not father, as in sonnets 1–17.

13 **cunning** skill, insight

24

Mine eye hath played the painter, and hath steeled
Thy beauty's form in table of my heart;
My body is the frame wherein 'tis held,
And perspective it is best painter's art;
For through the painter must you see his skill,　　　5
To find where your true image pictured lies,
Which in my bosom's shop is hanging still,
That hath his windows glazed with thine eyes:
Now see what good turns eyes for eyes have done:
Mine eyes have drawn thy shape, and thine for me　　10
Are windows to my breast, wherethrough the sun
Delights to peep, to gaze therein on thee;
　　Yet eyes this cunning want to grace their art:
　　They draw but what they see, know not the heart.

---

1 steeled] steeld *Q;* stell'd *Capell*　3 'tis] ti's　4 painter's] Painters　5 painter] Painter　6 image] Image　pictured] pictur'd　9 good turns] good-turns　11 wherethrough] where-through　sun] Sun

25 This sonnet contrasts the speaker, a private and obscure man securely happy in his loving friendship, with court favourites whose fame and fortune may be lost in an instant. The image in ll. 9–12 of the popular war hero would apply well either to the Earl of Essex, to whose expected success in Ireland Shakespeare alluded in *H5* (cf. also 125n.), or to his patron the Earl of Southampton, imprisoned and deprived of his rank for his part in the Essex rebellion in 1601.

1 **in . . . stars** lucky in their situation, blessed in their planetary influence; but also in positions of favour with the important people, or luminaries, on whom they depend

3 **whom . . . bars** who is denied by (ill) luck the possibility of boasting of worldly success; or who is excluded, through the chance of lowly status, from such glorious pageantry (*triumph*)

4 **Unlooked for** applies partly to *joy* – 'I experience unexpected joy' – partly to *I* – 'I am overlooked, not in the public eye'
   that . . . most what I, in contrast to the world in general, regard as most valuable: contrasted with the *public honour* of l. 2

5 **princes'** In Elizabethan usage these could be female or male, so an allusion may be present either to Elizabeth I or to James I or both.
   fair leaves Leaves (*OED* 2) were often petals rather than foliage; cf. *1H6* 4.1.92. Figuratively, the image suggests splendidly dressed courtiers glittering with silk and jewels.

6 **as . . . eye** The acknowledged characteristic of the Elizabethan marigold (roughly equivalent to the modern 'pot marigold') was that it opened and closed in response to the sun: cf. *WT* 4.4.105 and *Luc* 397.

7 Cf. the image of burial within a bud in 1.11: the suggestion here is presumably that the pride of favourites, which appeared to be reinforced by external signs, is shut up uselessly within them.

buried buri*èd*

8 **at a frown** Cf. 'Fear no more the frown o'the great', *Cym* 4.2.264.

9 **painful** painstaking; enduring pain (wounds)
   famoused famous*èd*: = made famous

9–11 ***worth . . . quite** The failure of ll. 9 and 11 to rhyme has prompted emendations of *worth* to 'fight' (Lewis Theobald) or 'might' (Capell), and of *quite* to 'forth' (Theobald) (Rollins, 1.73–4). Previous editors have generally accepted one of these three emendations in order to achieve a rhyme. However, none can be accounted for with reference to compositorial misreading or mishearing, and there are objections to all three. Either 'might' or 'fight' merely reinforces a point already made – the exemplum is of a court favourite who is a soldier; and 'fight' introduces a threefold alliteration on 'f' whose effect is somewhat ironical. *Worth* carries a very different sense – '*deservedly* famous' – and suggests that even those courtiers advanced on the basis of merit (such, in Shakespeare's eyes, may have been both Essex and Southampton) are subject to sudden falls. This seems too important a notion to be emended out of existence. Also, 'razed forth' would add another alliteration on 'f' as well as an assonance with *forgot* (12), and is a rather odd construction: elsewhere Shakespeare used either 'raze' simply, or 'raze out' (cf. *R2* 2.3.75, 3.1.25; *2H4* 5.2.127; *Mac* 5.3.42; *Cym* 5.5.70). It is possible that Shakespeare, never a brilliant rhymester, left these lines imperfect.

10 **foiled** defeated; dishonoured, defiled

11 figuratively, expelled from the ranks of the nobility; but since honours were denoted by means of official court documents, there may also be a reference to the expunging from such records, or books of honours, of disgraced noblemen.
   razed raz*èd*

14 in a place from which I cannot move myself (remove), or be shifted by others

25

Let those who are in favour with their stars
Of public honour and proud titles boast,
Whilst I, whom fortune of such triumph bars,
Unlooked for joy in that I honour most;
Great princes' favourites their fair leaves spread   5
But as the marigold at the sun's eye,
And in themselves their pride lies buried,
For at a frown they in their glory die.
The painful warrior famoused for worth,
After a thousand victories once foiled,   10
Is from the book of honour razed quite,
And all the rest forgot for which he toiled:
    Then happy I, that love and am beloved
    Where I may not remove, nor be removed.

---

5 princes'] Princes   6 marigold] Marygold   7 themselves] them-selues   9 famoused] famosed worth] might *Capell*   11 quite] forth *Ard¹*

26 This is a sonnet with some of the character of a dedicatory epistle, in which the speaker stresses his limited skill and promises not to make his declaration public until he has received public approbation or advancement. Despite the speaker's claim to write in order to signal his duty, not to display his skill, it is marked by conspicuous elaboration, for instance in the carefully-disposed feminine rhymes in ll. 6, 8, 9–12, 13 and 14.

1 **vassalage** absolute subjection, servitude; cf. 58.4

2 Your excellence has made powerfully binding the obligation (duty) which I already owed you.

2–5 **duty . . . duty . . . Duty** an example of anadiplosis, 'when the same sound is repeated in the ende of the sentence before, and in the beginning of the sentence following after' (Fraunce, 36–7)

3 **this written embassage** the sonnet itself, a formal written message which the friend is to read attentively (cf. 23.9). The phrase has courtly and chivalric associations, for it occurs in the account of the Iberian jousts in Sidney's *Arcadia*, which in turn is modelled on the late-Elizabethan Accession Day Tilts: 'then another from whose tent, I remember, a bird was made to fly with such art to carry a written embassage among the ladies' (*NA*, 256) (E.E.D.-J.).

4 **witness . . . wit** Though he claims to write in order to declare his duty, not display rhetorical skill, the line itself, in the repetition of the syllable *wit* in two senses, offers an example of the rhetorical trope epanodos, 'when one and the same sound is repeated in the beginning and middle, or middle and end' (Fraunce, 46–7).

6 **wanting . . . it** Half-way through the twenty-sixth sonnet, it is evident that this poet is by no means short of words, but is adopting a pose of modesty: concealed finesses here are the pun on *show it* and 'show wit', and a rhyme on the implied but unspoken word 'poet'.

7 **some . . . thine** some favourable opinion; some rhetorical ingenuity or poetic elaboration (*OED* 4a and 8a). There may be an implication that the addressee is also a poet, or at least skilled in language.

8 **(all naked)** placed in parentheses in Q. The nakedness may be either that of the friend's *soul*, or of his soul's thought, or that of the speaker's own *wit* or *duty*. Possibly there is a paradoxical suggestion that what is *naked* in the friend – his most intimate and unvarnished impulse or *thought* – has the capacity to clothe, enrich and adorn his friend's unvarnished *duty*.
bestow it The subject is still *duty*: *bestow* may suggest 'enrich'. The word was used analogously by Shakespeare in *Tit* 4.2.163 (and cf. *OED* 6c). Alternatively, *bestow* may = stow away, place (*Glossary*, 5): 'your good opinion will lodge my duty in your innermost thoughts'.

9 **that** The word is apparently superfluous, but underlines the speaker's uncertainty: 'whatever star it may be that . . . '.

10 **Points on me** directs its (favourable) beams towards me; cf. *R2* 1.3.146–7.
fair aspect term from astrology, denoting 'favourable angle of astral influence'

11 **my tattered loving** uses the commonplace classical conceit that 'words are the clothes of the mind': because of his poor wit (l. 4) the speaker is unable to dress his love in the splendour which would be fitting for the lord of his love. 'Tattered' was often spelt 'tottered'; cf. 2.4.

12 ***thy sweet respect** Q's 'their' is the first of fourteen apparent misreadings of *thy* as 'their'; cf. Jackson, 'Compositors'. The close similarity of *sweet respect* to *fair aspect*, suggests that the friend himself is the star which controls the speaker's life.

14 **not . . . me** not make myself conspicuous in places where you may put me to the test, or, perhaps, discover me

26

Lord of my love, to whom in vassalage
Thy merit hath my duty strongly knit:
To thee I send this written embassage,
To witness duty, not to show my wit;
Duty so great, which wit so poor as mine   5
May make seem bare, in wanting words to show it;
But that I hope some good conceit of thine
In thy soul's thought (all naked) will bestow it:
Till whatsoever star that guides my moving
Points on me graciously with fair aspect,   10
And puts apparel on my tattered loving,
To show me worthy of thy sweet respect;
   Then may I dare to boast how I do love thee;
   Till then, not show my head where thou mayst
      prove me.

---

3 embassage] ambassage   11 tattered] tottered   12 thy] *Capell;* their *Q*

27 This is the first of a series of five sonnets in which the solitary poet medi-
tates on his friend: 27–8 are on night
and sleeplessness, a traditional motif
in Petrarchan sonnet sequences;
29–30 on loneliness and failure, a
more unusual theme; 31 expands the
resolution of 30.

1 **Weary with toil** perhaps picked up
from '*cum lassa quiete*' (Ovid, *Met.*,
15.188)

2 **dear** precious; 'to which one is great-
ly attached' (*OED* 4, 5)
repose place of repose
travail labour; travel: not clearly distinguished in Elizabethan spelling; cf.
32.2

3 **journey** possibly with a play on Fr.
journée = day, or day-long task

4 **work** make it work; activate it

5 **from . . . abide** The source of his
thoughts is a long way from where he
lives.

6 **Intend** are purposefully fixed on: to
'intend a journey', from Lat. *iter
intendere*, was a regular expression; cf.

AC 5.2.201.

8 **Looking** The subject is still *thoughts.*
which . . . see all the blind see is darkness.

9 **Save** except
imaginary sight vision which is
imaginative, not physical

10 *thy another of Q's 'their' for 'thy'
errors: cf. 26.12n.

11 **like a jewel** Some precious stones
(especially carbuncles) were thought
to be capable of emitting light; cf. *Tit*
2.3.226–30.
ghastly terrifying, deathly

12 *Black* is here equated with 'ugly', and
night (Lat. *nox*, feminine) is thought
of as an ugly old woman (cf.
Michelangelo's sculpture in the
Medici chapel in Florence). However,
the final image of her *old face* being
made *new* also suggests the appearance of the new moon after preceding
moonless nights.

14 **For . . . for** on account of; on behalf
of

27

Weary with toil, I haste me to my bed,
The dear repose for limbs with travail tired;
But then begins a journey in my head
To work my mind, when body's work's expired:
For then my thoughts, from far where I abide,   5
Intend a zealous pilgrimage to thee,
And keep my drooping eyelids open wide,
Looking on darkness which the blind do see;
Save that my soul's imaginary sight
Presents thy shadow to my sightless view,   10
Which like a jewel hung in ghastly night
Makes black night beauteous, and her old face new:
    Lo, thus by day my limbs, by night my mind,
    For thee, and for myself, no quiet find.

5 from far] far from *Malone*   7 eyelids] eye-lids   10 thy] *Capell;* their *Q*   11 hung . . . night]
(hunge . . . night)

28 Continuing the theme of the preceding sonnet, the speaker describes day and night, natural opposites, competing to prolong his anguish. The repeated rhymes on *night* in ll. 1, 3, 9 and 11 suggest the victim's claustrophobia, though not so insistently as Sidney's *AS*, 89, which has 'night' and 'day' as its only end-words.

1   happy plight cheerful condition

5–6 each . . . me Day and night are viewed as a pair of rival tyrants who nevertheless make a league (*shake hands*; cf. *H5* 5.2.133) to seal a bargain to torment the speaker. Shakespeare may have known Spenser's translation of J. van der Noot's *Theatre for Worldlings* (1569), which opens with a woodcut showing black and white dogs, representing day and night, attacking a white hind, symbolizing Petrarch's Laura.

7–8 to . . . toil Night tortures him by causing him to lament his growing distance from his friend.

9–12 Like Katherina in *TS* 4.5.7, the speaker tries to master his situation by means of absurd and blatant denial. He praises the sun for his brightness and compliment to his friend (*him*) even when the sun is concealed by clouds, and tells the night that she gilds the evening at a time when no stars twinkle (*twire*). It may appear initially that *to please him* refers to *thee*, the poet's friend; but the succeeding *So flatter . . .* indicates that at this point it is the sun that the speaker seeks to gratify.

11 swart-complexioned black-faced

13 draw draw out, extend

14 grief's length Capell's emendation of Q's *length* to 'strength' undermines the subtlety of the distinction between day and night: night makes the speaker's grief, already experienced as long-drawn-out, even more intense; it also eliminates the chiastic pattern *sorrows longer . . . length . . . stronger*. The feminine rhymes of lines 13–14 reinforce the sense of prolongation.

28

How can I then return in happy plight
That am debarred the benefit of rest?
When day's oppression is not eased by night,
But day by night and night by day oppressed,
And each, though enemies to either's reign,   5
Do in consent shake hands to torture me,
The one by toil, the other to complain
How far I toil, still farther off from thee.
I tell the day to please him, thou art bright,
And dost him grace, when clouds do blot the
          heaven;   10
So flatter I the swart-complexioned night,
When sparkling stars twire not thou gild'st the even;
   But day doth daily draw my sorrows longer,
   And night doth nightly make grief's length seem
          stronger.

---

9 day] Day   11 swart-complexioned] swart complexiond   12 gild'st the even] *Malone*; guil'st th'
eauen *Q*   14 length] strength *Capell*

29 Lonely and outcast, the speaker envies the prosperity and talent of others, until he remembers his friend, whose love compensates him for everything.

1   **in disgrace** lacking grace or favour

2   **beweep** lament, weep for; cf. *KJ* 1.4.324.

    outcast state condition of being outcast, rejected

3   **bootless** hopeless, without remedy

4   **look upon myself** engage in self-contemplation

5   **one . . . hope** someone with better prospects, including prospects of wealth

6   **Featured like him** with features (by implication, beautiful) like his

7   **art** skill of any kind, not necessarily relating to creative art

    scope freedom, opportunity

8   least satisfied with the things of which I have most: what it is that the speaker 'most enjoys' is not indicated; perhaps his own skill with language.

10 **Haply** perhaps; with a suggestion also of 'happily'

10–11 **my . . . arising** Though this sonnet is not explicitly associated with night-time, as are 27 and 28, the comparison of his re-animated state to

that of 'the lark at break of day' suggests relief and illumination discovered at dawn. Cf. *Cym* 3.20.

12 **sullen earth** dark, shadowy earth, with some connotations of melancholy (*OED* sullen 4a): this image, too, suggests that the meditation belongs to the hours of night.

    sings . . . gate Instead of importuning heaven, as in l. 3, the speaker, or his *state*, now praises God.

13 **thy . . . remembered** the recollection of your sweet love for me; or the recollection of your sweet self, whom I love. However, there is a touch of undermining uncertainty in the word *remembered*, as if the speaker remembers his friend as loving him, but may not be in a position to know whether this love continues in the present.

14 **change** exchange

    kings plural; or plural possessive, 'kings''; or singular possessive, 'king's', = that of a king, e.g. James I, who may have enjoyed the company of the poet's friend at times when the poet did not; Q's capitalization reinforces the suggestion of allusion to a particular monarch.

29

When in disgrace with fortune and men's eyes
I all alone beweep my outcast state,
And trouble deaf heav'n with my bootless cries,
And look upon myself, and curse my fate,
Wishing me like to one more rich in hope,   5
Featured like him, like him with friends possessed,
Desiring this man's art and that man's scope,
With what I most enjoy contented least;
Yet in these thoughts myself almost despising,
Haply I think on thee, and then my state,   10
Like to the lark at break of day arising,
From sullen earth sings hymns at heaven's gate;
    For thy sweet love remembered such wealth brings
    That then I scorn to change my state with kings.

---

1 fortune] Fortune 2 outcast] out-cast 3 heav'n] heauen 6 Featured] Featur'd possessed]
possest 11 Like . . . arising,] (Like . . . arising) lark] Larke 12 heaven's] Heauens 14 kings] Kings

30 Still in solitude, the poet takes stock of his past losses and failures, rendered in legal and financial metaphors, weeping for them afresh, until he thinks, consolingly, of his friend.

1 **sessions** judicial proceedings or formal examination, with a play on the older meaning of 'session', 'the state or posture of being seated' (*OED* 1a)

2 **summon up** cause to appear as if in a judicial investigation; with a play on 'sum' (v.) = enumerate, call to financial account
   remembrance . . . past Cf. Wisdom of Solomon (OT Apocrypha), 11.12, 'For a double griefe came upon them, and a groaning for the remembrance of things past' (E.E.D.-J.)

3 **sigh** sigh for

4 **dear time's waste** the expiry of time that was loved by him, or valuable to him: to 'waste time' did not always have adverse connotations; cf. *VA* 24, *AYL* 2.4.95.

5 **unused to flow** Cf. Othello's description of his eyes as 'unused to the melting mood' (*Oth* 5.2.35) when in a vein of reminiscence and retrospection.

6 **dateless night** night that will never come to an end; cf. 14.14 and n.: suggests that legal restrictions are not here applicable

7 **cancelled** another legal term, denoting bonds which are no longer valid; cf. l. 12

8 **th'expense** loss, with financial associations (*OED* 1b, with this example)

9 **grievances** sorrows, traumas, which have gone before, belong to the past; perhaps also grievances for which, until now, he has *foregone* to grieve (cf. *OED* forgo, forego 5, 6)

10 **heavily** laboriously, sadly
   from . . . o'er count, enumerate each sorrow, *woe to woe* suggesting '"o" to "o"', and an account book full of (a) groans; (b) empty figures, noughts; and for 'tell o'er' as 'enumerate (griefs)', cf. *Oth* 3.3.171–2: 'O, what damned minutes tells he o'er / Who dotes yet doubts, suspects yet strongly loves.'

11 **account** narrative; financial reckoning
   fore-bemoaned moan the closeness of the phrase to *grievances foregone* only two lines before enacts the repetitive grieving that is described.
   fore-bemoaned fore-bemoanèd

13 **dear friend** picks up 'dear time' in l. 4: the friend's 'dearness', or value, compensates for all previous sorrows.

30

When to the sessions of sweet silent thought
I summon up remembrance of things past,
I sigh the lack of many a thing I sought,
And with old woes new wail my dear time's waste;
Then can I drown an eye (unused to flow)   5
For precious friends hid in death's dateless night,
And weep afresh love's long since cancelled woe,
And moan th'expense of many a vanished sight.
Then can I grieve at grievances foregone,
And heavily from woe to woe tell o'er   10
The sad account of fore-bemoaned moan,
Which I new pay, as if not paid before;
    But if the while I think on thee, dear friend,
    All losses are restored, and sorrows end.

1 sessions] Sessions   5 unused] vn-vs'd   7 afresh] a fresh   cancelled] canceld   foregone] fore-gon
13 thee, dear friend,] thee (deare friend)

31 The young man is universally loved,
and in the congress of those who love
him the lonely poet imaginatively
recovers his own lost (dead?) friends.

1 **bosom** heart, seat of intimate emotions; used as a synecdoche for the
youth as a whole. For its associations
with close male friendship, cf. *MV*
1.3.16–18: 'this Antonio / Being a
bosom lover of my lord, / Must needs
be like my lord'.

1–4 **endeared . . . supposed . . . buried**
The 'e' is sounded in the last syllable
of all three words, making an emphatic assonance with *dead* in ll. 2 and 7.

2 No longer enjoying the popularity
that the youth does, the speaker has
believed his friends to be dead, and/or
the capacity for love to be extinct.

3 **all . . . parts** all the aspects and capacities of love

5 **holy . . . tear** a tear of devotion shed
as part of an 'obsequy', or funeral: cf.
Tit 1.1.160, 'My tributary tears / I
render for my brother's obsequies'.

6 **religious** Cf. *OED* 4a, 'Scrupulous,
exact, strict, conscientious'.
stol'n Tears are paid or exacted, like
coins; for another application of this
metaphor, cf. Donne, 'A Valediction:
Of Weeping', 1–9 (Donne, 89).

7 **interest** continues the image of tears
as coins; they are the return or reward
owed to dead friends.
which The subject is *all those friends*.

8 **But things removed** but as things
which have moved; 'remove' was commonly used intransitively.
*thee Charles Gildon's emendation
of Q's 'there' (Rollins, 1.90–1) carries
conviction: 'there' may be a compositorial misreading comparable with the
many 'their'/'thy' errors; cf. 26.12n.
Though 'there' makes perfectly good
sense – 'in thy bosom' – it sounds

clumsy, and does not lead on so neatly
as *thee* to the *Thou* of the sestet.

9 **Thou . . . grave** Contrast 1.11–14, in
which the youth was his own grave,
and was reproached rather than
praised for so being: the young man's
bosom is now viewed as a spacious
memorial chapel or mausoleum.

10 **the . . . gone** *Trophies* suggests symbolic relics of past victories, such as
helmets or battle honours. Here they
probably correspond with 'their parts
of me' in the following line, the suggestion being that the speaker's past
triumphs in love are now transferred
to the young man. *Lovers* need not
carry any erotic charge, and may simply denote 'those who once loved me',
as in Psalms, 38.11, 'My lovers and
my friends stand aloof from my sore:
and my kinsmen stand afar off'.

11 **their . . . me** the parts of me that
belonged to them: presumably, his
love, as in *love's loving parts* in l. 3

12 **due of many** what was both owed by,
and paid to, many: cf. *the world's due*,
1.14. If this connection is made, an
implication may be discovered that
the young man is selfish or greedy in
gathering such diverse expressions of
love into himself.

13 **Their . . . loved** the images of those
whom I loved: *images* may denote a
picture or copy, or, conceivably, a
ghost (*OED* 4a and b; 5); and cf. *Ham*
1.1.8, 'our last king / Whose image
even but now appeared to us'.

14 **thou . . . me** You, who encompass or
encapsulate all those who love you,
also possess everyone whom I have
ever loved or been loved by: you also
possess my inmost essence – *all the
all*. Booth (176–8) raises, but eventually discards, the possibility that *all*
has a sexual sense.

31

Thy bosom is endeared with all hearts
Which I, by lacking, have supposed dead;
And there reigns love, and all love's loving parts,
And all those friends which I thought buried.
How many a holy and obsequious tear   5
Hath dear religious love stol'n from mine eye,
As interest of the dead, which now appear
But things removed that hidden in thee lie:
Thou art the grave where buried love doth live,
Hung with the trophies of my lovers gone,   10
Who all their parts of me to thee did give;
That due of many, now is thine alone.
    Their images I loved, I view in thee,
    And thou, all they, hast all the all of me.

---

1 endeared] indeared   3 love] Loue   love's] Loues   6 stol'n] stolne   8 removed] remou'd   thee]
Malone; there *Q, Benson*   13 loved] lou'd   14 thou, all they,] thou (all they)

32 If the young man outlives the poet, he may come to view his verse as old-fashioned, but is implored to cherish it for the devotion it conveys.

1 **well-contented day** the day when he pays his debt to nature in full: for 'content' in this sense (*OED* 4a) cf. *Oth* 3.1.1, 'Masters, play here, I will content your pains'. It is also a day with which he will be *well-contented*, i.e. satisfied, uncomplaining. For 'content' (adj.) in both senses, cf. Shylock's last line, *MV* 4.1.390.

3 **by fortune** by luck; by (good) fortune

4 **deceased** deceasèd
    lover the man who once loved you: not necessarily with erotic connotations; cf. 31.10n.

5 **the bett'ring . . . time** the improvement made in subsequent time; by implication, poems which reflect this improvement

6 **every pen** Cf. *every alien pen*, 78.3.

7 **Reserve** preserve; keep in a separate or private place

7–8 **their . . . men** *Rhyme*, though a rhyme-word, acts as a synecdoche for 'literary style': the *poor rude lines* of the poet will be transcended by the high style of more fortunate (*happier*) writers.

11 If the poet had lived to develop a more

sophisticated and up-to-date style, his love would have generated poems of more value (*dearer*). Whereas in sonnet 17 the poet anticipates the young man dying without progeny, their positions here are reversed, with the youth (supposedly) imagining the poet dying without worthy poetic offspring.

12 The primary image is military: the better poems that may be produced in a later age could have kept better company, with superior weaponry or equipment. There may also be a suggestion of more sophisticated poetic structures, with *ranks*, or successive lines of verse, organized in subtler or more complicated fashion, as, perhaps, in Donne's *Songs and Sonnets*. Shakespeare may also have been thinking of Sidney's criticism of the shapeless work of English poets, who write anything they think of, 'never marshalling it into any assured rank, that almost the readers cannot tell where to find themselves' (*Prose*, 112).

13 **better prove** turn out to be better

14 **style I'll** The internal rhyme, underlined by Q's spelling, seems to mock the supposedly greater finesse of subsequent poets.

32

If thou survive my well-contented day,
When that churl death my bones with dust shall
      cover,
And shalt by fortune once more re-survey
These poor rude lines of thy deceased lover:
Compare them with the bett'ring of the time,   5
And though they be outstripped by every pen,
Reserve them for my love, not for their rhyme,
Exceeded by the height of happier men.
O then vouchsafe me but this loving thought:
'Had my friend's Muse grown with this growing age,10
A dearer birth than this his love had brought,
To march in ranks of better equipage:
    But since he died and poets better prove,
    Theirs for their style I'll read, his for his love.'

1 well-contented] well contented   4 lover] Louer   6 outstripped] out-strip   13 poets] Poets
14 style I'll] stile ile

33 This sonnet and the following one treat of disappointment and betrayal, expressed in imagery of sun and cloud. The two are closely connected: for instance, in 33 the friend endures *disgrace* at the end of line 8; in 34, the poet.

1–8 The poet's experience is commonplace; cf. Tilley, S978, 'The morning sun never lasts a day.'

2 **Flatter . . . sovereign** Some reversal of traditional roles is suggested: most often courtiers flatter sovereigns; but this sovereign, a sun/son, flatters (deceives) inferiors.

3 **Kissing . . . face** A kiss bestowed by face, not lips, appears richly beneficent.

4 **heavenly alchemy** divine, or else merely pertaining to the sky/heavens: alchemy was suspect to most intelligent Elizabethans, and Q's phonetic spelling, 'alcumy', suggests the indiscriminate nature of the sun's blessing, bestowed on 'all comers'.

5 **ride** The clouds are upstart cavaliers, beggars on horseback; as they cross the sun's face they may also figure lines or wrinkles: cf. Fr. *se rider*, to become wrinkled.

6 **ugly rack** *rack* = 'a mass of clouds driven before the wind in the upper air' (*OED* 3a); the word is cognate with 'wrack' or 'wreck', suggesting an obstruction that is at once ruinous and fragile.

7 **forlorn** Metre requires stress on the first syllable, and Q's 'for-lorne' may also indicate it.

8 **disgrace** disfigurement, and consequent shame

11 **alack** Note the internal rhyme with *rack* in 6.

12 **region** belonging to the upper air, governed by the 'sovereign' sun: cf. *Ham* 2.2.487.

14 **Suns . . . world** Only when the end of the line is reached does it become apparent that the poet's exaltation of his friend as *my sun* has become reductive, for he is, punningly, 'a son of the world', a morally corrupt worldling, not a divine being.
stain primarily intransitive, = receive stain; but as the ensuing sonnet indicates, the sun-friend's *stain* also 'stains' the poet – injures him irreversibly.

33

Full many a glorious morning have I seen
Flatter the mountain tops with sovereign eye,
Kissing with golden face the meadows green,
Gilding pale streams with heavenly alchemy;
Anon permit the basest clouds to ride   5
With ugly rack on his celestial face,
And from the forlorn world his visage hide,
Stealing unseen to west with this disgrace:
Even so my sun one early morn did shine
With all triumphant splendour on my brow;   10
But out alack, he was but one hour mine,
The region cloud hath masked him from me now.
    Yet him for this, my love no whit disdaineth:
    Suns of the world may stain, when heaven's sun
       staineth.

---

4 gilding] Guilding   alchemy] alcumy   7 forlorn] for-lorne   9 sun] Sunne   10 all triumphant] all-triumphant *Ard¹*   12 masked] mask'd

34 This sonnet continues the theme and imagery of 33, with the speaker betrayed by his young friend, addressed as the sun.

1–2 Cf. Tilley, S968: 'Although the sun shines, leave not your cloak at home.'

2 **travail** as in Q. Both *travail* = labour, perhaps painfully, and *travel* = make a journey, are implied, the spellings being indistinguishable in Elizabethan orthography.

3 **base clouds** suggests unworthy companions, like the 'base contagious clouds' surrounding Prince Hal in Eastcheap, *1H4* 1.2.193

4 **brav'ry** splendour, courage, ostentatious beauty
rotten smoke Clouds were thought of as vapours carrying infections, such as plague.

8 **heals . . . disgrace** Cf. Tilley, W929: 'Though the wound be healed yet the scar remains', alluded to also in *Luc* 731. The use of *disgrace* in an identical position in 33 and 34 draws attention to the close linking of the two. Here, as in 33, the word implies both 'shame' and 'disfigurement, loss of grace (beauty)' – a visible scar.

9 **grief** pain which may be perceived as

in part physical; cf. Falstaff's question whether honour can 'take away the grief of a wound', *1H4* 5.1.132.

12 **loss** Capell's emendation to 'cross' has been accepted by virtually all subsequent editors; however, it transforms the speaker into a Christ-figure, a metaphor not used elsewhere in *Son*, and a Christ-figure who will not, contrary to Gospel accounts, forgive those who have crucified him. 42.12 uses the word in the same position, but in a context that suggests an identification with Simon of Cyrene, rather than with Christ himself. Though some of the religious connotations of repentance and forgiveness are invoked in 13–14, it is not clear that these are to be made fully explicit in the preceding line; Shakespeare may have been guilty of a non-rhyme. Booth (189) acknowledges that 'the repetition might be purposeful', illustrating the persistence of loss.

13 **pearl** adjectival, = made of pearl: suggestive of Christ's comparison of the kingdom of heaven to a pearl of great price, Matthew, 13.46
sheds Q's 'sheeds' made at least an eye-rhyme.

34

Why didst thou promise such a beauteous day
And make me travail forth without my cloak,
To let base clouds o'ertake me in my way,
Hiding thy brav'ry in their rotten smoke?
'Tis not enough that through the cloud thou break,   5
To dry the rain on my storm-beaten face,
For no man well of such a salve can speak
That heals the wound and cures not the disgrace;
Nor can thy shame give physic to my grief;
Though thou repent, yet I have still the loss;   10
Th'offender's sorrow lends but weak relief
To him that bears the strong offence's loss.
    Ah, but those tears are pearl which thy love sheds,
    And they are rich, and ransom all ill deeds.

2 travail] trauaile *Q;* travel *Malone*   12 loss] losse *Q;* cross *Capell*   13 sheds] sheeds

35 The young man has wronged his friend; in making excuses for him the poet colludes with him and shares his fault. From proverbial citations in the octave the poet moves to legal terminology in the sestet.

1 **grieved** Cf. *grief* in 34.9.

2 **Roses have thorns** proverbial: 'No rose without a thorn' (Tilley, R182). **silver fountains** Moving water was often described as 'silver'; cf. *R2* 5.3.59; *KJ* 2.1.339.

3 **stain** hide or darken; dishonour: clouds were thought of as carrying pollution and disease, and eclipses as portending disaster.

4 **loathsome . . . bud** proverbial: 'The canker soonest eats the fairest rose' (Tilley, C56); and cf. 70.7. *Canker* = a caterpillar or canker-worm (*OED* 4); 'bud' has already been established in 1.11 as a metonym for the young man.

5 **All . . . faults** yet another proverb: 'Every man has his faults' (Tilley, M116).

6 **Authorizing** The second and fourth syllables are stressed. The word is used in a legal sense for 'sanctioning, justifying', with a further play on 'author' as 'composer or writer' (*OED* 3a): he justifies the fault by writing a poem about it. **with compare** by means of the sententious comparisons in ll. 1–5.

7 In healing or forgiving the youth's offence, the poet morally compromises himself: cf. *salve* in 34.7.

8 *****Excusing . . . are** Either, offering more excuse for your sins than they deserve; or, offering more than they, as small sins, require. The common emendation of Q's 'their . . . their' to 'thy . . . thy' has been rejected in favour of 'these . . . these' on the

hypothesis that what the compositor saw was 'theis', which he misread as 'their' (RP).

9 **to . . . sense** In order to defend your fault, committed through the bodily senses, I invoke (common) sense, or reason: cf. *OED* bring in 18f, 'To introduce (into consideration, discussion)'.

10 Your (legal) opponent is also your (legal) defender.

11 **'gainst . . . commence** submit a legal (and just) complaint against myself

12 **civil war** internal war, war within the 'state of man' (*JC* 2.1.67); also a war conducted with civility, or courtesy, respect (*OED* civil 12) **in** both within my love and within my hate, and between the two of them

13 **accessory** Shakespeare's normal pronunciation was àccessòry (cf. *R3* 1.2.192 and *Luc* 922 and 1658); here used in a partly-legal sense to suggest the poet's complicity in his friend's offence.

14 to his still-loved friend, who has cruelly, hurtfully (*sourly*) injured him. The phrase *sweet thief* recurs in a more favourable sense in 99.2. What it is that has been taken away from the poet may be his reputation (cf. *disgrace*, 33.8 and 34.8), or the enjoyment of his friend's company (36.8), or both. Though the ostensible theme of 33 and 34 is forgiveness, the sustained analysis of the process of forgiveness renews and keeps alive the young man's fault. Yet another proverb is suggested: 'Forgive and forget' (Tilley, F593), cited four times in Shakespeare's plays; but unlike the proverbs in ll. 1–5 it is negated.

35

No more be grieved at that which thou hast done;
Roses have thorns, and silver fountains mud;
Clouds and eclipses stain both moon and sun,
And loathsome canker lives in sweetest bud.
All men make faults, and even I, in this,   5
Authorizing thy trespass with compare,
Myself corrupting, salving thy amiss,
Excusing these sins more than these sins are:
For to thy sensual fault I bring in sense;
Thy adverse party is thy advocate,   10
And 'gainst myself a lawful plea commence:
Such civil war is in my love and hate
   That I an accessory needs must be
   To that sweet thief which sourly robs from me.

---

3 moon] Moone   sun] Sunne   7 corrupting, salving] corrupting saluing *Q;* corrupt in salving
Capell   8 these . . . these] *this edn.;* their . . . their *Q*   10 advocate] Aduocate

36 Continues the theme of the speaker's participation in the youth's guilt, this time with emphasis on outward reputation rather than moral responsibility. The poet appears to act as a scapegoat or whipping boy, taking his friend's *blots* on himself and rejoicing, at a distance, in the young man's splendid reputation.

1 **confess** acknowledge, declare
   we . . . twain We must remain two separate beings, not united into 'one flesh', as husband and wife; also, we must remain at odds, in dispute. Cf. *RJ* 3.5.241, 'Go, counsellor! Thou and my bosom henceforth shall be twain'; and *OED* twain 3a.

2 **our undivided loves** They are united in affection, but physically separate.

3 **those blots** those disgraces, presumably corresponding with the *faults* of 35.5

4 (If they continue to be severed from each other,) the speaker can carry the full burden of the young man's shame, or, possibly, their mutual shame.

5 **respect** consideration, motive: cf. *Ham* 3.1.68–9, 'there's the respect / That makes calamity of so long life'; there may also be a reference to the

'mutual respect' in which the friends hold each other.

6 **separable spite** a mortifying situation (cf. *Ham* 1.5.188, 'O cursed spite') which causes separation

7 **love's sole effect** the tendency of love to make the two of us one, as in l. 1; and/or the unique condition or mode of fulfilment of our love

8 **steal sweet hours** An unexplained *separable spite* keeps us apart, diminishing the time spent together; it also detracts from the pleasures that are 'ours'.

9 I am not permitted to greet you openly at any future time (cf. *Glossary*, s.v. 'evermore').

10 **bewailed guilt** the shame that the poet has lamented and grieved for
   bewailed bewailèd

13–14 Do not jeopardize your reputation by making a public display of favour towards me; I love you to such an extent that your good reputation is also mine: i.e. I do not want to see you shamed, even if I myself would be the beneficiary. The couplet is repeated in identical form at the end of 96, another sonnet on the public reception of the young man's 'faults'.

36

Let me confess that we two must be twain,
Although our undivided loves are one;
So shall those blots that do with me remain,
Without thy help, by me be borne alone.
In our two loves there is but one respect,　　　　5
Though in our lives a separable spite;
Which, though it alter not love's sole effect,
Yet doth it steal sweet hours from love's delight.
I may not evermore acknowledge thee,
Lest my bewailed guilt should do thee shame,　　　10
Nor thou with public kindness honour me,
Unless thou take that honour from thy name:
　　But do not so; I love thee in such sort,
　　As thou being mine, mine is thy good report.

6 spite] spight　9 evermore] euer-more

37 Extending the notion that he partakes vicariously of the young man's good *parts*, the poet finds consolation, perhaps delusory, for his own unlucky and inferior status in his young friend's talents and good fortune.

1 **As . . . father** The poet adopts metaphorically the role he projected on to his friend in 2.13–14.

3 **made lame** Neither the poet's decrepitude nor his lameness should be taken literally; cf. *KL* (First Quarto) 4.6.225, where Edgar describes himself as 'A most poore man, made lame by Fortune's blows'. The burdens of age were traditionally seen in terms of damage to the feet, as in the proverb 'The black ox has trod on his feet' (*OED* ox; Tilley, O103).
dearest spite injury to the *dearest*, most intimate, part of him: the phrase picks up *separable spite* from 36.6.

4 **of** from
worth and truth Since 33–6 have dealt with the young man's betrayal of his friend, his *sensual fault* (35.9) and *blots* (36.3), the celebration here of his *worth and truth* must entail an appropriation of the young man's weaknesses so effective that he can now be regarded as faultless.

5–6 **beauty . . . more** Alliteration and quick-fire enumeration of categories produce a near-comic effect, as if the addressee is being mocked for his (supposed) superabundance of gifts, rather than praised for them.

7 **Entitled in** having a rightful claim to (*OED* 4); or named after
*thy parts *thy* emended from Q's 'their'; cf. 26.12 and n. The young man's *parts*, or beauties and talents,

have been celebrated in 17.4 and 31.3.
do crowned sit The gifts of fortune and nature enumerated in l. 5 (may) reach their greatest glory when located in you.
crowned crownèd

8 I fasten my love closely to this abundance of blessings; cf. *store* in 11.9 and 14.12. There may be an implication both that the speaker is almost parasitically attaching himself to the youth's plentiful good fortune, and that, in loving him so devotedly, he is adding one further blessing.

9 **despised** Cf. 29.9.

10 **this . . . give** a reversal of the usual relationship between 'substance' and 'shadow': the speaker's imaginative, delusory enjoyment of his friend's good fortune provides him with solid satisfaction.

11 **sufficed** fully satisfied or nourished: cf. *AYL* 2.7.131.

12 **all thy glory** all your splendour, with a recollection of the image of 'crowning' in l. 7, as in Fr. *gloire* = halo or crown of light

13 **Look what** whatever

14 either a conditional: '*If* I have this wish, it will give me tenfold happiness', with *happy* operating as a verb = make happy, as in 6.6; or an absolute statement: 'This wish is fulfilled; consequently I enjoy tenfold happiness'. Either way, the reader cannot escape a suspicion that what the speaker enjoys is 'the happiness of being well deceived'. The childish phrase *happy me* also suggests that, whether or not physically *lame*, he is at this point assuming the role of a 'lame' poet.

37

As a decrepit father takes delight
To see his active child do deeds of youth,
So I, made lame by fortune's dearest spite,
Take all my comfort of thy worth and truth:
For whether beauty, birth, or wealth, or wit,　　　5
Or any of these all, or all, or more,
Entitled in thy parts do crowned sit,
I make my love engrafted to this store:
So then I am not lame, poor, nor despised,
Whilst that this shadow doth such substance give　　10
That I in thy abundance am sufficed,
And by a part of all thy glory live:
　　Look what is best, that best I wish in thee;
　　This wish I have, then ten times happy me.

3 fortune's] Fortunes　7 Entitled] Intitled　thy] *Capell;* their *Q*, *Benson*　8 engrafted] ingrafted
9 despised] dispis'd　11 sufficed] suffic'd

38 Using a well-worn conceit, the speaker attributes his poetic skill – if any – to the inspiring nature of his subject-matter: cf. Sidney, *AS*, 3.

1 **want . . . invent** lack material for poetic *invention*

2 **While . . . breathe** while you live; with some echo of the divine 'breath' that created man (Genesis, 2.7)

3 **Thine . . . argument** the delightful subject-matter which is yourself (cf. *OED* argument 7 *fig.*)

4 **rehearse** narrate, describe

5 **aught** anything; or nothing, as in an 'ought', the figure 0, preparing for the multiplication-game of ll. 9–10

6 **stand . . . sight** meets your eye; but also 'rises up in competition with the sight of you', since a poetic image of the youth may, as in 18, transmit his beauty

7 **to thee** about you; addressing you

8 **dost . . . light** bring the light of inspiration to poetic creativity

9 **the tenth Muse** Since the nine Muses of classical mythology were all female, the conceit may, like 20.1 and 41.5–6, point to something quasi-feminine about the (male) addressee.

10 **rhymers** suggests inferior poets, mere versifiers (*OED*; and cf. 'scald rhymers', *AC* 5.2.214); yet the 'rhymers' who have called upon the nine Muses include the majority of

Greek, Latin and early Renaissance poets.

invocate This more elaborate form of the word 'invoke' suggests the redundant activity of the *rhymers*.

11 **he . . . thee** whoever invokes you: presumably above all, the present speaker

12 **Eternal numbers** everlasting verses, with a suggestion also of the generation of huge figures by the youth's application of the power of ten to previous sources of inspiration; for *Eternal*, cf. 18.12, and for *numbers*, 17.6.

to . . . date to live beyond even a very distant limit in time

13 **slight** slender, insignificant: the word picks up *sight* and *light* in ll. 6 and 8.

Muse the products of my pen: *Muse* here has a different application both from l. 7, where it denotes 'the source of my poetic creativity', and l. 9, where it refers to the young man. There is some awkwardness in the transition from the swaggering claim made for the superabundant *worth* of the *Muse* of l. 9 to the humbly diminished *Muse* of l. 13.

these curious days these days of exacting or fastidious readers of poetry

14 Let the labour (of writing) be mine, while the credit for the achievement is yours.

38

How can my Muse want subject to invent
While thou dost breathe, that pour'st into my verse
Thine own sweet argument, too excellent
For every vulgar paper to rehearse?
O give thyself the thanks, if aught in me   5
Worthy perusal stand against thy sight:
For who's so dumb, that cannot write to thee,
When thou thyself dost give invention light?
Be thou the tenth Muse, ten times more in worth
Than those old nine which rhymers invocate;   10
And he that calls on thee, let him bring forth
Eternal numbers to outlive long date.
    If my slight Muse do please these curious days,
    The pain be mine, but thine shall be the praise.

2 pour'st] poor'st   3 too] to   5 aught] ought   12 outlive] out-live

39 Resuming, from sonnets 35–7, the idea of his loving amalgamation with his young friend, the poet proposes a separation which will enable him to praise his friend better while contemplating his merits in absence.

1 'How can I celebrate your merits in a becoming fashion?': for *manners* = 'good manners, custom' (*OED* 4d), cf. *1H4* 3.1.184, 'Defect of manners, want of government'.

2 **the . . . me** Sidney used the expression 'my better half' in the context of devoted marriage (*NA*, 378), and the phrase quickly gained currency (Tilley, H49).

3 If our two selves are amalgamated, praising you achieves nothing, for it is merely self-praise.

4 **mine own** my own praise, praise of myself

5 **Even for this** for this precise reason

8 **That . . . thee** that recompense which is given to you

which . . . alone You alone deserve it; and you deserve to receive it independently, not with your identity merged in mine.

11 **entertain the time** while away the time; cf. 'The weary time she cannot entertain', *Luc* 1361.

12 The addressee is still absence: 'you, absence, who give such pleasurable distractions to solitary time and meditation'. The popular emendation of *dost* to 'doth', though adopted by Booth, seems unnecessary, and breaks the consistency of the address to absence throughout the sestet. To 'deceive the time' was a regular expression, analogous to 'entertain the time'. There is a repetitive feeling to the sestet which suggests restless loneliness.

14 by praising my friend in the place where I am (and in this poem), though he continues to be somewhere else

39

O how thy worth with manners may I sing,
When thou art all the better part of me?
What can mine own praise to mine own self bring,
And what is't but mine own, when I praise thee?
Even for this, let us divided live,   5
And our dear love lose name of single one,
That by this separation I may give
That due to thee which thou deserv'st alone.
O absence, what a torment wouldst thou prove,
Were it not thy sour leisure gave sweet leave   10
To entertain the time with thoughts of love,
Which time and thoughts so sweetly dost deceive,
   And that thou teachest how to make one twain
   By praising him here who doth hence remain.

6 lose] loose   7 give] give: 12 dost] do *Capell;* doth *Malone, Booth*

40 The speaker loves the young man so much that however much advantage the youth takes of his affection he can do him no wrong; or any wrong he does will be forgiven. Sonnets 41 and 42 enlarge the narrative implication: the youth has betrayed his friend by taking one of the poet's *loves*, i.e. love-objects. The same, or an analogous, situation is referred to in 133–4 and 144.

1 **Take . . . take** with possible connotations of 'take carnal possession of' (Partridge, 200)
my . . . love By addressing the youth as *my love* in the preceding phrase, the speaker hints that his own *loves* may be not merely 'varieties and abundance of affection', but 'love-objects, individuals whom I love'.

3 The additional love that the youth has appropriated cannot be called (or addressed as) *true love* partly because the speaker's *true love* was all his already; but also, perhaps, because in taking *this more* (l. 4) the youth is acting falsely, and/or causing another to act falsely.

4 **this more** It is tempting to find a pun on 'Moor' (note also l. 2), and detect here an anticipation of the sonnet alluding to 'a woman coloured ill' (144); but nothing else in this part of the sequence supports such a reference.

5–8 **receivest . . . refusest** Feminine rhymes here suggest a breach of customary boundaries.

5 **for my love** in return for my love; in place of my love

6 **for . . . usest** The word 'use' has been established as having sexual connotations; cf. 4.13–14 and n. The senses here seem to be (a) because you exploit or take advantage of my affection ; (b) for having sexual relations with one whom I love.

7 **be blamed** suggests that the youth is objectively blameworthy, although the speaker is determined, for his part, not to blame him
*__thyself__ emended from Q's 'this selfe', which appears to reflect the

compositors' tendency to make 'this'/'their'/'thy' errors.

8 **wilful . . . refusest** seems to refer back to 1–17: the youth is capriciously engaging in sexual activity that, in the context of marriage, he refuses; *wilful* also suggests 'self-willed, headstrong', and 'driven by sexual desire (will)'. 'Taste' as a verb was often used by Shakespeare to denote sexual enjoyment (of a woman): cf. *Oth* 3.3.345–7; and Partridge, *Bawdy*, 201–2. It seems likely that the noun here suggests 'sexual consumption'. Booth proposes an alternative, opposite sense of *what thyself refusest* as 'what you decline to give or grant', which, if pursued, could deepen the sonnet's bisexual undercurrents, leading us to the reading: 'you refuse to have sex with your devoted (male) lover, but wilfully have it with a woman (his mistress)'.

10 **thou . . . poverty** You take for yourself all that I have, which is very little, and/or worthless. The word 'steal' had associations with secret or illicit sexual activity, as in Edmund's reference to his being begotten 'in the lusty stealth of nature', *KL* 1.2.11.

11 **love knows** After seven uses of the word *love* with personal associations, *love* is here invoked as an abstract ideal, the effect being equivalent to 'heaven knows'.
grief sorrow; wound, injury; cf. 34. 9 and n.

12 to endure injuries inflicted out of love rather than out of hate, which are open or expected (*known*); the word *bear* recalls 34.12.

13 **Lascivious grace** you, who are graceful even when lustful. If the addressee is a nobleman, there may also be an allusion in *grace* to his high rank, as well as to his ability to confer *grace* or beneficence on others. The phrase strongly connects the youth with the seducer in *LC*, especially ll. 316–17: 'with the garment of a grace / The naked and concealed fiend he covered'.

40

Take all my loves, my love; yea, take them all;
What hast thou then more than thou hadst before?
No love, my love, that thou mayst true love call;
All mine was thine, before thou hadst this more:
Then if for my love thou my love receivest,   5
I cannot blame thee, for my love thou usest;
But yet be blamed, if thou thyself deceivest
By wilful taste of what thyself refusest.
I do forgive thy robb'ry, gentle thief,
Although thou steal thee all my poverty;   10
And yet love knows it is a greater grief
To bear love's wrong, than hate's known injury.
　　Lascivious grace, in whom all ill well shows,
　　Kill me with spites; yet we must not be foes.

---

all . . . shows all vices, when committed by you, come over as virtues. Booth explores the complex implications of a pun on 'well'/'will'/'Will'.

14 'Even if you kill me with injuries (cf. *Glossary*, spite), let us not become enemies.'

2, 12 than] then   7 blamed] blam'd   thyself] *Malone;* this selfe *Q , Benson, Oxf*

41 The speaker claims that his young friend's amorous proclivity is excusable because of his youth and attractiveness to women, but remonstrates with him for the double betrayal of engaging in sexual relations with his own mistress.

1 **pretty** childish, charming
that liberty commits that you commit while at large: *liberty* has associations with sexual licence, as in *MM* 1.2.129.

2 **sometime** at some time; for some while

3 **befits** The singular verb following a plural subject (*wrongs*) is not uncommon in Elizabethan usage.

5 combines the praise in 20 of the youth as possessing 'A woman's gentle heart' with the proverbial claim that 'All women may be won' (Tilley, W681), which Shakespeare invoked in *1H6* 5.3.78–9: 'She's beautiful, and therefore to be wooed; / She is a woman, therefore to be won'; cf. also *Tit* 2.1.82; *R3* 1.2.228.

6 **assailed** vigorously wooed ; cf. *AW* 1.1.126; *TN* 1.3.60; *Cym* 1.4.136.

7–8 Though this sounds like an obvious truism, Shakespeare's first published work, *VA*, described a 'woman's son', Adonis, who refuses the advances of the goddess of love: Shakespeare may have expected readers to remember

this still-popular poem, reprinted seven times by 1602.

8 **sourly** ungraciously, ill-naturedly
prevailed For the sexual application of 'prevail', cf. *2H6* 5.4.78.

9 **seat** the area designated for my sexual activity; cf. *Oth* 2.1.290–1, 'I do suspect the lustful Moor / Hath leap'd into my seat'.
forbear spare, refrain from

10 **chide** scold; banish

11 **riot** debauchery, wantonness: Shakespeare often associates the youthful Prince Hal with *riot* (*1H4* 1.1.85; *2H4* 4.4.62, 5.5.66; *H5* 1.1.56); and cf. the proverb 'Youth riotously led breeds a loathsome old age' (Tilley, Y47).

12 **truth** converges in meaning with 'troth', a binding promise of fidelity; cf. *BCP*, Solemnization of Matrimony, 'I plight thee my troth'.

10–14 The threefold repetition of *thy beauty*, especially in l. 13, where we might expect some allusion to the woman's beauty, gives the reprimand in the sestet an effect of exoneration and compliment. The young man is not really responsible for his sexual transgressions, for it is a case of 'Why was he born so beautiful?'

13 **Hers** her *truth* or 'troth', or pledge of constancy to the poet.

14 **Thine** the youth's bond of friendship with the poet

41

Those pretty wrongs that liberty commits
When I am sometime absent from thy heart,
Thy beauty and thy years full well befits;
For still temptation follows where thou art.
Gentle thou art, and therefore to be won;   5
Beauteous thou art, therefore to be assailed;
And when a woman woos, what woman's son
Will sourly leave her till he have prevailed?
Ay me, but yet thou mightst my seat forbear,
And chide thy beauty and thy straying youth   10
Who lead thee in their riot even there
Where thou art forced to break a twofold truth:
    Hers by thy beauty tempting her to thee,
    Thine by thy beauty being false to me.

2 sometime] some-time   12 twofold] two-fold

42 The poet grieves more for the loss of his young friend than for that of his mistress, but tries to persuade himself that the common ground between the young lovers is himself, and that, in loving the youth, the woman is manifesting her love for the poet with whom the youth, too, is united in love. An exercise in self-consolation, 42 explores what *may be said* (cf. l. 2) in the manner of Sidney's Astrophil's attempts 'to make myself believe that all is well' (*AS*, 2.13).

1–3 hast . . . hath with some of the connotations of 'have' as 'to possess carnally' (Partridge, 126)

1 grief sorrow; wound or injury: cf. 34.9 and n.

2 dearly fondly; but also with a sense of this affection as costly

3 is . . . chief is the loss I most lament; is the primary reason why I mourn or 'wail'

4 touches . . . nearly provokes emotion of a more intimate kind; has a more immediate bearing on me

5–8 Note the feminine rhymes *excuse ye . . . love her . . . abuse me . . , approve her*, which may draw attention to the unmanageable complexity of the situation; cf. 40.5–8.

5 Loving offenders Although he appears to address both lovers at this point, subsequent lines make it clear that the youth alone is the poet's true concern, the woman being referred to in the third person in ll. 6, 7, 8 and 10.
excuse ye find an excuse for you

7 even so in the same manner
abuse ill-treat, deceive, with some connotations of 'make a cuckold of' (Partridge, *Bawdy*, 63)

8 approve pronounce to be good, to commend (*OED* 6); to test or experience sexually

9–11 lose . . . losing . . . lose Q's 'loose . . . loosing . . . loose' permits additional senses: 'set you loose . . . setting her loose (as a "loose" woman) . . . set you two free'; in Elizabethan orthography 'lose' and 'loose' were not distinguished. However, images of 'gain' and 'loss' suggest that the primary image is of 'losing' rather than 'loosing', and the spelling has been adjusted accordingly. For a further possibly relevant application of 'loose', as 'experience sexual release', cf. Sidney, *AS*, 18.14.

12 lay . . . cross subject me to this trial or vexation (cf. *OED* cross 10a and b), with inescapable recollections of Simon of Cyrene being made to carry Christ's cross. If Capell's emendation is accepted at 34.12, the word occurs there in the same position and same relationship with 'loss'.

13 my . . . one In previous sonnets (e.g. 36–7) it is claimed that the speaker and his friend are, in the manner of husband and wife, 'one flesh'; but a reader who recalls Hamlet's mocking application of similar chop-logic (*Ham* 4.3.52–6) may be unpersuaded by its elaboration here.

14 Sweet flattery gratifying expression of affection, or consoling delusion
she . . . alone The claim that the woman, in loving the youth, actually loves only the poet, is both logically and emotionally weak. First, the argument that love for one person is really love for another is inherently implausible (cf. Sidney's use of it in *AS*, 91.12–14); and secondly, the poet has made it quite clear in preceding lines of the sonnet that what he cares about is the young man's defection, not the woman's.

42

That thou hast her it is not all my grief,
And yet it may be said I loved her dearly;
That she hath thee is of my wailing chief,
A loss in love that touches me more nearly.
Loving offenders, thus I will excuse ye: 5
Thou dost love her, because thou knowst I love her,
And for my sake even so doth she abuse me,
Suff'ring my friend for my sake to approve her;
If I lose thee, my loss is my love's gain,
And losing her, my friend hath found that loss;   10
Both find each other, and I lose both twain,
And both for my sake lay on me this cross:
    But here's the joy, my friend and I are one;
    Sweet flattery! Then she loves but me alone.

2 loved] lou'd   9 lose] loose   10 losing] loosing   11 lose] loose

43 In the first of three sonnets on absence, the poet uses a series of polyptotic paradoxes and oxymora to contrast his night-time visions of his friend with his daytime absence.

1 **wink** close my eyes

2 **unrespected** unvalued, lacking interest: cf. *Glossary*, respect, sense 4; also unlooked at, unseen: cf. *OED* respect 5b. The word is used again, with slightly different import, at 54.10.

4 **darkly . . . directed** Eyes were thought of as emitting light, as well as receiving it: cf. 24.11 and n. An approximate sense may be: '(My eyes,) illuminated by the darkness (secrecy) of night, are guided by or towards light through darkness.'

5 **whose . . . bright** 'whose imagined semblance illuminates the dark shade of night': for *shadow* here cf. *OED* 6a, 'An unreal appearance; a delusive semblance or image'; and 6b, 'an actor or a play'. Shakespeare often used the word in the latter sense, as in Macbeth's 'Life's but a walking shadow, a poor player'; cf. also *MND* 5.1.430; *R2* 4.1.292; *Cym* 5.4.97.

6 'How would the substance behind your imagined image (*shadow's form*)

create a joyful spectacle'.

8 **shade** 'unsubstantial image of something real' (*Glossary*); more or less synonymous with *shadow* in l. 5, and extending the paradox by which something apparently dark (a *shade*) emits light (*shines*)

9 **blessed** blessèd: the word was associated with healing as well as with happiness (*OED* 4b), so includes the suggestion that the sight of the youth would cure the poet's blindness

11 **dead night** dead of night; nighttime, which is associated with death and lifeless phantoms
thy . . . shade The image of the youth is incomplete (*imperfect*) because it is an appearance only, not a physical actuality; but a recollection of the allusions to the young man's moral defects in 33–5 permits a subsidiary oxymoron: 'the image of you, beautiful despite your moral imperfection'.

13 **to see** 'in visible aspect' (*OED* 16a)

14 **do . . . me** display you to me: possibly the need for a rhyme prompted the word order, which has the odd effect of leaving the final stress on *me* rather than *thee*

43

When most I wink, then do mine eyes best see;
For all the day they view things unrespected,
But when I sleep, in dreams they look on thee,
And darkly bright, are bright in dark directed.
Then thou whose shadow shadows doth make bright, 5
How would thy shadow's form form happy show
To the clear day with thy much clearer light,
When to unseeing eyes thy shade shines so?
How would (I say) mine eyes be blessed made
By looking on thee in the living day, 10
When in dead night thy fair imperfect shade
Through heavy sleep on sightless eyes doth stay?
    All days are nights to see till I see thee,
    And nights bright days when dreams do show
        thee me.

8 unseeing] vn-seeing   11 thy] *Capell;* their *Q*

44 This sonnet continues the theme of absence: the speaker wishes that his body could move with the same agility as his thoughts, instead of being confined to the elements of earth and water.

1 **dull** slow, inert, inactive (*Glossary*, 3); and cf. 51.2, where it is applied to a dilatory horse

2 **Injurious** malicious in wrongdoing: Shakespeare applied the epithet to the operation of time, rather than space, in *Luc* 930 and *Son* 63.2.
   stop my way impede my progress

3 **space** the distance or space that separates him from his friend

4 **limits** territories or regions defined by boundaries (*OED* 3a); and cf. *1H4* 3.1.75, 'The Archdeacon hath divided it / Into three limits very equally.'
   where to where, whither
   stay sojourn; remain

5 **my foot** common synecdoche for the whole body; cf. *R2* 1.1.63–6.

6 **the . . . thee** the region of the world furthest away (*removed* = separated, remote) from where you are; alternatively, *removed* may govern *foot*, yielding 'where I am removed from you in the furthest region of the world'.

7 **jump** 'to pass clear over by a leap' (*OED* 6a, with this example); cf. also *Mac* 1.7.7.

8 **think** think about, think of (*OED* 2a)
   he The primary subject is *thought*: 'thought can travel as swiftly as it conceives of a desired place' (and cf. Tilley, T240). But there may be an underlying sense of thinking about

where the young man may be.

9 **thought kills . . . thought** a self-infolded paradox: 'the thought that I am not thought (but lodged in heavy flesh) destroys me'.

11 'except that, since I am so exclusively fashioned of the (dull) elements of earth and water'

12 **I . . . leisure** Ingram and Redpath connect this with 'a petitioner waiting on a great man, Time'; there is probably also a sense of waiting for the young man's leisure time, as in 57.1–6.

13 **naughts** Q's 'naughts' has hitherto been emended to 'naught', on the ground that 'naughts' = 'A thing of no worth or value' (*OED* 3a) is rare, and not used by Shakespeare elsewhere. Partly on the *difficilior lectio* principle it has been retained here; also because Q's reading permits an extension of the image of the preceding line: instead of receiving hoped-for riches from the great lord Time, the earth-bound petitioner receives only round and leaden tears, which are like empty *noughts* in a ledger.

14 **But** no more than, merely
   heavy . . . woe Heaviness is the attribute of earth, and tears belong to water: the speaker's *woe* ensues from his imprisonment in these two elements; however, as Booth (206) observes, *either's woe* also suggests 'your woe and mine'. The final *woe* resonates as 'O', reinforcing *naughts* in the previous line.

44

If the dull substance of my flesh were thought,
Injurious distance should not stop my way;
For then, despite of space, I would be brought
From limits far remote, where thou dost stay;
No matter then although my foot did stand   5
Upon the farthest earth removed from thee,
For nimble thought can jump both sea and land
As soon as think the place where he would be.
But ah, thought kills me, that I am not thought,
To leap large lengths of miles when thou art gone, 10
But that so much of earth and water wrought,
I must attend time's leisure with my moan;
   Receiving naughts by elements so slow
   But heavy tears, badges of either's woe.

3 despite] dispight   6 removed] remoou'd   12 attend time's] attend, times   13 naughts] *Q;* nought
Ard¹   slow] sloe

45 This follows on immediately from the preceding sonnet's focus on the speaker's confinement in the elements of earth and water. The remaining, mobile, elements of air and fire have been dispatched from the poet to his friend, leaving him depressed and heavy.

1 **The other two** the other two elements in the human body: in the absence of his friend, it was established in 44.11, the speaker is composed only of 'earth and water'.

slight insubstantial, weightless (*OED* 3a and b)

purging Fire was associated with the purifying of metals, such as gold; symbolically, purifying fire was linked with the Second Coming and Last Judgement; cf. 'he is like a refiner's fire', Malachi, 3.3.

3 **The . . . other** Thought, the first, is airy; desire, the second, fiery.

desire Though *desire* is most frequently identified with sexual appetite, as in Sidney's *AS* and Shakespeare's *VA* 36, 386, 389, 547 and *passim*, its identification here with *purging fire* suggests, rather, an elevated form of affection which seeks to improve its object.

4 **present absent** absent from the poet; present with his friend; simultaneously present with the poet and absent from him: cf. Sidney, *AS*, 106.1, 'O absent presence!'

5 **quicker** speedier; fuller of life

6 **tender** loving; with some sense of the fragility and volatility of this loving message

7 **My . . . four** refers to the commonplace belief that the human body was composed of the four elements of fire, air, water and earth; cf. Marlowe, *Tamburlaine*, 2.7.18, and *TN* 2.3.9–10. Ill health was thought to result from an imbalance between

them.

8 **oppressed with melancholy** cast down, dejected. 'Melancholy' was not merely a state of transient misery, but a severe medical condition caused by 'black humour'. The extra-metrical syllable in *melancholy* reinforces the sense of congestion.

9 **life's composition** the balance of humours or elements

recured from Lat. *recurare*, to cure: there may or may not be a sense of restoring a previous state of health.

10 **those swift messengers** If these are equivalent to the poet's dispatch of *thought* and *desire*, they denote the friend's reciprocal sentiments, which may have been sent in a similarly insubstantial manner; however, the next two lines may allude to a message with some concrete actuality, such as a letter. It may be relevant to the plural *messengers* that in Elizabethan usage the plural 'letters' applied even to a single missive.

12 ***thy** another 'their'/'thy' emendation: cf. 26.12 and n.

fair health good health; continued beauty: *fair*, amalgamating *fire* and *air*, suggests the young man's appropriation of these elements.

13 **I joy** I rejoice.

but . . . glad Sidney's *AS*, 92, offers an analogue to this account of the lover unsatisfied by news of his beloved's well-being.

14 **them** the messengers, *air* and *fire* (= thought and desire): the suggestion may be that the poet instantly responds to the friend's literal or metaphorical greetings, rather than that he returns them in identical form.

sad The subsidiary sense, 'heavy' (*OED* 7a and b), continues the image of the poet *oppressed* by his watery and earthy condition.

45

The other two, slight air, and purging fire,
Are both with thee, wherever I abide:
The first my thought, the other my desire,
These, present absent, with swift motion slide;
For when these quicker elements are gone   5
In tender embassy of love to thee,
My life being made of four, with two alone
Sinks down to death, oppressed with melancholy,
Until life's composition be recured
By those swift messengers returned from thee   10
Who even but now come back again assured
Of thy fair health, recounting it to me.
   This told, I joy; but then no longer glad,
   I send them back again and straight grow sad.

2 wherever] where euer   5 elements] Elements   6 embassy] Embassie   9 life's] *Malone;* liues *Q,*
Benson   10 returned] return'd   12 thy] *Malone;* their *Q*

46 This sonnet and the following pursue a rhetorical debate between the speaker's eye, which can apprehend the youth physically, and his heart, which comprehends him imaginatively. The conceit was a traditional one; the sustained metaphor is that of a legal disputation.

1 mortal primarily suggests a fight to the death (*OED* 3); but there may be a secondary, subversive, suggestion that the conflict is itself *mortal* in the sense of being transient (*OED* 2), as in *Ham* 3.1.67.

2 divide the conquest distribute the spoils of war; share out the benefits of having seen the youth

thy sight the sight of you, or of an image of you

3 My eye wishes to deny my heart the sight of your image.

3, *13, 148 thy See 26.12n.

6 'Closet' could denote a small cabinet in which valuables were stored (*OED* 3a); but 'the closet of the heart' had a specific anatomical reference to the pericardium or area surrounding the heart (*OED* 6a). The transparency of eyes, which are *crystal* (cf. *H5* 2.3.54; *VA* 963), is implicitly contrasted with the opacity of the enclosed heart.

7 the defendant The heart prosecutes; the eye defends.

deny another term with legal connotations

9 *To 'cide Most modern editors accept George Sewell's (Rollins, 1.127–9) and Malone's interpretation of Q's 'side' as '(de)cide', which given the indifference of the copy-text writer or the compositors to 's'/'c' distinctions is plausible, yielding the sense 'determine or resolve'. Ingram and Redpath retain 'side', glossing it as a verb = 'to take the part of' or 'to clear or tidy up'; however, their supporting examples are not closely analogous. Another possible, but on balance less cogent, emendation would be 'cite', = 'testify to, be evidence of', as in *AW* 1.2.216; in this case the error might result from compositorial mishearing.

title claim, entitlement

empanelled empanellèd: = compelled to appear in a court

10 quest jury

11 determined determinèd: = resolved, adjudged

12 clear eyes' moiety the portion that belongs to the *clear eyes* – cf. *crystal eyes* in l. 6; the portion that clearly belongs to the eyes

dear heart's part the portion belonging to the heart, the intimate seat of feeling; the precious portion belonging to the heart: just as *clear* may govern either *eyes* or *moiety*, so *dear* may apply to either *eyes* or *part*. The internal rhyme in *heart's part* gives additional emphasis to the chiastic repetition, in the rhymes at 10, 12, 13, 14, of *heart . . . part . . . part . . . heart*.

13 mine eyes' due what is owed, as recompense, to the eyes; cf. *the world's due*, 1.14 and n.

14 my heart's right what belongs to my heart as of right

thy . . . heart suggests both 'my love of you, retained within my heart'; and, with a quick shift of emphasis, 'your heartfelt love of me'

46

Mine eye and heart are at a mortal war
How to divide the conquest of thy sight;
Mine eye, my heart thy picture's sight would bar;
My heart, mine eye the freedom of that right;
My heart doth plead that thou in him dost lie, 5
A closet never pierced with crystal eyes;
But the defendant doth that plea deny,
And says in him thy fair appearance lies.
To 'cide this title is empanelled
A quest of thoughts, all tenants to the heart, 10
And by their verdict is determined
The clear eyes' moiety, and the dear heart's part:
    As thus, mine eyes' due is thy outward part,
    And my heart's right, thy inward love of heart.

3, 8, 13, 14 thy] *Capell;* their *Q*   6 A . . . eyes;] (A . . . eyes)   9 'cide] *Malone;* side *Q*

47 In 46 eye and heart were in conflict; here they are in harmony, each consoling the other with thoughts or images of the young man.

1 **a . . . took** an agreement is made: in Elizabethan usage 'took' was an acceptable past participle (cf. Abbott, and *MM* 2.2.74).

2 **good turns** Cf. the similar use of the phrase in 24.9

3 **famished . . . look** for the notion of the eyes of an absent lover as 'famished', cf. Sidney, *AS*, 106.6

4 **with sighs** may be the object either of *in love* or of *smother*: the heart loves empty sighs, and consequently smothers itself; or, the loving heart smothers itself with sighing.

5 **my love's picture** appears to refer to a concrete depiction, not just a mental image

6 **bids** invites: the metaphor of the loving banquet recalls Spenser's *Amoretti* (1595), 77 (*Shorter Poems*, 646–7).

11 ***no** The MS may have read 'noe', rendered by the compositor as 'nor'.

12 **them . . . they** The subject is still *my thoughts*.

14 **eye's** kept in the singular, to conform with *eye* in ll. 1, 3, 5, 7, though Q's 'eyes' would permit 'eyes' '

47

Betwixt mine eye and heart a league is took,
And each doth good turns now unto the other;
When that mine eye is famished for a look,
Or heart in love with sighs himself doth smother,
With my love's picture then my eye doth feast,   5
And to the painted banquet bids my heart;
Another time mine eye is my heart's guest,
And in his thoughts of love doth share a part.
So either by thy picture or my love,
Thyself away, art present still with me: 10
For thou no further than my thoughts canst move,
And I am still with them, and they with thee;
   Or if they sleep, thy picture in my sight
   Awakes my heart to heart's and eye's delight.

10 art] *Capell;* are *Q*   11 no] *Capell;* nor *Q;* not *Benson, IR*

48 From meditations on the enclosure of his young friend's image within his heart, the speaker moves to a contrast between the vulnerability of this most precious commodity and the security of his earthly possessions.

1 **took my way** set out on my journey

2 **truest bars** most reliable locks or barricades

3 **unused** unusèd: = not stolen or tampered with
stay remain.

4 **From** away from, or safe from
wards guard, protection; also a technical term for the inner structure of a lock (*OED* 24a ; and cf. *Luc* 303)

5 **to whom** compared with whom; with an additional sense of 'in whose eyes'. To a wealthy young nobleman, the valuables of a professional playwright would no doubt seem trifling.

6 **Most worthy comfort** most valuable source of comfort or solace; with a possible play on *worthy* as 'distinguished, estimable' (*OED* 2a)
grief sadness; wound, injury; cf. 34.9 and n.

7 **best of dearest** best among those I love most dearly, or of the possessions I most cherish
care responsibility, source of anxiety

11 **gentle closure** loving containment
my breast The then fairly new sense of 'chest' as 'thorax' was used by Shakespeare in *TC* 1.3.163 and 4.5.10; here there may be a reference to its figurative application, as 'seat of the emotions and passions' (*OED* 9a and b), yielding the suggestion that 'the only chest in which I have you is my own chest (breast)'.

12 elliptically expressed for 'into which you may come and from which you may go (depart) according to your own pleasure'

14 **truth . . . dear** alludes to the proverb 'The prey entices the thief' (Tilley, P570), which Shakespeare adapted in *VA* 724, 'Rich preys make true men thieves'. Moving on from the allusion to *every vulgar thief* in l. 8, the poet concludes by suggesting that even a normally honourable person might break vows when confronted by the irresistible attractions of the young man, who is both *dear* = precious, and *dear* = loved, lovable.

48

How careful was I, when I took my way,
Each trifle under truest bars to thrust,
That to my use it might unused stay
From hands of falsehood, in sure wards of trust;
But thou, to whom my jewels trifles are,   5
Most worthy comfort, now my greatest grief,
Thou best of dearest, and mine only care,
Art left the prey of every vulgar thief.
Thee have I not locked up in any chest,
Save where thou art not, though I feel thou art,   10
Within the gentle closure of my breast,
From whence at pleasure thou mayst come and part;
    And even thence thou wilt be stol'n, I fear;
    For truth proves thievish for a prize so dear.

3 unused] vn-vsed   9 locked] lockt

49 The speaker prepares himself for the prospect of a future time when the young man no longer cares for him by invoking the irrationality of love. Since neither his own love nor that of the young man can be justified, the future cessation of the youth's affection needs no justification, either. The imagined situation is strongly reminiscent of Henry V's rejection of Falstaff.

1 **Against that time** in expectation of that time: cf. *MND* 3.2.99.

2 **defects** failings, deficiencies

3 **Whenas** at a time when
cast . . . sum made its final reckoning: cf. cast = 'To count or reckon so as to ascertain the sum of various numbers' (*OED* 37a, b, c.)

4 **audit** a formal examination of accounts: cf. 126.11.
advised respects sober considerations: cf. 'advised respect', *KJ* 4.2.214; there may also be a suggestion of the young man taking advice from a mature counsellor.

5 **strangely pass** walk by like a stranger, with an estranged or distant demeanour (cf. *OED* strange 11)

7 **converted . . . was** transformed from its former condition: cf. *2 H4* 5.5.56, 'Presume not that I am the thing I was' ; also 5.2.60–1, 'Harry lives, that shall convert those tears / By number into hours of happiness'.

8 **gravity** the mature judgement associated with age: cf. *2H4* 1.2.160.

9 **ensconce me here** establish myself firmly, as if in a 'sconce', or small fort

10 **mine own desert** Initially, it may appear that the speaker is consoling himself with the thought of his own merit; but the final couplet indicates that the implication is 'my own (lack of) merit'.

11 **this my hand** includes a reference to 'this my handwriting', i.e. the sonnet we are reading
uprear raise, as if raising a hand to affirm testimony given in a lawcourt: the speaker incriminates himself; there is also some suggestion of raising his hand towards physical self-injury.

12 **guard** protect, justify
on thy part on your side in a contest or legal dispute

13 **thou . . . laws** You are supported by legal right. The anticipated alliance between the youth and *laws* is analogous to Prince Hal's reconciliation with the Lord Chief Justice, *2H4* 5.2.

14 **why to love** cuts two ways. The speaker declares a self-disarming inability to discover any reason why *he* should be loved, but also hints that he cannot justify his own love for the young man: 'Why should you love me – but, come to that, why should I love you?'

49

Against that time, if ever that time come,
When I shall see thee frown on my defects;
Whenas thy love hath cast his utmost sum,
Called to that audit by advised respects;
Against that time when thou shalt strangely pass,   5
And scarcely greet me with that sun, thine eye;
When love, converted from the thing it was,
Shall reasons find of settled gravity;
Against that time do I ensconce me here,
Within the knowledge of mine own desert,   10
And this my hand against myself uprear,
To guard the lawful reasons on thy part:
    To leave poor me, thou hast the strength of laws,
    Since why to love, I can allege no cause.

---

3 Whenas] When as   4 Called] Cauld   advised] aduis'd

50 The speaker goes miserably on a journey which takes him away from the young man, and his slow horse seems to sympathize with his reluctance. The sonnet may allude ironically to Sidney, *AS*, 49, in which Astrophil rides his horse and is in turn ridden by love.

1 **heavy** partly adverbial, governing *journey*; partly adjectival, governing *I*; suggests both a physical and an emotional burden (cf. *OED* 27a)

2 **my . . . end** the object of my tedious journey, with a possible play on 'travail'

3 **that . . . repose** the leisure and rest that await him at his destination

5 **tired . . . woe** The conceit is that the horse is weary not because of the speaker's literal weight, but because of his sadness: though never used, the word 'sad', with its connotations of solidity and heaviness (cf. *OED* 7), is everywhere implied.

6 **dully* Q's 'duly' is so emended by editors from Benson onwards; *dull bearer* in l. 2 of the following sonnet seems to support the emendation. Though 'duly' is not nonsensical, the double 'bears . . . to bear' seems rather vacuous in Q's reading, whereas *dully* makes a distinction between the general function of the horse – 'The beast that bears me' – and his specific response to the additional burden of misery – 'that weight in me' – which

makes his movement *dull*.

7 **the wretch** often used with a sense of mingled pity and affection: cf. the Nurse's reference to the infant Juliet as a 'pretty wretch' (*RJ* 1.3.44), or Gertrude's to Ophelia as 'the poor wretch' (*Ham* 4.7.183).

9 **The bloody spur** the spur that draws blood; with a suggestion that the spur is already bloody from previous attempts to make the animal move

10 **sometimes** every now and again
anger By personifying anger, the speaker rhetorically disclaims responsibility for his cruelty to the horse, preparing for his empathetic response to the horse's suffering in 11–12.

11 **heavily** The repetition of the partly-adverbial *heavy* from l. 1 underlines the sympathy between horse and rider.

12 **sharp** painful, either physically (to the horse), or emotionally (to the speaker); cf. *OED* 5c.

14 The analogy between the horse's physical wound and the speaker's mental one is strengthened if the reader remembers that *grief* could refer to physical injury, as in *1H4* 1.5.132 and *Son* 33.9. What the horse's groan prompts the speaker to think is something he already knew at the beginning of the sonnet, thus enacting a process of weary repetition. *Onward* and *behind* refer to time as well as space: sorrow is in the future, joy in the past.

50

How heavy do I journey on the way
When what I seek, my weary travel's end,
Doth teach that ease and that repose to say,
'Thus far the miles are measured from thy friend.'
The beast that bears me, tired with my woe,   5
Plods dully on to bear that weight in me,
As if by some instinct the wretch did know
His rider loved not speed being made from thee:
The bloody spur cannot provoke him on
That sometimes anger thrusts into his hide,   10
Which heavily he answers with a groan,
More sharp to me than spurring to his side,
    For that same groan doth put this in my mind:
    My grief lies onward and my joy behind.

---

4 measured] measurde   6 dully] *Benson;* duly *Q*   8 loved] lou'd   10 sometimes] some-times

51 This sonnet develops the theme of 50.
The horse continues to move slowly as
he takes the speaker away from his
friend; but on the return journey the
poet hopes to fly at the speed of love,
outstripping or abandoning his slow-
paced steed.

1 **Thus** in the manner to be expounded
in l. 3

2 **dull bearer** his slow horse, which in
50.6 *Plods dully on*
speed to go with speed (*OED* 13):
ironic, since both the previous sonnet
and this indicate that he travels slowly
and reluctantly

4 **posting** travelling swiftly, like the
bearers of important messages

5 **then** when it is time to return

6 **swift extremity** the greatest extreme
of swiftness

7 **spur** probably metaphorical, = 'put
on speed', in contrast to the physical
application of spurs to the unhappy
horse in 50.9

8 I will move with such speed (as if fly-
ing) that I shall seem not to move
winged wingèd

10 ***perfect'st** The build-up of conso-
nants makes this an awkward reading;
yet it is hard to account otherwise for
the presence of 's' at the end of the
word 'perfects' in Q, and in *MA*
2.1.317. Shakespeare wrote the almost
unsayable line 'Silence is the per-
fectest herald of joy'. Love, as in 45, is
composed of the elements of fire and
air, in contrast to the earthy dullness

of the horse.

11 **neigh . . . flesh** None of the many
attempts to emend or improve this
phrase offers a convincing alternative
to the Q reading; for a detailed discussion, see Booth, 218–20. The Q reading can be glossed as 'not neigh in the
manner of commonplace (horse)
flesh': instead of uttering an equine
non-verbal 'neigh', the poet's love will
speak ll. 13–14. The Dauphin's
extravagant praise of his horse in *H5*
3.7 has some analogies with this line,
and includes the claim that 'his neigh
is like the bidding of a monarch'.
his fiery race his fiery trajectory (cf.
OED race 5). The subject is still *desire*,
which moves with the speed of fire, or
of the sun travelling across the airy
heavens. For this application of *race*,
cf. the 'dazzling race', probably that of
a lamp, in Sidney, *AS*, 105.6.

12 **love . . . jade** love (synonymous with
desire in l. 10) out of affection will
excuse my (low-grade) horse; there
may also be a hint of 'love in recompense for love'.

13–14 The couplet is imagined as spoken
by the poet's *love*.

13 **wilful slow** deliberately (wilfully)
slow; or willing to move, but nevertheless slow

14 **give . . . go** allow the horse to travel at
his own pace (in contrast to the speed
of desire); or dispense with the
horse's services altogether

51

Thus can my love excuse the slow offence
Of my dull bearer, when from thee I speed:
From where thou art, why should I haste me thence?
Till I return, of posting is no need.
O what excuse will my poor beast then find,   5
When swift extremity can seem but slow?
Then should I spur, though mounted on the wind;
In winged speed no motion shall I know;
Then can no horse with my desire keep pace;
Therefore desire, of perfect'st love being made,   10
Shall neigh no dull flesh in his fiery race,
But love, for love, thus shall excuse my jade:
    Since from thee going he went wilful slow,
    Towards thee I'll run, and give him leave to go.

10 perfect'st] *Capell;* perfects *Q;* perfect *Malone*   11 neigh no] *Booth;* naigh noe *Q;* neigh-no *Ard¹;* neigh to *Malone;* rein no *Oxf*

52 Still trying to come to terms with separation from his friend, the poet compares absence with the physical and
temporal constraints by means of
which the preciousness of jewels and
special holidays is sustained. The sonnet's number alludes to the number of
weeks in a year.

1 **So . . . rich** I am like the rich (man).
The image is broadly reminiscent of
the opening scenes of Marlowe's *Jew
of Malta* and Jonson's *Volpone,* in both
of which the protagonist surveys his
treasure; in neither of these, however,
is it suggested that this is an infrequent activity.
blessed blessèd

2 **bring him to** bring him to a sight of
up-locked up-lockèd

4 for fear of dulling the keenness of
pleasure, which is sustained by infre-
quency

5 **rare** special, choice; not often
encountered: the idea is strongly analogous to Prince Hal's image, applied
to his absence from court, in *1H4*
1.2.199–201: 'If all the year were playing holidays, / To sport would be as
tedious as to work; / But when they
seldom come, they wish'd for come, /
And nothing pleaseth but rare accidents.' Cf. also 3.2.55–9, in which

Henry IV speaks of his careful control
of his public appearances: 'and so my
state / Seldom, but sumptuous,
show'd like a feast, / And wan by
rareness such solemnity'.

6 **in . . . year** arranged in the year which
for long stretches lacks holidays

7 **placed** placèd

8 **captain** chief, principal
carcanet 'an ornamental collar or
necklace, usually of gold or set with
jewels' (*OED*)

9 **So . . . you** in the same manner, the
time that keeps you separate from me
is

11 to 'make special' = indicate specially,
specify; the sense is 'to mark out as
especially fortunate some particular
moment'

12 **his imprisoned pride** the splendour
of the moment, previously hidden by
the time of absence; the occluded
magnificence of the youth

13 **Blessed** blessèd: expanded from the
word's previous occurrence in l. 11 as
a single syllable

14 (Your merits ensure that) those who
enjoy your presence experience a
sense of triumph; those who are separated from you can at least enjoy the
the pleasure of hoping for it.

52

So am I as the rich, whose blessed key
Can bring him to his sweet up-locked treasure,
The which he will not every hour survey,
For blunting the fine point of seldom pleasure;
Therefore are feasts so solemn and so rare,   5
Since, seldom coming, in the long year set,
Like stones of worth they thinly placed are,
Or captain jewels in the carcanet.
So is the time that keeps you as my chest,
Or as the wardrobe which the robe doth hide,   10
To make some special instant special blessed
By new unfolding his imprisoned pride.
   Blessed are you, whose worthiness gives scope,
   Being had, to triumph; being lacked, to hope.

3 every] eu'ry 8 jewels] Iewells 10 wardrobe] ward-robe 12 imprisoned] imprison'd 14 lacked] lackt

53 The fair youth is claimed as the archetype or defining image of all beauty,
whether human or natural, male or
female; but according to the Platonic
idea of externals as a shadow of
inward realities, he is (apparently)
praised above all for moral excellence.

1 **substance** used in the philosophical
sense: cf. *OED* 3a, 'That which
underlies phenomena; the permanent
substratum of things'; cf. 5.14 for a
similar application of the word.

2 **millions . . . tend** 'numberless
images of other individuals accompany you': *strange* suggests both 'foreign'
and 'belonging to another person or
place, not one's own' (*Glossary*); *shadows* suggests various kinds of simulacra, such as ghosts, portraits or
actors; and to *tend* may be to wait
upon, take care of, or follow.

3 'since each one of the *strange shadows*
has a single image or appearance'

4 The young man's plurality is contained in singleness. Though he is
only *one* (cf. sonnets 1–17, especially 3
and 8, with their stress on his 'singleness'), he is able to impart or bestow
something on all the others. Initially it
seems that *lend* = 'lend an appearance
of'; but ll. 5–6 define it as 'bestow
fresh attributes upon'.

5–6 Presumably refers to Shakespeare's
own *VA*, with its celebration of the
irresistible though immature beauty
of 'rose-cheeked Adonis': the implication is therefore not only that 'anyone who attempts to describe Adonis
will produce something which resembles you, but falls far short', but also:
'look at my own poetic shadowing of
Adonis, and you will find that it is an
inadequate representation of yourself'. Southamptonites may find support in this second reading, since *VA*
was dedicated to Southampton; however, the allusion would work equally
well as a claim that Shakespeare's first
published poem was an unconscious
(as well as inadequate) foreshadowing
of another fair youth, and/or patron.

7 '"Set out" (portray) Helen of Troy in
such a way as to exemplify the highest

ideal of beauty'; however, the act of
imitating or counterfeiting seems to
be partly transferred from artist to
subject, with connotations of cosmetics and false beauty. Like *Son, TC* was
printed in 1609, and ll. 7–8 may carry
an allusion to Shakespeare's own published play, in which, however, Helen
is rather unflatteringly portrayed.

8 **Grecian tires** Greek costume or
attire, or, specifically, head-dress, continuing the suggestion that the
imitable features of Helen of Troy are
not her natural beauties but her artificial adornments. The idea of a young
man adorned with a Greek woman's
costume or head-dress seems a shade
grotesque, but it is of course such an
image that Elizabethan audiences
would have seen either in Marlowe's
Doctor Faustus or Shakespeare's *TC*
3.1.

9 Shakespeare's reference to his own
writings here comes even closer to
home, since sonnet 18 has deployed
imagery of spring and summer, 12 of
autumn and harvest; *foison* = abundance; by extension, abundant harvest, the season of harvest.

10 **The one** spring; despite the denial, in
sonnet 18, that *a summer's day* could
be an adequate metonym for the youth
shadow appearance, representation,
with an oxymoron in the notion of a
shadow, supposedly dark, representing
the freshness and clarity of spring and
youthful beauty

11 **bounty** munificence, like the abundance of harvest; however, the suggestion may be rather of bountiful
endowments than of largesse in distributing them.

12 may be read either as 'and you (are
manifested) in every fair image we
perceive'; or 'and we acknowledge
(*know*) you in every fair image'
blessed blessèd

13 **external grace** grace, or beauty, of
exterior form

14 primarily hyperbolic praise: (a) 'There
is no resemblance between you and
anyone else when it comes to the interior virtue of constancy', with some

53

What is your substance, whereof are you made,
That millions of strange shadows on you tend?
Since every one hath every one one shade,
And you, but one, can every shadow lend;
Describe Adonis, and the counterfeit   5
Is poorly imitated after you;
On Helen's cheek all art of beauty set
And you in Grecian tires are painted new;
Speak of the spring, and foison of the year:
The one doth shadow of your beauty show,   10
The other as your bounty doth appear,
And you in every blessed shape we know.
   In all external grace you have some part,
   But you like none, none you, for constant heart.

---

reminiscence, prompted by the Helen simile of ll. 7–8, of 20, 3–4, in which the youth has a woman's facial beauty but lacks her emotional instability; however, if *like* is construed as a verb, a contrary sense (b) emerges, one which conforms better with 40–42: 'But you are attracted to (*like*) no one for the sake of his or her constant heart, nor is that the source of your own attractiveness'. Shakespeare often used 'like' (v.) for 'be sexually attracted to'; cf. *CE* 3.2.7, *AC* 3.3.13 and many other instances. In this reading *But* introduces a radical mod-

ification of all that has gone before, rather than an extension: (a) suggests 'your beauty is paramount, and so is your constancy'; (b) 'your external beauty is paramount, but does not match up to your inward qualities, since you are inconstant'. For an image analogous to (b), of excelling beauty which fails to correspond with moral worth, cf. *TN* 3.2.375–9. Booth (226) suggests that *constant heart* could have been readily heard as 'constant art', which would link the youth further with the seductive wiles of Helen in ll. 7–8.

5 Adonis] *Adonis*   7 Helen's] *Hellens*   8 Grecian] *Grecian*

54 This sonnet continues the theme of substance and show through a distinction between *roses* and *canker blooms,* the former alone being susceptible of distillation into rose-water; this process is analogous to the poet's artistic preservation of the young man's quintessential substance.

1   seem Though the assertion is that inward *truth* manifests itself as the crowning glory of external *beauty,* the word *seem* introduces at the outset a faint uncertainty about the friend's integrity. Also, if the previous sonnet's final line is read in sense (b) (see 53.14n.), ll. 1–2 express a longing for what is lacking, rather than a eulogy of what the youth embodies.

2   By on account of, reinforced by

3   deem judge

4   cf. 'As sweet as a rose' (Tilley, R178): roses were prized by the Elizabethans as much for their culinary and medicinal properties as for their appearance. The herbalist John Parkinson said that their virtues were so many that a whole book could be written about them (*Theatrum Britannicum. The Theater of Plants* (1640), 1021).

5   canker blooms Previous editors have identified these with 'an inferior kind of rose; the dog-rose' (*OED* 5), an interpretation which seems right for Shakespeare's uses of 'canker' as a plant in *1H4* 1.3.173–4 and *MA* 1.3.25–6. Here, however, it is possible that he refers, rather, to the colloquial name for wild red poppies, which was 'cankers' or 'canker rose'; cf. John Gerard, *Herball* (1636), index under 'canker rose'; Parkinson, op. cit., 367; and for a fuller discussion cf. Duncan-Jones, 'Canker blooms'.

as deep a dye as intense a colour; roses were chosen for distillation which were deep red or crimson. While 'dog-roses' or wild roses could not be claimed as being as strongly coloured as crimson garden roses, wild poppies could.

6   perfumed tincture the fragrant essence and flavour of roses extracted by distillation; cf. *OED* tincture 5.

perfumed perfumèd

7   Hang . . . thorns In *1H4* 1.3.175 the 'canker' seems synonymous with a 'thorn'; but the assertion here that their thorns are indistinguishable from those of true roses comes across as poetic exaggeration, whether *canker blooms* are identified with wild roses or with wild poppies. Possibly *thorns* is used here for 'stalks' or 'stems'; cf. *LLL* 4.3.110, part of a poem which occurs also in *PP* 238.

8   'when a summer breeze releases them from the buds which mask them'

masked maskèd

9   'because their merit lies only in their appearance, without inward worth': *virtue* is used here in the technical sense of 'power, efficacy', especially applied to flowers and plants. Roses (see 1. 3n.) have many 'virtues'; dog-roses have the same 'virtues', but in much less powerful form; poppy flowers have none, and their petals were not used for distillation. Their seeds, however, induce sleep and forgetfulness, a property undesirable in the subject of the poet's verse.

10   unwooed not sought after; with a strong implication that what is really at issue is the attractiveness of shallow but ostentatious young people

unrespected not looked at; not esteemed or treated with respect: cf. 43. 2 and n.

11   Die to themselves They die alone; they are as if dead; they are their own *dye*, furnishing no colour or value to others; and, possibly, they experience orgasm in solitude.

Sweet roses suggests both 'roses which, unlike cankers, are sweet'; and 'roses which are sweet, as distinct from those which are not'. The second reading would be compatible with an identification of *canker blooms* with poppies, which were also called 'corn roses'; cf. Duncan-Jones, 'Canker blooms'.

12   sweet deaths Roses died sweetly, because they enjoyed a further life as rose-water, syrup or conserve; and the products of dead roses were literally

54

O how much more doth beauty beauteous seem
By that sweet ornament which truth doth give!
The rose looks fair, but fairer we it deem
For that sweet odour which doth in it live;
The canker blooms have full as deep a dye   5
As the perfumed tincture of the roses,
Hang on such thorns, and play as wantonly,
When summer's breath their masked buds discloses;
But for their virtue only is their show
They live unwooed, and unrespected fade,   10
Die to themselves. Sweet roses do not so;
Of their sweet deaths are sweetest odours made;
    And so of you, beauteous and lovely youth;
    When that shall vade, by verse distils your truth.

---

sweet, because the process of conservation required the addition of a large quantity of sugar.

13 **And . . . you** 'and the same principle applies to you'; or, 'and so the beauty which is yours'
   youth primarily suggests 'you, my young friend'; but we may if we choose read the assertion as applying to the general condition of 'beauteous and lovely youth'. There may be a threatening distinction between the *youth* which is *beauteous and lovely*, which will enjoy a second life in poetry, and that which is empty and shallow (like poppy blooms?) and will be quickly forgotten.

14 **that** *beauty*, the announced subject of the sonnet; or *youth*, now interpreted as the condition of being young
   vade go away (cf. Lat. *vadere*), often used in a sense which overlaps with 'fade' (as in l. 10); cf. Sidney, *AS*, 102.5, 'How doth the colour vade of those vermilion dyes'.
   by . . . truth 'by means of verse your truth is preserved and transmitted to future generations': whereas in sonnets 1 and 5 procreation was recommended as the means of preserving *beauty's rose*, that power is here attributed to poetry. The suggestion that ageing (and death?) must occur before poetic distillation is fully accomplished is effective if chilling: even as plucked roses are boiled with sugar, so (dead) human beauty is conserved with rhetoric. Capell's widely accepted emendation of *by* to 'my' narrows down the exploration of large principles that characterizes this sonnet.

3 rose] Rose   5 canker] Canker   6, 11 roses] Roses   10 unwooed] vnwoo'd   14 by] my *Capell*

55 Building on the end of the previous sonnet, the speaker claims that his *powerful rhyme* will outlast palaces and cities, keeping the youth's virtues alive until the Last Judgement. For an account of the classical resonances of this claim, see Leishman, 37 and *passim*.

1 *monuments Q's 'monument' may be a compositorial error, with abbreviated '-es' read as a comma.

1–2 the . . . princes suggests gilded tombs of monarchs in marble chambers, such as that of Henry V in Westminster Abbey

3 these contents the *contents* of this book; these poems, which contain *you*; these poems, which are a source of lasting happiness or contentment

4 unswept stone The rhetorical dynamic of comparison is reversed: in ll. 1–2 the poet's *rhyme* outlives what is supposed to be lasting; in 4 it outshines what is, because of the eroding process of time, no longer shining, and has come to be neglected. The image evokes a ruined, deserted city, such as those described in Spenser's *Ruines of Time* (1595), 92–8 (*Shorter Poems*, 231–4).

besmeared . . . time Time is personified as a sluttish housewife who has allowed stone buildings to crumble and blacken.

5 wasteful war war which lays cities and monuments waste

7 The forward thrust of the sonnet obscures the awkwardness of making *sword*, as well as *fire*, the subject of *burn*. 'Sword and fire' was a familiar phrase; cf. *OED* fire, 5a; and *1H4* 2.4.312–13. The assonance between *Mars* and *war's* also helps to bond the two agents of destruction.

8 living record presumably, a record which transcends the fragile paper it is written on, which would fall victim to *quick fire* even sooner than would statues and stone buildings. The assertion can be read as support for Shakespeare's intention to publish

Son, to ensure the proliferation of copies.

9 'Gainst in the face of, in opposition to
all oblivious enmity enmity which desires that the youth is forgotten; or enmity which is itself unaware of your worth ; or enmity which forgets everything, is oblivious to *all*

10 pace a surprisingly gentle word, where we might expect something more assertive, such as 'stride'; perhaps chosen both for its similarity to 'peace', in contrast to the images of warfare which precede it, and for its rhyme with the ensuing *praise*
room space, a place in which the youth's merit is expounded, with a possible pun on 'Rome', suggesting the perpetuation, in the artistic image of the youth, of ancient splendour. Shakespeare used this pun in *JC* 1.2.156 and *KJ* 3.1.180.

11–12 all . . . out 'all those succeeding generations through whom the world moves to its decay, when it is "worn out"'; cf. *KL* 4.6.136–7, Gloucester commenting on Lear's decay, 'This great world / Shall so wear out to naught'. Shakespeare, like Donne, played with the idea that nature, or at least mankind, was decaying and declining; cf. 'mankind decays so soon, / We are scarce our fathers' shadows cast at noon' (Donne, *An Anatomy of the World*, 143–4).

12 ending doom the (Last) judgement, with which the world will end

13 that when ; cf. *AYL* 3.2.163.

14 this this *powerful rhyme*, referring presumably not just to sonnet 55 but to the sequence as a whole
dwell . . . eyes Lovers will see you in this verse, and take you as a model; your image will be reflected in the eyes of lovers; you will dwell in the eyes of readers who will learn to love you by reading this verse. However, since *lovers' eyes* were notoriously unreliable, as in the proverb 'Love is blind' (Tilley, L506), the image introduces a subversive doubt.

55

Not marble, nor the gilded monuments
Of princes, shall outlive this powerful rhyme;
But you shall shine more bright in these contents
Than unswept stone, besmeared with sluttish time.
When wasteful war shall statues overturn　　　　5
And broils root out the work of masonry,
Nor Mars his sword, nor war's quick fire, shall burn
The living record of your memory:
'Gainst death, and all oblivious enmity,
Shall you pace forth; your praise shall still find room
Even in the eyes of all posterity　　　　11
That wear this world out to the ending doom.
　　So till the judgement that yourself arise,
　　You live in this, and dwell in lovers' eyes.

---

1 monuments] *Malone;* monument *Q*   2 princes] Princes outlive] out-liue   4 Than] Then
besmeared] besmeer'd   5 statues overturn] *Statues* ouer-turne   7 Mars] *Mars*   9 enmity] emnity

56 Addressing the quality of love –
whether his own, his friend's, or that
of both is not clear – the poet pleads
for it to be charged with fresh vigour
and for a separation between the
friends to function as a device to
renew the intensity of their devotion.
Because *Sweet love* is unlocated, the
reader is left unsure whether the
speaker has wearied of his friend or
his friend of him.

2 **than appetite** than that of appetite:
the word *feeding* in the following line
suggests 'appetite for food'; but since
the comparison is with *love*, sexual
appetite is primarily implied, which is
more common in Shakespeare than
the application to food, as in *VA* 34,
Luc 546; and cf. Partridge, *Bawdy*, 66,
for more examples.

5 **So . . . thou** Despite the personal-
seeming address, which invites the
reader to identify the addressee as a
human individual, the subject seems
still to be 'the emotion of love';
whose, is not clear.

6 **wink** close; eyes, like two mouths,
being so amply 'fed' with the sight of
the beloved that they shut themselves
against further cramming

8 **dullness** lethargy; bluntness, perhaps
with a sense of sexual torpor; cf.
Adonis' 'dull disdain', *VA* 33.

9 **interim** an intervening time, interval
of time (*OED* 7); in Shakespeare most
often suggesting a period of inactivity
or absence: cf. *Oth* 1.3.258–9, in which
Desdemona declares that 'I a heavy
interim shall support / By his dear
absence; let me go with him.' The following sonnet may imply that the *sad
interim* experienced by the speakers is

caused by the young man's withdrawal.

9–11 **ocean . . . banks** The image
appears to be one of a wide river or
estuary, rather than an 'ocean' in the
normal sense, with a newly betrothed
couple standing on opposite sides of
the water and gazing across in the
hope of a sight of each other. The
notion of two lovers separated by a
sound of water is irresistibly reminiscent of the Hero and Leander story
(as in Marlowe's poem); but its tragic
conclusion is presumably not invoked
here. The application to the friends of
the image of marriage (*contracted new*)
shows how far the speaker has come
from sonnets 1–5, in which the youth
was *contracted* only to his own beauty,
but urged to marry a woman.

11–12 **when . . . love** Presumably the
betrothed lovers are imagined as gazing across the water *daily*, being eventually rewarded either with a sight of
each other and/or with a fresh meet-
ing.

13 *****Or** Q's 'As', though defended by
Sisson (1.212), cannot readily introduce the sense which seems to be
required: 'here is another consoling
analogy . . .'.
   winter The association of *winter* with
misery or absence is conventional; cf.
Sidney, *AS*, 69.7; *R3* 1.1.1. It is picked
up and developed in sonnet 97.

14 **summer's welcome** the eagerness
with which we respond to summer;
the *welcome*, or bountiful reception,
that summer gives to us
   wished wished for
   rare choice, valuable; especially valuable because perceived as infrequent

56

Sweet love, renew thy force; be it not said
Thy edge should blunter be than appetite,
Which but today by feeding is allayed,
Tomorrow sharpened in his former might;
So, love, be thou; although today thou fill   5
Thy hungry eyes even till they wink with fullness,
Tomorrow see again, and do not kill
The spirit of love with a perpetual dullness;
Let this sad interim like the ocean be
Which parts the shore, where two contracted new   10
Come daily to the banks, that when they see
Return of love, more blessed may be the view;
    Or call it winter, which being full of care
    Makes summer's welcome thrice more wished,
        more rare.

56] *sonnet omitted by Benson* 3, 5 today] too daie 4 sharpened] sharpned 7 Tomorrow] Too morrow 8 love] Loue 9 interim] *Intrim* ocean] Ocean 12 blessed] blest 13 Or] *Capell;* As *Q*, *Riv Cam*[3] winter] Winter 14 summer's] Sōmers wished] wish'd

57 Claiming to be wholly subservient, physically and mentally, to the wishes and commitments of his young friend, the speaker none the less indicates that he is aware that his absent friend may not be employing his time well.

1 **tend** attend; wait for, care for, be solicitous towards

2 **your desire** Initially, especially after the plea for strengthened affection in the preceding sonnet, we may read this as 'your love for me'; but the lines that follow redefine it as 'your desire for me which is at present in abeyance', or 'your desire for others, which I must perforce accommodate'.

5 **chide** blame, complain of

the world-without-end hour the hour that seems everlasting, seems to occupy a *world* of time; cf. *OED* world 6b, and *LLL* 5.2.779. The phrase is equivalent to Lat. *in secula seculorum*.

6 **my sovereign** a development of the imagery used in 33, where the young man was compared with the *sovereign* brightness of the sun, and addressed as *my sun*. The word may here have an ironical tinge; the youth is a *sovereign* to the speaker only because of the latter's devotion.

9 **question with** ask questions by means of

10 **affairs** business, concerns: although the association of the word with 'sexual involvement' is not found before 1709 (*OED* 3), the context suggests that some of the young man's preoccupations may be amorous.

suppose speculate on, guess at

11 **naught** Though *naught* is modified by the next line, its sense of 'having no moral value', especially in a sexual context (cf. *R7* 1.1.98), is possibly also applicable: while claiming to think no evil of his friend, the speaker hints that he is aware of the likelihood that he is up to no good.

12 **those** those who are with you

13 **So . . . love** so trusting a fool; such a complete, utter fool

in your will Q's capitalization irresistibly suggests 'in the case of your own William Shakespeare', as well as 'with regard to your desire'.

14 **Though . . . anything** This broad concession indicates that the speaker's *jealous thought* encompasses the possibility of considerable wrongdoing by the youth – why else would he need to emphasize his, or love's, ability to 'think no ill' of what the youth is doing? The couplet activates the very suspicions which it claims to suppress.

57

Being your slave, what should I do but tend
Upon the hours and times of your desire?
I have no precious time at all to spend,
Nor services to do, till you require;
Nor dare I chide the world-without-end hour   5
Whilst I, my sovereign, watch the clock for you,
Nor think the bitterness of absence sour
When you have bid your servant once adieu;
Nor dare I question with my jealous thought
Where you may be, or your affairs suppose,   10
But like a sad slave stay and think of naught,
Save, where you are, how happy you make those.
    So true a fool is love, that in your will,
    Though you do anything, he thinks no ill.

5 world-without-end] world without end   6 I, my sovereign,] I (my soueraine)   13 will] Will
14 Though . . . anything,] (Though . . . any thing)

58 Continuing the image of the speaker as a slave to his young friend, the poet reluctantly tells him that he is entitled to act as independently as he wishes. While in 57 he made subjection to his friend's whims sound easy, it is here shown as requiring superhuman effort.

1 **That god forbid** subjunctive: = may that god forbid. Perhaps the god referred to is Cupid (not named until the penultimate sonnet); but Q's capitalized 'God' causes the reader initially to register an oath, 'God forbid'.

that The use of the less personal *that*, rather than 'who', serves to filter out the conjecture that the Christian God is invoked.

2 that I should (even) in my own mind seek to regulate your enjoyments, or times when it 'pleases' you to see me; cf. l. 14 and note.

3 or seek to ask you for an itemization (*account*) of how you spend your time. The collocation of *hand* and *account* suggests a written enumeration, like a financial account-book; cf. 30.11 and n.

4 **vassal . . . leisure** your slave, who is obliged (*bound*) to wait until you have time for him

5 **suffer** endure, acquiesce in; with some undertow of 'sustain loss or injury' (*Glossary*, 2, 4)

being . . . beck awaiting your summons, or 'beckoning' gesture

6 a dense conceit: = 'my prolonged absence from you, a consequence of the freedom of which you avail yourself, which to me is a form of imprisonment'

7 **patience tame** *Tame* appears to be a verb governed by *let me* in l. 5: '(Let me) govern and control my (im)-

patience.' Most earlier editors, with the exception of Capell, have taken *tame* as an adjective.

to . . . check 'endure (*bide*) every reverse or disappointment, subjecting it to endurance'; or 'command (bid) every disappointment to a condition of patient forbearance'. For this sense of *sufferance*, cf. *Glossary*, 2.

8 'without holding you blameworthy for injuring me'

9 **where you list** wherever you feel like being; cf. 'the wind bloweth where it listeth', John, 3.8. That Shakespeare saw the wind as the archetypal image of freely chartered liberty is suggested by *AYL* 2.7.48 and *H5* 1.1.48.

charter privilege, entitlement

10 **privilege** authorize, license; cf. the analogously ironic application in *Luc* 621, 'To privilege dishonour'. The wider implication seems to be that 'your position (of privilege?) entitles you to spend your time however you like'.

11–12 **to . . . crime** 'It is up to you (or, it is your prerogative) to exonerate yourself of wrongs done by yourself, or to yourself': *self-doing* seems to suggest that the use the young man makes of his freedom may be morally injurious to himself, as well as harmful to his absent friend.

13 **wait** suggests, besides 'spend time in passive expectation', 'be in attendance, as on a monarch or lord'

14 suggests both 'not blame you for your demeanour towards me, whether it is friendly or adverse' (cf. the still-current phrase 'the Queen's pleasure') and 'not reprimand you for indulging in pleasure, whether you are spending your time well or badly'

58

That god forbid, that made me first your slave,
I should in thought control your times of pleasure,
Or at your hand th'account of hours to crave,
Being your vassal bound to stay your leisure.
O let me suffer, being at your beck,   5
Th'imprisoned absence of your liberty,
And patience tame, to sufferance bide each check,
Without accusing you of injury.
Be where you list, your charter is so strong
That you yourself may privilege your time   10
To what you will; to you it doth belong
Yourself to pardon of self-doing crime.
   I am to wait, though waiting so be hell,
   Not blame your pleasure be it ill or well.

---

1 god] *Ard¹*; God *Q*, *Malone*   5 suffer, being . . . beck,] suffer (being . . . beck) *Q*, *Malone*, *Cam²*
6 imprisoned] imprison'd   11 To] Do *Malone*, *Ard¹*

59 If (as some ancient writers suggest) the world goes through a succession of repetitive cycles, the young man's beauty may have both existed and been described poetically in the past; but the speaker ends by asserting that earlier poets have praised *subjects worse*.

1–2 **If . . . new** 'The thing that hath been, it is that which shall be; and that which is done is that which shall be done: and there is no new thing under the sun' (Ecclesiastes, 1.9). This chapter was ordained to be read at Evening Prayer on 29 October (*BCP*, 45).

2–4 **brains . . . child** The image of the brain as a womb, giving birth to ideas and language, was commonplace; cf. Sidney, *AS*, 50.11; *Son* 76.8.

3 **amiss** adverbial: = erroneously, in a wrong way

4 a child (concept) of earlier times which is laboriously brought into being once again

5 **record** recòrd: memory, the power of recollection, as in *TN* 5.1.253 and *Ham* 1.5.99

6 **Even of** even to the extent of
five . . . sun The immediate impression is of the mind looking back 'a very long time': cf. *Tit* 1.1.350; but some have detected a reference to the 'Platonic' or Pythagorean Great Year, a period of time after which all the moving bodies in the cosmos were believed to return to their previous positions. Shakespeare was probably most familiar with this notion from the speech attributed to Pythagoras in Ovid, *Met.*, 15.66ff.; cf. especially ll. 431–48, describing the 500-year life-cycle of the Phoenix.

7 **antique** ancient, with a suggestion of 'old-fashioned, out of date' (*Glossary*)

8 (a book) produced soon after the time when men first learned to express their thoughts in writing

9–10 **what . . . this** both 'how much writings of ancient times could say, when compared with this'; and 'what writers of former times could say if (an archetype of) this were their subject'

10 **composed . . . frame** refers both to the young man's body and to the poet's image of it: (a) the ordered beauty of your bodily harmony; (b) the amazing beauty of your body as articulated and ordered (*composed*) in my verse
composed compposèd

11 **mended** improved

12 **whether . . . same** 'whether the cycle of time has brought about an exact replication'; cf. l. 6n.

14 **worse** primarily suggests that the young man's beauty excels that of past ages, early poets having praised 'less excellent' persons; but undercut by a swaggering tone which invites the reading '*even* worse': all poets lie and exaggerate, it is implied, but the *wits of former days* were exaggerating even more than I am.

59

If there be nothing new, but that which is
Hath been before, how are our brains beguiled,
Which, labouring for invention, bear amiss
The second burden of a former child?
O that record could with a backward look   5
Even of five hundred courses of the sun
Show me your image in some antique book,
Since mind at first in character was done,
That I might see what the old world could say
To this composed wonder of your frame;   10
Whether we are mended, or whe'er better they,
Or whether revolution be the same.
     O sure I am, the wits of former days
     To subjects worse have given admiring praise.

1 there] *Benson;* their *Q*   5 backward] back-ward   6 sun] Sunne   11 whe'er] where

60 Developing the temporal meditations of the preceding sonnet, the speaker considers the inevitable process of maturity and decay in the natural world, only to be counteracted by his own verse in praise of the young man. It is artfully placed at this numerical point in the sequence; cf. l. 2n.

1–4 Cf. Ovid, *Met.*, 15.181–4, trans. Arthur Golding, *The XV Bookes of . . . Metamorphoses* (1567), ed. J.F. Nims (1965) (200–5): 'But looke, / As every wave dryves other foorth, and that that commes behynd / Both thrusteth and is thrust itself: even so the tymes by kynd / Doo fly and follow bothe at once, and evermore renew / For that that was before is left, and streyght there doth ensew / Anoother that was never erst.' Whereas the previous sonnet concerned the possibility of infinite cyclical repetition, this posits a cycle of perpetual movement and loss.

1 **towards** one syllable

2 **our minutes** plays on 'hour-minutes', the total of minutes in an hour being suggested by the sonnet's number

4 **sequent toil** successive effort(s)
contend strive, with a sense of effortful forward movement

5 **Nativity** portmanteau word for 'that which is born', suggesting human beings both collectively and individually
main broad expanse (*OED* 5b); an application extended from the sense of 'open sea'

6 **Crawls to maturity** suggests at once a crawling infant and a person tottering with age
wherewith with maturity

7 **Crooked eclipses** Eclipses are both the product of asymmetrical move-

ments by the planets, and *crooked* in the sense of 'malign' in their effects on humanity; also, old people become bent.
glory beauty or magnificence; highest state of prosperity; also, perhaps, the light like a halo that 'crowns' the human being at the peak of perfection (*OED* 6, 8, 9a)

8 'The Lord giveth, and the Lord taketh away' (*BCP*, Order for the Burial of the Dead, from Job, 1.21): *confound =* destroy.

9 Time is imagined as armed with a sharp-pointed instrument (such as his traditional scythe) which pierces ('transfixes') the flourishing beauty of the young. To 'transfix' generally at this period meant to 'pierce or impale' cf. Spenser, *FQ*, 1.v.50; however, a counteracting sense of 'fix, imprint' is developed by the following line, which implies that time destroys the lineaments of beauty not by destroying them but by caricaturing them.

10 **delves the parallels** digs parallel lines, with a reference to *parallels* as military trenches (*OED* 3)

11 **rarities** choice specimens, marvels; perhaps developing the implied identification of the youth with the Phoenix in sonnet 59
nature's truth nature's essential integrity; an integrity which is natural, as in 54.2

12 **nothing . . . mow** All that comes into existence is subject to time's destruction; particularly so, perhaps, is the human capacity for reproduction which is associated with *nothing* ; cf. 12.13–14 and nn.

13 **to . . . hope** until future, or hoped for, times; but *in hope* seems also to modify and make provisional the poet's assertion that his verse will defy time.

60

Like as the waves make towards the pebbled shore,
So do our minutes hasten to their end,
Each changing place with that which goes before,
In sequent toil all forwards do contend.
Nativity, once in the main of light,   5
Crawls to maturity; wherewith being crowned
Crooked eclipses 'gainst his glory fight,
And time, that gave, doth now his gift confound.
Time doth transfix the flourish set on youth,
And delves the parallels in beauty's brow;   10
Feeds on the rarities of nature's truth,
And nothing stands but for his scythe to mow.
   And yet to times in hope my verse shall stand,
   Praising thy worth, despite his cruel hand.

1 pebbled] pibled   2 minutes] minuites   12 scythe] sieth   14 despite] despight

61 Reverting to the theme of dreams of the beloved (cf. 43), the speaker asks, in the octave, whether his friend deliberately projects the image of himself in order to trouble and spy on him, concluding, in the sestet, that it is his own obsessive devotion that keeps him awake.

2 **weary night** transferred epithet: = night that induces weariness

4 **shadows** false likenesses: the word could be applied to portraits, or to actors, and does not necessarily suggest a lack of light.
mock delude, tantalize (*OED* 3a)

6 **So . . . home** 'so far away from your body, which is your spirit's natural residence'; with an additional suggestion that the speaker is being spied on while *far from home*

8 '(Is the scrutiny of my ill-spent time) your object and meaning in jealously watching over me?' *Scope* = an end in view, purpose, aim (*OED* 2a); *tenor* = drift, purpose (*OED* 11a).

10–11 **my love . . . Mine own true love** (a) my feeling of love; (b) the object of my love (either applied to either phrase)

12 **To . . . watchman** 'One good friend watches for another' (Tilley, F716).

13 **watch . . . wake** The speaker's 'watching' is associated with care and assiduity, while the young man 'wakes', it is implied, in *OED*'s sense 1d, 'To sit up late for pleasure or revelry; to turn night into day'; and cf. *Ham* 1.4.8, 'The king doth wake tonight, and takes his rouse'.

61

Is it thy will thy image should keep open
My heavy eyelids to the weary night?
Dost thou desire my slumbers should be broken
While shadows like to thee do mock my sight?
Is it thy spirit that thou send'st from thee   5
So far from home into my deeds to pry,
To find out shames and idle hours in me,
The scope and tenor of thy jealousy?
O no, thy love, though much, is not so great;
It is my love that keeps mine eye awake,   10
Mine own true love that doth my rest defeat,
To play the watchman ever for thy sake.
    For thee watch I, whilst thou dost wake elsewhere,
    From me far off, with others all too near.

---

1 image] Image   8 tenor] *Booth, Oxf, Kerrigan;* tenure *Q Benson;* tenour *Capell*   jealousy] Ielousie
12 watchman] watch-man   14 too] to

62 In the first of two sonnets on his own
decrepitude, the speaker first rejoices
in his own merit and beauty, then
acknowledges that the beauties he
boasts of belong to the young man
whom he loves, and only vicariously
to himself.

1 **self-love** Cf. 3.8, where the
addressee's self-tombed *self-love*
inhibits reproduction: the sequence is
in process of tracing a circle from the
youth's sterile narcissism to the poet's.

4 **inward** inwardly

6 **No . . . true** no body so well-propor-
tioned: cf. *KL* 1.2.8, where Edmund
claims 'my shape as true / As honest
madam's issue'.
   of such account of such value; to be
so highly esteemed

7 **for myself** for my own benefit; with
regard to myself

8 (I calculate my value) in such a way
that I excel everyone else in every area
of excellence.

10 **Beated** acceptable form of 'beaten' =
battered, weather-beaten, with perhaps a shade of 'experienced' (*OED*
4); cf. *AYL* 2.4.50.
   chopped cracked, fissured
   tanned antiquity the process of ageing, personified as itself *tanned* with
age; the process of ageing which 'tans'
human skin, making it brown and
leathery. According to the Grave-
digger in *Ham* 5.1.162–8, tanners'
skins became toughened with their
trade; since Shakespeare's father was a
'whittawer', who prepared leather for
gloves, Shakespeare may well have
believed his own skin to have undergone this process (Chambers,
Shakespeare, 1.12).

11 **quite . . . read** I interpret in a quite
opposite sense

12 A self engaging in that kind of self-
love would be guilty of sin (*iniquity*);
or of 'inequity', failure to achieve a
correct estimation.

14 **Painting my age** adorning, decorat-
ing my (old) age; or describing it in
terms of your youthful beauty

62

Sin of self-love possesseth all mine eye,
And all my soul, and all my every part;
And for this sin there is no remedy,
It is so grounded inward in my heart.
Methinks no face so gracious is as mine,   5
No shape so true, no truth of such account,
And for myself mine own worth do define
As I all other in all worths surmount.
But when my glass shows me myself indeed,
Beated and chopped with tanned antiquity,   10
Mine own self-love quite contrary I read;
Self, so self-loving, were iniquity;
   'Tis thee (myself) that for myself I praise,
   Painting my age with beauty of thy days.

---

10 Beated] 'Bated *Malone* chopped] chopt *Q, Cam²* tanned] tand 11 self-love] selfe loue
12 self-loving] selfe louing 13 Tis] T'is

63 Anticipating a time when the fair youth will be as old and decrepit as he is now, the speaker makes provision against the youth's loss of beauty by preserving it in poetry. It is surely not by chance that this sonnet on the severe changes brought about by the ageing process is positioned as number 63, the 'grand climacteric', = 7 × 9, a figure associated with major life changes. Also, we are now exactly half-way through the 'fair youth' sequence, which ends with the imperfect 126 (see Introduction, p. 100).

1 **Against** in preparation for the time when; cf. *MND* 3.2.99; *R2* 3.4.28.

2 **injurious** 'wilfully inflicting injury or wrong' (*OED* 1); cf. *TC* 4.4.41–2: 'Injurious Time now with a robber's haste / Crams his rich thiev'ry up, he knows not how'.
o'erworn worn out, like a piece of shabby cloth

3 **filled** Though Q's 'fild' has been modernized to *filled*, the possibility cannot be excluded that the word should be 'filed', suggesting both 'carved with lines' and 'defiled': cf. Duncan-Jones, 'Modernizing'.

5 **travailed** As at 34.2, Q's spelling has been retained, to ensure that modern readers do not lose the simultaneous sense of 'labouring' and 'journeying'.
steepy difficult to ascend, like a steep hill; cf. *Tim* 1.1.75.

8 **Stealing away** The verb functions both (a) intransitively – the young man's beauties 'steal away', flee stealthily; and (b) transitively, with *time's injurious hand* and/or *hours* as the subject, which 'steal' the glories of

youth: cf. 'the stealing hours of time', *Ham* 5.1.71.

9 **For** in preparation for; a resumption of the sense of *Against* in l. 1
fortify make a fortification or buttress; cf. 16.3–4, where progeny, rather than *barren rhyme*, was the means by which the youth was advised to *fortify* himself.

10 **age's cruel knife** repeats the rhythm of *age's steepy night* in l. 5, but conflates *age* with *time*, who is so often armed with a sharp implement, as in 60.9–10

12 **though . . . life** 'though (he will cut from human memory) the life of my lover': the apparent synonymity here of *my love* and *my lover* is disconcerting, but there is a possibility that *My sweet love's beauty* refers to the poet's imaginative vision of his beloved, in contrast to the mortal specificity of *my lover's life*.

13 **black lines** lines of poetry, forming black lines on the page; they appropriate and redefine the *lines and wrinkles* of l. 4.

14 **he . . . green** 'he will remain, in the poet's verses, fresh and youthful.' However, the word *green* also has associations with rawness and unripeness which introduce an acidic note; cf. *VA* 806; *AC* 1.5.74. Where we might anticipate a conventional paradox of black ink revealing the brightness or fairness of the love-object, as in 65.14, *green* suggests that the poet's lines may preserve the young man's callowness and immaturity as much as his consummate beauty.

63

Against my love shall be as I am now,
With time's injurious hand crushed and o'erworn;
When hours have drained his blood, and filled his brow
With lines and wrinkles; when his youthful morn
Hath travailed on to age's steepy night,   5
And all those beauties whereof now he's king
Are vanishing, or vanished out of sight,
Stealing away the treasure of his spring;
For such a time do I now fortify
Against confounding age's cruel knife,   10
That he shall never cut from memory
My sweet love's beauty, though my lover's life.
  His beauty shall in these black lines be seen,
  And they shall live, and he in them still green.

2 crushed] crusht   3 drained] dreind   filled] fild   5, 10 age's] Ages   6 king] King   7 vanished]
vanisht   8 spring] Spring

64 Viewing the operation of time in the
world, the poet is prompted to reflect
on the death of his *love*, which he
laments in anticipation. The sonnet is
formally organized, with three quatrains opening 'When I have seen',
and a couplet which declares his
response to what he has seen.

2   suggests the expensive splendour of
elaborate funeral monuments, such as
those to be seen in Westminster
Abbey or St Paul's. The three components of *rich proud cost*, = opulent,
arrogant expenditure, are matched
and counteracted by *outworn buried
age*, = men who have grown old and
exhausted, or who lived long ago, and
are now interred.

3   **sometime lofty towers** buildings
which were once lofty: 'tower' (*OED*
1, 2) could refer to any tall building,
such as a church, castle or monastery.
down razed deliberately swept away
or demolished (*OED* raze 5a and b);
perhaps with specific reference to
large religious buildings pulled down
or reconstructed for secular use after
Henry VIII's dissolution of the
monasteries

4   **brass . . . rage** Even brass, though
durable by nature, is perpetually subject to the depredations of humanity;
eternal refers both to brass's supposed
lastingness and to its continued vulnerability. If a specific reference is
intended to Horace's claim that in his
Odes he has constructed a monument
aere perennius, 'more lasting than
brass' (*Odes*, 3.30.1), there may be a
covert suggestion that poetry, too, is
vulnerable.

5–8 The poet turns his gaze from human

artefacts to nature, viewing land and
sea as greedy competitors.

7   **main** ocean; cf. *R3* 1.4.20.

8   Each side's gain is the other side's
loss. The word *store* played a crucial
part in sonnets 1–17, suggesting, at
11.9 and 14.12, the vital essence of the
youth which requires to be reproduced; but here it seems to carry no
promise of perpetuity.

9   **interchange of state** alternation or
vicissitude of condition; with a secondary reference to 'state' in the political sense, anticipated in the image of
dry land's *kingdom* in l. 6. For readers
in 1609 an allusion to the end of
Elizabeth's long reign and the beginning of James's in 1603 must have
been irresistible.

10 **to decay** functions both as a noun,
indicating the condition that a *confounded*, confused or destroyed condition may be brought to, and as an
infinitive verb, governing both the
interchange of state and *state . . . confounded* which the poet has seen
decaying

11 *Ruin* has taught the speaker to *ruminate* partly because of the similarity of
the verb 'ruinate', into which the consonant from *me* has been injected:
'my' thoughts are embraced by *ruin*,
and even the word *taught* is only an
aspirate away from *thought*. The proximity of 'ruminating' to 'ruinating'
anticipates the swift removal of *my
love*.

12 **my love** the object of my love; the
feeling of love that I experience

14 **weep to have** weep while in possession of; weep with desire to possess

64

When I have seen by time's fell hand defaced
The rich proud cost of outworn buried age;
When sometime lofty towers I see down razed,
And brass eternal slave to mortal rage;
When I have seen the hungry ocean gain   5
Advantage on the kingdom of the shore,
And the firm soil win of the wat'ry main,
Increasing store with loss, and loss with store;
When I have seen such interchange of state,
Or state itself confounded, to decay,   10
Ruin hath taught me thus to ruminate:
That time will come and take my love away.
    This thought is as a death, which cannot choose
    But weep to have that which it fears to lose.

2 rich proud] rich-proud *Malone* 3 razed] rased 5 ocean] Ocean 6 kingdom] Kingdome
10 itself] it selfe 11 ruminate:] ruminate 12 time] Time 14 lose] loose

65 Recapitulating his survey of time's power to transform the world, the speaker searches desperately for a means to preserve human beauty, finding a fragile possibility of this in his own writing.

1–2 Since . . . power ellipsis for 'since (none of these elements) is exempt from the operation of *sad mortality*'

1 **brass** This example, from l. 4 of the previous sonnet, may be placed first because of of its traditional association with poetry. If the 'brass' to which Horace compared his poetic monument (see 64.4n.) is itself vulnerable, it is hinted at the outset that to hope to counter the operation of time by means of language may be futile.

2 **o'er-sways their power** is more powerful than they are; *o'er-sways* has political connotations which recall the images of *kingdom* and *state* in the preceding sonnet.

3 **with** against, confronted by

4 **action** partly a continuation of the legal metaphor of *hold a plea*, = legal process, legal action (*OED* 7, 8); partly a more general sense of 'agency,

force or influence' (*OED* 1, 2). Neither as litigant nor as agent generally can a *flower* be imagined as potent.

6 **wrackful** causing 'wrack' or destruction; 'wrack' is interchangeable, in Elizabethan usage, with modern 'wreck'.

7 **stout** strong, resolute

9 **fearful meditation** a meditation which is born of fear and/or provokes fear

11 **his swift foot** Time is here personified as a speedy runner, as in the proverb 'Time flees away without delay' (Tilley, T327).

12 **spoil** pillage, destruction, resuming the warfare metaphor of ll. 5–6
*o'er Both compositors consistently print 'o'er' as 'ore': cf. 5.8, 12.4, 23.8, 30.10 and many other examples, such as l. 2 of the present sonnet. It seems likely therefore that Q's 'or' represents 'ore' (= o'er), rather than being a mistake for 'of', as Malone and most modern editors have suggested.

13 **might** efficacy

14 **my love** my object of love; my feeling of love

65

Since brass, nor stone, nor earth, nor boundless sea,
But sad mortality o'er-sways their power,
How with this rage shall beauty hold a plea,
Whose action is no stronger than a flower?
O how shall summer's honey breath hold out   5
Against the wrackful siege of batt'ring days
When rocks impregnable are not so stout,
Nor gates of steel so strong, but time decays?
O fearful meditation! Where, alack,
Shall time's best jewel from time's chest lie hid?   10
Or what strong hand can hold his swift foot back,
Or who his spoil o'er beauty can forbid?
    O none, unless this miracle have might:
    That in black ink my love may still shine bright.

---

3 this] his *Malone*   10 jewel] Iewell   12 o'er] *Capell;* or *Q, Booth;* of *Malone*

66 Weary of the corruption and hypocrisy of the age he lives in, the speaker longs for death, restrained only by the thought of abandoning his *love*. The catalogue of eleven wrongs is analogous to the sevenfold catalogue in Hamlet's 'To be or not to be' speech, *Ham* 3.1.70–6, though it is fear of 'something after death', not of deserting his love, that restrains Hamlet. This despairing poem is probably located where it is by design. Multiples of six have adverse connotations, alluding to the biblical 'beast' associated with universal corruption: all human beings 'had the marke, or the number of his name . . . and his number is, six hundred threescore and sixe' (Revelation, 13.16–18).

1 **Tired with** tired of; cf. *Per* 2 Gower 37.

2 **desert** synecdoche for 'those who are deserving'

3 **needy . . . jollity** empty, worthless people dressed up in extravagant (by implication, costly) clothes. The boorish Cloten, who adorns himself in Posthumus's clothes, is described as 'that harsh, noble, simple nothing' (*Cym* 3.4.135; cf. also 4.2.192–3, where 'Triumphs for nothing' are identified with 'jollity for apes'). For *jollity* as 'finery of dress or array', cf. *OED* 7.

4 **unhappily forsworn** suggests both those who have kept vows and then regrettably broken them, and those who have kept their own vows truly but have been maliciously betrayed by others: cf. *OED* unhappily.

5 'honours and adornments disgracefully bestowed on undeserving recipients'

6 **strumpeted** suggests both chastity calumniated by being accused of whoredom, as in the defamation of Hero in *MA*, Desdemona in *Oth* and Hermione in *WT* ; and chaste girls raped and made into 'strumpets'. The resemblance of the word to 'trumpeted' accentuates the public and notorious nature of the disgrace done to *maiden virtue*.

7 **right** true, absolute: while the previous line suggests the sexual degradation of women, this points to wider – possibly male – qualities of *perfection* which are slandered or dishonoured.

8 'strength deprived of its effect by an authority which is itself weak': the image suggests the power exercised over young male courtiers by the ageing Elizabeth during the last years of her reign, the most conspicuous example being the house arrest imposed on the Earl of Essex in 1600/1. To form a rhyme with *strumpeted* the last word needs to be pronounced as 'disable-led', which generates a further play on *strength* as governed (led) by *limping sway*.

9 Though 'art' normally alluded to skills generally, not especially to creative art, the image of it as *tongue-tied* suggests a reference to censorship of literature, to which Elizabethan dramatists were frequently subject.

10 **doctor-like** *Doctor* is here used in *OED*'s sense 2a, 'One who, by reason of his skill in any branch of knowledge, is competent to teach it'.

11 plain truth wrongly described as folly or stupidity: reminiscent of Lear's dismissal of Cordelia for plain speaking. The phrase *simple truth* is differently applied in 138.8.

12 Another version of the concept in l. 8, with the metaphor changed from political to military: *good* is enslaved to, and in the service of, *captain ill*. The rank of captain had some associations with corruption and false authority, as in *2H4* 2.4. 136–47.

13 **Tired with** Like the repetitions in the catalogue itself (cf. previous note), the repetition of the opening phrase enacts the wearying, tedious experience of living in a corrupt society.

14 **to die** if I die; in order to die; and the rhyme of *die* with *cry* in l. 1 suggests further iterance.
I . . . alone, 'I leave my beloved lonely'; or 'I withdraw from my emotion of love'; or 'I desist from importuning my love-object'; or even 'I leave only my love, nothing else' (cf. Booth, 249–50).

66

Tired with all these for restful death I cry:
As to behold desert a beggar born,
And needy nothing trimmed in jollity,
And purest faith unhappily forsworn,
And gilded honour shamefully misplaced,   5
And maiden virtue rudely strumpeted,
And right perfection wrongfully disgraced,
And strength by limping sway disabled,
And art made tongue-tied by authority,
And folly, doctor-like, controlling skill,   10
And simple truth miscalled simplicity,
And captive good attending captain ill:
    Tired with all these, from these would I be gone,
    Save that to die I leave my love alone.

1, 13 Tired] Tyr'd   3 nothing] Nothing   trimmed] trimd   5 misplaced] misplast   7 disgraced] disgrac'd   10 folly, doctor-like,] Folly (Doctor-like)   11 simple truth] simple-Truth   miscalled] miscalde   simplicity] Simplicitie   12 captive good] captiue-good   captain] Captaine

67 This follows on from the preceding sonnet's account of a hopelessly corrupt society, replacing the question of the speaker's death-wish with that of whether his friend should live. In existing in this environment, the fair youth lays himself open to exploitation and imitation; but he is kept alive by nature as an exemplar of what beauty was like in earlier, better, days.

1 **with infection** primarily 'in the company of moral corruption'; but there is a secondary implication that, as in sonnets 34–5, the addressee himself is 'infected', i.e. morally faulty.

3–4 'so that sinful persons may advance themselves at his expense, or through his example, bestowing specious adornments on themselves by association with him': *lace* here = 'To ornament or trim with lace' or 'To mark as with (gold or silver) lace or embroidery' (*OED* 5, 6a).

6 **steal dead seeing** appropriate a lifeless appearance; the suggestion is that the youth's authentic beauty is falsely mimicked either in art, such as portraiture, or in vain attempts by others to copy his appearance in their own.

7 **poor beauty** primarily, perhaps, 'inferior beauty, beauty which falls short of the youth's glorious archetype'; but *poor* inevitably carries some undertones of sympathy for individuals manifesting lesser attractiveness.

8 **Roses of shadow** The 'rose', as in *beauty's rose*, 1.2, encapsulates the idea of the highest summation of human beauty; *Roses of shadow* therefore suggests 'imitation roses', which mimic, but do not transmit the inner worth of, the youth's beauty.

9 **bankrupt** Nature is *bankrupt* in the sense that all her wealth of human beauty has, supposedly, been bestowed on the fair youth, leaving none to bestow on other human progeny.

11 **exchequer** source of revenue, like the 'King's exchequer', or treasury; cf. *OED* 2 and figurative application in 5a.

12 **proud of many** puzzling phrase, for nature's 'pride' is hard to reconcile with the analysis of her bankruptcy; or the sense may be 'proud (mother) of many offspring', who consequently need to be nourished or adorned with what the youth has 'gained' from her. Capell's plausible emendation to 'prov'd' would yield the sense 'as many have discovered'. Another possible emendation is 'mon[e]y' for *many*, suggesting that nature flaunts the wealth she borrows from the youth; in combination with Kerrigan's emendation of 'proud' to ''prived', this would spell out nature's *bankrupt* condition.

13 **stores** keeps in her *store*, as in 11.9; but the speaker no longer proposes that progeny should perpetuate the stored-up beauty contained in the youth.

67

Ah, wherefore with infection should he live,
And with his presence grace impiety,
That sin by him advantage should achieve,
And lace itself with his society?
Why should false painting imitate his cheek,   5
And steal dead seeing of his living hue?
Why should poor beauty indirectly seek
Roses of shadow, since his rose is true?
Why should he live, now nature bankrupt is,
Beggared of blood to blush through lively veins?   10
For she hath no exchequer now but his,
And proud of many, lives upon his gains.
    O, him she stores, to show what wealth she had
    In days long since, before these last so bad.

---

8 rose] Rose   10 Beggared] Beggerd   12 proud] prov'd *Capell;* 'prived *Kerrigan*

68 Still on the theme of the present age's decadence, the poet celebrates the youth's authentic beauty, a throwback to an earlier, better, age, before wigs and borrowed adornments created false beauty. Whatever the original date of composition, it is unlikely that it could have been published during the lifetime of the period's most celebrated wearer of false hair, Elizabeth I. Wigs and false hair must have often been in Shakespeare's thoughts both because he himself was a bald actor, and also because in 1604, and possibly for some time earlier, he lodged in Silver St, the centre of the wig trade (Schoenbaum, *Life*, 209).

1 **map** The metaphorical application of the word to the human face, as an index of the whole body, began very early; cf. *2H6* 3.1.203; *TN* 3.2.85. In the early twentieth century the word became a slang expression for a face (*OED* 1a, 2a, 2d).

2 **as . . . now** primarily suggests the authenticity of natural, living beauty; but with strong undertones of transience, as in Job, 14.2, quoted in *BCP*, Order for the Burial of the Dead, as 'He cometh up and is cut down like a flower'; cf. also the proverb 'It fades like a flower' (Tilley, F386).

3 **borne** Q's spelling has been retained, giving the sense 'carried, displayed' or 'endured, tolerated'; but there is doubtless also a play on 'born', especially after the word *bastard*, suggesting a contrast between recent, illegitimate births and the youth's

embodiment of an archetype of beauty.

4 **inhabit on** dwell on; with a play on the 'habit', or adornment, assumed by the *living brow*

6 **the . . . sepulchres** what justly belongs to or is owned by the graves of the deceased; cf. 'So are those crisped snaky golden locks / Which make such wanton gambols with the wind / Upon supposed fairness, often known / To be the dowry of a second head, / The skull that bred them in the sepulchre' (*MV* 3.2.92–6).

8 **beauty's dead fleece** transferred epithet: = the fleece [hair] of dead beauty. For a woman's hair as 'golden fleece', cf. *MV* 1.1.170.

9 **holy antique hours** metonym for the beauty (of the youth's cheek) which was the product of those hours, connected by rhyme to the authentic *flowers* of l. 2

10 **itself** The implied subject is still *his cheek*, representing *beauty*, as in ll. 1–2.

11 'not exploiting the youthful beauty of another to reinforce his own'

12 **old** old (beauty); former (beauty). There is a subtle distinction between the poet's claim that the youth's beauty derives legitimately from the distant past – *holy antique hours* – and his scorn for beauty falsely composed of the appurtenances of those lately dead.

13 **store** retain in store; fill with beauties

14 **of yore** long ago, with a reinforcing pun on 'of your(s)'

68

Thus is his cheek the map of days outworn,
When beauty lived and died as flowers do now,
Before these bastard signs of fair were borne,
Or durst inhabit on a living brow;
Before the golden tresses of the dead, 5
The right of sepulchres, were shorn away,
To live a second life on second head;
Ere beauty's dead fleece made another gay:
In him those holy antique hours are seen,
Without all ornament, itself and true, 10
Making no summer of another's green,
Robbing no old to dress his beauty new;
    And him as for a map doth nature store
    To show false art what beauty was of yore.

1 outworn] out-worne   2 lived and died] liu'd and dy'ed   13 nature] Nature   14 art] Art

69 To outward view, the youth's beauty and merit is faultless, and is so reputed; but those whose gaze extends to his moral character find it degraded.

1 The *parts* = beauties and/or accomplishments that are visible to everyone; cf. 17.4, 37.7 and *passim*. For a comparable distinction between visible beauty and unknown inward qualities, cf. *Cym* 1.6.17.

2 **Want** lack

that . . . mend that heartfelt thoughts could improve: i.e., the youth's parts could not, to outward view, be bettered in imagination.

3 *due** Q's 'end' may be the result of compositorial error, resulting from 'turned letters' ('u' for 'n') and/or a failure of the usual process of converting the correct order to 'mirror-writing' as viewed on the composing-stick; cf. McKerrow, 257, 9–10. Alternatively or additionally, the compositor's eye may have slipped to *mend* in the previous line. Booth (253) describes this sonnet as 'sloppily printed throughout'.

4 **even . . . commend** *Even* probably governs *foes*, = 'so that even your enemies praise you', rather than 'in such a manner as enemies give praise'.

5 *Thy** one of Q's 'thy'/'their' errors; cf. 26.12n.

7 **other accents** other (less favourable) tones

confound undermine, destroy (cf. 60.8); but there may also be a sense of 'confuse, complicate'.

9 **look into** investigate closely; with the possible suggestion of 'look to see if there is any . . .' (*OED* look 16 a–c)

10 **that** refers to 'the beauty of thy mind'

in guess by conjecture, estimate

11 **Then . . . thoughts** Most modern editors (e.g. Ingram and Redpath, Booth) enclose *churls* by commas, making it an adjective applied to *those same tongues*; however, an antithesis seems to be set up between 'kind eyes' and 'churlish thoughts'.

12 **weeds** often used by Shakespeare as an image of moral corruption; cf. e.g., *R2* 3.4.38; *2H4* 4.1.11; *H8* 5.1.52.

14 *soil** Neither Q's 'solye' nor any of the many proposed emendations yields a wholly satisfactory sense; but *soil* is the most plausible, both because reversals of letter-order are a feature of this part of Q (cf. 'end' for 'due', l. 3; rn'wd' for 'ruin'd', 73.4), and because it yields a reasonable, if slightly strained, sense: 'the basis (ground, soil) of the disparity between your fair appearance and foul moral reputation is that you are debasing yourself, perhaps by keeping unworthy company'. The ease with which the word 'common' could slide from 'widespread' to 'morally obnoxious' is illustrated in *Ham* 1.2.72–4. Alternatively or additionally, *soil* may derive from the obsolete verb, a variant of 'assoil', meaning 'To resolve, clear up, expound or explain' (*OED* 3), functioning here as if it meant 'the solution'. Shakespeare could have selected the odd word 'soil' in preference to some more familiar word such as 'cause' because it opens up an additional play on 'common soil': 'you keep common, or vulgar, company'.

69

Those parts of thee that the world's eye doth view
Want nothing that the thought of hearts can mend;
All tongues, the voice of souls, give thee that due,
Utt'ring bare truth, even so as foes commend:
Thy outward thus with outward praise is crowned. 5
But those same tongues that give thee so thine own
In other accents do this praise confound,
By seeing further than the eye hath shown;
They look into the beauty of thy mind,
And that in guess they measure by thy deeds; 10
Then churls their thoughts (although their eyes were
        kind)
To thy fair flower add the rank smell of weeds.
    But why thy odour matcheth not thy show,
    The soil is this, that thou dost common grow.

3 tongues, the . . . souls,] toungs (the . . . soules)   3 due] *Capell;* end *Q*   4 commend] Commend
5 Thy] *Capell;* Their *Q*   8 further] farther   14 soil] *Benson;* solye *Q*

70 Continuing the theme of the youth's bad reputation, the poet sets out to defend him on the ground that his surpassing beauty inevitably makes him the target of envious slander.

1　**shall . . . defect** will not be attributed to your weakness: the declarative *shall not be* heralds a sustained rhetorical attempt to exonerate the youth from the allegations of the hostile *tongues* in 69: 'shall not be (viewed as) your defect (if I can help it)'.

2　'Envy shoots at the fairest mark' (Tilley, E175): the fact that beauty and virtue were subject to calumny was a strong Renaissance preoccupation, often linked with the most famous painting of antiquity, the *Calumny* of Apelles. Hamlet warns Ophelia 'be thou as chaste as ice, as pure as snow, thou shalt not escape calumny', *Ham* 3.1.137–8; cf. also *Ham* 1.3.38 and *MM* 3.2.174.

3　**suspect** suspèct; suspicion is the adornment (or invariable accompaniment) of beauty. The hyperbole is such an unusual one that it is difficult to filter out a counterpointing suggestion that beauty's ornaments are *suspect* (adj.), i.e. questionable, specious.

4　**A crow** adjectival noun applied to *suspect*, which inauspiciously blackens beauty's fairness.

5　**So . . . good** so long as you are good
approve prove, demonstrate

6　***Thy** Cf. 26.12n.
being . . . time perhaps suggests,

referring back to 69.1–5, 'being so admired and sought after at the present moment'. The concept of *time's love* in 124.3 seems comparably to denote love or popularity that is merely temporal, influenced by current reputation.

7　**canker vice** vice which is like the canker-worm or caterpillar (*Glossary* 2)

8　**thou present'st** you exhibit, display, are characterized by (*OED* present *v.* 4a)
unstained unstainèd
prime prime of life, youth or early manhood: it is not clear whether the youth's *prime* is now complete, as *passed by* might imply, or whether he is still in it.

9　**the . . . days** the vices lying in wait to ensnare the young; the military image resumes the suggestion of archery from *mark* in l. 2.

10　either not tempted, or triumphant over the onslaughts of temptation

11　**cannot . . . praise** 'cannot exalt your reputation to such an extent as to'

12　**envy, evermore enlarged** *enlarged* = set at liberty: the image of envy as perpetually at large is strongly reminiscent of Spenser's *FQ*, 6.xii.38–41, in which the many-tongued Blattant Beast is bound in chains by Calidore, but soon escapes, and attacks everyone he can find, including the poet.

13　**suspect** suspicion, as in l. 3

14　**owe** possess, own

70

That thou art blamed shall not be thy defect,
For slander's mark was ever yet the fair;
The ornament of beauty is suspect,
A crow that flies in heaven's sweetest air.
So thou be good, slander doth but approve   5
Thy worth the greater, being wooed of time;
For canker vice the sweetest buds doth love,
And thou present'st a pure unstained prime.
Thou hast passed by the ambush of young days,
Either not assailed, or victor, being charged;   10
Yet this thy praise cannot be so thy praise,
To tie up envy, evermore enlarged:
   If some suspect of ill masked not thy show
   Then thou alone kingdoms of hearts shouldst owe.

---

1 blamed] blam'd 4 crow] Crow 6 Thy] *Capell;* Their *Q* wooed] woo'd 7 canker] Canker
8 unstained] unstayined 9 passed] past 10 assailed] assayld charged] charg'd 12 enlarged]
inlarged 13 masked] maskt

71 Anticipating the aftermath of his death (threescore and ten sonnets being now accomplished), the poet implores the youth to forget him quickly, and to forget even that he was the author of the sonnets, so that he will not be compromised by association with the dead poet. Like Christina Rossetti's sonnet 'Remember', this plea for oblivion must inevitably, if read at all, function as a memorial.

1–2 Do not let your mourning for me, after my death, last longer than the sound of the funeral bell that will be tolled for me. It would be in the power of the dead speaker's heirs to commission a prolonged tolling of the bell, as Shakespeare appears to have done for the burial of his actor brother Edmund on 31 December 1607 in St Saviour's, Southwark, paying twenty shillings for 'a forenoone knell of the great bell' (Chambers, *Shakespeare*, 2.18; Schoenbaum, *Life*, 26).

2 **surly sullen** stern, gloomy (*OED* surly, with this example); and 'Of a deep, dull or mournful tone' (*OED* sullen 3b).

4 **From . . . world** Cf. *AC* 5.2.311–12: '*Cleo.* What should I stay? – / *Char.* In this vile world', where Capell is surely correct in emending F's 'wilde' to 'vile' (Elizabethan spelling 'vilde');

cf. also Young Clifford's exclamation on seeing his father dead, 'O let the vile world end', *2H6* 5.2.40.

with . . . dwell 'I have said to corruption, Thou art my father: to the worm, Thou art my mother and my sister' (Job, 17.14).

6 **so** so much; in such a manner

8 **make you woe** cause you to be sorrowful

10 **compounded** combined with; cf. *2H4* 1.2.8.

11 **rehearse** repeat, utter: if the friend was accustomed to call him 'William', he would find 'Will' assonated in *bell . . . dwell* in ll. 2 and 4, and *I am* in 1 and 3, hinting at a chiming of the poet's name in the tolling of the bell. Cf. Portia's use of rhymes in '-èd' to prompt Bassanio to choose 'lead', *MV* 3.2.63–5.

12 **decay** fall away, die; cf. *Luc* 23.

13 **wise world** sarcastic: = the world in its wisdom, especially since the phrase echoes *vile world* in l. 4.

look . . . moan investigate the cause of your sorrow

14 **And . . . me** If, as sonnets 135–6 suggest, the youth shares the poet's Christian name, William, the repetition of this name would inevitably implicate him in his grief, confusing mourner and mourned.

71

No longer mourn for me when I am dead
Than you shall hear the surly sullen bell
Give warning to the world that I am fled
From this vile world, with vilest worms to dwell:
Nay, if you read this line, remember not   5
The hand that writ it, for I love you so
That I in your sweet thoughts would be forgot,
If thinking on me then should make you woe.
O if (I say) you look upon this verse,
When I, perhaps, compounded am with clay,   10
Do not so much as my poor name rehearse,
But let your love even with my life decay;
    Lest the wise world should look into your moan,
    And mock you with me after I am gone.

4 vilest] vildest *Q, Riv*   10 I, perhaps,] I (perhaps)

72 Continues from the end of the preceding sonnet, with another plea for oblivion which functions as a reminder. If the young man is pressed to say what virtues his dead friend had, he should not lie on his behalf, but suppress the recollection of him.

1 task ... recite challenge you to tell (*OED* task 2b, with this example)

2 lived in me was in me (while I lived)

4 nothing worthy prove (a) 'apprehend (*prove*) nothing of value'; possibly undercut by (b), 'demonstrate that even *nothing* has value'

7 hang ... I the image derives from the practice of suspending epitaphs and trophies on the hearse or funeral monument of the deceased. The use of *I* for 'me' not only achieves the needed rhyme with *lie*, but activates a pun on the poet's 'deceasèd eye' – 'I shall not live to see it'.
deceased deceasèd

8 niggard miserly

9 in this in this respect

10 speak ... untrue 'speak well of me at the price of being untruthful'; 'speak well of me, who am "untrue", i.e. morally flawed'

13 'That which cometh out of the man, that defileth the man. For from within, out of the heart of men, proceed evil thoughts, adulteries, fornications, murders. Thefts, covetousness, wickedness, deceit, lasciviousness, an evil eye, blasphemy, foolishness: All these evil things come from within, and defile the man' (Mark, 7.20–3): though generally read as referring to the production of poems, as in 38.11 or 103.1, there is a connected suggestion of shameful actions and desires.

14 so should you so you too ought to be ashamed; or so will you, too, be brought into disgrace if you stand by me.
things nothing worth Primarily suggests 'that which is of no value, i.e. the dead poet'; but there may also be a reference to the poet's words, as in 'who will make me a liar, and make my speech nothing worth?' (Job, 24.25).

72

O, lest the world should task you to recite
What merit lived in me that you should love,
After my death (dear love) forget me quite,
For you in me can nothing worthy prove;
Unless you would devise some virtuous lie   5
To do more for me than mine own desert,
And hang more praise upon deceased I
Than niggard truth would willingly impart;
O, lest your true love may seem false in this,
That you for love speak well of me untrue,   10
My name be buried where my body is,
And live no more to shame nor me, nor you:
    For I am shamed by that which I bring forth,
    And so should you, to love things nothing worth.

2 lived] liu'd   13 shamed] shamd

73 This sonnet explores the young man's perception of the poet's decrepitude through a series of images of decay, concluding that this strengthens, or should strengthen, his love.

2 yellow . . . few The reversal of the steadily diminishing order – the reader expects 'or few, or none' – ensures that we focus on several stages of the process of seasonal decay, which includes both the leafless trees of midwinter and the partly stripped trees of mid-autumn, rather than simply on the period when the stripping of vegetation is complete. Since Shakespeare was bald, a visual analogy may be implied between an almost-leafless tree and the almost-hairless head, a process which may in a specific as well as a general sense be viewed *in me*.

3 shake against shiver in anticipation of (cf. the temporal use of *Against* in 63.1); shiver in response to

4 *Bare ruined choirs Primarily, the tree branches are imagined as those 'Quires and places where they sing' (*BCP*, Morning and Evening Prayer) which in summer were the haunts of songbirds; however, the phrase *Bare ruined choirs* also inevitably evokes visual recollections of chancels of abbeys left desolate by Henry VIII's dissolution of the monasteries. Q's 'rn'wd' is one of several errors of reversal made by Compositor B in sigs E1ᵛ – E4ᵛ; cf. 'end' for *due* in 69.3; cf. also 'whit' for *with,* 23.14, also the work of Compositor B; and 'stainteh' for *staineth,* 33.14, this time Compositor A. Here there is also a minim error, the MS having presumably read 'ruin'd' or 'rvin'd'.

5 twilight Shakespeare's only use of the word, whose relative unfamiliarity may be indicated by Q's hyphenation **such day** such a day; or such day-

light, in the form of afterglow

8 Death's second self Sleep, rather than night, is commonly called 'the elder brother of death' (cf. Sidney, *OA*, 88, and Tilley, S526); but the metonymic transfer to night is easily made.

seals . . . rest suggests both 'closes everything up in repose, as in a coffin which is "sealed"'; and 'closes all eyes', as in 'seel' = sew up the eyes of a falcon. The word *rest* hints at death as an end which is as much desired as feared.

10 his youth Since Elizabethan English lacked the genitive 'its', *his* should not automatically be construed as personalizing *fire;* however, followed by *deathbed,* it does naturally suggest the dying embers of a human life.

12 'Eaten up by that which it ate up', cf. *tempus edax rerum, tuque, invidiosa vetustas,* Ovid, *Met.,* 15.234–6, a phrase which immediately follows an image of Helen looking at her wrinkled face in a mirror. The larger subject of *that* is presumably time, as in Ovid; the human body was brought to maturity (*nourished*) by the same temporal process which destroys it.

13 which . . . strong tonally ambivalent: = either declarative of the existing strength of the youth's love, or carrying a note of hope: 'which (will) make your love more strong'; or simply descriptive, 'yours must be a very strong love, to be capable of being bestowed on a transient object'

14 To . . . well to love that (love-object) fully, heartily; conceivably there is a play on 'Will', i.e. 'to love that man called William'.

leave picks up *leaves* from l. 2, re-applying it as a verb, = 'be separated from'

73

That time of year thou mayst in me behold,
When yellow leaves, or none, or few do hang
Upon those boughs which shake against the cold,
Bare ruined choirs where late the sweet birds sang;
In me thou seest the twilight of such day   5
As after sunset fadeth in the west,
Which by and by black night doth take away,
Death's second self that seals up all in rest;
In me thou seest the glowing of such fire
That on the ashes of his youth doth lie,   10
As the deathbed, whereon it must expire,
Consumed with that which it was nourished by;
   This thou perceiv'st, which makes thy love more
      strong,
   To love that well, which thou must leave ere long.

---

4 Bare ruined choirs] *Benson;* Bare rn'wd quiers *Q;* Barren'd of quires *Capell*   5 twilight] twi-light
6 sunset] Sun-set   west] West   11 deathbed] death bed   12 Consumed] Consum'd   nourished]
nurrisht

74 Revoking his appeal to the youth in 71 to forget the author of these sonnets, the poet implores him to retain the *better part* of him, which will survive in his verse after death.

1 **be contented** stress should fall strongly on *be,* since the implication is: 'despite what I said in the preceding sonnet about loving my ageing body, remain untroubled'.
 that fell arrest the arrival of death, seen as an officer coming to apprehend a criminal; *fell* = fierce, terrible, as in 'one fell swoop', *Mac* 4.3.219.

2 **Without all bail** without any possibility of release from prison

3 **in . . . interest** some right of possession or continued residence in the line of verse which you read: for *interest* cf. 'where life hath no more interest but to breathe', *AYL* 5.1.8. Though *line* might also suggest the thread of human life spun by the Fates, or the *line* of offspring, neither seems applicable here.

5 **reviewest** survey, or resurvey
 review see once more

6 **very part** true portion: cf. 'thou art all the better part of me', 39.2.

7 **The earth . . . earth** 'We therefore commit his body to the ground, earth to earth, ashes to ashes, dust to dust', The Order for the Burial of the Dead, *BCP*, 310.

9–11 The three metaphorical phrases *the dregs, The prey,* and *The coward con-*

quest all describe *my body being dead.*

9 **the . . . life** literalizes *spirit* in the previous line, treating death as a process of distillation in which the physical body is left behind as *dregs*

11 A much-discussed line: momentarily it may seem that the poet anticipates self-slaughter, but it is more likely that the *wretch* whose sharp implement has taken possession of the speaker's body is personified death, seen in ll. 1–2 as a relentless officer carrying the dead man to judgement, and now as a ruthless assassin. However, the tone is confusing, both because it is not clear whether *coward* applies chiefly to the terror of the dying man or to the 'cowardly' attack made on him, and because elsewhere Shakespeare often uses *wretch* in terms of pity or tenderness; cf., e.g., *VA* 680, *Oth* 3.3.90, *KL* 3.4.28.

12 **remembered** rememberèd: = (a) recollected; (b) brought back to life, with the bodily 'members' put together again

13–14 The distinction between *that* (body due to be destroyed by death) and *this* (poem that you are reading) is developed from ll. 1 and 5, and here, because of the threefold repetition of *that* and twofold repetition of *this,* produces an effect of quickfire quibbling, with *this* ultimately cracked open to reveal its underlying relationship with *thee.*

74

But be contented when that fell arrest
Without all bail shall carry me away;
My life hath in this line some interest,
Which for memorial still with thee shall stay.
When thou reviewest this, thou dost review   5
The very part was consecrate to thee;
The earth can have but earth, which is his due,
My spirit is thine, the better part of me;
So then thou hast but lost the dregs of life,
The prey of worms, my body being dead,   10
The coward conquest of a wretch's knife,
Too base of thee to be remembered:
    The worth of that, is that which it contains,
    And that is this, and this with thee remains.

10 prey] pray   12 Too] To

75 This sonnet sustains a metaphor of the friend's image and presence as nourishment to the poet, in relation to which he alternately starves and feasts.

1 **as food to life** equivalent to the nourishment which sustains (human) life

2 **sweet seasoned showers** suggests both showers that fall in a 'sweet season', spring, and, continuing the metaphor of eating, showers which are 'sweetly seasoned', delicious in flavour

3 'in order to attain the peace which is embodied in you I engage in such conflict': the odd expression *peace of you* supports a pun, which extends the metaphor of hunger and anticipates that of money, on 'piece of you'. According to Booth (263) 'This line passes all understanding'.

6 **Doubting** fearing that; cf. 'I doubt some danger does approach you nearly', *Mac* 4.2.67.

8 **Then bettered** elliptical: may suggest 'then bettering that *best* in the desire . . . '; or, as Booth (263) has it, 'made better, made happier'

9 **Sometime** at times; cf. 18.5.

10 **clean** utterly, wholly (*OED adv.* 5b) **starved** starvèd

11 **Possessing or pursuing** anticipates the depiction of sexual desire in 129.9, 'Mad in pursuit, and in possession so'

12 **must . . . took** must be derived from you in the future; or, can be derived from you alone

13 **pine and surfeit** suffer from too little food or too much

14 **Or** either **all** The young man is the speaker's *all*; cf. 31.14, 40.1, 109.14, 112.5.

75

So are you to my thoughts as food to life,
Or as sweet seasoned showers are to the ground;
And for the peace of you I hold such strife
As 'twixt a miser and his wealth is found:
Now proud as an enjoyer, and anon   5
Doubting the filching age will steal his treasure;
Now counting best to be with you alone,
Then bettered that the world may see my pleasure;
Sometime all full with feasting on your sight,
And by and by clean starved for a look,   10
Possessing or pursuing no delight
Save what is had, or must from you be took.
   Thus do I pine and surfeit day by day,
   Or gluttoning on all, or all away.

2 sweet seasoned] sweet season'd *Q;* sweet-season'd *Malone*   8 bettered] betterd *Q;* better *Capell*
9 Sometime] *Ard¹;* Some-time *Q*   14 away.] away,

76 Apologizing for the stylistic mono-
tony of his verse, the poet ascribes this
to the constancy of his affection and
its object. The sonnet resumes the
theme of 38 (which is 38 sonnets further back), where the *sweet argument*
of the youth was expected to inspire
unlimited *invention*.

1 **barren of** deficient in, lacking

4 To new literary styles and unusual
combinations (of genre, types of
rhetoric, or poetic diction): *OED* cites
this line under 'compound' *sb.* 2c,
defining it as 'A compound word, a
verbal compound'. Shakespeare himself may be glancing aside at
Drayton's ongoing revision and
republication of his sonnet sequence
Idea, originally published in 1594, but
appearing in extensively revised and
expanded versions in 1599, 1600, 1602
and 1605 (see Introduction, pp.
14–15); or Daniel's revised and
expanded sonnet sequence *Delia* in
1601–2. According to Drayton's editors, 'In his new sonnets [Drayton]
emphasizes his difference from other
sonneteers . . . and his lighthearted
readiness to experiment, to range
sportively "in all Humors", "wilde,
madding, jocond, & irreguler"'
(Drayton, 5.138–9).

5 **Why . . . one** Why do I persist in
writing in the same manner?
However, *all one* may also anticipate
alone in 79.2; the poet writes in isolation as well as in a solipsistic style.

6 **a noted weed** a distinctive, recognizable garb or livery: a metaphor for a
characteristic literary style

7 In his poem prefixed to the First Folio
Jonson stressed the distinctive and
authentic character of the lines
Shakespeare fathered: 'Looke how the
fathers face / Liues in his issue, euen

so, the race / Of *Shakespeares* minde,
and manners brightly shines / In his
well torned, and true-filed lines'
(Jonson, 8.392).
*tell Q's 'fel' is probably one of
Compositor B's errors of reversal, in
this case the result of a confusion
between 't' and 'f'; cf. 73.4n.

8 **their** that of his words, considered
collectively

9 **of** about, concerning: cf. Lat. *de*; there
is also a suggestion that what he writes
derives directly from the youth.

10 **argument** subject-matter; with a
subsidiary suggestion of contention
or dispute between *you and love*: cf.
thy lovely argument, 79.5.

11 **all my best** the best I can do
dressing . . . new rearranging old
words, or ornamenting old words to
make them seem like new ones; continues the clothing metaphor of ll.
7–8, in which words are personified as
children dressed in their parent's livery

12 suggests that his words are like old
coins, capable of supporting repeated
transactions, or like sexual emissions
from an almost-exhausted source; cf.,
4.1–2n.

13 The identification of the poet's verse
and its subject-matter with the sun's
cycle simultaneously elevates the
youth and makes him sound tedious;
there may be an association also
between iterative 'sonnets' and iterative 'suns'.

14 **still . . . told** suggests both the
repeated relation of an old narrative
and the repeated counting (*telling*) of
a hoard of coins. The close links with
sonnet 38, with which 76 shares both
a general subject and four key words,
invention, sweet, write and *argument*,
also reinforce the notion of repetition.

76

Why is my verse so barren of new pride,
So far from variation or quick change?
Why with the time do I not glance aside
To new-found methods and to compounds strange?
Why write I still all one, ever the same,   5
And keep invention in a noted weed,
That every word almost doth tell my name,
Showing their birth, and where they did proceed?
O know, sweet love, I always write of you,
And you and love are still my argument: 10
So all my best is dressing old words new,
Spending again what is already spent:
　　For as the sun is daily new and old,
　　So is my love still telling what is told.

1 pride,] pride?   4 new-found] new found   7 tell] *Capell;* fel *Q*   13 sun] Sun

77 As if to reinforce his self-description as a monotonous and old-fashioned poet in the previous sonnet, the speaker deploys the hackneyed figure of *correlatio*, much used by Sidney, and popular in sonnets of the early 1590s; it was parodied by Sir John Davies in the fifth of his 'Gullinge Sonnets' (Davies, 165–6, 392). Taking three objects, a mirror, a timepiece and a notebook, he defines three processes by means of which the youth may achieve self-improvement, culminating in his illumination from the perusal of his own words. Though it has often been suggested that the poem is designed to accompany three gifts, or a gadget incorporating all three, there is no clear indication of this, and the echo of *thy glass* in 3.1 counts against the notion. Metaphorically, all three may be found in *Son* itself, which offers an admonitory image of the youth, a chronicle of his subjection to time and pages which await his annotation.

    At this, the half-way point in the total of 154 sonnets, it appears that the poet is relinquishing his own pen in favour of that of his beloved.

1   *wear Though Charles Gildon's emendation of Q's 'were' (Rollins, 1.198) has been adopted, yielding the sense 'wear out, endure the on-slaughts of time', there is no doubt also a sense of 'once were': 'looking at how your beauties are now will remind you painfully of how they used to be'.

2   dial probably a portable, and mechanical, clock or watch, as in *AYL* 2.7.20, rather than a sundial, which would not be a personal possession with the same intimacy

    waste are spent, pass away, with a subsidiary sense of 'are squandered'

3   vacant leaves (a) the blank pages of a notebook; (b) white spaces in *Son* which await annotation by the beloved: the speaker's capacity for self-denigration may extend to the description of pages with his own sonnets on them as *vacant*.

4   this book The natural presumption on first reading is that *this book* = the volume *Son*, as in *this*, 74.5, 14; but whether the reference is to *Son* or to a blank notebook, it becomes apparent in ll. 11–14 that the youth is to be instructed by his own writings, not the poet's.

5   While sonnet 3 ('Look in thy glass . . . ') suggested that the youth's mirror would show him youthful perfection, with *wrinkles* in l. 12 a future hazard, it appears that time has elapsed, for the speaker is now in no doubt that he will see wrinkles, which are *truly* reflected.

6   mouthed graves graves which are wide open in readiness to devour the youth, like the grave which 'doth gape' in readiness to swallow Falstaff (*2H4* 5.5.57); cf. also 'What is thy body but a swallowing grave?', *VA* 757.

    mouthed mouthèd

    memory a reminder (*Glossary*, 1); a *memento mori*

7   dial's shady stealth Though this image has been used to support an interpretation of 'dial' as a sundial, casting a varying shadow, it applies equally well to the slow movement of the hands of a mechanical clock or watch which cast a shadow on the face. In either case the indicator of time moves 'stealthily' as it 'steals' each successive moment, but a clock, with its pair of hands, is more anthropomorphic in theft.

8   Time's thievish progress Cf. 'the pilot's glass / Hath told the thievish minutes how they pass', *AW* 2.1.164–5. Time, the 'ceaseless lackey to eternity' (*Luc* 967), moves forward by stealing from the present moment.

6   memory here used in the sense of 'power of recall'

10 *waste blanks The conventional emendation of Q's 'blacks', based on a plausible supposition that the MS used a contraction sign for 'n', has been adopted with some reluctance. Reading (b) of l. 3 permits the description of pages of *Son*, though marked

77

Thy glass will show thee how thy beauties wear,
Thy dial how thy precious minutes waste,
The vacant leaves thy mind's imprint will bear,
And of this book, this learning mayst thou taste:
The wrinkles which thy glass will truly show   5
Of mouthed graves will give thee memory;
Thou by thy dial's shady stealth mayst know
Time's thievish progress to eternity;
Look what thy memory cannot contain,
Commit to these waste blanks, and thou shalt find   10
Those children nursed, delivered from thy brain,
To take a new acquaintance of thy mind.
    These offices, so oft as thou wilt look,
    Shall profit thee, and much enrich thy book.

with *black lines* (63.13), as *waste*, containing nothing of value until they bear the impress of the youth's reflections on his own image.

11 'your own thoughts, born from your brain and nourished by further contemplation': the placing of *nursed* before *delivered* 'may have been prompted by Shakespeare's desire to stress the idea that what the mind gives it also receives' (Booth, 268).

12 **a new acquaintance** Reading the written version of his thoughts, he will encounter them afresh.

13 **offices** functions, duties: presumably

refers, not just to writing and reading, but to the threefold stages of self-contemplation proposed in ll. 1–4, all of which entail *looking*.

14 will promote your moral improvement, and add to the value of your (note)book: a tritely predictable admonition; however, if the allusion is not to a blank notebook, but to the youth's *book* of his friend's sonnets, a more complex suggestion is made that the value of the book called *Shakespeare's Sonnets* derives, not from what the poet has written, but from the (written) response to it of the youth.

1 wear] *Capell (Gildon);* were *Q*   2 minutes] mynuits   3 The] *Q, Ard¹;* These *Capell*   10 blanks] *Capell;* blacks *Q*   11 nursed] nurst   delivered] deliuerd   14 enrich] inrich

78 Continuing the enlargement of poetic self-awareness initiated in 76, the speaker claims that his celebration of the youth as his (male) Muse has provoked many other writers to invoke him as their patron; he appeals to the young man to cherish his poems most, because his dependence on him is most absolute.

2   **fair assistance** suggests both favourable help as a patron, and the directly inspiring quality of the fair youth's beauty

3   **alien** The italicization and capitalization of this word in Q appears to underline the 'alienness', or otherness, of the rival writers. The word primarily suggests 'foreign' or 'immigrant' (*OED* 1a, 3a), but is here presumably figurative (*OED* 2). It might, however, suggest a pen employed, learnedly, in translating *alien*, i.e. non-English, writings.
    got my use appropriated my custom (of invoking you as my Muse)

4   **under . . . disperse** distribute their poems under your patronage; dispersal could take the form of manuscript circulation or printing or both.

5–8 **taught . . . majesty** traces a fourfold process of amelioration, with two negatives positived and two forms of talent enhanced: the dumb sing; the ignorant are raised up; the learned are made more so; grace and dignity are enhanced.

5   **taught . . . sing** taught those previously dumb to sing *high*, or compose 'lofty' verses: could apply both to the original inspiration afforded by the

youth to the poet, and to his subsequent inspiration of others. If 'Mr. W.H.' (Dedication, l. 3) is William Herbert, there could be an allusion to Captain Tobias Hume, *The First Part of Ayres* (1605), dedicated to William Herbert by a soldier who claims to lack eloquence, yet translates songs and composes airs.

7   suggests both the process of 'imping' feathers on to birds' wings in falconry, and the reinforcement of the goose quill which is the instrument of writing

9   **compile** compose: cf. 'Longaville / Did never sonnet for her sake compile', *LLL* 4.3.131–2; and *OED* 3.

10 **Whose . . . thine** The poems the speaker writes are wholly inspired by the addressee.

11 **mend** improve; cf. 103.9.

12 'Your graciousness (or gracefulness) adds lustre to manifestations of literary skill'; a further layer is added if the addressee is a nobleman who may at times be addressed as 'your grace', and/or consorts with other such *graces*, though this term is correctly applied only to those of ducal rank or above (*OED* grace 16b).
    graced gracèd

13 **thou art . . . art** Cf. Sidney, *AS*, 64.14, 'Thou art my wit, and thou my virtue art', with a similar play on *art* = you are / *art* = literary skill.

14 The speaker is the least learned or lofty of all those who address the youth, but because of his primacy in invoking the youth he is elevated to the level of the most learned.

78

So oft have I invoked thee for my Muse,
And found such fair assistance in my verse,
As every alien pen hath got my use,
And under thee their poesy disperse.
Thine eyes, that taught the dumb on high to sing,   5
And heavy ignorance aloft to fly,
Have added feathers to the learned's wing,
And given grace a double majesty.
Yet be most proud of that which I compile,
Whose influence is thine, and born of thee: 10
In others' works thou dost but mend the style,
And arts with thy sweet graces graced be;
    But thou art all my art, and dost advance,
    As high as learning, my rude ignorance.

---

1 invoked] inuok'd   3 alien] *Alien*   8 majesty] Maiestie   10 born] borne   12 arts] Arts

79 Continuing his discussion of other poets who celebrate the fair youth, the speaker argues that the other writer needs no thanks, for the merit of his writing derives entirely from the merit of its subject. The strained logic of the poem resembles the chop-logic of Shakespeare's jesters when they seek to displace rival aspirants to favour.

2 (a) My poetry enjoyed the exclusive benefit of your patronage; (b) my writings alone encompassed the topic of your nobility and favour.

3 **gracious numbers** verses elevated by your *grace*
are decayed suggests both that the poetry has lost its lustre because of the wider diffusion of the youth's favour, and that it is old and ailing (as in *sick Muse*, next line); also, possibly,

that the *numbers* – numerals – of the sonnets themselves, post-70, bespeak decadence

4 **give another place** cede room to another Muse, or poet

5 **thy lovely argument** the beautiful subject-matter which is yourself

7 **of thee** about you, concerning you: chiastic reversal of the phrase in the second foot of the succeeding line (*thee of*) enacts the notion of bestowing what is lent.

11 **in thy cheek** synecdoche for the beauty of the youth's whole form, as in 68.1
afford supply, furnish; with a play on 'have the means, bear the expense', since the poet owes all his rhetorical wealth to his subject (*OED* 7, 3)

14 **owes thee** is obliged to furnish you with

79

Whilst I alone did call upon thy aid
My verse alone had all thy gentle grace;
But now my gracious numbers are decayed,
And my sick Muse doth give another place.
I grant, sweet love, thy lovely argument   5
Deserves the travail of a worthier pen;
Yet what of thee thy poet doth invent
He robs thee of, and pays it thee again;
He lends thee virtue, and he stole that word
From thy behaviour; beauty doth he give,   10
And found it in thy cheek; he can afford
No praise to thee, but what in thee doth live:
    Then thank him not for that which he doth say,
    Since what he owes thee, thou thyself dost pay.

---

3 decayed] decayde   5 grant, sweet love,] grant (sweet loue)   7 poet] Poet

80 Acknowledging the superiority of the 'rival poet', the speaker pleads for his generous patron at least to recognize the value of his love, as in 32.14. The contrast between himself and his rival is shown in terms of the contrast between the small, mobile ships used by the English at the time of the Spanish Armada and the larger, more impressive and more heavily armed Spanish galleons; cf. *Armada*, 236.

1 **faint** quail, lose heart (*OED* 1)

2 **a better spirit** suggests both a superior being and a more inspired writer, supported by a more powerful *spirit* than the *sick Muse* of 79.4
use may have some adverse connotations, suggesting 'exploit', or even 'consume', as well as 'cite'

4 **To . . . tongue-tied** suggests destructive competitiveness, as if the *better spirit* is as much concerned to silence his rival as to exalt his patron

5 **wide . . . is** which is as wide as the ocean: for the identification of a noble or royal person with the sea, cf. *Luc* 652, ' "Thou art", quoth she, "a sea, a sovereign king" '; or Daniel's *Delia* (1592), 1.1–2: 'Unto the boundless Ocean of thy beautie / Runs this poore river, charg'd with streames of zeale.' See also *AC* 3.12.7–9.

7 **saucy bark** small boat which is presumptuous, insolent towards a superior

8 **broad main** wide expanse of water; cf. 64.7 and n.
wilfully reinforces *saucy*, suggesting a capricious, thoughtless venturousness

9 Being a lightweight vessel, the speaker needs only minimal support from his ocean-like patron.

10 **soundless** deep beyond 'sounding'; but also 'noiseless'
ride often used of ships moving on water; cf. 137.6; also *R3* 4.4.434; *Per* 4.4.31, 5.1.18.

11 **I . . . boat** I am (only) a worthless vessel, not deserving of rescue or support.

12 **tall building** lofty structure, like that of the most advanced galleons of the period
pride self-assurance; splendour

14 **my love . . . decay** primarily, 'I was destroyed because of my devotion to you'; but secondarily, if *my love* is taken to refer to the object rather than the emotion, 'the person I love let me down'. This, it would then be implied, was his *worst* affliction.

80

O how I faint when I of you do write,
Knowing a better spirit doth use your name,
And in the praise thereof spends all his might,
To make me tongue-tied speaking of your fame.
But since your worth, wide as the ocean is,   5
The humble as the proudest sail doth bear,
My saucy bark, inferior far to his,
On your broad main doth wilfully appear.
Your shallowest help will hold me up afloat,
Whilst he upon your soundless deep doth ride;   10
Or, being wracked, I am a worthless boat,
He of tall building, and of goodly pride.
    Then if he thrive, and I be cast away,
    The worst was this: my love was my decay.

---

5 worth, wide . . . is,] worth (wide . . . is)   ocean] Ocean   7 bark, inferior . . . his,] bark (inferior
. . . his)   9 afloat] a floate   11 Or, being wracked,] Or (being wrackt)   13 if] If

81 After 'fourscore', a figure associated with extreme old age (cf. Psalm 90.10; *KL* 4.7.61), as after 'threescore and ten', the speaker anticipates his death, but this time includes the possibility that his friend may pre-decease him. When the poet dies, he will be quickly forgotten; but when the youth dies, he will continue to live as the subject-matter of the poet's verse. The paradoxical claim that *Son* will be remembered for its subject-matter (the fair youth), not for its author, is here taken to its furthest extremes.

1–2 Or . . . Or whether . . . or

1 your . . . make to pen your epitaph; to survive as your living epitaph

3 your memory the memory of you

4 in me in my case
each part includes the sense 'each gift', suggesting a reference to the speaker's poetic skill (cf. *OED* part 12)

5 from hence henceforward; from here, the sonnet sequence we are in the middle of reading

6 to . . . world to the whole of posterity; to all outward appearance

7 a common grave an ordinary grave; a grave shared with others. The fact that Shakespeare was buried in an honorific position in the chancel of Holy Trinity Church, Stratford, is not, as has been suggested, especially ironical (Brown and Feavor, 27 ff.), for the contrast here is between any physical form of burial and the living monument of verse.

8 entombed entombèd
lie At first it seems that *lie*, rather than 'live', has been chosen to rhyme with *die*; but the oddity of 'lying' may

be deliberate, especially given the plays with lies and lying in later sonnets, such as 138. The youth will die in men's eyes, rather than live in them, for he will be seen as in a recumbent effigy ; and he may also be falsely represented in them.

9 my gentle verse The suggestion may be that the noble subject makes the (low-born) poet's verse *gentle* in the sense of 'gentlemanly'; also there is an implied contrast between the earthy grave that entombs the poet and the *gentle*, or tender, solicitous, containment of the youth in language (*OED* gentle 1a, 6, 8). Jonson famously applied the epithet to Shakespeare himself in the poem 'To the Reader facing the title-page of the First Folio': 'This Figure, that thou here seest put, / It was for gentle Shakespeare cut' (Jonson, 8.390).

11 tongues to be tongues of people yet to be, not yet born
rehearse repeat, re-enact

12 all . . . world all those at present alive; cf. 'I will chide no breather in the world but myself', *AYL* 3.2.297.

13 such . . . pen such power or efficacy is in my writing; with a subsidiary suggestion that the writing celebrates moral *virtue*. The first reading is hard to square with the assertion in l. 4 that the pen's wielder will be instantly *forgotten*.

14 breath suggests both the breath that distinguishes a living body from a dead one, and the 'breath' of rumour or fame; for the second sense, cf. *TC* 1.3.244.

81

Or I shall live, your epitaph to make;
Or you survive, when I in earth am rotten;
From hence your memory death cannot take,
Although in me each part will be forgotten.
Your name from hence immortal life shall have,   5
Though I, once gone, to all the world must die;
The earth can yield me but a common grave,
When you entombed in men's eyes shall lie.
Your monument shall be my gentle verse,
Which eyes not yet created shall o'er-read,   10
And tongues to be your being shall rehearse,
When all the breathers of this world are dead.
    You still shall live, such virtue hath my pen,
    Where breath most breathes, even in the mouths
        of men.

---

1 epitaph] Epitaph   5 I, once gone,] I (once gone)   8 entombed] intombed   13 live, such . . . pen,]
liue (such . . . Pen)

273

82 At first acknowledging that the youth
is not obliged to read one poet only,
the speaker suggests that the more
elaborate forms of verse used by others may better express the young
man's excellence; but then claims that,
since he needs no flattery, he is best
celebrated in his own plain style.

1 **grant** concede, acknowledge

2 **attaint** disgrace, moral infection; cf.
Luc 825.
o'erlook examine, peruse; cf. *TGV*
1.2.50.

3 the words used by writers in dedicating their works to you; also the works
themselves

4 **Of . . . subject** concerning their
excellent subject-matter, yourself; cf.
lovely argument, 79.5.
blessing which blesses, bestows
benefits on

5 **hue** external appearance, colour
(*OED* 1, 2, 3a); cf. 20.7 and n.

6 **a . . . praise** 'an area extending
beyond my capacity to praise it in
verse': for *limit* as 'extensive region',
cf. 44.4 and n.

8 some newer creation (with a suggestion, in *stamp*, of a newly printed
book) which is the product of recent,
improved times: *time-bettering days*
suggests 'times or fashions which
improve on the old days'. But as
Booth (280–1) suggests, there may be
a touch of irony because of the simi-

larity of the phrase to 'time-serving'
or 'time-pleasing'. If compound epithets are thought of as the distinguishing mark of more fashionable
poets (cf. *compounds strange*, 76.4
and n.), there is a touch of insouciant display in the use of such an epithet to
describe their activities.

9 **do so love** and accordingly, or in
these terms, you love the *dedicated
words* of the other poets; or, you have
my permission to love in this way.

10 **strained touches** 'artificial devices
or conceits'; with suggestions of a
painter's brush-strokes, in anticipation of *painting* in l. 1 of the following
sonnet
strained strainèd

11 **sympathized** '(presented in) a perfectly matching or corresponding
manner' (*OED* sympathize 3b); cf.
'True sorrow then is feelingly suffic'd
/ When with like semblance it is sym-
pathiz'd' (*Luc* 1113).

13 **gross painting** excessive, inappro-
priately profuse rhetoric, with suggestions of flattery

14 **Where . . . blood** to elevate individuals who lack beauty; the youth's *cheek*
is frequently used as a synecdoche for
the beauty of his entire body: cf.67.5,
68.1, 79.1, 99.4.
in . . . abused with reference to you,
such rhetoric is misapplied; your taste
for it is inappropriate

82

I grant thou wert not married to my Muse,
And therefore mayst without attaint o'erlook
The dedicated words which writers use
Of their fair subject, blessing every book.
Thou art as fair in knowledge as in hue,   5
Finding thy worth a limit past my praise,
And therefore art enforced to seek anew
Some fresher stamp of the time-bettering days,
And do so love; yet when they have devised
What strained touches rhetoric can lend,   10
Thou, truly fair, wert truly sympathized
In true plain words, by thy true-telling friend;
    And their gross painting might be better used
    Where cheeks need blood; in thee it is abused.

5 hue] hew   8 time-bettering] time bettering   days,] dayes   9 devised] deuisde   10 rhetoric] Rhethorick
11 sympathized] simpathizde   12 true-telling] true telling   13 used] vs'd   14 abused] abus'd

83 Following immediately on the end of the previous sonnet, the speaker claims that he has refrained from applying rhetorical praises to the youth's beauty, but should not be reproached for this, since the young man's living excellence transcends any words used of it.

1–2 painting . . . painting primarily suggests 'falsely profuse rhetoric', as in the *gross painting* of 82.13; but may also denote, more broadly, 'description or delineation'

2 fair fairness, beauty; cf. 18.7; *LLL* 4.1.17.
set applied

3 or . . . found Presumably the speaker questions his previous belief that the youth needed no flattery because he has now been rebuked for his *silence*, as in l. 9.

4 'the sterile or worthless benefit that a writer has to offer': *debt* accommodates both an acknowledgement that the present poet ought to have 'painted' his friend, and a sense that such an activity would have been merely dutiful, not an expression of true feeling.

5 slept . . . report have been ineffectual, inactive in describing you (cf. *OED* sleep 4a)

6 That so that

7 a modern quill an ordinary, commonplace style of writing; cf. 'wise saws and modern instances', *AYL* 2.7.156. 'Trite', rather than 'recent or contemporary', is Shakespeare's usual

application of *modern*; cf. *OED* 4.

7–8 too . . . of worth The inevitability of literary praise falling short of the youth's excellence is reinforced by the syntactical brevity of the clause, in which we would expect 'short *of* . . . '.

8 grow suggests not only that written descriptions of the youth's excellence fall short, but that the excellence itself may be burgeoning or increasing, rendering description obsolete

9 impute consider, regard

10 Which my *silence*: behind ll. 9–10 may lie a recollection of Sidney's *AS*, 54.13–14: 'Dumb swans, not chattering pies, do lovers prove; / They love indeed, who quake to say they love.'

11 Since I am silent, I do not misrepresent or damage your beauty.

12 When whereas
others . . . tomb In seeking to evoke your living beauty in verse, the other poets kill it. The speaker now assigns to other writers the role he attributed to his own verse in 17.3, where he called it *but . . . a tomb*. Cf. *Cor* 4.7.51–3.

14 both your poets does not necessarily indicate that there is only one 'rival poet', for Shakespeare sometimes uses *both* to govern three or more objects, as in *VA* 747 and *1H6* 5.5.107 (and cf. *OED* B 1b); however, in combination with 'one of your fair eyes' it implies that even two poets per eye would not be enough.

83

I never saw that you did painting need,
And therefore to your fair no painting set;
I found (or thought I found) you did exceed
The barren tender of a poet's debt;
And therefore have I slept in your report,   5
That you yourself, being extant, well might show
How far a modern quill doth come too short,
Speaking of worth, what worth in you doth grow.
This silence for my sin you did impute,
Which shall be most my glory, being dumb;   10
For I impair not beauty, being mute,
When others would give life, and bring a tomb.
    There lives more life in one of your fair eyes
    Than both your poets can in praise devise.

4 poet's] Poets   14 poets] Poets

84 This sonnet continues the discussion of whether the youth is best praised in the speaker's supposedly plain terms, or the elaborate rhetoric of others. Though he makes a case for plain style, he undercuts it with an allegation that the youth himself has a weakness for flattery.

1–4 Booth (284) calls these four lines 'a stylistic palimpsest'. However, if Malone's insertion of a question mark after *most* is accepted, the remaining three and a half lines yield a reasonably coherent sense: 'Which (of the poets competing to praise the fair youth) can say more than that you are uniquely and splendidly yourself, and that within you alone the fountain and archetype (*store*) of worth is contained (*immured*) which alone offers a simile which can match you in excellence? That is, you can be compared only with yourself: any other comparison fails to do you justice.' There may be a reminiscence of Sidney, *AS*, 35.1–2: 'What may words say, or what may words not say, / Where truth itself must speak like flattery?' Also, the phrase *rich praise* could allude covertly to Sidney's many plays on 'rich' in *AS*, as in 35.11.

3 **immured** immurèd

5 the play on *pen* and *penury* reinforces an allusion to the commonplace idea that 'learning and poverty will ever kiss' (cf. Marlowe, *Hero and Leander*, 469: *Poems*, 26). However, the primary

reference here is to poverty of invention, as in 103.1.

8 **so** in so doing
dignifies his story elevates his writing, makes it worthy of you

9 Cf. Sidney, *AS*, 3.12–14: 'in Stella's face I read / What love and beauty be; then all my deed / But copying is, what in her nature writes'.

10 **clear** lucid; beautiful (*OED* 8, 3c)

11 **counterpart** 'A person or thing so answering to another as to appear a duplicate or exact copy of it' (*OED* 3; no example offered before 1680): apparently used here as a synonym of 'counterfeit'
fame his wit make his poetic skill famous

12 **admired** admirèd

13 **You** Presumably the addressee here, as in ll. 2–4, is the fair youth, rather than the poet who celebrates him.

14 **fond on** foolishly eager for, desirous of
makes . . . worse The desire you have for praise is a weakness which undermines the praise you receive; or, because of your weakness for being praised, the praise you receive is specious, flattering rhetoric, not the plain statement 'That you are you' recommended by the present poet. The conclusion is strongly reminiscent of *KL* 1.1.36–106, in which Cordelia, who loves her father most, is least able to gratify his desire for flattery.

84

Who is it that says most? Which can say more,
Than this rich praise: that you alone are you,
In whose confine immured is the store
Which should example where your equal grew?
Lean penury within that pen doth dwell   5
That to his subject lends not some small glory;
But he that writes of you, if he can tell
That you are you, so dignifies his story.
Let him but copy what in you is writ,
Not making worse what nature made so clear,   10
And such a counterpart shall fame his wit,
Making his style admired everywhere.
    You to your beauteous blessings add a curse,
    Being fond on praise, which makes your praises
       worse.

---

1 most?] *Malone;* most, *Q*   5 pen] Pen   11 counterpart] counter-part

85 Still playing the Cordelia role, the
speaker concedes and confirms the
glorious praises voiced by a rival poet,
but claims that his own silent, inter-
nalized devotion merits equal favour.
There are further echoes here of
Sidney's *AS*, especially of 54, with the
same paradox that the reader is asked
to accept a carefully elaborated sonnet
as an image of inarticulate love.

1 **in . . . still** out of courtesy maintains
her silence: though the primary suggestion of *in manners* is that the speaker's Muse is showing deference to the
rival poet, there may also be an implication that the other's elaborate language is not 'mannerly'; and *still* suggests not only 'in silence' but 'in
continuance'.

2 **comments . . . praise** expositions of
or commentaries on your praisewor-
thy qualities, possibly in the form of
illustrative matter rather than the central text (cf. *OED* comment 1, 3).
compiled collected into a volume or
treatise (*OED* 1)

3 *****Reserve your character** retain,
preserve your appearance, demeanour:
for this sense of *reserve*, cf. *Son* 32.7,
MM 5.1.467; for *character* cf. *MM*
1.2.151. Pooler's suggested emendation of Q's 'their' to *thy* (Ard¹) has
been rejected in favour of 'your' (RP).
golden quill suggests a beautifully
elaborate, 'aureate', style of writing

4 **precious phrase** following on from
golden, denoting language of the
utmost value. The adverse literary

application of the word, following Fr.
précieux, as 'affected, over-refined',
was not current until the mid seventeenth century.

5 **other** others

6 **unlettered clerk** The function of the
parish clerk was to lead the congrega-
tion in responses and 'amens': cf. *R2*
4.1.172–3.

7 **hymn** song of praise, perhaps with a
pun on 'him' = 'every Tom, Dick or
Harry'
that . . . affords which that talented
genius lends to you; or, which is provided by poetic ingenuity interpreted
more broadly. The following sonnet,
with its reference to the *spirit* of a single writer, would support the first
reading.

8 **well-refined** well-refinèd: in the
sophisticated style produced by a
writer whose style is successfully
purified (cf. *OED* refine 1a and b; 3a);
there may also be a suggestion that the
writer's language has benefited from
immersion in such a *well* of inspiration as the youth.

10 **most** utmost

12 **holds . . . before** maintains first position in the hierarchy (of those who
love you)

13 **respect** love; esteem; cf. *TGV*
1.2.131.

14 **speaking in effect** which speak in
external action or in truth, rather than
in mere *breath of words*, which is here
treated as insubstantial and suspect:
cf. *OED* effect 8.

85

My tongue-tied Muse in manners holds her still,
While comments of your praise richly compiled
Reserve your character with golden quill,
And precious phrase by all the Muses filed;
I think good thoughts, whilst other write good words, 5
And like unlettered clerk still cry 'Amen'
To every hymn that able spirit affords
In polished form of well-refined pen.
Hearing you praised, I say,' 'Tis so,'tis true',
And to the most of praise add something more;   10
But that is in my thought, whose love to you
(Though words come hindmost) holds his rank before;
   Then others for the breath of words respect,
   Me for my dumb thoughts, speaking in effect.

---

2 compiled] compil'd,   3 your] *this edn.* (RP) their *Q*   thy *Ard¹ conj.* character] Character   4 filed]
fil'd   7 hymn] Himne   8 well-refined] well refined   9 praised] prais'd   10 something] some-thing
12 hindmost] hind-most

86 Undaunted by the splendour of his rival's verses, the speaker quails only at his appropriation of the young man's favour. The imagery of 80, in which the addressee offers an *ocean* of favour to those who are able to navigate it, is here resumed; and both sonnets are paralleled in Thomas Fuller's account of Shakespeare and Jonson in his *Worthies of England* (1662), 126: 'Many were the *wit-combates* betwixt him and *Ben Johnson*, which two I behold like a *Spanish great Gallion*, and an *English man of War* ; Master *Johnson* (like the former) was built far higher in Learning; *Solid*, but *Slow* in his performances. *Shake-spear* with the *English-man of War*, lesser in *bulk*, but lighter in *sailing*, could turn with all tides, tack about and take advantage of all winds, by the quickness of his Wit and Invention.' Possibly Fuller alludes to these sonnets, and believed Jonson to be the chief 'rival poet'; or believed that some of Shakespeare's and Jonson's published writings (perhaps specifically the latter's *Epigrammes* (1616) and the former's *Sonnets)* reflect such an emulation. The 'wit-combats' need not have been oral, as Schoenbaum (*Lives*, 57) and others have assumed.

1 **the . . . verse** like the *tall building* and *goodly pride* attributed to the rival poet's vessel in 80.12, suggests a mighty ocean-going galleon, figuring an ambitious and perhaps highly elaborated form of verse

2 **Bound . . . prize** The image is of a privateer setting out for the Indies or elsewhere in the hope of capturing valuable booty.

3 As in the final line of the preceding sonnet, the speaker claims to be unable to voice his thoughts of love: they are ready for utterance (*ripe*), but remain buried (*in-hearsed*) in his brain because he is intimidated by his rival.

4 causing them to die even before they were born (uttered): the image of the brain as a *womb*, fairly common, also recalls Thorpe's identification of

Mr. W.H. as the sonnets' *only begetter* (Dedication, ll. 1–3).

5 **spirit** intellectual power, energy (*Glossary*, 2, 1)
spirits suggests supernatural beings, such as the *spirits* of dead writers; George Chapman, for instance, was inspired by Musaeus and Christopher Marlowe to complete the latter's *Hero and Leander* (1598) (cf. 3.123–198); and by Homer to translate the *Seaven Bookes of the Iliades* (1598), expanded into a twelve-book version in the winter of 1608/9. But the word could simply refer to the rival poet's own powerful *spirits*, or reserves of creative energy.

6 **mortal pitch** height attainable by mere mortals
struck me dead stunned me into (dead) silence (*OED* strike 46b): there seems to be a parallel to Touchstone's remark, sometimes taken as an allusion to the death of Marlowe, 'When a man's verses cannot be understood, nor a man's good wit seconded with the forward child, understanding, it strikes a man more dead than a great reckoning in a little room' (*AYL* 3.3.9–14).

7 **his . . . night** once taken as an allusion to the 'School of Night', a supposed coterie whose members included Ralegh, Chapman, Harriot and others (cf. Bradbrook): *compeers* = companions, associates. The implication is that the rival poet is dependent on the promptings of others for his creations.

8 **astonished** astonishèd: stunned, struck dumb with amazement (cf. *Luc* 1730)

9 **that . . . ghost** that benign and friendly guardian spirit (cf. *OED* familiar 2d, *familiar angel*). The phrase seems to carry an allusion to some well-known relationship between a poet and his Muse or inspiring genius, such as Chapman's with the spirit of Homer.

10 **gulls . . . intelligence** tricks him with (false) communications

86

Was it the proud full sail of his great verse,
Bound for the prize of all-too-precious you,
That did my ripe thoughts in my brain in-hearse,
Making their tomb the womb wherein they grew?
Was it his spirit, by spirits taught to write   5
Above a mortal pitch, that struck me dead?
No, neither he, nor his compeers by night,
Giving him aid, my verse astonished.
He, nor that affable familiar ghost
Which nightly gulls him with intelligence,   10
As victors of my silence cannot boast;
I was not sick of any fear from thence.
　　But when your countenance filled up his line,
　　Then lacked I matter, that enfeebled mine.

---

11 **victors . . . boast** (Those *spirits*) cannot claim to have been the cause of my (poetic) *silence.*

12 **sick of** sick because of; cf. *TN* 1.5.97, 'O, you are sick of self-love, Malvolio'.

13 **your countenance** your face; your favourable regard: the word has strong biblical associations with divine favour, as in Numbers, 6.26, 'The Lord lift up his countenance upon thee, and give thee peace.'
filled up suggests both a patronage which reinforces and strengthens the rival poet's *great verse*, and, resuming the sailing imagery of ll. 1–2, a favourable breath which 'fills' the sails of his project, as in Prospero's appeal for 'Gentle breath' (*Tem* Epilogue 11–12). Though Q's spelling 'fild' permits the reading 'filed' as polished, refined, as in l. 4 of the preceding sonnet, the *full sail* of l. 1 makes *filled* more probable; and a *countenance*, viewed as emitting light, warmth and breath, cannot readily be imagined as 'filing'.

14 **matter** substance, subject-matter (*OED* 11a)

2 all-too-precious] (all to precious) 3 in-hearse] inhearce 7 compeers] compiers 13 countenance] countinance filled] fild 14 lacked] lackt enfeebled] infeebled

87 Using legal and financial imagery, the
speaker relinquishes his claim to the
young man, which was based on a
misjudgement or *misprision*, the youth
having underestimated his own value
and overestimated that of the speaker.
The use of feminine rhymes in every
line except 2 and 4 draws attention to
the sonnet as unusual in form (cf. 20
and headnote), perhaps to mark a new
phase in the sequence: the rival poet is
forgotten, but all is not well with the
friends. There may be a structural
allusion to Sidney's *AS* 87, which, following four songs, initiates a phase of
sonnets on separation and misunder-
standing.

1 too . . . possessing a paradox: on an
emotional level = 'I love you so much
that I cannot keep you', undercut by
the financial sense, = 'you are too
valuable for someone of my lowly status'

2 estimate value, reputation (*Glossary*,
1 and 2); suggests both 'you know
your true value' and 'you know how
you are esteemed by others'

3 charter of thy worth privilege you
enjoy because of your merit; cf. the
similar application of *charter* in 58.9.
gives thee releasing entitles you to
free yourself (from me)

4 'all that binds me finds its limit or
terms of expiry in you': for *determinate* in this sense, cf. *OED* A. In a sonnet where every other rhyme is disyl-
labic the use of a monosyllabic rhyme
here reinforces a sense of severance.

6 riches suggesting 'a person of
immense value because so much
loved', cf. 'The riches of the ship is
come on shore', *Oth* 2.1.83.

7 The . . . gift the warrant for your
bestowing on me the beautiful gift of
yourself
wanting lacking; there is probably no
play on 'desiring', as Booth suggests,
since this sense is not recorded until
the early eighteenth century (cf. *OED*
wanting; want 5a).

8 patent privilege, right of ownership
swerving turning, deviating; here a

slightly strained application, the word
being partly dictated by the rhyme, to
suggest that the speaker's rights of
ownership have lapsed or become
void. The word is elsewhere associated with moral deviance: cf. *H5*
2.2.233; *AC* 3.11.50.

10 else probably governs *me* rather than
mistaking, the larger sense being 'you
gave yourself to me either in ignorance of your own worth, or else in
ignorance of my lack of worth'
mistaking misapprehending, mis-
judging; cf. *AYL* 1.3.64.

11 upon misprision growing coming
into existence as the result of a false
estimate

13 had thee possessed you, possibly
with sexual undertones ; cf. 129.10
(and *OED* have 14e).
flatter deceive, beguile with pleasing
illusion (*OED* 6, 7a and 7b): cf. 'For
now reviving joy bids her rejoice, /
And flatters her it is Adonis' voice'
(*VA* 976–7).

14 in . . . king primarily suggests that
the speaker has enjoyed intense happiness: cf. 'As merry (happy) as a king'
(Tilley, K54). Q's capitalized 'King'
could alternatively suggest that he has
enjoyed his presence in a way analogous to James I; or *king* could apply to
the addressee, elevated to kingly status, or the status of a specific King,
only by the speaker's imagination ; cf.
R2 5.1.1–9.
waking The internal rhyme on *a king*,
which also picks up *mistaking . . . making* from ll. 10 and 12, suggests a quib-
ble. Conceivably the elevenfold repetition of the particle *-ing* hints at
'ingle', = a boy favourite, a catamite
(*OED*); some such innuendo may also
be underlined by the 'feminine'
rhymes and the word *had* in the previous line. There may additionally or
alternatively be an allusion to
Shakespeare having acted kings; cf.
John Davies of Hereford, Epigram
159, 'To our English Terence Mr.
Will: Shake-speare': 'Some say (good
Will) which I, in sport, do sing, /

87

Farewell, thou art too dear for my possessing,
And like enough thou knowst thy estimate;
The charter of thy worth gives thee releasing;
My bonds in thee are all determinate.
For how do I hold thee but by thy granting,   5
And for that riches where is my deserving?
The cause of this fair gift in me is wanting,
And so my patent back again is swerving.
Thyself thou gav'st, thy own worth then not knowing,
Or me, to whom thou gav'st it, else mistaking;   10
So thy great gift upon misprision growing
Comes home again, on better judgement making.
    Thus have I had thee as a dream doth flatter,
    In sleep a king, but waking no such matter.

Had'st thou not plaid some kingly parts in sport, / Thou had'st bin a companion for a *King*; / And, beene a King among the meaner sort' (*The Scourge of Folly* (1611), 76–7).

3 charter] Charter   14 king] King

88 Continuing the theme of severance between the friends deriving from their disparity in value, the poet promises to endorse the young man's rejection of him by enumerating his own deficiencies, thus doubly affirming the young man's integrity.

1   **disposed . . . light** in a mood to think little of me

2   and look on my merits with a scornful eye, or cause others to do so

4   demonstrate your integrity or truthfulness, despite your false aspersions on my *merit*

6   **a story** a narration, a recital

7   **attainted** tainted, morally compromised; (rightfully) accused, as if in a court of law

8   **That** so that, with the consequence that
    losing me destroying my reputation;

cf. *OED* lose 1b, and example from *KL* 1.1.236: 'Such a tongue / That I am glad I have not, though not to have it / Hath lost me in your liking'.

11–12 Cf. *KL* 2.4.302–6: 'to wilful men / The injuries that they themselves procure / Must be their schoolmasters'.

12   In bestowing benefit on you, (this procedure) will doubly benefit me (in reinforcing your merits and so making you even more lovable).

13   **so** in such a manner, so utterly

14   In order to do the right thing by you, to affirm your *right* to be loved and admired, I will take all faults on to myself: recalls the self-abnegating denial of Shakespeare's heroines, such as Desdemona's 'Nobody, I myself, farewell' (*Oth* 5.2.125), or Cordelia's 'No cause, no cause' (*KL* 4.7.75).

88

When thou shalt be disposed to set me light
And place my merit in the eye of scorn,
Upon thy side, against myself, I'll fight,
And prove thee virtuous, though thou art forsworn:
With mine own weakness being best acquainted,   5
Upon thy part I can set down a story
Of faults concealed, wherein I am attainted,
That thou, in losing me, shall win much glory;
And I by this will be a gainer too,
For bending all my loving thoughts on thee,   10
The injuries that to myself I do,
Doing thee vantage, double vantage me:
    Such is my love, to thee I so belong,
    That for thy right myself will bear all wrong.

1 disposed] dispode *Q;* dispos'd *Benson*   7 concealed] conceald   8 losing] loosing   12 me:] me.

89 Continuing from the end of the previous sonnet, the speaker expands further on his willingness to assume the faults of which he is accused, and to be excluded therefore from the young man's company.

1 **Say that** if you claim that

2 **comment** enlarge, expatiate; or meditate, ponder (*OED* 2, 5); cf. 15.4.

3 Taken literally, this is evidence against, rather than for, Shakespeare's being lame, since it suggests that if charged with lameness he will feign it; however, as Booth suggests (293), the reference could equally well be to 'lame' verses, with defective 'feet'.

4 **reasons** statements, assertions; grounds for forsaking me (*Glossary*, 1, 2)

6 The line is rather obscure: probably, 'to find a formal cause for your desire to leave me'; 'by setting out the manner in which you would like me to change (for the better)'; or, 'to make the change which you want to see in me attractive'; cf. *MND* 1.1.232–3. **desired** desirèd.

7 **knowing thy will** knowing your determination to cast me off; with

perhaps a secondary suggestion of 'knowing your Will[iam Shakespeare], myself'

8 I will suppress my familiarity with you and behave as if I do not know you: *strange* = distant or cold in demeanour (*OED* 11; and cf. *TGV* 1.2.103).

9 **thy walks** the places where you walk; cf. *JC* 3.2.252.
in my tongue i.e. I shall not speak of you.

10 **beloved** belovèd

11 **profane** perhaps used in its root Lat. sense, 'standing outside a sacred place or temple'; also suggests, more broadly, 'unacceptable in good company', as in Henry V's dismissal of Falstaff as 'so surfeit-swelled, so old and so profane', *2H4* 5.5.54. The implication in the next line that he may unwisely speak 'of our old acquaintance' also recalls Falstaff.

12 **haply** possibly, or by chance or 'hap'; there may be some ironical sense also of '(un)happily'.

13 **vow debate** determine to engage in conflict

89

Say that thou didst forsake me for some fault,
And I will comment upon that offence;
Speak of my lameness, and I straight will halt,
Against thy reasons making no defence.
Thou canst not, love, disgrace me half so ill,   5
To set a form upon desired change,
As I'll myself disgrace, knowing thy will;
I will acquaintance strangle and look strange,
Be absent from thy walks, and in my tongue
Thy sweet beloved name no more shall dwell,   10
Lest I, too much profane, should do it wrong,
And haply of our old acquaintance tell.
    For thee, against myself I'll vow debate;
    For I must ne'er love him whom thou dost hate.

5 not, love,] not (loue)   11 I, too much profane,] I (too much prophane)

90 Following on from the end of the previous sonnet, the speaker urges his friend, if he must reject him, to do so now, while his fortunes are at a low ebb, so that his other misfortunes can dwindle in comparison to this overwhelming one.

1 **Then** in that case (*OED* 4a); but with some sense also of a temporal reference, picking up the *When* of 88.1: 'When (and if) you feel like repudiating me . . . let the time be now.'

2 **bent . . . cross** determined to frustrate everything I do. This sounds like a specific personal reference, but in default of external evidence we cannot hope to connect it with documented reverses.

3 **bow** give in, submit to the crushing blows of fortune

4 **drop . . . after-loss** descend on me with an additional blow after I have already received others: it has been thought that *drop in* might be a technical term from sport or warfare, but no convincing analogy has been found. The only faint parallel elsewhere in Shakespeare is 'Certain friends that are both his and mine / Whose loves I may not drop', *Mac* 3.1.122.

5 **this sorrow** the sorrow of being spurned by you

6 elliptical military metaphor: = bring up the rear in assailing an opponent who is, to his grief, already defeated

7 do not redouble my miseries by making worse follow bad: resumes the meteorological imagery of 33–4, in which the young man's favourable regard is equated with sunshine, his neglect, treachery or unkindness with storm and rain.

8 military again: = to prolong the defeat of me which you intend

9 **do . . . last** do not be the last to leave me: implies that the other misfortunes alluded to in l. 2 also take the form of rejections by friends

10 **petty griefs** minor injuries

11 **taste** experience

13 **strains** varieties, levels; or perhaps (musical) sounds (*OED* 9a, b; 13)
    seem woe seem (truly) woeful, grievous

14 **so** so grievous: since 'O' was used to represent the sound of a groan (cf. *KL* (First Quarto) 5.3.308; *R3* 3.3.90), the thrice-repeated 'O' sounds in *woe . . . woe . . . so* mimic redoubled grief.

90

Then hate me when thou wilt, if ever, now,
Now, while the world is bent my deeds to cross,
Join with the spite of fortune, make me bow,
And do not drop in for an after-loss.
Ah, do not, when my heart hath 'scaped this sorrow, 5
Come in the rearward of a conquered woe;
Give not a windy night a rainy morrow,
To linger out a purposed overthrow.
If thou wilt leave me, do not leave me last,
When other petty griefs have done their spite; 10
But in the onset come, so shall I taste
At first the very worst of fortune's might;
    And other strains of woe, which now seem woe,
    Compared with loss of thee, will not seem so.

4 after-loss] after losse   5 'scaped] scapte   6 conquered] conquerd   8 purposed] purposd   10 spite] spight   11 shall] *Benson;* stall *Q*   14 Compared] Compar'd

91 The poet spurns the material blessings in which others delight, declaring that all his pleasure is invested in his friend, who therefore has it in his power utterly to deprive him of happiness. *Correlatio* is employed, more subtly than in 77, in the enumeration and recapitulation of blessings.

1–4 'Some trust in chariots, and some in horses: but we will remember the name of the Lord our God' (Psalm 20.7).

1 **glory in** boast of; cf. 'Of such an one will I glory, yet of my selfe I will not glory, but in mine infirmities' (2 Corinthians, 12.5).

3 **new-fangled ill** fashionable but absurd: a conventional dismissal of the impracticality of modish dress; cf. *KL* 2.4.270–2.

4 **horse** plural or collective

5 **humour** temperament, individual bent

his its

adjunct joined, associated

7 **particulars** personal interests, concerns (*Glossary*, 2); itemized matters

8 **better** improve on, excel

9–11 **high . . . horses** recapitulates the eight worldly benefits enumerated in ll. 1–4, but reduces them to five

9 *better Q's 'bitter' may be an aural spelling.

10 **garments' cost** expensive splendour of raiment; cf. *rich proud cost* in 64.2 (*OED* cost 4).

12 **of . . . boast** I brag of pleasures excelling those of all (other) men.

13–14 a variant on the couplet of 64: the speaker's sole source of misery lies in his awareness of the possibility of loss, so that instead of being happier than *all men*, as in l. 12, he is in danger of being, of all men, *most wretched*.

91

Some glory in their birth, some in their skill,
Some in their wealth, some in their bodies' force,
Some in their garments, though new-fangled ill,
Some in their hawks and hounds, some in their horse,
And every humour hath his adjunct pleasure,   5
Wherein it finds a joy above the rest;
But these particulars are not my measure;
All these I better in one general best.
Thy love is better than high birth to me,
Richer than wealth, prouder than garments' cost,   10
Of more delight than hawks or horses be;
And having thee, of all men's pride I boast –
    Wretched in this alone, that thou mayst take
    All this away, and me most wretched make.

---

4 hawks] Hawkes   hounds] Hounds   horse] Horse   9 better] *Benson;* bitter *Q*   11 hawks] Hawkes
horses] Horses

92 Following from the end of the preceding sonnet, the speaker reassures himself with the thought that if the friend withdraws his love, he will immediately die, and so become immune to further injury from the young man's whims; however, this thought does not protect him against injuries of which he is not (yet) aware.

1   **steal thyself away** 'steal away' = to depart or withdraw secretly (*OED* 9a); with a secondary suggestion here that the young man removes from the speaker that which he has just described as *Richer than wealth* (91.10)

2   **term of life** legal phrase applying to marriage and/or property rights; the next line makes it clear that '*my* life' is understood.
    assured mine firmly assigned to me (*OED* assure 3): another legal term
    assured assurèd

3   **stay** remain, inhere

4   **depends upon** is governed by, is contingent upon
    that . . . thine that love that you bestow on me

5–6 **the . . . them** Since the preceding sonnet has identified the withdrawal of the young man's love as the *worst* injury the speaker can experience, it is hard to know how to interpret *the least of them* ; but perhaps the suggestion is,

'I need not fear the ultimate injury, the complete withdrawal of your love, since I shall die at the first hint of it.'

7   **a better state** a happier condition or place; here, by implication, 'a state beyond mortal life'. Though the speaker's natural life depends on the youth's favour, his heritage is heaven, which transcends it.

8   **humour** mood, inclination (*OED* 5, 6)

9   **vex . . . mind** grieve me with (your) variable moods or intentions

10 **revolt** change of sides or opinion (*OED* 1c, with this example)

11–12 The threefold *happy* appears to cancel the double *wretched* at the end of the preceding sonnet, suggesting both 'joyful', 'fortunate', and (in the third occurrence) 'contented'.

11 **title** right of possession, entitlement

13 **blessed fair** beneficently beautiful; happily equitable
    blessed blessèd
    fears no blot is not at risk of pollution or diminution

14 **Thou . . . false** you may be false to me in the future; you may already be false to me now
    yet nevertheless; for the time being
    not Malone follows this with a colon, suggesting an introduction to 93.

92

But do thy worst to steal thyself away;
For term of life thou art assured mine,
And life no longer than thy love will stay,
For it depends upon that love of thine.
Then need I not to fear the worst of wrongs,   5
When in the least of them my life hath end;
I see a better state to me belongs
Than that which on thy humour doth depend.
Thou canst not vex me with inconstant mind,
Since that my life on thy revolt doth lie.   10
O what a happy title do I find,
Happy to have thy love, happy to die!
    But what's so blessed fair that fears no blot?
    Thou mayst be false, and yet I know it not.

14 not.] not: *Malone*

93 The speaker develops from the last line of the previous sonnet the notion of being happily deceived: the young man's appearance suggests that he is incapable of being anything but loving, which makes the deceptiveness of his appearance – if it is deceptive – the more disastrous.

1 **So** in this manner (as defined in the preceding sonnet)
supposing believing

2 **Like . . . husband** the kind of husband Othello would like to have been, *Oth* 3.3.351–3.
deceived deceivèd

3 **May . . . me** may still appear to me as the quintessence of love; may still seem expressive of love towards me
altered new newly altered; the beloved's face here seems like that of the changing moon.

4 Cf. 61.14.

7 **many's looks** the appearance of many other men, or their facial expression
the . . . history the record of the heart's falsity

8 **moods** (expressions of) varying states of mind or feeling, with particular connotations of anger; cf. *TGV* 4.1.51, *H5* 4.7.38.
wrinkles strange odd contortions of the facial muscles: see *OED* wrinkle 3a; its associations are with displea-

sure rather than age.

11 **workings** Cf. Othello's comment on Iago's words: 'They are close denotements, working from the heart', *Oth* 3.3.127.

12 **thence** from the heart, a source of authentic impulse
tell speak of; enumerate

13 **Eve's apple** a fruit which, like that eaten by Eve in Genesis, 3.6, looks attractive but has evil effects when consumed; cf. the image applied by Antonio to Shylock, 'a goodly apple rotten at the heart', *MV* 1.3.102.

14 **virtue** suggests both moral virtue and the medicinal 'virtue' residing in a plant or fruit; cf. 54.9 and n.
answer . . . show does not correspond with your appearance: both here and in the next sonnet Shakespeare draws on the Neoplatonic idea that physical beauty is, or should be, a trustworthy index of inner virtue; cf. 'beautie commeth of God . . . Wherupon doth very seldom an ill soule dwell in a beautifull bodie. And therfore is the outwarde beautie a true signe of the inward goodnesse, and in bodies this comelines is imprinted more and lesse (as it were) for a marke of the soule, whereby she is outwardly knowne' (Castiglione, 360).

93

So shall I live, supposing thou art true,
Like a deceived husband; so love's face
May still seem love to me, though altered new,
Thy looks with me, thy heart in other place;
For there can live no hatred in thine eye,   5
Therefore in that I cannot know thy change.
In many's looks, the false heart's history
Is writ in moods and frowns and wrinkles strange;
But heaven in thy creation did decree
That in thy face sweet love should ever dwell;   10
Whate'er thy thoughts or thy heart's workings be,
Thy looks should nothing thence but sweetness tell.
   How like Eve's apple doth thy beauty grow,
   If thy sweet virtue answer not thy show.

3 altered] alter'd   5 there] their   13 Eve's] *Eaues*

94 Picking up from the conclusion of the previous sonnet the notion that the youth's beauty ought to be an index of sincere goodness, the speaker develops the idea that the gift of beauty carries with it an obligation to behave virtuously. Those who, despite their beautiful appearance, behave viciously deserve more obloquy than those whose appearance marks them out as *weeds*.

1 **power to hurt** because of their beauty: cf. 'To be able to do harm, and not to do it, is noble' (Tilley, H170).

2 **the . . . show** Presumably the reference is to sexual activity, which is 'shown' in them in the sense that thoughts of it are provoked by their attractive appearance.

3 **as stone** cold and unmoved, as in 'as still as a stone' (*OED* stone 3a, b); or powerfully attractive, like lodestone (*OED* 8b)

4 **Unmoved** unmovèd

5 **rightly** as of right; truly, properly

6 **husband** preserve, administer with thrift and prudence (*OED* 2a)
   from expense from (unnecessary) expenditure, with a play on refraining from the emission of semen; cf. 129.1–2 and n.; also 6.3–4 and n., 20.14 and n.

7–8 **lords . . . stewards** Those who are self-controlled are rightful possessors of their natural beauty; those who are not merely administer it for the benefit of others, like *stewards*.

9 **summer's flower** the flower that pertains to the summer, with connotations of the fragile beauty of (female) sexuality: cf. 'Women are as roses, whose fair flower / Being once displayed, doth fall that very hour' (*TN* 2.4.37–8). Both here and in l. 11 *flower* is linked by rhyme and position to *power* in l. 1.
   to the summer as perceived by the (personified) summer; with regard to the summer

10 Contrast the undesirable *canker blooms* of 54, which *Die to themselves*, and so lack value; cf. also 'Things growing to themselves are growth's

abuse', *VA* 166. The phrase *it only* suggests both '(though) it lives and dies alone' and '(though) it does no more than live and die'. There seems to be a parallel with Romans, 14.7–8: 'For none of us liveth to himself, and no man dieth to himself. For whether we live, we live unto the Lord; and whether we die, we die unto the Lord'.

11 **base infection** degrading pollution or disease: cf. 67, 'Ah, wherefore with infection should he live', where also there was an identification of the youth with a flower (*rose*) of archetypal splendour.

12 **outbraves** outdoes in beauty or splendour of array (*OED* 2b): cf. John Gerard, *Herball* (1597), Preface, of King Solomon, 'The Lillies of the field out-braved him'; there is probably a reference to the Sermon on the Mount, Matthew, 6.28–9: 'consider the lilies of the field, how they grow; they toil not, neither do they spin. And yet I say unto you, That even Solomon in all his glory was not arrayed like one of these'. The lordly youth's *dignity*, like that of Solomon, can be outdone by a simple flower.

13 **sweetest . . . deeds** conflates two proverbs: 'What is sweet in the mouth is oft sour in the maw', Tilley, M1265, and cf. *R2* 1.3.235, *Luc* 699; and 'The corruption of the best is the worst' (Tilley, C668)

14 Though there may be an allusion to the proverb 'The lily is fair in show but foul in smell' (Tilley, L297), the primary suggestion is that, untainted, the lily would smell sweet; a foul smell is worse in it than in a mere weed because of the expectations of virtue (moral and botanical) activated by its beauty. The line occurs in identical form in the anonymous *The Reign of King Edward the Third* (1596), 2.1.41, (*Edward III*, 79). Whether or not Shakespeare had a hand in the play, verbal parallels leave no doubt that he was familiar with it and with the application of the line to the lustful Edward, who tries to use his high rank

94

They that have power to hurt, and will do none,
That do not do the thing they most do show,
Who, moving others, are themselves as stone,
Unmoved, cold, and to temptation slow:
They rightly do inherit heaven's graces,   5
And husband nature's riches from expense;
They are the lords and owners of their faces,
Others, but stewards of their excellence.
The summer's flower is to the summer sweet,
Though to itself it only live and die,   10
But if that flower with base infection meet,
The basest weed outbraves his dignity:
    For sweetest things turn sourest by their deeds;
    Lilies that fester smell far worse than weeds.

to compel the Countess of Salisbury to yield to him. (Cf. Proudfoot, 181). The line occurs in the Countess's sententious rejection of the King: 'That sinne doth ten times agreuate it selfe, / That is committed in a holie place: . . . / That poyson shewes worst in a golden cup; / Darke night seemes darker by the lightning flash; / Lillies that fester smel far worse then weeds; / And euery glory that inclynes to sin, / The shame is treble, by the opposite' (2.1.441–2, 449–53).

1 power] powre   7 lords] Lords   9, 11 flower] flowre   12 outbraves] out-braues

95 The speaker alters the angle from which he views the discrepancy between outward fairness and inward faultiness in the addressee, stressing the dangerous freedom from reproach that his beauty allows him.

1 **lovely** beautiful; lovable: for the concept of an individual so attractive that moral faults appear only as beauties, cf. *AC* 1.1.49–50, 2.2.238–40; and, with more immediate application here, *LC* 316–22.

2 **canker** caterpillar or canker-worm (*OED* 4)

3 **spot** stain, sully; reproach, vilify (*OED* 1a, b)

budding name suggests both 'burgeoning reputation' and 'role as a young scion of an aristocratic family'; cf. 'bud of nobler race', *WT* 4.4.95.

4 **sweets** sweet things, as in 12.11, with perhaps a more specific allusion to sugar and flower syrups or conserves 'enclosed' in a jar or box; but here the paradox is that, rather than being tightly enclosed, the sweets themselves enclose *sins*.

5 **the (collective) tongue** of those who comment on how you spend your time

6 **lascivious comments** ellipsis for 'comments on or accusations of lasciviousness'

sport pleasure, with connotations of sexual pleasure; cf. *VA* 24, *MM* 3.2.120–1, *Oth* 2.1.228–9.

7 **kind** manner, fashion; with a hint that they will speak kindly

8 suggests that, though the youth is charged with lasciviousness, the distinction of his *name* exonerates him, making unfavourable accounts appear favourable. There is some uncertainty here about whether it is high birth or beauty that chiefly protects him from censure. The opening phrase may echo Sidney, *AS* 35.10–11: 'now long needy fame / Doth even grow rich, naming my Stella's name'.

9 **mansion** dwelling, place of residence

10 **habitation** place of abode (*OED* 2a), with a subsidiary play on 'habit' = apparel, clothing

12 **turns** Q's reading is surely right, the subject of both *doth cover* and *turns* being the transforming *veil* of beauty.

13 **dear heart** primarily a form of intimate and affectionate address, but also suggests a concern with the *dear heart*, or most intimate interior impulses, of the addressee; cf. *dear heart's part*, 46.12.

14 sounds proverbial, but not found elsewhere in quite this form: cf. 'Iron with often handling is worn to nothing' (Tilley, 192); and Polonius's sententious 'borrowing dulls the edge of husbandry', *Ham* 1.3.77. The surprising new field of imagery may carry an implication that ill-judged promiscuity threatens the young man's potency, especially given the sexual connotations of *use*, as in 6.5.

95

How sweet and lovely dost thou make the shame
Which like a canker in the fragrant rose
Doth spot the beauty of thy budding name:
O in what sweets dost thou thy sins enclose!
That tongue that tells the story of thy days,   5
Making lascivious comments on thy sport,
Cannot dispraise; but in a kind of praise,
Naming thy name, blesses an ill report.
O what a mansion have those vices got,
Which for their habitation chose out thee,   10
Where beauty's veil doth cover every blot,
And all things turns to fair that eyes can see!
    Take heed, dear heart, of this large privilege;
    The hardest knife ill used doth lose his edge.

2 rose] Rose   3 name:] name? *Q;* name! *Ard¹*   6 Making . . . sport,] (Making . . . sport)   12 turns]
turn *Ard¹*   13 heed, dear heart,] heed (deare heart)   14 used] vs'd

96 The youth is admired as much for his faults as for his youthful attractions, whose charm is so powerful that he could, if he wished, mislead (seduce?) even more of his admirers than he does at present.

1–2 Though the lines are parallel in construction, there is a distinction between l. 1, in which two separate groups of people identify the youth's moral faultiness either with *youth* or with *wantonness*, and l. 2, in which a single group of people finds charm (*grace*) in his combination of *youth* and *gentle sport* – a phrase which suggests, rather than 'lasciviousness' or 'caprice, whim' (*OED* wantonness 1a, g), 'aristocratic diversion' (*OED* gentle 2b), and so hints that it may be rank, as well as beauty, that glosses over his imperfections.

3 **more and less** those of higher and lower rank

4 The image is of a great lord whose suitors arrive as *faults*, but are immediately elevated to *graces*.

5–6 suggests both a literal reference to a queen, such as the dead Elizabeth, with her great love of elaborate jewellery, and a general metaphoric reference to unworthy court favourites who are admired because of their proximity to the throne

5 **throned** thronèd

8 **translated** transformed, metamorphosed; cf. *MND* 3.1.122.

9–10 There is a general reference to Matthew, 7.15, 'Beware of false prophets, which come to you in sheep's clothing, but inwardly they are ravening wolves', and cf. also *2H6* 3.1.77–8; but more specifically the image here suggests sexual rapacity, as at the moment of rape in *Luc* 677: 'The wolf hath seiz'd his prey, the poor lamb cries', which in turn derives from Ovid, *Fasti*, 2.800: '*Parva sub infesto cum jacet agna lupo*'.

10 At first it may seem that the suggestion is that it is lambs which change their appearance, but probably the suggestion is 'transform his appearance so that he looks like a lamb'.

11 **gazers** possibly implies a play on 'grazers', sheep-like admirers who will be misled, as in *WT* 4.4.109

12 **the . . . state** suggests both 'the power that comes from your condition of youthful beauty' and 'the force of your high rank'

13–14 repeated exactly from the end of 36 (sixty sonnets earlier, perhaps a significant interval?), but here deployed with different effect: in 36 the speaker views himself as the repository of shame on behalf of both friends; here the suggestion is that the young man's good reputation, which so far has been enhanced rather than undermined by his *faults*, will eventually be jeopardized if he takes too much advantage of his privileged position, and the speaker will be implicated in this disgrace.

96

Some say thy fault is youth, some wantonness;
Some say thy grace is youth and gentle sport;
Both grace and faults are loved of more and less;
Thou mak'st faults graces, that to thee resort:
As on the finger of a throned queen   5
The basest jewel will be well esteemed,
So are those errors that in thee are seen
To truths translated, and for true things deemed.
How many lambs might the stern wolf betray
If like a lamb he could his looks translate?   10
How many gazers mightst thou lead away
If thou wouldst use the strength of all thy state?
   But do not so; I love thee in such sort,
    As thou being mine, mine is thy good report.

---

3 loved] lou'd   5 queen] Queene   6 jewel] Iewell   esteemed] esteem'd   8 deemed] deem'd
9 lambs] Lambs   wolf] Wolfe   10 lamb] Lambe

97 The first of three sonnets on the speaker's separation from the youth. Their position may allude to Sidney's *AS*, in which 87–98 (and possibly also 99) relate to a period of physical separation. While Sidney's 97 treats absence as a form of 'night', during which the sun, Stella, shines elsewhere, Shakespeare's treats it as a form of winter.

2 **pleasure** that which makes the year pleasurable; with a subsidiary suggestion that the year is using the addressee at his *pleasure* (*OED* pleasure 5a)

fleeting year the year that flies swiftly past; cf. 19.5, where time is instructed to 'Make glad and sorry seasons as thou fleet'st'.

4 **old December's bareness** December is personified as an old man, perhaps with a bald head; the bareness of former Decembers, former winters, is experienced; also suggests that the bareness is that of late December, when the month itself is *old*.

5 **time removed** time when I was removed (from you)

summer's time As the next three lines make clear, this denotes the whole period presided over by summer, which extends from spring to harvest; it is astronomically reckoned from the summer solstice (21 June) to the autumnal equinox (22 or 23 September).

6 **The teeming autumn** Autumn is personified as an abundantly fertile woman; cf. Gaunt's description of England as 'This nurse, this teeming womb of royal kings', *R2* 2.1.51: to 'teem' = 'bring forth young' or 'be full, as if ready to give birth' (*OED* 1, 2).

big with great with (young), ready to give birth to (*OED* big 4)

7 **Bearing** as in 1.4, suggests both

'transmitting' and 'giving birth to'

wanton . . . prime ellipsis for 'the burden (of fertility) begotten by the lascivious spring'

8 as the wombs of pregnant widows do: here the 'father', the spring, has died, but autumn brings forth his abundant issue. The image is strongly reminiscent of 1.3–4.

9 **seemed** The past tense reinforces the sense that the summer period of separation is now over, and is being viewed from the perspective of late autumn.

10 no more than the benefits hoped for (in vain) by orphans and fatherless issue: the identification of the absent youth with spring and summer makes nature's autumnal bounty seem forlorn.

11 **summer . . . thee** 'Summer and his pleasures' are personified as courtiers or suitors who attend on the youth as their king or lord. Whereas in Nashe's *Summer's Last Will and Testament* (1600; Nashe, 3.233–95), with which this sonnet seems strongly connected, Summer predictably ends up by making Autumn his 'adopted heire', here his withdrawal is associated with the removed youth.

12 **thou away** while or because you are away

the . . . mute pathetic fallacy: the literal time is autumn or later, but the poet attributes the silence of the birds to the young man's absence.

13–14 **Or . . . pale** While appearing to modify the preceding conceit, the poet elaborates it: such birdsong as there is is so dismal as to provoke the leaves to fade.

13 **cheer** mood, disposition

14 **winter's near** Rhyme and rhythm link the dreaded onset of winter with the *fleeting year* of l. 2.

97

How like a winter hath my absence been
From thee, the pleasure of the fleeting year!
What freezings have I felt, what dark days seen,
What old December's bareness everywhere!
And yet this time removed was summer's time,   5
The teeming autumn big with rich increase
Bearing the wanton burden of the prime,
Like widowed wombs after their lords' decease:
Yet this abundant issue seemed to me
But hope of orphans, and unfathered fruit;   10
For summer and his pleasures wait on thee,
And thou away, the very birds are mute;
   Or if they sing, 'tis with so dull a cheer
   That leaves look pale, dreading the winter's near.

---

1 winter] Winter   2 year!] *Ard¹; yeare? Q*   3 seen,] seene?   4 everywhere!] *Malone;* euery where? *Q*
5 removed] remou'd   6 autumn] Autumne   8 lords'] Lords   9 seemed] seem'd   10 orphans]
Orphans   unfathered] vn-fathered   11 summer] Sommer   14 winter's] Winters

98 This continues from the preceding sonnet, but with a retrospective view of the flowers of spring rather than of the fruits of *teeming autumn*: the speaker took no pleasure in the season because the youth, its archetype, is elsewhere.

2 proud pied splendid and variegated; there seems no need to hyphenate the double epithet, as most editors since Thomas Ewing and Malone have done. April is personified, as is conventional, as a gaudily dressed young man.

trim adornment, array (*OED* 4a); cf. *1H4* 4.1.113, where Hotspur describes the splendidly arrayed troops of Prince Hal as 'like sacrifices in their trim'.

3–4 put . . . That ellipsis for 'put such a spirit . . . that (even)'

4 heavy Saturn The planetary deity Saturn is associated with old age, coldness and disaster; cf. Chaucer, *Knight's Tale*, 2453–69 ; *MA* 1.3.12; *Tit* 2.3.31. Here he is seen as *heavy* in the sense of 'grave', 'ponderous' or 'slow, sluggish' (*OED* 13, 18, 19).

5 ¹nor neither

6 flowers which differ from each other in scent and colour; elaborates the *pied* effect of April

7 summer's story (cheerful) narrative suitable for summer; apparently Shakespeare's invention of a counterpart and opposite to the proverbial 'winter's tale', told by the fire in winter; cf. Marlowe and Nashe, *Dido Queen of Carthage*, 3.3.59; *Mac* 3.4.65; and, most pertinently, *WT* 2.1.25, 'A

sad tale's best for winter'.

8 their proud lap presumably a metonym for 'the lap (of April, or of earth) which is proud to bear them'

9 lily's white This could be modernized alternatively as 'lilies white' = white lilies, or 'lilies' white' = whiteness of (plural) lilies. However, both the singular *rose* in the following line and the proverbial 'As white as a lily' (Tilley, L296) make a collective singular the most plausible reading.

10 vermilion bright red or scarlet (*OED* 2); not used by Shakespeare elsewhere

11 but sweet sweet, but no more than that; suggests a superficial acknowledgement of the pleasantness of spring flowers

but figures of delight merely forms or outlines of pleasure

12 after in imitation of, like (*OED* 14c): suggests that the addressee is the Platonic archetype of beauty of which spring and summer are mere copies. Cf. *Oth* 5.2.11, 'thou cunning'st pattern of excelling nature'; and *Son* 19.12, *beauty's pattern*.

14 Undercuts the speaker's previous denial that he has taken pleasure in the delights of spring, for he acknowledges after all that he did *play*, that is, sport, frolic, perhaps sexually (*OED* 10a, b, c), with the simulacra of youth which the season offered. There may be a parallel with Sidney, *AS*, 91.10, in which Astrophil admits that in absence he has been pleased by the beauty of other ladies, but only because 'of you they models be'.

98

From you have I been absent in the spring,
When proud pied April, dressed in all his trim,
Hath put a spirit of youth in everything,
That heavy Saturn laughed, and leaped with him.
Yet nor the lays of birds, nor the sweet smell   5
Of different flowers in odour and in hue,
Could make me any summer's story tell,
Or from their proud lap pluck them where they grew;
Nor did I wonder at the lily's white,
Nor praise the deep vermilion in the rose;   10
They were but sweet, but figures of delight,
Drawn after you, you pattern of all those.
   Yet seemed it winter still, and, you away,
   As with your shadow I with these did play.

2 proud pied] proud pide *Q;* proud-pied *Malone* April, dressed . . . trim,] Aprill (drest . . . trim)
4 Saturn] *Saturne* laughed] laugh't leaped] leapt 9 lily's] Lillies 10 rose] Rose 11 were] weare
13 seemed] seem'd winter] Winter

99 This develops from the end of the preceding sonnet the conceit that the delightful attributes of spring flowers are only *figures* of the archetypal beauty of the youth. Some editors, closing 98 with a colon, have seen the whole sonnet as an account of the manner in which the speaker has 'played' with the spring flowers. Uniquely, the sonnet is fifteen lines long: this reinforces the sense of a potentially unlimited catalogue of flowers.

1 **forward violet** The violet is *forward* both because it flowers very early and because it has been bold or presumptuous in appropriating the youth's fragrance (*OED* forward 7, 8). Elsewhere Shakespeare associates violets with young courtiers; cf. *R2* 5.2.45–6: 'who are the violets now / That strew the green lap of the new-come spring?'
chide rebuke

2 **Sweet thief** fragrant thief; thief of fragrance
thy . . . smells your sweetness that smells (sweet)

3–5 **The . . . dyed** The conceit is that the violet, invading the youth's body in order to steal his breath, has left behind tell-tale traces of purple in his veins.
purple pride purple colour in which you glory, take pride

5 **too grossly dyed** too obviously, manifestly stained, no doubt with a play on 'died', suggesting that the violets have perished in the youth's body and left purple streaks behind. Technically this appears to be the additional line, adding a third rhyme

to l. 1; but alternatively we may count l. 1 as an introduction, and treat the sonnet proper as starting with l. 2.

6 I blamed the lily for stealing whiteness from your hand; I condemned it as an inadequate representation of your hand. Adonis' hand is identified with a lily, *VA* 362.
condemned condemnèd

7 **buds of marjoram** small tight curls which are also fragrant; the reference may be specifically to knotty or knotted marjoram, an aromatic herb used in cookery.

8 **on thorns** literally, 'on thorny stems'; but 'to stand on thorns' = 'to be in a painful state of anxiety or suspense' (*OED* thorns 1, 2). The roses are presumably imagined as fearful because they are guilty of stealing their colours from the youth.

10 **had . . . both** This one is presumably pink or 'carnation' = flesh pink in colour.

11 to his theft of red and white had added the further crime of stealing scent (breath)

12 **in . . . growth** when he was resplendent in reaching his fullest growth

13 **A vengeful canker** a canker-worm or caterpillar (cf. 35. 4, 95.2)
ate . . . death consumed the rose to the point where it was killed

14 **noted** observed, took note of; cf. *Luc* 414.

15 **But** except that. This somewhat lame conclusion fails to modify, undercut or refine what has gone before: the extra-long sonnet is slack rather than rich.

99

The forward violet thus did I chide:
'Sweet thief, whence didst thou steal thy sweet that
      smells,
If not from my love's breath? The purple pride
Which on thy soft cheek for complexion dwells
In my love's veins thou hast too grossly dyed.'   5
The lily I condemned for thy hand,
And buds of marjoram had stol'n thy hair;
The roses fearfully on thorns did stand,
One blushing shame, another white despair;
A third, nor red, nor white, had stol'n of both,   10
And to his robb'ry had annexed thy breath;
But for his theft, in pride of all his growth,
A vengeful canker ate him up to death.
    More flowers I noted, yet I none could see,
    But sweet, or colour, it had stol'n from thee.   15

3 breath?]; breath, *Q*   4 dwells]; dwells? *Q*   5 dyed] *Capell;* died *Q*, *Benson*   6 lily] Lillie   8 roses]
Roses   9 One] *Malone;* Our *Q*, *Benson*   10, 15 stol'n] stolne   11 annexed] annext

100 The poet rebukes his Muse for abandoning her true subject, *my love*, and exhorts her to resume the war on time that will rescue the youth's beauty from decay. A new beginning, though one which resumes the war on time conducted in sonnets 1–19. We may imagine either that a period of poetic silence has elapsed between 99 and 100, or that the speaker's absence and preoccupation with mere shadows of the youth (cf. 98.14) constitutes a poetic desertion of him.

3 **Spend'st . . . fury** do you exhaust your inspiration? *Fury* presumably refers to the technical term *furor poeticus*, derived from Plato via Ficino. Cf. Sidney, *AS*, 74.4–5: 'Some do I hear of poet's fury tell, / But, God wot, wot not what they mean by it' ; also E.K.'s gloss on Cuddie's last speech in the 'October' eclogue of Spenser's *Shepheardes Calender* (1579) – 'He seemeth here to be ravished with a Poetical furie' (*Shorter Poems*, 182).

some worthless song suggests either that the poet has frittered his energies away on other verses, or that some of the preceding sonnets, such as 97–99, with their seasonal preoccupations, constitute a deviation. Whatever *worthless song* refers to, it can surely not be a play.

4 compromising or shadowing your poetic energies in order to elevate or brighten unworthy topics or individuals; may also suggest that the poet's Muse has directed her attention to commoners – *base subjects* – abandoning the kingly or aristocratic youth.

5–6 **redeem . . . time** save (time) from being lost (*OED* redeem 8; and cf. *1H4* 1.2.241) by means of verses which are gracious and/or aristocrat-

ic; there may also be suggestion that 100 is a 'gentler' number than those which have gone before.

7 **the . . . esteem** The first indication in *Son* that the addressee is an appreciative reader.

9 **resty** sluggish, indolent (*OED* 2a); and cf. *Cym* 3.7.3.

9–10 **survey / If** gaze at ('my love's sweet face') to see whether

10 **graven** inscribed; as in many preceding sonnets, time and the poet compete, the one seeking to inscribe lines of ageing, the other to counteract these with lines of verse.

11 **If any** if (you find) any

be . . . decay be a satirist in attacking (and so counteracting) the process of decay (cf. *OED* satire II. 4, with quotation from the anonymous *ULYSSES upon Aiax* (1596), E1ᵛ, 'Harke in thine eare, *Misacmos* is a *Satire*, a quipping fellow'). *Satire* in this sense is associated with the rough and hairy 'satyr', so the Muse, normally conceived of as female, is being enjoined to change both sex and function.

12 cause time's conquest of beauty, or marring of it (*spoils* suggests both), to be universally scorned

despised despisèd

14 **So** in this manner; on condition that

prevent'st outrun, outstrip (*OED* 3d), with perhaps some sense also of 'outdo, excel' (ibid. 3b)

scythe . . . knife presumably a poetic tautology, in which time's curved scythe or sickle is alternatively described as a *crooked knife* ; cf. *age's cruel knife*, 63.10; but the effect here is to make time seem doubly armed, and unlikely to be effectively outdone by the poet's languid Muse.

100

Where art thou, Muse, that thou forget'st so long
To speak of that which gives thee all thy might?
Spend'st thou thy fury on some worthless song,
Dark'ning thy power to lend base subjects light?
Return, forgetful Muse, and straight redeem,   5
In gentle numbers, time so idly spent;
Sing to the ear that doth thy lays esteem,
And gives thy pen both skill and argument.
Rise, resty Muse: my love's sweet face survey,
If time have any wrinkle graven there;   10
If any, be a satire to decay,
And make time's spoils despised everywhere:
    Give my love fame faster than time wastes life,
    So thou prevent'st his scythe and crooked knife.

11 satire] *Satire*   14 prevent'st] preuenst   scythe] sieth

311

101 This sonnet continues the dialogue between the poet and his Muse: she claims that the youth's beauty needs no poetic embellishment, but he exhorts her to immortalize it in verse.

1 **what . . . amends** how can you make amends?

2 **truth . . . dyed** truth which is an integral part of the beauty it inhabits

3 **depends** are subordinate to; wait in expectation upon (*OED* 3, 6); the youth is treated as the Platonic archetype of truth and beauty, like the Phoenix and the Turtle (*PT* 62). For singular verb used with plural subject, cf. 41.3.

4 **and therein dignified** and you derive dignity from your own dependence on *my love*

5 **haply** perhaps

6 Since truth's *colour*, or beauty, is integral to it (picking up *dyed* from l. 2), it needs no additional *colour*, or pretext for embellishment.

7 **pencil** brush or instrument for painting, metaphorically 'transferred to word-painting or descriptive skill' (*OED* 1b, with this example); cf. *time's pencil*, 16.10.
   to lay to put upon a surface in layers; to put or arrange colours on canvas

(*OED* 41a, with this example); cf. Sidney, *NA*, 232, 'Shall I labour to lay marble colours over my ruinous thoughts?', and a discussion of Sidney's revision of this passage, *OA*, xxx–xxxiin.

8 what is best is at its best without adulteration or addition; sounds proverbial, but appears not to be, though we may find a parallel in *WT* 4.4.87–8

11 **much outlive** survive much longer than
   a gilded tomb Cf. 'the gilded monuments / Of princes' in 55.1–2, which is also 'outlived' by poetry.

12 **ages . . . be** Cf. 'The age to come', 17.7.

13 **office** duty, obligation
   I . . . how implies that this and surrounding sonnets are written without the aid of the Muse, and are therefore uninspired; yet if they serve an exemplary function to the Muse, perhaps the poet does not really need her?

14 **seem . . . shows** Although in the octave the speaker has stressed the absolute authenticity of the youth's beauty, the wording here suggests that poetic art can offer only a 'seeming' beauty in contrast to the immediate appearance which *he shows now*.

101

O truant Muse, what shall be thy amends
For thy neglect of truth in beauty dyed?
Both truth and beauty on my love depends;
So dost thou, too, and therein dignified:
Make answer, Muse, wilt thou not haply say,   5
'Truth needs no colour with his colour fixed,
Beauty no pencil, beauty's truth to lay,
But best is best if never intermixed'?
Because he needs no praise, wilt thou be dumb?
Excuse not silence so, for't lies in thee   10
To make him much outlive a gilded tomb,
And to be praised of ages yet to be.
    Then do thy office, Muse: I teach thee how
    To make him seem long hence as he shows now.

2 dyed] di'd   4 dignified] dignifi'd   6 fixed] fixt   8 intermixed] intermixt   11 outlive] out-liue
12 praised] praisd   13 Muse: . . . how] Muse, . . . how

102 Still claiming to have fallen silent, the poet claims that he loves just as much, though he shows it less, for fear of wearisome repetition.

1 **in seeming** in appearance, in show

3 **merchandised** reduced to the value of a saleable commodity (cf. *OED* 2, with this example): cf. 'There's beggary in the love that can be reckon'd', *AC* 1.1.15.
rich esteeming the high value placed on it by its *owner*

4 **publish** broadcast, make public

5 **but in the spring** Cf. Proteus's 'spring of love', *TGV* 1.3.84; also *CE* 3.2.3.

7 **Philomel** the nightingale, supposedly metamorphosed from the princess Philomela after her rape by her brother-in-law Tereus; cf. Ovid, *Met.* 6.424–674.
summer's front the first period or beginning of summer (*OED* summer 6b, with this example): cf. 'April's front', *WT* 4.4.3.

8 *****her** The use of *her* in ll. 10 and 13 suggests that Q's 'his' is a misreading

of the MS, which may have read 'hir'. However, both Pooler (Ard[1], 98) and Booth (330) defend 'his'.
in . . . days as summer days develop and lengthen: the nightingale was believed to stop singing at the end of July; cf. Sidney, *OA*, 66.13–14, where, however, the nightingale is male.

9, 11 **that** because

11 **wild . . . bough** every tree branch is filled with the songs of wild birds: suggests both that the boughs are physically burdened with crowds of birds, and that the *burdens*, or refrains, that they sing crowd the air (*OED* burden 10)

12 pleasures which have become familiar are no longer so intensely enjoyable: cf. the proverb 'Familiarity breeds contempt' (Tilley, F47); and *Son* 12.11, 'sweets and beauties do themselves forsake'.

13 **sometime** sometimes (cf. 18.5); for some time

14 **dull you** bore you, be tedious to you; represent you in a tedious manner in my verse

102

My love is strengthened, though more weak in
          seeming;
I love not less, though less the show appear.
That love is merchandised, whose rich esteeming
The owner's tongue doth publish everywhere.
Our love was new, and then but in the spring,   5
When I was wont to greet it with my lays,
As Philomel in summer's front doth sing,
And stops her pipe in growth of riper days.
Not that the summer is less pleasant now
Than when her mournful hymns did hush the night; 10
But that wild music burdens every bough,
And sweets grown common lose their dear delight:
     Therefore, like her, I sometime hold my tongue,
     Because I would not dull you with my song.

3 merchandised] marchandiz'd   7 Philomel] *Philomell*   8 her] *IR;* his *Q, Booth, Kerrigan*   11 burdens] burthens   bough] bow   13 sometime] some-time

103 Continuing to apologize for his inadequate or scanty verse, the speaker tells the youth to look in his glass to see his true excellence. This is the third time he has told him to look in his glass: cf. sonnets 3 and 77.

2 **That** in that, in so far as
scope . . . pride opportunity to display her rhetorical splendour, or to reveal the youth of whom she is 'proud' (*OED* pride 7, 5a)

3 **argument** essential subject-matter, i.e. the youth: cf. *thy lovely argument,* 79.5.

3–4 **all . . . beside** has even less value at that time when my (poetic) praise has been bestowed on it: that is, my attempts to glorify you in verse have failed to enhance their subject-matter, yourself.

6 **Look . . . glass** an echo of 'Look in thy glass' (3.1), a hundred sonnets earlier; but whereas the previous injunction was admonitory – the youth's sight of himself was to prompt him to reproduce himself physically – this appears purely eulogistic.

7 **overgoes** transcends, overcomes (*OED* 4, 5a); cf. Gabriel Harvey's account of Spenser's ambition to 'overgo' Ariosto's *Orlando Furioso* in his *Faerie Queene,* in Spenser and Harvey, *Three Proper, and wittie Letters* (1580): Spenser, *Prose Works,* 471.

8 showing up my verse as dreary and inadequate and bringing me to shame

9–10 **striving . . . mar** while attempting to improve (my writing), to make (the subject I was trying to embellish) worse: cf. Sidney's account of Musidorus writing a verse letter, *NA,* 310, 'marring with mending, and putting out better than he left'.

10 **well** good, perfect

11 **pass** event, completion (of project) (*OED* 5, with this example)
tend aim

13 **sit** be enthroned (*OED* 1b); cf. *Luc* 288.

103

Alack, what poverty my Muse brings forth,
That, having such a scope to show her pride,
The argument all bare is of more worth
Than when it hath my added praise beside.
O blame me not if I no more can write!   5
Look in your glass, and there appears a face
That overgoes my blunt invention quite,
Dulling my lines, and doing me disgrace.
Were it not sinful, then, striving to mend,
To mar the subject that before was well?   10
For to no other pass my verses tend
Than of your graces and your gifts to tell;
    And more, much more, than in my verse can sit
    Your own glass shows you, when you look in it.

7 overgoes] ouer-goes   10 well?] *Capell;* well *Q* , *Benson*

104 It seems that the youth has obeyed the injunction in 103.6, 'Look in your glass', and has, as in 77.5, discovered signs of ageing, for this sonnet is devoted to reassuring him that in the speaker's eyes he will never age; or, if he does, the poet will transmit an image of his perfect beauty to posterity.

1   Though apparently a loving compliment, this line suggests that in the eyes of himself and others the youth *can* be seen as old.

2   **your . . . eyed** a witty epanodos (= 'regression, turning to the same sound, when one and the same sound is repeated in the beginning and middle, or middle and end', Fraunce, ch. 23) which also plays on the conceit 'your I' = your identity

3   **seems** appears: at first this reads as a confident assertion that the youth's beauty is undiminished, but the acknowledgement in l. 12 that 'mine eye may be deceived' leads to a subsequent reinterpretation of *seems* as 'seems – perhaps falsely'.

    three winters cold This apparently precise time reference, suggesting that three years have elapsed since poet and youth first met, should not be taken too literally. If it carries any literal allusion, it does not help us, since we do not know at what date the sonnet was written. But in any case, as Lee pointed out, a three-year passage of time was suggested by other sonneteers, such as Ronsard, Desportes, Vausquelin de la Fresnaie, and Daniel (Rollins, 1.255–6). Perhaps Tennyson, whose *In Memoriam* we know to have been composed over more than fifteen years, was following in this tradition when he imposed a three-year time-

scheme on his sequence of lyrics (see Introduction, p. 21).

4   **three summers' pride** Trees' foliage is identified with the *pride*, or splendour, of summer; cf. *RJ* 1.2.10.

6   **process** progression (*OED* 1a)

8   **fresh . . . green** If *fresh* and *green* are treated as synonymous, the *fair friend* is undiminished in *beauty*; but on a second reading it may seem that there is a distinction between *fresh*, which may be equated with the fragrance of *April*, and *green*, which may be associated with the summer heat of June. Note also the adverse connotations of *green*: cf. 63.14n.

9   **like . . . hand** like the hand of a mechanical timepiece: cf. 77.7–8 and n.

10 **Steal . . . figure** (beauty) moves stealthily away from his outward appearance (cf. *OED* figure 4, and Fr. *figure* = face, visage); alternatively, if *Steal* is treated as transitive, 'steals from the sum (figure) of his allotted days or years'

    no pace perceived There is no perceptible movement or stepping.

11 **hue** used, as in 20.7 and 82.5, to stand for 'beauty of complexion or outward appearance'

    still doth stand stands still, appears to be motionless

13 **age unbred** posterity; future age of human beings not yet conceived; there may also be a suggestion of future readers who lack 'breeding', or aristocratic blood-lines.

14 The consummation (or *eternal summer*, as in 18.9) of human beauty lived and died before you were born. As in some earlier sonnets (cf. 63) this affirmation of the durability of the youth's beauty in art is undercut by the reminder that the fair youth will die.

104

To me, fair friend, you never can be old;
For as you were when first your eye I eyed,
Such seems your beauty still: three winters cold
Have from the forests shook three summers' pride;
Three beauteous springs to yellow autumn turned   5
In process of the seasons have I seen;
Three April perfumes in three hot Junes burned,
Since first I saw you fresh, which yet art green.
Ah, yet doth beauty, like a dial hand,
Steal from his figure, and no pace perceived;   10
So your sweet hue, which methinks still doth stand,
Hath motion, and mine eye may be deceived;
    For fear of which, hear this, thou age unbred,
    Ere you were born was beauty's summer dead.

---

2 eyed] eyde   3 still: three winters] still: Three Winters *Q;* still.Three winters *Malone*   5 autumn
turned] *Autumne* turn'd,   7 burned] burn'd   9 dial] Dyall   10 perceived] perceiu'd   11 hue] hew
methinks] me thinkes

105 While ostensibly exonerating himself from a charge of *idolatry*, the speaker celebrates his friend in threefold terms which recall the Trinity, and in particular the Trinitarian rhetorical formulas of the Athanasian Creed.

1 **idolatry** immoderate attachment to or veneration for any person or thing (*OED* 2)

2 **idol** subject of such devotion, which should properly be directed to God: cf. Hamlet's praise of Ophelia as 'my soul's idol', *Ham* 2.2.109.

4 **still such** Cf. 'such as the Father is, such is the Son: and such is the Holy Ghost', *BCP*, 65.

6 **still** perpetually

7 **to constancy confined** restricted to (the celebration of) undeviating kindness

9 **argument** subject-matter, as in 76.10, with which this sonnet has strong links

10 **Fair, kind and true** By repeating the three epithets from the preceding lines the speaker exemplifies the *constancy* of his verse, yet immediately undercuts it in 'varying to other words'.

11 **this change** this attempt to vary the terms in which the beloved's threefold virtues are expressed
spent exhausted

12 **wondrous scope affords** offers marvellous scope (for poetic invention)

13 'Beauty and honesty seldom meet' (Tilley, B163); and cf. *AYL* 1.2.40, 3.3.28.

14 **seat** residence, abode (*OED* 14, 15)

105

Let not my love be called idolatry,
Nor my beloved as an idol show,
Since all alike my songs and praises be,
To one, of one, still such, and ever so.
Kind is my love today, tomorrow kind,   5
Still constant in a wondrous excellence;
Therefore my verse, to constancy confined,
One thing expressing, leaves out difference.
Fair, kind and true is all my argument;
Fair, kind and true, varying to other words,   10
And in this change is my invention spent,
Three themes in one, which wondrous scope affords.
    Fair, kind and true have often lived alone,
    Which three, till now, never kept seat in one.

1 called] cal'd   idolatry] Idolatrie   2 idol] Idoll   7 confined] confin'de   10 varying] varrying
13 lived] liu'd

106 Looking at accounts of beautiful men and women in the past, the speaker claims that his friend excels them all: strongly parallel to Daniel's *Delia* (1592), 46, opening: 'Let others sing of knights and Palladins / In aged accents, and untimely words', but changed to masculine gender. The sonnet occurs in two MSS, Pierpont Morgan MA 1037 p.96 and Rosenbach MS 1083/16 p.256, in which it is entitled 'On his Mistris Beauty': see Appendix, p. 457.

1 **chronicle . . . time** account of time which is past or consumed, with some suggestion of time spent 'idly or unprofitably' (*OED* waste 9e; and cf. *R2* 5.5.49)

2 **wights** persons; the archaic word, which by this period often had contemptuous associations, suggests their old-fashioned, obsolete character; cf. *Oth* 2.1.158–60.

3 beauty of the individuals chronicled lending beauty to the (possibly rather antiquated) poetry in which they are described

4 **lovely knights** We might normally expect 'loveliness' to be the distinguishing attribute of chivalric *ladies*; the application of the epithet here to *knights* prepares for the claim that the (male) addressee is the consummation of human loveliness.

5 **blazon** description, record of virtues or excellences (*OED* 4, with this example); the heraldic origins of the word are apt in this backward-looking sonnet.
   sweet beauties best best and sweet(est) beauties, envisaged either as individual beautiful components – *hand, foot,* etc. – or as beautiful individuals. The traditional emendation

to 'beauty's' seems uncalled for, though it cannot be excluded as an alternative reading permitted by Q's spelling.

6 The exclusion of 'hair' and 'breasts' from this wittily compact *blazon* of bodily beauties continues the subtle accentuation of masculine attributes; see n. on l. 4.

7 **antique pen** Cf. 19.10, where *time* wields an *antique pen* (a phrase unique to Shakespeare). However, the pen here is presumably collectively wielded by those who have composed the *descriptions* of l. 2.

8 **master** possess, have at your disposal (*OED* 6a, with this example): note again masculine language, reminiscent of *master mistress* in 20.2; the youth is claimed as superior to all women and men.

10 **all you prefiguring** all offering prophetic images of you: the mild blasphemy of the preceding sonnet's Trinitarian claims is here compounded with a suggestion that the youth's appearance was forecast in old chivalric literature, as Christ's was in the Old Testament.

11 **for** because, since
   but . . . eyes only with the eyes of divination, not having full sight of you

12 **skill** Though Sisson (1.213) defended Q's 'still' as 'as yet', in conjunction with *enough* it is almost impossible to gloss. If Thomas Tyrwhitt's emendation to *skill* (Rollins, 1.260–2) is adopted, the larger suggestion is that older writers, lacking the direct inspiration of the youth's beauty, could not do it justice; the present speaker and his contemporaries, who do see it, are dumbfounded by it.

106

When in the chronicle of wasted time
I see descriptions of the fairest wights,
And beauty making beautiful old rhyme,
In praise of ladies dead, and lovely knights;
Then in the blazon of sweet beauties best,   5
Of hand, of foot, of lip, of eye, of brow,
I see their antique pen would have expressed
Even such a beauty as you master now:
So all their praises are but prophecies
Of this our time, all you prefiguring;   10
And for they looked but with divining eyes
They had not skill enough your worth to sing;
    For we which now behold these present days
    Have eyes to wonder, but lack tongues to praise.

---

1 chronicle] Chronicle 4 ladies] Ladies knights] Knights 5 beauties] *Q*, *Benson;* beauty's *Malone* 7 pen] Pen expressed] exprest 11 looked] look'd 12 skill] *Capell;* still *Q*

107 A great change has taken place in the public sphere, which has turned out much better than expected; in the private realm, both poet and youth flourish, and the speaker claims that his verse will outlive both this and further changes. The topical allusions seem to conform best with the death of Elizabeth I and accession of James I in March to April 1603, followed by James's coronation and progress through the City of London in March 1604; for further discussion, see Introduction, pp. 21–4.

1 Not neither

the prophetic soul the inward speculations (of the generality of people); cf. *Ham* 1.5.41, 'O my prophetic soul! My uncle!'

2 **the wide world** the world in general, presumably here a metonym for 'all those who inhabit the globe' – a rather different application from 'the wide world and all her fading sweets', 19.7

3 can regulate or set a limit to my right to possess *my true love* (*OED* control 5, 1). Booth (343) calls *yet* here 'nearly meaningless', but it may serve both to govern the two previous lines – 'not *even* my fears or others' prophecies . . . ' – and to hint at 'as yet': 'it may have looked as if my time was up, but as yet it is not'.

4 presumed to be surrendered to a sentence of limitation or confinement: if *my true love* is taken as referring to the person loved, rather than to the (shared or separate) emotion of love, an allusion to literal imprisonment can readily be discovered here. Shakespeare's early patron, the Earl of Southampton, was released from prison on the accession of James; his later one, William Herbert, was received back at court after a spell of imprisonment, followed by banishment, in 1601.

5 most readily glossed as 'the moon-Queen, Elizabeth, subject to death, has now been eclipsed by it' – i.e. she always was mortal, and now she is dead. (Cf. *OED* eclipse 1b, 'deprivation of light, temporary or perma-

nent'; s.v. endure, 3, 4, 'to undergo, sustain, submit to'.)

6 Sombre or gloomy soothsayers laugh at their own predictions. The Roman associations of the word *augurs* (cf. *OED* augur *sb.* 2) suggest prophecies of long standing, as well as ones authorized by the state.

7 outcomes of which the world was unsure are now securely 'crowned', or brought to a happy consummation (cf. *OED* crown 10; *Tem* 3.1.69). This could readily be construed as an allusion to James I's accession and coronation (see Introduction, pp. 22–3).

8 The *olives* seem here to denote a 'period free from conflict' (cf. *2H6* 4.4.87; *Tim* 5.4.82; *AC* 4.6.7), so that the suggestion is 'the peace we now enjoy announces further, unending, phases of peace'. The suggestion that olive trees planted at this moment will live for ever can only be symbolic, since olives do not grow in Britain; cf. *2H4* 4.4.87, 'Peace puts forth her olive everywhere'.

9–10 **Now . . . fresh** 'Balm' is frequently associated by Shakespeare with the anointing of a monarch, as in *R2* 3.2.55, *H5* 4.1.277; but also more generally with healing. The 'balm' which characterizes this period of unexpected but welcome peace bestows its blessing on the youth – and/or the speaker's affection for him – who consequently looks blooming or flourishing.

10 **death . . . subscribes** Death submits to me (*OED* subscribe 8, with this example): there is a particular appropriateness in death's 'subscribing', literally = 'writing beneath', the poet, whose *poor rhyme* will triumph over him.

12 **insults o'er** exults over, triumphs in an insolent way (*OED* insult 1b)

13 **this** this *poor rhyme*: the fact that it has been so described somewhat detracts from the apparent compliment.

14 **tyrants' crests** the crowns or heraldic crests that identify monarchs: the use here of the word 'tyrant' serves both

107

Not mine own fears, nor the prophetic soul
Of the wide world, dreaming on things to come,
Can yet the lease of my true love control,
Supposed as forfeit to a confined doom.
The mortal moon hath her eclipse endured,   5
And the sad augurs mock their own presage;
Uncertainties now crown themselves assured,
And peace proclaims olives of endless age.
Now with the drops of this most balmy time
My love looks fresh, and death to me subscribes,   10
Since 'spite of him I'll live in this poor rhyme,
While he insults o'er dull and speechless tribes;
    And thou in this shalt find thy monument,
    When tyrants' crests and tombs of brass are spent.

to hint that the present period, however apparently *balmy*, may be
presided over by a 'tyrant', and that
the previous regime (Elizabeth's?) was

a tyranny.
spent passed, come to an end (*OED*
2b, with this example)

4 Supposed] Supposde   confined] confin'd   5 moon] Moone   endured] indur'de   6 augurs] Augurs
7 Uncertainties] Incertenties *Q;* Incertainties *Ard¹, Cam³*   themselves] them-selues   assured] assur'de
8 olives] Oliues   11 'spite] spight

108 Reaching 108, the total number of sonnets in Sidney's *AS* (imitated by several other sonneteers; see Introduction, p. 99), the poet takes stock of his achievements. He can find no new way of representing either himself or the youth in words, but is compelled to reiterate what he has often said before; in so doing he continually rediscovers his first love and the young man's first beauty, revivified in language though vanished in nature.

1 **character** write, inscribe; cf. *Ham* 1.3.59.

2 **figured** portrayed, represented (*OED* figure 4)

3 *****new to register** Booth (348) defends Q's 'now', glossing the phrase as 'what now remains unrecorded'; but it seems more likely to be a compositorial slip for *new*, ll. 3–4 being constructed on the parallelism of trying *speak . . . my love* in a new way, and *register . . . thy . . . merit* in a new way. *Register* = record, note.

5 **sweet boy** the only time the youth is so addressed, though the epithet *sweet* has often been applied to him in other forms (cf. 1.8, 4.10, 13.4, 35.4, 38.3 and *passim*). Falstaff unwisely greets the newly acceded Henry V as 'my sweet boy', *2H4* 5.5.43. The phrase has caused embarrassment, for Benson altered it to 'sweet love', and a German editor, Richard Flatter, to 'sweet joy' (Rollins, 1.271–2).

like prayers divine another application of religious formulas (cf. 105, 106.9–10 and n.): the speaker is obliged to repeat his daily praises of the youth just as Elizabethans were required, morning and evening, to repeat 'divine prayer'. Such applications of repetitive religious devotion

to secular love were not uncommon: cf. Sidney's account of Leicester saying his rosary by adding 'and Elizabeth' to 'Our Father' (Sidney, *Prose*, 31).

8 **hallowed . . . name** revered your name as holy, as in 'hallowed be thy name' in the Lord's Prayer (*BCP*); there may also be a play on 'halloo', to shout or call (*OED* 3); and cf. 'halloo your name to the reverberate hills', *TN* 1.5.291. Falstaff appears to conflate the two words in his claim that 'For my voice, I have lost it with hallooing, and singing of anthems', *2H4* 1.2.187–8.

9 **eternal . . . case** love which is everlasting enclosed in the outward form of a new kind of love; *eternal love* again has strong religious connotations, as in Sidney's *CS*, 32.13–14: 'Then farewell, world, thy uttermost I see; / Eternal love, maintain thy life in me'.

10 **Weighs not** does not pay heed to, care about (*OED* weigh 14a, b)

   injury of age the injuries done by age to the body

11 nor yields to the wrinkles which are inevitable (cf. *OED* give 23)

12 makes the object of love, though aged, for ever his boy *page* or attendant (this follows well from the *sweet boy* of line 5); or makes ancient love, love of long standing, for ever his subject-matter – the *page* on which he writes (this follows well from the *ink* of l. 1)

13–14 finding the original impulse of love generated in the very place (by implication, your body) in which the passage of time and external appearance appear to show (the beauty which prompted love as no longer present: cf. 104, which also closes with a rhyme of *unbred / dead*.

108

What's in the brain that ink may character
Which hath not figured to thee my true spirit?
What's new to speak, what new to register,
That may express my love, or thy dear merit?
Nothing, sweet boy; but yet, like prayers divine,   5
I must each day say o'er the very same,
Counting no old thing old; thou mine, I thine,
Even as when first I hallowed thy fair name:
So that eternal love, in love's fresh case,
Weighs not the dust and injury of age,   10
Nor gives to necessary wrinkles place
But makes antiquity for aye his page,
 Finding the first conceit of love there bred,
 Where time and outward form would show it dead.

1 ink] Inck   2 figured] figur'd   spirit?] spirit,   3 new . . . new] *Malone;* new . . . now *Q, Benson*
5 boy] love *Benson*

109 The first of two sonnets on the speaker's voluntary absence from the youth. He claims that his *soul* still resides in the young man, and that nothing else in the world has value for him.

2 **my . . . qualify** to modify or reduce the strength of my love's ardency (*OED* qualify 8, 11)

3 **easy** easily, readily
   depart separate, be divided: cf. Solemnization of Matrimony (*BCP*, 292), 'till death us depart'.

5 **home of love** Like the first quatrain, this suggests the domesticity of marriage.

7 exactly at the time appointed, not altered by the passage of time (cf. *OED* exchange 5, with this example); however, the second phrase probably also plays with the notion 'not given away or altered in response to a changing environment', as in 'Why with the time do I not glance aside', 76.3. Booth (351) finds in this line a display of 'Falstaff-like gall in solemnly making a logical-sounding equation between two non-comparable things: the journeys of a traveler and the promiscuous sexual liaisons of an unfaithful lover'.

8 **water for my stain** water to wash away my faults: another image with religious associations. As Booth (352) observes, 'The essential idea of the line is the implied argument that since

the speaker's crime was his departure, his return cancels it.' There may also be a suggestion of repentant tears, expressed in the sonnet itself.

9 **reigned** prevailed, predominated

10 **blood** passion, appetite (*OED* 5, 6)

11 **it** my nature
   preposterously unnaturally, absurdly (*OED* 1): cf. Brabantio's indignation at the idea of his daughter being attracted to Othello: 'For nature so preposterously to err, / (Being not deficient, blind, or lame of sense,) / Sans witchcraft could not' (*Oth* 1.3.61–3).
   stained polluted, morally compromised: cf. 33.14, 35.3.

12 **nothing** something of no value, in contrast to the microcosmic *sum of good* embodied in the addressee; *for nothing* also suggests 'for no cause'.

13 **wide universe** expands on the *wide world* of 107.2, perhaps partly to accommodate the sound *you*, the second person plural, alluding to 'everyone else in the world except thou'. Shakespeare uses *universe* only once elsewhere, in *H5* 4 Prol. 3.

14 **my rose** Cf. *beauty's rose*, 1.2; *his rose*, 67.8. As a form of address, *rose* = a peerless or matchless person, a paragon (*OED* 5), most often applied to women, though Ophelia calls Hamlet the 'rose of the fair state' (*Ham* 3.1.154).

109

O never say that I was false of heart,
Though absence seemed my flame to qualify;
As easy might I from myself depart
As from my soul which in thy breast doth lie:
That is my home of love; if I have ranged,   5
Like him that travels I return again,
Just to the time, not with the time exchanged,
So that myself bring water for my stain;
Never believe, though in my nature reigned
All frailties that besiege all kinds of blood,   10
That it could so preposterously be stained,
To leave for nothing all thy sum of good:
    For nothing this wide universe I call,
    Save thou, my rose; in it thou art my all.

2 seemed] seem'd   5 ranged] rang'd   7 exchanged] exchang'd   9 reigned] raign'd   11 stained]
stain'd   13 universe] Vniuerse   14 rose] Rose

110 The speaker acknowledges that he has strayed in affection from the youth, but claims that this has served only to strengthen his original and continuing devotion.

1 **here and there** in this place and that; in various places (*OED* here 9a; and cf. *Ham* 1.1.93)

2 **motley . . . view** fool in appearance; and since the *motley* worn by fools was particoloured, there is also a suggestion of visible fickleness.

3 **Gored** (1) pierced, wounded (*OED* 1); or (2) divided up with differently coloured wedges or 'gores' of cloth; or (3) defiled as with filth or congealed blood: (2) follows on best from the image of *motley*, and could be linked with *TN* 1.5.63, 'I wear not motley in my brain'; but (3) leads on better to the next phrase.

4 turned my new attachments into old (or former) injuries or wrongs; or offences against my *old* affections

5 **truth** true love (mine and/or yours) embodied in you. The youth has previously been associated with *truth* in 14.11,14; 37.4; 54.2; 60.11; and 101. 3, 6.

6 **Askance and strangely** disdainfully or obliquely, and in a 'strange' or unfriendly manner; cf. 49.5, and *look strange*, 89.8.

7 **blenches** sidelong glances (*OED* 2, with this example)
another youth a renewed period of youth; another young man: as Booth (356) points out, 'In context of the speaker's infidelity and the relative ages of lover and beloved . . . *another youth* carries incidentally self-incriminating suggestions of "a different boy".'

8 and experiments with or trials of inferior (love) demonstrated you to offer me the best experience of love (cf. *OED* essay 11, with this example)

9 **all is done** suggests both 'all my infidelity is at an end' and 'my life is complete'
*****save . . . end** Malone's emendation of Q's first 'have' to *save* has been adopted, because the open-endedness of 'have what shall have' does not seem to

square with the absolute claim made in *never more* in the following line; also, the invocation of the divine seems consistent with *by all above* in l. 6 and *next my heaven* in l. 13: the speaker claims that his reaffirmation of love for the addressee is now lifelong, to be ended or transcended only by 'what shall have no end' – divine love.

10–11 **grind / . . . proof** sharpen or intensify by experiments elsewhere: an elaboration of the notion of making an appetite *keen*, as in 118.1, with the appetite as a knife whose grindstone is other objects of love

11 **to . . . friend** to test out (by comparison) the worth of a former friend; to cause suffering to a friend who is older: like l. 7, this hints strongly that the speaker's affections have deviated towards one (even) younger than the addressee.

12 **A . . . love** one god-like in capacity for love; a god who is *in love*; one made a god in the transaction of love, so perhaps deified by the speaker's adoration. The invocation of his love for the youth in terms of religious devotion, initiated in 105, reaches a climax here. **confined** limited, restricted: apart from the extravagance of claiming that he can love only his friend when a few lines earlier he acknowledged that he has strayed to other loves, the word *confined* introduces suggestions of unwelcome restrictions such as imprisonment or even torment; cf. old Hamlet, 'for the day confin'd to fast in fires', *Ham* 1.5.11.

13 In which case you, who are for me the best thing in the world short of heaven, (should) receive me warmly: contrast with 21.1–3, in which the speaker distinguished himself from the poets who elaborated their themes with reference to *heaven itself.*

14 **most most loving** As Booth points out (359), although this registers initially as an extravagant compliment, it also 'carries perverse overtones', and may be read as suggesting that the addressee outdoes the speaker in his ability to find *affections new.*

110

Alas, 'tis true, I have gone here and there,
And made myself a motley to the view,
Gored mine own thoughts, sold cheap what is most
     dear,
Made old offences of affections new.
Most true it is that I have looked on truth   5
Askance and strangely; but by all above,
These blenches gave my heart another youth,
And worse essays proved thee my best of love.
Now all is done, save what shall have no end;
Mine appetite I never more will grind   10
On newer proof, to try an older friend,
A god in love, to whom I am confined:
    Then give me welcome, next my heaven the best,
    Even to thy pure and most most loving breast.

3 Gored] Gor'd   5 looked] lookt   6 Askance] Asconce   strangely; but] strangely: But   8 proved] prou'd   9 save] *Malone;* haue *Q;* have *Ard¹*   10 grind] grin'de   12 god] God   confined] confin'd

111 The speaker blames Fortune for his public, and therefore publicly compromised, way of life; he implores the young man to pity him and to impose on him any *penance* he wishes. Like the preceding sonnet, but more plausibly, this has been frequently read as an allusion to Shakespeare's public profession as an actor-dramatist.

1 **do you** a command: = do it, you
*with Fortune chide Although not adopted by Benson, the correction of Q's 'wish' to *with* seems clearly correct, especially since 'chide . . . with', signifying 'complain against, dispute angrily with' (*OED* 2b), was a regular expression; cf. *Ham* 4.2.167.

2 **guilty . . . deeds** the goddess who is morally responsible for, or guilty of, the things I have done wrong

3 **That** who
my life my means of living, my support; cf. *Tem* 2.1.47–8: '*Gon.* Here is everything advantageous to life. / *Ant.* True; save means to live'.

4 **public means** public methods; public money, such as that paid by those who attend the 'public' theatres. The line can be read with *public means* as either subject or object – breeding *public manners*, or bred by them.
public manners breeds causes or generates (or is caused by) a style of behaviour appropriate to a public way of life: John Davies of Hereford's comment on Shakespeare having jeopardized his social position by his career as an actor may be pertinent here; cf. 87.14n.

5 **my . . . brand** my name is marked or stigmatized, as in the Roman practice of public censure, or 'branded' with a hot iron, like the hand or face of an Elizabethan criminal (*OED* brand 4b)

6 **almost . . . subdued** Probably *almost* governs *subdued* rather than *thence*:

'(as a result of my occupation) my nature is almost reduced to the level . . . '. For *subdued* in this sense, cf. *KL* 3.4.70: 'nothing could have subdued nature / To such a lowness but his unkind daughters'; cf. also *Oth* 1.3.25, 'My heart's subdued / Even to the very quality of my lord'.

7 **the dyer's hand** As the dyer's hand is stained by dye, so is the speaker's nature by his *public* occupation. In so far as Shakespeare's occupation was writing, rather than acting, his own hand could also be imagined as darkened with ink.

8 **renewed** restored to what I would have been if not polluted or stigmatized in the manner described in the octave. The word has biblical associations, as in 'thy youth is renewed like the eagle's', Psalms, 104.5, or 'though our outward man perish, yet the inward man is renewed day by day', 2 Corinthians 4.16.

9 **a willing patient** one who suffers pain willingly; one who is willingly sick, or compliant in accepting treatment (*OED* patient 1a, 2)

10 **Potions of eisell** concoctions of vinegar; cf. *Ham* 5.1.271: 'Woo't drink up eisel, eat a crocodile?' Though many medicines, including some used against the plague, were indeed made with vinegar, the word is probably used here, as in *Ham*, to suggest drinks of extreme bitterness like the 'vinegar . . . mingled with gall' offered to Christ on the cross (Matthew 27.34).

11 **No bitterness** (there is) no bitterness

12 **Nor double penance** 'nor (will I protest at) double penance'

14 If the friend's *pity* suffices for the speaker's cure, perhaps he will not, after all, be required to consume the bitter potions of ll. 9–12.

111

O, for my sake do you with Fortune chide,
The guilty goddess of my harmful deeds,
That did not better for my life provide
Than public means, which public manners breeds;
Thence comes it that my name receives a brand,   5
And almost thence my nature is subdued
To what it works in, like the dyer's hand;
Pity me, then, and wish I were renewed,
Whilst like a willing patient I will drink
Potions of eisell 'gainst my strong infection;   10
No bitterness that I will bitter think,
Nor double penance to correct correction.
    Pity me then, dear friend, and I assure ye,
    Even that your pity is enough to cure me.

---

1 with] *Capell;* wish *Q, Benson*   6 subdued] subdu'd   7 dyer's] Dyers   8 renewed] renu'de   10 eisell] Eysell

112 This continues directly from the preceding sonnet, adding to the idea that the addressee has it uniquely in his power to expunge the speaker's faults, a more hyperbolic conceit of nothing in the world, except his friend, registering with the speaker.

1–2 doth . . . brow smooths over (by filling up) the dent made in my reputation by popular repute: *scandal* is here imagined as a physical stumbling-block or stone (*OED* scandal 1b) which has made a depression or indentation (*OED* impression 2a) in the speaker's *brow*, or visible public image. There may also be a notion of a printed book, perhaps written by the poet (cf. 111.6–7), whose title-page is *stamped*, or printed, in a disgraceful manner, but redeemed by the young man's *love and pity;* cf. *2H4* 1.1.60: 'This man's brow, like to a title-leaf, / Foretells the nature of a tragic volume'. If this reading is accepted, we may discern here an allusion to Jaggard's piratical publishing of *PP* (twice) in 1599, with Shakespeare's name on the title-page, which, according to Thomas Heywood, caused Shakespeare to be 'much offended with M*aster* Jaggard that altogether unknowne to him presumed to make so bold with his name' (T. Heywood, *Apology for Actors* (1612), sig. G4).

3 calls . . . ill gives me a good or a bad name

4 So provided that
o'er-green . . . allow gloss over what I have done wrong and praise my good deeds: though commentators have made heavy weather of *o'er-green*, emending it to 'o'er-skreen', 'o'er-grieve' or 'o'er-grain', and others have engaged in elaborate expositions (see, for instance, Everett, 'Greening'), Malone and *OED* are probably correct in glossing Q's reading as a nonce word meaning 'To cover with green, clothe with verdure; hence *fig.* to cover so as to conceal a defect, embellish'. 'Allow' (*OED* 1) = praise, commend, sanction.

5 my all-the-world Cf. Constance's lament for her absent son Arthur, *KJ* 3.3.103–4: 'O Lord! my boy, my Arthur, my fair son! / My life, my joy, my food, my all the world!'

7–8 *George Steevens called these two lines 'purblind and obscure' (Rollins, 1.284), but it is the second only that poses major problems. Line 7 presumably means '(because it is your opinion only that I care about) it is as if no one but you is alive as far as I am concerned, and I live in the opinion of no one else'. Line 8 is more difficult, but if T.G. Tucker's emendation (Rollins, 1.284) of Q's 'or changes' to *o'er-changes* is adopted (cf. 'o'er-silvered', the accepted rendering of Q's 'or siluer'd', 12.4) it yields up: 'so that my resolute (strengthened) perceptions transmute both right and wrong'. With *steeled* cf. *VA* 376; *R2* 5.2.34; *R3* 1.1.148; for *o'er-changes*, see *OED* overchange (*obsolete*), 'to change into something else or into another condition; to transmute'.

9 profound abysm deep gulf or bottomless pit; 'abysm' is most often associated with hell, as in *AC* 3.13.146, but can also suggest a mental gulf, as in *Tem* 1.2.50, 'the dark backward and abysm of time' in Miranda's memory. These three are the only occurrences of the word in Shakespeare.

9–10 care / Of anxiety about, heed to
10 adder's sense my senses, which are collectively deaf or unreceptive: cf. 'As deaf as an adder', Tilley, A32, with this example.

11 stopped stopped

12 how . . . dispense how, given my neglect of or obliviousness to (the opinions of others); or, given my condition of being neglected, I excuse myself, or disregard (the world); cf. *OED* dispense 9, 12.

13 in . . . bred brought into existence in my discourse or preoccupations (*OED* purpose 4b, 5)

14 None of the proposed emendations to Q's 'y'are' yields easier sense. The line as it stands can be read as '(because I have excluded the rest of the world

112

Your love and pity doth th'impression fill
Which vulgar scandal stamped upon my brow;
For what care I who calls me well or ill
So you o'er-green my bad, my good allow?
You are my all-the-world, and I must strive   5
To know my shames and praises from your tongue;
None else to me, nor I to none, alive,
That my steeled sense o'er-changes right or wrong.
In so profound abysm I throw all care
Of others' voices, that my adder's sense   10
To critic and to flatterer stopped are.
Mark how with my neglect I do dispense:
   You are so strongly in my purpose bred
   That all the world besides me thinks you're dead.

---

from my consciousness) I believe that to everyone except me you are dead – you have existence only for me'. The simplest, and, as Booth (364–72) says, 'most popular of the emendations', is to 'That all the world, besides, methinks, are dead' – i.e. 'that every-one in the world seems dead to me except you'. However, this merely repeats the claim in l. 5 that 'You are my all-the-world', whereas Q's reading elaborates it, taking the supposed consequences of the speaker's solip-sism to their furthest extreme.

2 stamped] stampt   4 o'er-green] *Ard¹;* ore-green *Q*   5 all-the-world] *Capell;* All the world *Q*, *Benson*   8 steeled] steel'd   o'er-changes] *this edn. (Tucker)* ; or changes *Q*   9 abysm] *Abisme*   10 adder's] Adders   14 you're] y'are *Q;* are *Capell*

113 This sonnet resumes the absence motif of 109, combining it with a further elaboration of the claim in 112 that 'You are my all-the-world': he sees the outside world only in terms of his friend.

1 **mine . . . mind** My 'mind's eye', which continues to see you while I am physically absent, is all that is operative.

2 **that which** guides me where to walk (that is, my physical eyesight)

3 **Doth part** partly performs

4 **out** put out, extinguished

5 **it . . . heart** (Physical eyesight) transmits no images to my interior consciousness: for the eye/heart relationship, cf. 24.

6 *****latch** Capell's emendation of Q's 'lack' has been adopted; the copy MS may have read 'lach'. For 'latch' = grasp, seize (with the mind), cf. *OED* 1a; and *Mac* 4.3.195.

7 **his quick objects** the live things that the eye encounters

8 **Nor does** the eye that sends messages

to the inner consciousness retain the image of what it sees.

10 *****sweet-favoured** Although Q's 'sweet-fauor', = 'beautiful appearance', makes sense, the hyphenation suggests an adjectival application, and its positioning as an alternative and opposite term to *deformed'st* seems to match the exact parallelism of *mountain/sea, day/night, crow/dove*, so Nikolaus Delius's emendation (Rollins, 1.286) has been adopted.

12 **shapes . . . feature** transforms their appearance so that it becomes yours (cf. *OED* shape 2a, 7a)

13 **Incapable** unable to take in, receive or keep (*OED* 1a, with this example) **replete** full to capacity

14 *****Though** many editors have tried to rationalize this line by emending Q's *mine*, Malone is surely correct in saying '*Untrue* is used as a substantive. *The sincerity of my affection is the cause of my untruth;* i.e. of my not seeing objects truly, such as they appear to the rest of mankind.'

113

Since I left you, mine eye is in my mind,
And that which governs me to go about
Doth part his function, and is partly blind;
Seems seeing, but effectually is out:
For it no form delivers to the heart   5
Of bird, of flower, or shape which it doth latch;
Of his quick objects hath the mind no part,
Nor his own vision holds what it doth catch:
For if it see the rud'st or gentlest sight,
The most sweet-favoured or deformed'st creature,   10
The mountain, or the sea, the day, or night,
The crow, or dove, it shapes them to your feature.
   Incapable of more, replete with you,
   My most true mind thus maketh mine untrue.

---

6 latch] *Capell;* lack *Q*   10 sweet-favoured] *this edn (Delius);* sweet-fauor *Q;*   12 crow] Croe   dove]
Doue   13 more, replete] more repleat,   14 My] Thy *Malone*   mine] mine eye *Capell*

114 Picking up from the preceding sonnet the idea that ugly things, as well as beautiful, are transformed in his mind's eye to images of the friend, the speaker considers whether his mind is 'flattered' by his eye or truly instructed by it.

1–3 Or whether . . . Or whether Is it the case that . . . or that . . . ? For the *or whether* construction framing alternatives, cf. *Cor* 1.3.63; *MV* 3.2.116–18.

1 being . . . you being honoured, blessed with your love: cf. 87.14, in which the speaker believes he enjoys the youth's love as *a king* (and *OED* crown *v.* 10).

2 greedily consume this flattery (pleasing delusion), which is the disease incident to kings. For another association of flattery with drinking, cf. *Tim* 1.2.132–4.

4 your love your love to me; my love of you

this alchemy this power to transmute base and ugly things to precious and beautiful; cf. the sun's *heavenly alchemy*, 33.4.

5 make of make out of

things indigest things which are shapeless and crude, therefore not beautiful

6 cherubins youthful angels: Shakespeare associates *cherubins* (the form of the word he normally uses) with delicate beauty as well as with goodness: cf. Othello's address to Desdemona as 'thou young and rose-lipped cherubin', *Oth* 4.2.63.

8 to his beams The eye was thought of by the Elizabethans as emitting *beams* of light which illuminate what is seen (cf. Sidney, *AS*, 6.3 and *passim*).

10 most kingly most like the king subject to flattery, as defined in l. 2

11 what . . . greeing what best suits the individual taste or appetite (of my mind): cf. *OED* gust 2, with this example: 'greeing', *ppl. a.*, concordant.

12 to adjusted to, to suit

13–14 'tis . . . begin The weakness of the mind, in preferring the *poisoned* cup of falsehood to the pure cup of truth, is mitigated by the fact that in his eagerness (*loves it*) he drinks it first – performing the tasting function normally exercised by a menial servitor, not a monarch.

114

Or whether doth my mind, being crowned with you,
Drink up the monarch's plague, this flattery?
Or whether shall I say mine eye saith true,
And that your love taught it this alchemy,
To make of monsters and things indigest   5
Such cherubins as your sweet self resemble,
Creating every bad a perfect best
As fast as objects to his beams assemble?
O, 'tis the first, 'tis flatt'ry in my seeing,
And my great mind most kingly drinks it up: 10
Mine eye well knows what with his gust is greeing,
And to his palate doth prepare the cup.
   If it be poisoned, 'tis the lesser sin,
   That mine eye loves it and doth first begin.

---

1 crowned] crown'd   4 alchemy,] *Alcumie?*   13 poisoned] poison'd

115 This sonnet plays with the paradoxes of a love claimed as absolute, yet still increasing, and therefore altering. Donne's 'Loves Growth', possibly inspired by this sonnet, explores similar paradoxes; cf. 'Me thinks I lied all winter, when I swore, / My love was infinite, if spring make it more' (5–6).

2 Pooler (Ard¹) asks, unnecessarily, 'Can this refer to lost sonnets?' Many of the preceding sonnets make such a claim, either directly or obliquely; see for instance 91, 105.

3 **Yet** but, however; as yet

4 **most full flame** flame (of love) burning at what appeared to be maximum intensity; the image of love's ardency is resumed from 109.2.

5 **But reckoning time** The loose syntax of this quatrain makes it hard to parse: at first it may appear that *time* (anticipating the images of time calling nature to account in 126) is the subject of *reckoning*; also, as Booth (379–80) points out, *reckoning* has some aural similarity to 'wrecking'. However, on a second or later reading it may seem to work better if we take the speaker to be the subject of *reckoning*, who was making absolute claims for the strength of his love, 'without reckoning on, or paying regard to, the operation of time'.
millioned accidents unforeseen occurrences or unusual events (*OED* accident 1) which are numbered by the million: see *OED* million 1, with this example; *OED* observes however that Q's 'milliond' may simply be a dialectal form of 'million'.

6 **'twixt vows** between vows and their fulfilment

7 **Tan** darken and toughen, like leather which is tanned; cf. *Ham* 5.1.162–5.
sacred beauty beauty which had appeared to be consecrated and therefore unchanging

8 cause strongly resolute intentions to be diverted (1) 'into the direction dictated by things as they change'; but probably also (2) 'into the *current* of changing circumstances' (IR)

9 **fearing of** fearing

10 **Might . . . say** Was it not reasonable for me at that time to say?

11 **certain o'er uncertainty** perhaps, 'confident of triumphing over changes or uncertainties'; or, as Booth (384) proposes as an alternative, 'I was more certain than even uncertainty [which is the surest thing in life]'

12 **Crowning the present** resumes image from 114.1: suggests 'identifying the present moment with complete fulfilment or happiness'
doubting of fearful of, uncertain of

13 **Love . . . babe** because identified with the baby Cupid, not mentioned by name until **153**
then . . . so repeats the claim of l. 10 that it was reasonable or natural for the speaker to assert, in the past, that his love was absolute. The simplest interpretation of *then* is 'since love is a baby, it was natural that I, in the full ardency of love, was naive and lacking in insight about the future'. For an account of several other readings of ll. 13–14, see Booth, 382–4.

115

Those lines that I before have writ do lie,
Even those that said I could not love you dearer;
Yet then my judgement knew no reason why
My most full flame should afterwards burn clearer.
But reckoning time, whose millioned accidents   5
Creep in 'twixt vows, and change decrees of kings,
Tan sacred beauty, blunt the sharp'st intents,
Divert strong minds to th' course of alt'ring things;
Alas, why, fearing of time's tyranny,
Might I not then say, 'Now I love you best',   10
When I was certain o'er uncertainty,
Crowning the present, doubting of the rest?
   Love is a babe; then might I not say so,
   To give full growth to that which still doth grow?

---

5 millioned] milliond   6 kings] Kings   11 uncertainty] in-certainty *Q;* incertainty *Ard¹*   13 babe] Babe

116 Building on the preceding sonnet's attempt to define love's constancy in a world of change, the speaker now sets up an ideal of true love as unaltered and unalterable, which he claims is embodied in himself – or in his sonnet. For a musical adaptation of this sonnet, see Appendix, p. 465.

1   Let me not may I never; I hope that I shall not

1–2 marriage . . . impediments 'acknowledge objections to the fulfilment of the union of true (truly loving) minds or intentions': legal terminology which recalls the marriage service in the Book of Common Prayer: 'if any man do allege and declare any impediment why they may not be coupled together in matrimony . . . then the Solemnization must be deferred until such time as the truth be tried' (*BCP*, 291). The challenge offered resembles the calling of banns, but the *marriage* proposed is *of true minds*, not (necessarily) of bodies.

2   love . . . love presumably, '(apparent) love is not true love'; cf. 'A perfect love does last eternally', Tilley, L539, with this example; also ibid., L573, 'Love without end has no end.'

4   bends turns (itself), deviates (*OED* 13)

       with . . . remove to move in response to, or in harmony with, the change or departure of the love-object

5   ever-fixed mark permanent beacon or signal for shipping; cf. Othello's penitent words to the dead Desdemona, *Oth* 5.2.268–9: 'Here is my journey's end, here is my butt, / And very sea-mark of my utmost sail'; also *Cor* 5.3.74.

       ever-fixed ever-fixèd

7   star guiding star; most readily identified with 'the northern star' (*JC* 3.1.60–2), or Pole Star

       wand'ring bark lost ship; in 80.7 the speaker compared himself to a *saucy bark*.

8   Whose worth's unknown the value of which is beyond human measurement: there seems again to be some

association with 80, where the speaker praises 'your worth, wide as the ocean'.

       his . . . taken its altitude is scientifically measured: 'take height' was a regular term in navigation and astronomy (*OED* take 32b).

9   Time's fool Something mocked by Time, because Time has power over it; cf. and contrast *1H4* 5.4.81: 'And thought's the slave of life, and life, time's fool'.

9–10 though . . . come though physical beauty falls within the range of time's sickle: *bending* suggests, in addition to its curved shape, a capacity to scoop up even what may appear to lie far from it.

11   his Time's

12   bears it out sustains without giving way, endures; see *OED* bear 15b; cf. also *AW* 3.3.5–6, 'we'll strive to bear it for your worthy sake / To th'extreme edge of hazard'.

       edge of doom first onset of Doomsday, the Last Judgement (cf. *OED* edge 11): though the marriage service opens with an injunction to the couple to affirm the lawfulness of their union 'as you will answer at the dreadful day of judgement, when the secrets of all hearts shall be disclosed' (*BCP*, 291), it is clear that the death of either partner dissolves the bond; the love defined here appears not merely life-long but world-long. Though Booth (386) argues for the possibility that *doom* also means merely 'death', with reference to 14.14 and the proverb 'Death's day is doomsday' (Tilley, D162), this does not seem in key with the hyperbole of the rest of the sonnet.

13–14 Booth (387–92) discusses this sonnet at length, and in particular defends its ending against the charge of 'bombast', which he defines vividly as 'high-sounding, energetic nonsense that addresses its topic but does not indicate what is being said about it'. However, reading this sonnet in the context of the preceding one, on love's inevitable changeableness, as well as the three following, on the

116

Let me not to the marriage of true minds
Admit impediments; love is not love
Which alters when it alteration finds,
Or bends with the remover to remove.
O no, it is an ever-fixed mark,   5
That looks on tempests and is never shaken;
It is the star to every wand'ring bark,
Whose worth's unknown, although his height be taken.
Love's not Time's fool, though rosy lips and cheeks
Within his bending sickle's compass come;   10
Love alters not with his brief hours and weeks,
But bears it out even to the edge of doom.
   If this be error and upon me proved,
   I never writ, nor no man ever loved.

speaker's deviations from love of the addressee, it is difficult not to feel that in the final couplet Shakespeare is living up to his surname, originating as a 'nickname for a belligerent person, or perhaps a bawdy name for an exhibitionist' (Hanks and Hodges, 482). At 116 sonnets into the sequence, it is clear enough that the speaker has *writ*,

and the challenge seems a Pistol-like piece of swaggering.

13 **upon me proved** proved against me; or proved (to be error) with reference to myself: language of legal or chivalric challenge, as in *KL* 5.3.110–13, 'If any man will maintain upon Edmund, supposed Earl of Gloucester, that he is a manifold traitor'.

116] 119   5 ever-fixed] euer fixed   8 height] higth   9 Love's] Lou's   *For a MS adaptation, see Appendix, p. 465*

117 Continuing the legal challenge suggested by the couplet of the preceding sonnet, the speaker subjects himself to his friend's (supposed) allegations of ingratitude and unfaithfulness, defending himself on the ground that he was testing his friend's constancy.

1 **scanted all** withheld or neglected all those things: see *OED* scant 2; and cf. *KL* 1.1.281, 'You have obedience scanted'.

2 in which I ought to recompense you in the magnificent terms which you deserve; or for the great things you have done for me: *your great deserts* may also suggest that the addressee is a *great* (= aristocratic) man, who is therefore especially deserving of service; cf. *Duty so great*, 26.5.

3 **upon . . . call** to invoke or appeal to your most precious (most affectionate) love: cf. *OED* call 23b, c.

4 **bonds** moral and/or personal ties or obligations: this line suggests that the speaker has received concrete favours from his friend, as well as being loved by him in the abstract.

5 **frequent** familiar, in company (with):

cf. *WT* 4.2.33–4, 'he is of late much retired from court, and is less frequent to his princely exercises'.

unknown minds strangers, individuals not known to you: perhaps so described to distinguish them from the *true minds* of 116.1

6 elliptical for 'given (away) your own richly earned right to spend time with me'

7 **hoisted sail** As in 116.5–8 and 80.5–12, the speaker sees himself as a small sailing boat, here one which has allowed the winds of favour or friendship to carry it all over the place.

9 **Book** record, itemize, as if drawing up a list of charges or accusations

10 pile up conjectures (of my misdeeds) on the basis of what has been clearly demonstrated

11 **within the level** within the aim or firing range (archery term); cf. *OED* level 9.

12 **wakened hate** your hate which has been activated by my derelictions

13 **my appeal says** my defence against your accusation claims
   prove test; demonstrate

117

Accuse me thus: that I have scanted all
Wherein I should your great deserts repay,
Forgot upon your dearest love to call,
Whereto all bonds do tie me day by day;
That I have frequent been with unknown minds,   5
And given to time your own dear-purchased right;
That I have hoisted sail to all the winds
Which should transport me farthest from your sight.
Book both my wilfulness and errors down,
And on just proof surmise accumulate;   10
Bring me within the level of your frown,
But shoot not at me in your wakened hate:
    Since my appeal says I did strive to prove
    The constancy and virtue of your love.

6 dear-purchased] deare purchas'd   10 surmise accumulate;] surmise, accumilate,   14 love.] loue

118 The speaker continues to attempt to defend himself against allegations that he has been unfaithful to his friend, this time through the analogy of bitter foods or medicines used to improve appetite or health, elaborating such proverbs as 'Sweet meat must have sour sauce' (Tilley, M839), or 'Sweet sauce begins to wax sour' (S97).

1 **Like as** just as, even as; cf. the opening of 60, where, however, the analogy is straightforward and cogent.

2 **eager compounds** pungent or bitter-tasting concoctions (*OED* eager 1a, with this example): cf. the image applied to the action of poison on old Hamlet's bloodstream, *Ham* 1.5.68–70: 'with a sudden vigour it doth posset /And curd, like eager droppings into milk, / The thin and wholesome blood'.

urge stimulate, excite (*OED* 7a)

3 **As** as (also)

4 **sicken . . . sickness** make ourselves ill to ward off illness: alludes to the practice of taking regular 'purges' at certain times of year (e.g. spring) to ward off infection

5 **ne'er cloying** In Q's spelling 'nere cloying' suggests a pun on 'nearly cloying' = unpleasantly sweet.

6 **frame my feeding** adjust my (social) diet

7 **welfare** being well, being healthy (*OED* 1a); cf. also the late-medieval sense (*OED* 3b), 'abundance of meat, drink'; activates the often dormant notion contained in 'farewell'

meetness appropriateness, fittingness

8 **To be** in being

9–10 **policy . . . assured** My (supposed) wise stratagem in our relationship, (adopted) to forestall non-existent evils, produced or led to definite wrongs.

11 applied a healthy condition to medical treatment (or vice versa)

12 **rank of** abounding in, (excessively) luxuriant with

14 **so . . . you** became ill in this manner because of you; grew weary of your company. The identification of love with sickness is conventional; cf. Sidney, *OA*, 41.8.

118

Like as, to make our appetites more keen,
With eager compounds we our palate urge;
As, to prevent our maladies unseen,
We sicken to shun sickness when we purge;
Even so, being full of your ne'er-cloying sweetness,   5
To bitter sauces did I frame my feeding,
And, sick of welfare, found a kind of meetness
To be diseased ere that there was true needing.
Thus policy in love, t'anticipate
The ills that were not, grew to faults assured,   10
And brought to medicine a healthful state
Which, rank of goodness, would by ill be cured;
    But thence I learn, and find the lesson true,
    Drugs poison him that so fell sick of you.

5 ne'er cloying] nere cloying   7 welfare] wel-fare   8 diseased] diseas'd   10 were not,] were, not

119 Building on the last line of the previous sonnet, in which he has been 'poisoned' by his own misguided efforts to maintain the health of his relationship with his friend, the speaker sees himself as maddened and confused, yet, once recovered, strengthened and increased in love.

1 siren tears Sirens – for the Elizabethans, more or less synonymous with mermaids – are normally thought of as exercising their fatal enchantments through singing, rather than weeping, though in so far as they are also thought of as serpents, or serpent-like, they might conceivably merge with crocodiles, which certainly were associated with deceptive tears, as in *2H6* 3.1.226; *Oth* 4.1.257. John Dickenson, *Greene in Conceipt* (1598), 48, closely associates sirens' tongues and crocodiles' tears. However, it is possible that Q's '*Syren*' additionally or alternatively refers to 'serene' or 'serein', 'A light fall of moisture or fine rain after sunset in hot countries, formerly regarded as a noxious dew or mist' (*OED*). This, if drunk, would certainly be regarded as toxic, as in Sidney's lines in the double sestina of Strephon and Klaius: 'Meseems I feele the comfort of the morning / Turnde to the mortall serene of an evening' (*OA*, 71.41–2). Four of the MS texts of Sidney's *Old Arcadia* spell the word '*Siren*', and in one of *OED*'s examples (Moryson, 1617) it is spelt '*Syren*'. For a more detailed discussion, see Duncan-Jones, '*Syren* teares'.

2 limbecks alembics, or gourd-shaped vessels used in distillation, whose beak conveyed vapours to a receiver in which they were condensed (*OED*)

3 Applying administering: continues the sense of medical treatment

4 saw . . . win believed myself to be about to conquer, or in process of conquering, my sickness

5 cf. Desdemona's 'Alas, what ignorant sin have I committed?', *Oth* 4.2.70, and Othello's interpretation of 'commit' as 'commit (adultery)', as, also, in *KL* 3.4.80, 'commit not with man's sworn spouse'.

6 so blessed never never so blessed; as blessed or happy as can be

7 spheres the circuit or celestial location of stars; the round sockets in which eyes are contained

blessed blessèd

fitted forced by fits or paroxysms out of (the usual place), *OED* fit *v.*[2], with this example only. W.N. Lettsom's 'flitted' (Rollins, 1.300–1) would make good sense (cf. *OED* flit *v.* 1, 'To remove or transport to another place'), but the fact that Shakespeare does not use this word elsewhere is against it. The concordance of *fitted* with the sustained disease image of the following line, together with the iteration of the sound in *benefit*, l. 9, supports Q's reading.

8 distraction . . . fever confusion caused by this fever which drives me mad: with *distraction* cf. *TC* 5.2.41, 5.3.85; with *madding*, *AW* 5.3.212.

10 better . . . better That which is better – in the sense of being good, not evil – is always made *even* better after recovering from an onslaught of evil.

11 An adaptation to a building metaphor (identifying love with a ruined house rebuilt) of the popular Latin proverb, derived from Terence by way of Erasmus, *amantium irae amoris redintegratio*, 'The falling-out of lovers is a renewing of love' (Tilley, F40). The word 'falling-out', used in most English versions of the proverb, may have suggested the idea of love as a collapsing building. Cf. also Richard Edwards's poem elaborating the aphorism in *The Paradise of Dainty Devices* (1576).

13 return . . . content come back, corrected in a way that makes me happy; come back to my happiness, suitably rebuked

14 gain . . . spent suggests an allusion both to the idea of the *felix culpa* or 'fortunate fall' – man's sin which occasioned the Redemption – and to the parable of the talents (Matthew, 25.14–30), in which the servants who have increased their lord's money (possibly by means of usury, which most Elizabethans saw as 'ill') are praised by their master.

119

What potions have I drunk of siren tears
Distilled from limbecks foul as hell within,
Applying fears to hopes, and hopes to fears,
Still losing when I saw myself to win?
What wretched errors hath my heart committed, 5
Whilst it hath thought itself so blessed never?
How have mine eyes out of their spheres been fitted
In the distraction of this madding fever?
O benefit of ill: now I find true
That better is by evil still made better, 10
And ruined love when it is built anew
Grows fairer than at first, more strong, far greater:
So I return rebuked to my content,
And gain by ills thrice more than I have spent.

---

1 siren] *Booth; Syren Q;* Siren *Ard¹* 2 Distilled] Distil'd limbecks] Lymbecks 7 spheres]
Spheares 10 is by] is, by 11 ruined] ruin'd 13 rebuked] rebukt 14 ills] ill *Malone*

120 Reminding himself of how he felt when his friend betrayed him, the speaker finds pain in the recollection of his anguish, but comfort in the thought of his own forgiveness at that time, and hopes to receive equivalent forgiveness himself.

1 **once unkind** unkind to me at some former time; the sonnet appears to refer back to 33–5, especially 34; cf. also 57–8.

   befriends me stands me in good stead; possibly also, 'ensures that I retain your friendship'

2 **for** for the sake of

3 **my transgression** my (own) error, equivalent to your unkindness in the past

   bow bend, submit (myself to shame) (*OED* 5)

4 **nerves** muscles; that which constitutes strength or energy (*OED* 1, 2): the sense of 'nerves' as 'feeling' (8b) was rare at this period, but may be present as a subsidiary suggestion.

6 **hell of time** period of hellish emotional torment; cf. 58.13: 'I am to wait, though waiting so be hell'.

8 **weigh** consider, estimate

9–10 **remembered . . . sense** reminded my deepest capacity for feeling, or capacity for deepest feeling

11–12 This is most readily understood with reference to 34.7, where the young man has offered to heal his injured friend through the *salve* of penitent tears: 'I ought to have offered you promptly, as you then offered me, the healing penitence which is what best suits the injured heart.'

13–14 The fact that my friend once injured me constitutes payment: the speaker's *trespass* cancels out that of his friend, and his friend's – he hopes – will cancel out his. Cf. *TGV* 5.4.75: 'If hearty sorrow / Be a sufficient ransom for offence / I tender it here'. These lines seem again to refer to 34.13–14.

120

That you were once unkind befriends me now,
And for that sorrow, which I then did feel,
Needs must I under my transgression bow,
Unless my nerves were brass or hammered steel:
For if you were by my unkindness shaken,   5
As I by yours, you've passed a hell of time,
And I, a tyrant, have no leisure taken
To weigh how once I suffered in your crime.
O that our night of woe might have remembered
My deepest sense how hard true sorrow hits,   10
And soon to you, as you to me then, tendered
The humble salve which wounded bosoms fits!
   But that your trespass now becomes a fee;
   Mine ransoms yours, and yours must ransom me.

---

1 befriends] be-friends   4 nerves] Nerues   6 you've] *Ard¹*; y'haue *Q;* you have *1R*   passed] past
time] Time   9 remembered] remembred   11 tendered] tendred

121 This sonnet is a reflection on false reputation, and on the corrupted judgements of those who disseminate damaging rumours about the speaker.

1 Cf. 'There is small difference in the eye of the world in being nought and being thought so' (Tilley, D336, with this example); however, Shakespeare elaborates the proverb, suggesting that it is actually better to be *vile* (here more or less synonymous with 'nought', = immoral, vicious, *OED* 1; cf. also *OED* vile 1, 'Of actions, character etc., Despicable on moral grounds') than to be falsely thought so.

2–3 When . . . lost when the subject of the adjudication of others, though in fact not *vile*, is blamed for being so, and yet has missed the rightful or legitimate pleasure (that might have accompanied genuine 'vileness')

3 which The subject is not clear, but is probably the *pleasure* wrongly identified by reproachful commentators.
so deemed judged to be (sexual?) pleasure

5 adulterate (themselves) defiled with adultery; counterfeit, of base origin (*OED* 1, 2): the association of eyes with adultery suggests an allusion to the Sermon on the Mount: 'whosoever looketh on a woman to lust after her hath committed adultery with her already in his heart', Matthew, 5.28.

6 Give salutation to greet, be familiar with; cf. *R3* 5.3.210–11, 'The early village cock / Hath twice done salutation to the morn'. The word also suggests an ironical allusion to the Annunciation and the Virgin Mary's anxiety about 'what manner of salutation this should be' when visited by the Angel Gabriel, Luke, 1.29.
my sportive blood my (supposed) propensity to be wanton or out of control; cf. 109.10, 'All frailties that besiege all kinds of blood'.

7 frailties moral weaknesses, shortcomings; cf. *2H4* 3.3.164–8.
why are why are there

frailer spies people, or people's eyes, even more faulty or susceptible than myself

8 in their wills 'in their desires or inclinations; with overtones both of sexual desire and of wilfulness' (*OED* will 2; and cf. 57.13, *in your will*). Booth (409–10) suggests 'a farfetched pun on "in their Williams"', pointing out the conjunction of *wills* with *I am . . . I am* in the following line, yielding a possible play on 'will-I-am'.

9 I am . . . am Cf. 'And God said unto Moses, I AM THAT I AM: and he said, Thus shalt thou say unto the children of Israel, I AM hath sent me unto you' (Exodus, 3.14). No doubt Shakespeare was aware of the semi-blasphemous effect of the divine self-definition appropriated by a wilful human individual, for he twice put similar statements into the mouth of the demi-devil Richard III: 'I am myself alone', *3H6* 5.6.83; and 'Richard loves Richard, that is, I am I', *R3* 5.3.184 (Folio text). According to Booth (410), the biblical echo makes 'the speaker sound smug, presumptuous and stupid'.
level guess at, aim (weapons) at (*OED* 8b, 7a)

10 abuses misdeeds, injuries (to others)
reckon up enumerate, list

11 bevel zigzag (heraldry); oblique (carpentry); an odd word for 'crooked', perhaps chosen both for the rhyme and for its echo of *be vile* in l. 1

12 By according to the estimation or judgement of
rank profuse; rotten; sexually uncontrolled; cf. 118.12.

13 maintain assert; argue in favour of

14 in . . . reign (1) flourish, triumph in their viciousness; or (2) use their own badness as sanction for their pursuit of others; or (3) are governed by their own particular form of badness, as a 'ruling' or 'reigning' passion: (3) is roughly synonymous with Jonson's phrase 'every man in his humour'.

121

'Tis better to be vile than vile esteemed,
When not to be, receives reproach of being,
And the just pleasure lost, which is so deemed
Not by our feeling, but by others' seeing.
For why should others' false adulterate eyes   5
Give salutation to my sportive blood?
Or on my frailties why are frailer spies,
Which in their wills count bad what I think good?
No, I am that I am, and they that level
At my abuses, reckon up their own;   10
I may be straight, though they themselves be bevel.
By their rank thoughts my deeds must not be shown,
    Unless this general evil they maintain:
    All men are bad, and in their badness reign.

7 spies,] spies;   11 themselves] them-selues

122 The speaker has parted with a notebook or manuscript volume given him
by his friend, but claims that his own
memory provides a more lasting
memento. The sonnet recalls *Ham*
1.5.95–110, in which Hamlet needs no
external help to retain the memory of
his father 'Within the book and volume of my brain', but turns to his
tables to note down the smiling vil-
lainy of Claudius. Cf. also 77, in
which the poet appears to give the
young man a book with *vacant leaves*
for him to write in.

1 tables either 'A small portable tablet
for writing upon, especially for notes
or memoranda' (*OED* table 2b) or,
more probably, synonymous here with
'table-book', a pocket notebook, as in
2H4 2.4.264.

1–2 are . . . memory This can be read as
suggesting either that the notebook
itself was *Full charactered,* that is,
amply inscribed, and that its contents
are firmly lodged in the speaker's
mind; or that, though the notebook
itself is blank, in the speaker's memory it is *Full charactered* – amply written on – with recollections of the
donor. For 'character' = write, see
108.1.

3 Which can refer either to the *tables* or
to their imagined or actual contents
that idle rank that worthless row or
level (of other persons or writings);
perhaps comparable with the 'trivial
fond records' which Hamlet expunges
from his memory in favour of recollection of his father's ghost

4 all date all limit or end of a period of
time (*OED* date 5); cf. 14.14 and 30.6.

5–6 so . . . subsist At first this may seem
to revert to the theme of the youth's
immortality, suggesting, like 18.13–14,

that the poet's thoughts, articulated in
verse, will ensure that he lives as long
as human faculties survive in the
world. However, the sestet makes it
clear that the focus is here on the
speaker's own *brain and heart* only, not
on their representation in words.

6 faculty capability, power, with perhaps some reference to the specialized
application of the word to 'One of the
several "powers" of the mind, will,
the reason, memory' (*OED* 3, 4)

7 razed oblivion oblivion which causes
mental images to be *razed*, or eradi-
cated

8 thy record the recollection or documentation of you: *OED* record *n.* 7,
5a; cf. also *TN* 5.1.253, *Son* 55.8
missed lost, missing

9 That poor retention the notebook, a
feeble means, compared with the
brain, of 'retaining' the image of the
beloved

10 tallies . . . score physical objects on
which to measure and record the value
of your love, which is so precious as to
be immeasurable: a 'tally' was a stick
on which the amount of a debt or payment was marked, or 'scored', with
notches; cf. *OED* tally 1, 2a; score 10c;
also *2H6* 4.7.32–3, 'our forefathers
had no other books but the score and
the tally'.

11 give . . . me give them (it) away

12 those tables the *tables* of memory, as
in *Ham* 1.5.98

13 adjunct something additional or auxiliary (*OED* 1); cf. *LLL* 4.3.314,
'Learning is but an adjunct to our
self'.

14 import imply, betoken (*OED* 5a, b)
forgetfulness a poor memory, a tendency to forget

122

Thy gift, thy tables, are within my brain
Full charactered with lasting memory,
Which shall above that idle rank remain
Beyond all date, even to eternity;
Or at the least, so long as brain and heart   5
Have faculty by nature to subsist;
Till each to razed oblivion yield his part
Of thee, thy record never can be missed.
That poor retention could not so much hold,
Nor need I tallies thy dear love to score;   10
Therefore to give them from me was I bold,
To trust those tables that receive thee more;
   To keep an adjunct to remember thee
   Were to import forgetfulness in me.

2 charactered] characterd   7 razed] raz'd   8 missed] mist

123 Building on his claim in the preceding sonnet that his own steadfast love provides a better bulwark against oblivion than any physical object can do, the speaker now defies time and pours scorn on the physical monuments of the past, or reminiscent of the past, rephrasing the claim made in 116.9 that 'Love's not Time's fool'. Sonnets 123–5 can be read as three comments on the 'wonderful year' 1603–4, during which many poets wrote tributes to James I, but Shakespeare did not; see Introduction, p. 26.

1 **boast** brag triumphantly; cf. 86.11.

2 **pyramids** tall structures with a sloping-sided apex, possibly in the form of what would now be called an obelisk or steeple (*OED* 3). The obelisks which adorned the triumphal arches built to greet James I in the the City of London on 15 March 1603/4 were described as *pyramids;* cf. Stephen Harrison, *The Arch's of Triumph* (1604), D1ʳ, E1ʳ, F1ʳ. Shakespeare's refusal to be impressed by pyramids, old or new, is suggested by his two references to them in *AC*, especially the gullible Lepidus' drunken reflection: 'Nay, certainly, I have heard that the Ptolomies' pyramids are very goodly things; without contradiction I have heard that' (*AC* 2.7.33–5; cf. also 5.2.61).
built . . . might constructed with strength more recent (than that which built the pyramids of antiquity); perhaps there is also a sense of 'using more recent technology'.

3 **nothing novel . . . strange** in no way new or extraordinary; alternatively, *nothing* can be read as a noun, = no new or extraordinary thing; *novel* (*OED sb.* 1) was a regular word for 'a novelty'.

4 **dressings . . . sight** reworkings or adornments of something seen before (cf. *MM* 5.1.59)

5 **Our dates** the limits of our lives; cf. 38.12, 122.4; for the idea, cf. Sidney, *OA*, 75.91, 'we last short while, and build long lasting places'.

admire marvel at

6 **foist upon us** palm off on us, fasten on us unwarrantably (*OED* foist 3c, a term from cheating with dice)

7 **make them** make them out to be, claim them as
born . . . desire brought into being to satisfy our wishes: though Q's 'borne' could be left so spelt and construed as 'brought, conveyed', *born* applies better to monuments apparently newly created.

8 **Than think** than cause or allow us to think
heard them told heard them mentioned, with perhaps some sense also of itemized, described (*OED* tell 1–3, 21).

9 **registers** records, chronicles (*OED* 1–2): suggests both written documents and monuments like the *pyramids:* cf. *LC* 52, and the use of *register* in a similar context, but as a verb, in 108.3.
both applies presumably to 'Thy registers and thee', not to *defy*
defy despise, challenge; cf. Romeo's and Hamlet's defiance of providence, *RJ* 5.1.24, *Ham* 5.2.211.

11 **For thy records** suggests both '(not wondering) . . . at your records', and 'for your records are . . . (made more or less)'.
records recòrds
what . . . lie that which lies before our eyes; what, as we see, is lying or deceptive

12 Because time moves so fast, the *registers* or *records* he leaves are constantly altered, either actually, through physical erosion, or apparently, through changing temporal viewpoints.

14 **thy . . . thee** While time's attempts to daunt mankind through created monuments, such as *pyramids* or *registers,* have been challenged in the first twelve lines, we are now reminded of time's conventional image as a destructive mower-down of men, as in 12.13 and 60.12. Booth (418–19) suggests that *scythe* may have been heard as a pun on *sight,* which is attractive because of the emphasis in l. 11 on *what we see.*

123

No! Time, thou shalt not boast that I do change;
Thy pyramids, built up with newer might,
To me are nothing novel, nothing strange;
They are but dressings of a former sight:
Our dates are brief, and therefore we admire   5
What thou dost foist upon us that is old,
And rather make them born to our desire
Than think that we before have heard them told:
Thy registers and thee I both defy,
Not wond'ring at the present, nor the past,   10
For thy records, and what we see doth lie,
Made more or less by thy continual haste:
    This I do vow, and this shall ever be,
    I will be true despite thy scythe and thee.

1 No! Time,] *Q*; No, Time, *Ard¹*; No, time, *Capell*   7 born] borne   14 scythe] syeth

124 Continuing from the previous sonnet the notion of his love as transcending the operation of time, the speaker contrasts its constancy with the vacillating fortunes of those who are subject to political control and therefore vulnerable to sudden changes of government.

1   **my dear love** the love which is so precious to me, and so strongly felt: *It* in the following line indicates that the reference here is to the affection located in the speaker, rather than its object.
    child of state derived from or dependent on the state, or 'the product of circumstances' (Booth, 419)

2   **for . . . unfathered** be rejected or disallowed, as the dubiously legitimate product of changed or changeable forces: readers in 1609 might recall that both the long-reigning and lately dead Elizabeth and her sister Mary had been declared illegitimate by their father in 1536; and theatre-goers might be reminded of Lear's rejection of Cordelia, his 'sometime daughter', now 'stranger'd with our oath', *KL* 1.1.108ff. *OED* points out an earlier use of *unfathered* as 'deprived of a father, made fatherless' in Sidney's *NA*, 403.

3   **time's love . . . hate** *Time* is here used, as in 76.3, to suggest 'the present time, currently prevailing ideas' (*OED* 3a): love which was merely a *child of state* would be at the mercy of what was in fashion.

4   When out of fashion, his love would take its place among despised *weeds;* when in favour, among *flowers* subject to being plucked; in either case at risk of destruction. The word *gathered* has strong biblical associations with death, as in the accounts in Genesis of Abraham being 'gathered to his people', 25.8; cf. also 49.29, 33; Numbers, 20.24, 27.13; Isaiah, 27.12.

4–8 While previous commentators, such as Ingram and Redpath and Booth, have seen a polarity between good and ill fortune for the love which is the *child of state,* I think, rather, that the suggestion is that to be subjected to either is damaging, whether as a spurned *weed* or a plucked *flower*, an obedient subject to smilingly false authority or a punished dissident.

5   **builded . . . accident** established in a place far removed from the vagaries of fortune; cf. time's *millioned accidents*, 115.5.

6   **suffers . . . pomp** does not endure pain, or acquiesce in whatever is required (*OED* suffer 3, 13a), in periods when it is subject to fortunate authority: *smiling* may here suggest not so much the propitious benevolence of *smiling* Fortune as the dangerously malign hypocrisy of a tyrant like Claudius who demonstrates 'That one may smile, and smile, and be a villain', *Ham* 1.5.8.

6–7 **falls . . . discontent** collapses under the oppression or imprisonment inflicted on those who resist current authority: *thralled* (thrallèd) is cited by Abbott, par. 374, as one of the 'passive participles . . . used as epithets to describe the state which would be the result of the active verb'. Discontented subjects are punished by being *thralled*, imprisoned or enslaved.

8   A puzzling line, partly because the referent of *Whereto* is not clear: perhaps the suggestion is that – for those of us whose love is the *child of state* – time summons us to a form of behaviour – *our fashion* – which leads inevitably to the suffering or thraldom defined in the previous two lines; alternatively, *fashion* may be the subject of *calls*, and *th'inviting time* the object. Ingram and Redpath gloss 'To which the temptations of today expose the likes of me', defending their rendering of *our fashion* as 'the likes of me' with reference to *TGV* 5.4.61 (IR); but this seems counter to the wider suggestion that the speaker and his love are *not* subject to the timebound perils that beset dependents on the state.

9   **policy** expediency, political cunning, dissimulation (*OED* 3, 4a): for the adverse, Machiavellian connotations

124

If my dear love were but the child of state
It might, for fortune's bastard, be unfathered,
As subject to time's love or to time's hate,
Weeds among weeds, or flowers with flowers
       gathered.
No, it was builded far from accident;   5
It suffers not in smiling pomp, nor falls
Under the blow of thralled discontent,
Whereto th'inviting time our fashion calls:
It fears not policy, that heretic,
Which works on leases of short-numbered hours,   10
But all alone stands hugely politic,
That it nor grows with heat, nor drowns with showers.
  To this I witness call the fools of time,
  Which die for goodness, who have lived for crime.

of the word, cf. *Tim* 3.2.88–9: 'Men must learn now with pity to dispense, / For policy sits above conscience'; cf. also 'Policy with his long nails has almost scratched out the eyes of religion', Tilley, P463.

heretic religious dissident, or 'one who maintains opinions upon any subject at variance with those generally received or considered authoritative' (*OED* 1, 2). As the previous note shows, *policy* in its adverse sense was seen as opposed to religious and ethical values, so the image of *policy* as itself a *heretic* underlines the speaker's definition of an independent value-system.

10 which operates in terms of limited periods of time measured by conventional units: *short-numbered hours* suggests hours which are both short and few in number. There may be some connection between the image of fast-moving cycles of (twenty-four) *hours* and the number of the sonnet; cf. 12 headnote.

1 If] Yf   4 gathered] gatherd   8 our] or *Capell*   9 heretic] *Heriticke*   10 short-numbered hours] short numbred howers   13 fools] foles   14 lived] liu'd

11 **hugely politic** enormously wise,
prudent: after the adverse connotations of *policy* only two lines earlier,
the speaker's claim for his own *politic*
power is disconcerting.

12 **That** so that
nor . . . nor neither . . . nor: the indication that both poles of variation to
which other kinds of love are subject
are threatening confirms the reading
of ll. 4–8 as presenting unpleasant
alternatives.

13 **To . . . call** to testify to what I claim,
I summon
fools of time presumably, 'those
whose love *is* determined by and subject to particular political circum-
stance', unlike the true love defined in

116, which is *not Time's fool*. Here *fool*
= plaything, dupe (*OED* 3).

14 presumably, 'who are regarded as
martyrs when they die, but as wrong-
doers while they live'. This has often
been seen as referring to Catholics
executed for their faith, and could be
applied to many such episodes, the
most recent and spectacular being the
Gunpowder Plot of 1605, followed by
the trial and execution of the conspirators in January 1606. However, the
words could refer almost equally well
to various other eminent figures who
were celebrated at the time of their
death or soon after, such as Mary,
Queen of Scots, or the Earl of Essex.

124

If my dear love were but the child of state
It might, for fortune's bastard, be unfathered,
As subject to time's love or to time's hate,
Weeds among weeds, or flowers with flowers gathered.
No, it was builded far from accident;   5
It suffers not in smiling pomp, nor falls
Under the blow of thralled discontent,
Whereto th'inviting time our fashion calls:
It fears not policy, that heretic,
Which works on leases of short-numbered hours,   10
But all alone stands hugely politic,
That it nor grows with heat, nor drowns with showers.
   To this I witness call the fools of time,
   Which die for goodness, who have lived for crime.

125 Continuing to define a space for his love as separate from, and more lasting than, political structures and the public ceremonial that expresses them, the speaker defends the pure simplicity of his love as the best bastion against the assaults of time.

1 **Were't . . . me** would it signify anything to me, what value would it have for me?

   bore the canopy carried a ceremonial canopy over a monarch or great person in procession (*OED* canopy 1a): the word's strong association with monarchy is suggested by Henry VI's meditation, *3H6* 2.5.42–5: 'Gives not the hawthorn bush a sweeter shade / To shepherds looking on their silly sheep, / Than doth a rich embroidered canopy / To kings that fear their subjects' treachery?' If there is a specific allusion here, James I's triumphal procession through London seems, as in 123, the most likely.

2 honouring exterior (displays of power) with my own exterior (appearance): for another use of *extern* in *OED*'s sense 1, 'pertaining to or connected with the outside', cf. *Oth* 1.1.63.

3 **bases** probably bases (foundations) for columns or pyramids, as in 123.1–2

   for eternity to support or celebrate *eternity*; (supposedly) to last for ever

4 which (though designated *eternity*) turns out in the event to last no longer than onslaught and decay permit; therefore, paradoxically, *ruining* is more durable than *eternity*.

5 **Have . . . seen** While ll. 3–4 suggest a long historical perspective in which ruined physical monuments of the past testify to the frailty of human attempts to create something lasting, the speaker now limits himself to his own memory and his experience of mutability in the sphere of courtly ambition.

   dwellers . . . favour those preoccupied with outward beauty or ceremonial and the favour of the great and powerful: cf. *RJ* 2.2.288, 'Fain would

I dwell on form', where Juliet wishes to stay within the bounds of courtly behaviour.

6 **paying . . . rent** paying too high a price: recalls the 'leases of short-numbered hours' in 124.10

7 neglecting simple tastes for the sake of a sweet (by implication, rich and unwholesome) mingling of flavours: in culinary terms, *compound sweet* suggests the tarts and sweetmeats served at aristocratic banquets, in contrast with the plain ingredients consumed by the common people. Cf. the proverbial 'Things sweet to taste prove in digestion sour' (*R2* 1.3.236; Tilley, M1265), which derives from Revelation, 10.9–10. It is tempting also to find in *compound sweet* a reference to the Earl of Essex, who as a young courtier was rewarded, *c.* 1590, with 'the farm of sweet wines' – the right to charge tax on all imported sweet wine – but lost it in September 1600 after his unlicensed return from Ireland, and was executed for his failed coup in February 1601; see Introduction, pp. 27–8.

8 pitiable (or contemptible) aspirants after success, or individuals who thrive poorly, who in their steadfast gazing (on *form and favour*) are destroyed: suggests an allusion to being blinded by looking directly at the sun, which could supposedly be done with impunity only by an eagle (cf. *3H6* 2.1.91–2). This, too, would apply aptly to Essex, who on his return from Ireland burst in on the undressed Queen in her bedchamber.

9 **obsequious** obedient, dutiful, especially with reference to the dead and their funeral 'obsequies' (*OED* 1a, b): the word may subliminally prepare the reader for the anticipation of the youth's death in the next poem.

10 **oblation** offering, especially in a religious context, as in the offering of sacramental bread and wine to God (*OED* 2, 3)

   poor but free applies both to the *oblation*, simple but freely, generously given, and to the speaker, who is *poor*

125

Were't ought to me I bore the canopy,
With my extern the outward honouring,
Or laid great bases for eternity,
Which proves more short than waste or ruining?
Have I not seen dwellers on form and favour   5
Lose all, and more, by paying too much rent,
For compound sweet forgoing simple savour,
Pitiful thrivers, in their gazing spent?
No, let me be obsequious in thy heart,
And take thou my oblation, poor but free,   10
Which is not mixed with seconds, knows no art,
But mutual render, only me for thee.
    Hence, thou suborned informer, a true soul
    When most impeached, stands least in thy control.

---

but *free* from courtly subservience

11 **seconds** material, e.g. flour, grapes, of secondary or inferior quality (*OED* 5) **knows no art** is not experienced in any artful mingling of elements, or courtly wiles

12 **render** surrender, making over to another (*OED n.* 2, with this example)

13 **suborned informer** bribed false witness, hired spy. Previous commentators have taken the phrase to refer cryptically to some 'actual' individual, but most probably the reference is to

Time, the explicit addressee of sonnets 123–5: cf. *VA* 655, where jealousy is described as a 'sour informer'. Here, Time is seen as the false witness who claims that the speaker is in his power by 'boasting' of his *change* (123.1).

14 **impeached** challenged, disparaged; accused of treason or other major crime (*OED* 3, 5): cf. also *MND* 2.1.214, for an instance of 'impeach' = jeopardize, put at risk.

7 sweet forgoing] sweet; Forgoing   11 mixed] mixt   13 suborned informer] subbornd *Informer*
14 impeached] impeacht

126 This six-couplet poem marks the completion of the 'fair youth' sequence. The young man's power over time is shown as bestowed on him by his patroness, nature, who must eventually hand him over (to decay and death). The number six, associated with perfection that is merely human, not divine (cf. Philo Judaeus quoted by Hopper, 47–8), and with the dreaded Beast of Revelation (cf. 66 headnote) is signalled both by the six-couplet verse form and by the figure at the head of the poem, which may be construed as 12/6. As 63 × 2 it suggests the completion of two 'grand climacterics', shadowing the deaths of both poet and youth (see Introduction, p. 100).

1 **my lovely Boy** Though some commentators have identified the *lovely Boy* with Cupid, the context makes it clear that the addressee is the speaker's beloved, and a mortal, not a deity. In 108.5 the youth had been addressed as *sweet boy*. The phrase caused embarrassment to Sidney Lee and others; yet compare Richard Barnfield's *The Affectionate Shepheard* (1594), 11–12: 'If it be sinne to love a lovely Lad; / Oh then sinne I, for whom my soule is sad'.
in thy power The youth's alleged power over time is presumably contrasted with the limited *control* over love exercised by the *suborned informer*, Time, at the end of 125; cf. also 20.7, 'all hues in his controlling'.

2 **fickle glass** presumably the hourglass traditionally held by personified Time, which is *fickle* because the sands perpetually trickling down mark time's inexorable movement, causing it to be changeable, unreliable (*OED* fickle, with this example)
*****his sickle hour** It seems initially tempting to follow Bernard Lintott and others (Rollins, 1.319–21) in emending Q's *sickle* to 'fickle', especially since the 'fi' and 'si' ligatures in Q are almost identical (see for instance the second *sins* in 35.8), and a compositor might readily pick up one in

error for the other: the sense would be 'his fickle hour (-glass)'. However, on the *difficilior lectio* principle it is preferable to retain *sickle*, construed as an adjectival noun: 'the hour when Time's (=death's) sickle cuts off life'. In 116.10 the speaker had proclaimed love's ability to stand out of reach of Time's *bending sickle's compass;* and The unique phrase *sickle hour* – time of harvest, when ripe corn is cut – matches the field of imagery of *waning*, *withering* and 'growing' in the next two lines. The youth, though growing, has the ability to hold back or defer the moment of harvest when what is fully ripe is reaped with a sickle.

3 **Who . . . grown** who, through the *waning* or diminution of time, has grown (to maturity or beyond): there may be a suggestion both of the *waning* hourglass with its descending grains of sand, and of a *waning* moon, visually prefigured in *his sickle hour*, the hour when the moon is diminished to a slender sickle; and an additional play on 'weaning', often in this period spelt 'wayning' or 'waning' (cf. *OED*'s example from Foxe) and probably identical in sound.

4 The same process which brings the youth to perfection brings the speaker to decay. Q's 'louers' permits modernization as 'lovers' ', = the withering of all those who love you; but the proprietorial and singular claim of 'O thou my lovely Boy' tips the balance in favour of the singular *lover's* as predominant.

5 **sovereign . . . wrack** supreme or paramount ruler over destruction, or over the destructive processes of time (cf. *OED* wrack 2b); in the context of love and loveliness, there is also an implication that nature is a supreme *mistress*, Venus-like, in a sexual sense.

6 As you move forward (into maturity) she continually pulls you, or desires (*will*) to pull you back (from decay): the image of nature, personified here as a mature woman devoted to a fair youth, 'plucking' him back from the

126

O thou my lovely Boy, who in thy power
Dost hold time's fickle glass, his sickle hour,
Who hast by waning grown, and therein show'st
Thy lover's withering, as thy sweet self grow'st;
If nature, sovereign mistress over wrack,   5
As thou goest onwards still will pluck thee back,
She keeps thee to this purpose: that her skill
May time disgrace, and wretched minute kill.
Yet fear her, O thou minion of her pleasure:
She may detain, but not still keep, her treasure!   10
Her audit, though delayed, answered must be,
And her quietus is to render thee.
      (   )
      (   )

---

jaws of destruction recalls the myth of
the nymph Thetis, who tried to preserve her son Achilles from mortality
by plunging him in the river Styx,
holding him back by the heel.

7   **keeps** holds, retains; preserves, cares
     for (you) (*OED* 16–20)
     her skill her skill in maintaining your
     youthful appearance and apparent
     invulnerability to decay

8   **time disgrace** put time to shame by
     eclipsing or outdoing him (*OED* dis-
     grace *v.*2); perhaps with an additional

suggestion that the boy's beauty
(grace) makes Old Father Time look
ugly

wretched minute kill destroy that
hateful unit of time which, by its
relentless repetition, brings mortal
beings to their destruction. It is surprising that so many editors, including Kerrigan, emend to 'minutes', for
'wretched minutes', like the 'damned
minutes' endured by the jealous husband in *Oth* 3.3.173, would be
tedious, unpleasant minutes, better

126] *sonnet omitted by Benson*   2 sickle hour,] *IR;* sickle, hower: *Q;* sickle, hour; *Ard¹;* sickle-hour;
Oxf; fickle hour: *Cam²* (*Lintott*)   5 nature, sovereign mistress . . . wrack,] Nature (soueraine mis-
teres . . . wrack)   7 skill] skill.   8 minute] mynuit *Q;* minutes *Capell*   11 audit, though delayed,]
Audite (though delayd)   answered] answer'd   12 quietus] *Quietus*

killed off than experienced, thus trivializing what is claimed here for nature. She is surely not trying merely to 'kill time', in the sense of expunging tedious minutes in favour of enjoyable ones, but attempting to challenge time's power in an absolute sense. As Booth (433) points out, the singular *minute* 'appears in company with the curious use of *hour* in line 2'. In addition, in Q's spelling, 'mynuit' may operate as a visual pun on Fr. *minuit*, midnight, suggesting that nature seeks to cancel the wretchedness of the midnight hour so often associated with death, despair and the expiry of legal contracts, as in Marlowe's *Doctor Faustus*, 19.137.

9 **Yet fear her** In spite of what I have just said, you should fear her: although this poem is not a sonnet, the sense of a break and a modified viewpoint after the first eight lines – as if they were an octave – is here strongly marked.

O . . . pleasure recalls and redefines the opening phrase: the youth is in nature's possession, not just the speaker's, and as 'nature's darling' is subject to the adverse as well as positive aspects of her *pleasure*, as in the sense of doing something 'at pleasure', or when one pleases (*OED* pleasure 5b). The word *minion* also, in addition to its ironical or contemptuous associations, suggests one vulnerable because exclusively dependent on the favour of a sovereign or great person (*OED* 1a, b, c).

10 **detain** keep back, restrain from (delivery to time) (*OED* 4, 5)
still keep retain always; retain in a motionless state, unaltered by time

11 **audit** summons to a final statement (literally, 'hearing') of accounts, in which nature must settle her score with time: underlying ll. 11–12 is the commonplace image of death as payment of a 'debt to nature', Tilley, D168; and cf. *1H4* 5.1.126–8: '*Prince.*

Why, thou owest God a death. / *Falstaff.* 'Tis not due yet, I would be loath to pay him before his day'.
answered satisfied, made good; cf. *1H4* 1.3.183–4: 'To answer all the debt he owes to you, / Even with the bloody payment of your deaths'.

12 The method by which nature is obliged to acquit herself of debt is by handing you over in payment (cf. *OED* render 11): for *quietus*, clearing of accounts, as an image of death, cf. *Ham* 3.1.75. Though ll. 11–12 make a perfectly complete sentence, they leave the reader with a sense of incompleteness or sudden ending, which is reinforced by the empty parentheses which follow, as if they figure the emptiness which will ensue – 'The rest is silence' (*Ham* 5.2.363). The parentheses themselves, omitted in all previous modernized editions, not only mark off the end of the 'fair youth' sequence, but suggest a range of apt significances. They resemble marks in an account-book enclosing the final sum, but empty. As Graziani has pointed out, they sketch out the shape of an hourglass, but one that contains no sand; and as Lennard (41–3) has suggested, the round brackets or *lunulae*, little moons, image a repeated waxing and waning of the moon, pointing to fickleness and frailty. Lennard sees the spaces as representing 'either the silence (quiet) of the grave, or the empty grave into which the corpse of the *lovely Boy* must sooner or later fall'. Also, since these brackets enclose an expected couplet, they may image a failure to 'couple'. The poet had warned the youth in 8.14 that 'Thou single wilt prove none': unless he 'couples' himself in marriage, he will fail to preserve his beauty for posterity. Even the poet's *black lines* (63.13) are finally missing. The poet's verse is incomplete, and so is the youth's life.

126

O thou my lovely Boy, who in thy power
Dost hold time's fickle glass, his sickle hour,
Who hast by waning grown, and therein show'st
Thy lover's withering, as thy sweet self grow'st;
If nature, sovereign mistress over wrack,   5
As thou goest onwards still will pluck thee back,
She keeps thee to this purpose: that her skill
May time disgrace, and wretched minute kill.
Yet fear her, O thou minion of her pleasure:
She may detain, but not still keep, her treasure!   10
Her audit, though delayed, answered must be,
And her quietus is to render thee.
  (   )
  (   )

127 Initiating the 'dark lady' sequence, the speaker claims that 'fairness' of complexion is no longer esteemed, since it can be falsely appropriated by means of cosmetics; fashionably, therefore, he rejoices in a mistress with dark eyes (by implication, dark complexion), whose eyes seem to mourn in mocking regret for the false reputation for beauty enjoyed by other women, while asserting their own aesthetic superiority.

1 **the old age** former times: although, as Ingram and Redpath point out, this is 'not necessarily a long time ago' (IR, 290), there must be some suggestion of the Golden Age, a time when ideals were fully realized, as in the 'antique world' recalled by Adam's generous faithfulness in *AYL* 2.3.57.
black . . . fair a dark (complexion) was not adjudged to be blonde (beautiful): the paradoxical assertion that what is black (dark) is now regarded as fair (light) identifies this sonnet, like 130 and 132, as a conceited exercise in mock-encomium.

2 presumably, 'if dark was adjudged to be light (in those days), it still was not described as beautiful': the concession may be that though some dark complexions were admired in the past, they were not celebrated in language, poetic or otherwise.

3 **black** blackness (of complexion)
beauty's successive heir the (legitimate) heir to beauty, or inheritor of beauty

4 **beauty . . . shame** What used to be called *beauty* – a '*fair* complexion' – has acquired a bad reputation through the imputation of falseness, which excludes it from the inheritance of beauty.

5 **since** since (the time when); because
each . . . power each and every hand can assume the power (to fashion beauty) that originally belonged to nature alone

6 **Fairing the foul** beautifying the ugly; for 'fair' as a verb cf. *OED* 2, with this example; also *unfair*, = 'deprive of beauty', 5.4.

art's . . . face the falsely appropriated *face* or appearance created by artifice

7 **hath no name** is not verbally identified as *beauty*, as in l. 1; has no legitimate inheritance, as in l. 4; has no eminence or reputation: cf. *OED* name 5b, 'of no name, implying obscurity and unimportance', exemplified in Job 30.8; and cf. *H5* 4.8.107.

8 is made commonplace, not sacred, or even lives in disgrace: though as Booth (435–6) points out, such a simplistic summary does not do justice to this sonnet's syntactic and semantic complexities, which aptly mirror 'false identities that pass for real and real ones that seem false'.

9 suggests either that, in order to be in tune with the times, the speaker has selected a black-eyed mistress; or, more fantastically, that his mistress has chosen her own fashionable eye-colour

10 **Her . . . suited** Though the overwhelming majority of editors have felt the repetition of *eyes* to be an error, and have either emended the *eyes* of the previous lines or these ones, to introduce an allusion to some other part of the mistress's appearance, Q's text makes perfectly good sense. The speaker's mistress's *eyes* are, in respect of their blackness (*so*), well matched both to the present age and to each other. To add some other part – 'brow', 'hair' or whatever – multiplies the number of *mourners* in the next phrase, so confusing the otherwise consistent use of anatomical synecdoche: *eyes* alone figure the mistress's beauty, just as in l. 5 *hand* figures all the agents of artificial beauty, and in the final line *tongue* represents a multitude of commentators.
mourners Cf. Sidney's *AS*, 7, on the blackness of Stella's eyes, which concludes that she chooses to dress 'Love' (Cupid) in 'mourning weed, / To honour all their deaths, who for her bleed'. The mistress's 'mourning' here includes a sense of 'deplore' or 'regret', as in *OED*'s sense 5; and cf. *Oth* 1.3.204.

127

In the old age black was not counted fair,
Or if it were, it bore not beauty's name;
But now is black beauty's successive heir,
And beauty slandered with a bastard shame:
For since each hand hath put on nature's power, 5
Fairing the foul with art's false borrowed face,
Sweet beauty hath no name, no holy bower,
But is profaned, if not lives in disgrace.
Therefore my mistress' eyes are raven black,
Her eyes so suited, and they mourners seem 10
At such who, not born fair, no beauty lack,
Sland'ring creation with a false esteem;
    Yet so they mourn, becoming of their woe,
    That every tongue says beauty should look so.

11–12 (lamenting or deploring) those (women) not naturally beautiful, but amply furnished with artificial beauty, who give natural beauty, or nature itself (*creation*), a bad name by being judged as beautiful on the basis of false appearance. This 'mourning' seems to contain an element of triumphant mockery: the poet's mistress's eyes are at least genuine.

13 **becoming . . . woe** assuming their mourning black in a manner which 'becomes' them, makes them appear beautiful

14 so that everyone now agrees that (true) beauty should look as the mistress's black eyes do: completes the process initiated in ll. 1–4 by which *black* beauty replaces *fair*ness

4 beauty slandered] Beautie slanderd 5 nature's] Natures 6 art's] Arts borrowed] borrow'd
8 profaned] prophan'd 9 mistress'] Mistersse raven] Rauen 10 eyes] hairs *Capell;* brow *IR;*
brows *Kerrigan* 11 born] borne 12 creation] Creation

128 Using the popular conceit of erotic empathy with an object close to the mistress, the speaker contemplates his mistress playing the virginals, envying the instrument its physical contact with her. As Herford and Simpson point out (Jonson, 9.461), 'it was a stale lover's conceit', satirized by Marston in *The Scourge of Villanie* (1598), 8.117–37, as well as by Jonson in his attribution of it to the affected courtier Fastidious Briske, who wishes to be his mistress's viol, *Every Man Out of his Humour*, 3.9.101–6. The Jonson analogy, originally proposed by Gerald Massey, but scorned by R. M. Alden and Rollins (Rollins, 1.326–7), seems nevertheless apt. Though Shakespeare had used a version of the conceit without apparent irony in *Tit* 2.4.44–6, he may here be satirizing it, for the reader of *Son*, if not for the imagined mistress. For an early MS transcription, see Appendix, p. 466.

1   **thou . . . play'st** you, who are *my music*, or highest, most harmonious delight, play music: the rhetorical trope (identified by Booth, 439, as antistasis, repetition of a word in a different sense) alerts the reader to the conspicuously 'conceited' character of the sonnet.

2–3 **whose . . . fingers** which is made to move, and consequently to resound, by your sweet fingers

3   **sway'st** wield, manipulate, perhaps with some sense of undulation (*OED* sway 8b, with this example)

4   **wiry . . . confounds** the harmony produced by plucked wires which (pleasingly) confuses my ear: cf. the 'musical confusion' of Theseus' dogs, *MND* 1.1.149.

5   **envy** pronounced envỳ (rhyming with 'die').

jacks Strictly speaking these should refer to pieces of wood 'fixed to the back of the key-lever, and fitted with a quill which plucked the string as the jack rose on the key's being pressed down' (*OED*); however, it seems that these objects are in direct contact with the woman's fingers, and *OED* is probably right in suggesting that Shakespeare erroneously applies the word to the keys. The word also evokes a 'knave' or 'ill-bred fellow' (*OED* 2a, b), personifying the keys as unworthy sexual rivals. It has not been established whether the expression 'nimble Jack', or 'Jack be nimble', was yet current.

6   **tender . . . hand** The palm of the hand was especially associated with erotic intimacy, as in *Oth* 2.1.168, 251–2; *WT* 1.2.125–6.

7   **harvest** harvest (of kisses), abundance of kisses

8   **by . . . stand** The conceit that the speaker's lips stand motionless *blushing* at the sauciness of the virginals parallels that of the mistress's eyes as *mourners* for made-up women in 127.10.

9   **tickled** Cf. Fastidious Briske (with tobacco-taking parenthesis) on Saviolina and her viol: 'Oh, shee tickles it so, that (*Tab.*) shee makes it laugh most divinely', Jonson, *Every Man Out of his Humour*, 3.9.101–3.
     would perhaps punning on 'wood': the lips desire to be 'wood', not flesh

9–10 **change . . . situation** change their *state* from flesh to wood; their *situation* from distance to the proximity enjoyed by the *jacks*

10   **chips** according to *OED* 1a, 'unless otherwise specified, understood to be of wood'

11, 14 ***thy fingers** two more of Q's 'their'/'thy' errors: cf. 26.12 and n.

128

How oft when thou, my music, music play'st
Upon that blessed wood whose motion sounds
With thy sweet fingers, when thou gently sway'st
The wiry concord that mine ear confounds,
Do I envy those jacks that nimble leap,   5
To kiss the tender inward of thy hand,
Whilst my poor lips, which should that harvest reap,
At the wood's boldness by thee blushing stand?
To be so tickled they would change their state
And situation with those dancing chips,   10
O'er whom thy fingers walk with gentle gait,
Making dead wood more blessed than living lips.
   Since saucy jacks so happy are in this,
   Give them thy fingers, me thy lips to kiss.

5, 13 jacks] Iackes   11, 14 thy fingers] *Malone;* their fingers *Q*   12 blessed] blest   *For a MS version, see Appendix, p. 466.*

129 This poem contrasts the moral and physical effects of *lust in action* with the anticipated pleasure that compels men to pursue it, casting a retrospective light back on the two preceding sonnets, as possibly untrustworthy eulogies by a lust-driven lover.

1–2 Th'expense . . . action Sexual intercourse (*lust in action*) is the (ultimate) means of squandering energy and becoming morally compromised: physical as well as moral degradation is suggested, *spirit* alluding both to semen as a 'vital spirit' and to the soul or higher part of man (*OED* 16a,1a), and *waste of shame* both to 'shameful waste' and to 'an action that isn't worth the shame it entails' (Booth, 443); *waste of shame* also suggests 'waste place possessed by shame'; cf. *wastes of time*, 12.10. There is additionally an association of sexual emission with failing eyesight: cf. Bacon, *Sylva Sylvarum* (1627), sect. 693: 'It hath been observed by the ancients, that much use of Venus doth dim the sight . . . the cause of dimness of sight . . . is the expence of spirits'. If this association is activated, it subverts the encomia of 'black beauty' in surrounding sonnets, for the speaker's eyesight may have been damaged by sexual activity.

3 Is perjured breaks promises (presumably those made to the love-object)

bloody brutal

blame blameworthiness, culpability (*OED* 3)

4, 10 extreme intense, excessive (in desire), possibly with shades of 'severe, harsh' (*OED* 4e, citing Psalms 129.3, Coverdale Bible).

4 rude unmannerly, violent

not to trust not to be trusted; untrustworthy

5 Enjoyed often used with reference to sexual fruition, as in *Tit* 2.3.134–5, *KL* 5.3.79; see also Partridge, 107–8. In Q's spelling the word chimes with the *in* . . . phrases in ll. 1, 2, 9, 10, 11.

despised despisèd

6 had sexually possessed; cf. *R3*

1.2.228–30.

7 a swallowed bait The lust-driven man, who appeared to be 'hunting' his prey, is himself caught like a fish; cf. Cleopatra's fancy of catching fish: 'and as I draw them up, / I'll think them every one an Antony, / And say, "Ah ha! y'are caught"' (*AC* 2.5.12–14).

8–9 *mad; / Mad Q's 'Made' may be an accurate compositional reading of copy which could be construed, in original spelling, as either 'mad' or 'made'. But since emphatic repetition is a feature of this sonnet (cf. *action . . . action*, in 2; *Past reason . . . Past reason*, 6–7; *extreme . . . extreme*, 4, 10; *well . . . well*, 13), the context seems to favour 'mad' as the dominant sense, with a subsidiary sense of 'made mad'. The two words were similar enough in sound to be punned on, as in *TN* 3.4.50–3.

9 so equally so; as mad in possession of the sexual love-object as in pursuit of it: the portmanteau use of *so* here is similar to that in *so suited* in 127.9

11 A . . . proof an intense pleasure while it is being experienced or tried out; cf. *OED* proof 4a; *RJ* 1.1.166–7: 'Alas that love so gentle in his view / Should be so tyrannous and rough in proof'. Cf. also *KL* 4.6.187.

proved . . . woe a truly wretched state once the experience is complete: this line, and the sonnet as a whole, may bear some reference to the post-classical tag *Post coitum omne animal triste* ('After coition, every creature is sad'; *ODQ*). Also, as Booth (446) points out, puns on 'woman' as 'woe (to) man' were common in the period; and cf. Tilley, W656, 'Woman is the woe of man.' Q's *and* may derive from 'a' read as an ampersand, or from attraction from the previous *and*. The capitalized 'In' in l. 9 suggests that the compositor's concentration was poor at this point.

12 a dream Cf. Tarquin's anguished anticipation of rape: 'What win I if I gain the thing I seek? / A dream, a breath, a froth of fleeting joy' (*Luc* 211–12).

129

Th'expense of spirit in a waste of shame
Is lust in action; and till action, lust
Is perjured, murd'rous, bloody, full of blame,
Savage, extreme, rude, cruel, not to trust;
Enjoyed no sooner but despised straight;   5
Past reason hunted, and no sooner had,
Past reason hated as a swallowed bait,
On purpose laid to make the taker mad;
Mad in pursuit, and in possession so,
Had, having, and in quest to have, extreme;   10
A bliss in proof, and proved, a very woe;
Before, a joy proposed; behind, a dream.
    All this the world well knows, yet none knows well
    To shun the heaven that leads men to this hell.

---

13 **the world** probably, as the following line suggests, = all *male* persons in the world

14 **heaven** the *bliss* of l. 11; perhaps also, women's 'heavenly' beauty
this hell the *hell* of shame and hatred

described in the preceding lines; the female sex organ: the identification of hell with the vagina is made in Boccaccio's *Decameron*, 3.10; and cf. 144.12 and *KL* 4.6.129.

1 spirit] Spirit   3 perjured] periurd   5 Enjoyed] Inioyd   9 Mad in] *Malone;* Made In *Q*
11 proved, a] *Malone;* proud and *Q*   12 proposed] proposd

373

130 As in the sestet of 127, the speaker boasts defiantly of his mistress's dark colouring and lack of the conventional attributes of female beauty. Following immediately on his analysis of the driving force of male lust, this may suggest that the traditional forms of beauty celebrated in love poetry are unnecessary to provoke desire: all that is necessary is that the object of desire is female and available. This strongly parallels Touchstone's wooing of the honestly ugly and wanton Audrey, *AYL* 3.3.1–57.

1   **My** Both here and in l. 12, it seems that *My* should receive strong emphasis: the speaker is distinguishing himself from the majority of other love poets: contrast, for instance Sidney's *AS*, 8.9, praising Stella's 'faire skin, beamy eyes, like morning sun on snow'. Rollins compares *Poems, Written by the . . . Earl of Pembroke* (1660), sig. D4: 'One Sun alone moves in the skye, / Two Suns thou hast, one in each eye; / Onely by day that sun gives light, / Where thine doth rise, there is no night'.
nothing like the sun in no way resembling the sun: cf. the similarly adverbial *nothing* in 123.3.

2   Cf. *TS* 1.1.129, 'I saw her coral lips to move'; *VA* 542, 'That sweet coral mouth'; *Luc* 420, 'her coral lips, her snow-white dimpled chin'; also Richard Barnfield, *Cynthia, With Certaine Sonnets* (1595), sonnet 17.12, 'His teeth pure Pearle in blushing Correll set'. Q's 'lips' could alternatively be modernized as 'lips'' or 'lip's'.

3   If snow is used as the standard by which to judge whiteness, her breasts, in comparison with it, are a dull greybrown: though Booth (454) argues that 'the thrust of the line is at least as much toward mocking inexact hyper-

bolic metaphor . . . as toward depreciating the lady's complexion', some readers may judge otherwise.

4   **If . . . wires** Hairs and wires must have been readily compared because of the lavish use of gold wires in 'tires' and hair ornaments, so it may be that (gold) *wires* might be implied: 'Whereas (poets' mistresses') hairs are normally compared with (gold) wires, mine possesses black ones.'

5   **damasked** ornamented with variegated colours; or, having the hue of the damask rose (*OED* damask *v.* 3; damasked 4, with this example)
red and white The 'damask' rose was red, but the suggestion here is both that he has seen variegated roses, and that he has seen red roses *and* white roses.

7   **some perfumes** suggests, sarcastically, that not all aromas classified as *perfumes* are delightful; cf. Hotspur's disgust with a fop's perfumes, *1H4* 1.3.36.

8   **reeks** exhales or emits steam or smoke (*OED* 2a, b): the word does not seem to have had quite such unpleasant associations for the Elizabethans as it was later to acquire (see Swift example, *OED* 3a), but was frequently linked with sweat, blood and bad breath; cf. *Cor* 3.3.120–1: 'You common cry of curs! whose breath I hate / As reek o'th'rotten fens'; and *Cym* 1.2.2.

11 **a goddess go** goddesses were supposedly recognized by their gait; *go* = walk.

13 **rare** choice, special

14 **any . . . compare** any woman misrepresented through deceptive similes: for *she* as 'woman' cf. *AYL* 3.2.10, in which Orlando prepares to write bad verses celebrating 'The fair, the chaste, and unexpressive she'.

130

My mistress' eyes are nothing like the sun;
Coral is far more red than her lips' red;
If snow be white, why then her breasts are dun;
If hairs be wires, black wires grow on her head;
I have seen roses damasked, red and white,　　　　5
But no such roses see I in her cheeks;
And in some perfumes is there more delight
Than in the breath that from my mistress reeks.
I love to hear her speak, yet well I know
That music hath a far more pleasing sound;　　　　10
I grant I never saw a goddess go;
My mistress when she walks treads on the ground.
　　And yet, by heaven, I think my love as rare
　　As any she belied with false compare.

1 mistress'] Mistres   sun] Sunne   2 Coral] Currall   5 roses damasked] Roses damaskt   6 roses] Roses   8, 12 mistress] Mistres   10 music] Musicke   14 belied] beli'd

131 Celebrates the speaker's mistress, who exercises as much power over him as more conventional beauties do over their lovers. Although some allege that, because of her appearance, she must lack this power, he claims that she does have it; but he acknowledges that she is *black* in behaviour.

1 **tyrannous** a stock epithet applied to 'Petrarchan' mistresses: cf. Spenser, *Amoretti* (1595), 10.5, where the mistress is called 'the Tyrannesse'; or Sidney, *AS*, 2.11, 'I call it praise to suffer Tyrannie'.

so as thou art such as you are, so lacking in conventional beauty as you are: another highly charged *so*, as in 127.10 and 129.11

2 **As . . . cruel** as those who, being generally regarded as beautiful, have some cause to take pride in their looks and their power over their lovers

3 **dear doting heart** my own heart, which loves you devotedly; perhaps with some suggestion, if *dear* is read as an adverb, of 'paying a high price for this infatuation'

4 **jewel** For the image of a *jewel* for the most precious love-object, cf. *Oth* 3.3.159–60: 'Good name in man and woman's dear, my lord; / Is the immediate jewel of their souls', and many other instances.

5 **in good faith** either the speaker's expletive, or a phrase governing the speech of others: 'surprisingly enough, some say'; or, 'some say, and say sincerely'

6 **make love groan** cause lovers to complain: like 'tyranny', the 'groans' of unhappy lovers belong to Petrarchan tradition, as in Sidney's *AS*, 54, in which Astrophil lists conventional signs of love, such as

'give each speech a full point of a grone'; cf. also *RJ* 1.1.197–8.

9–10 **I . . . groans** suggests that he uses groans to reinforce and validate the truth of what he swears by groaning while he swears; but because *groans* are ambivalent, being more frequently associated with 'pain or distress' (*OED* groan 1a) than with erotic delight, the hyperbole of *A thousand groans* activates a suspicion that the speaker's response to his lady is not wholly adoring, and may even hint at the possibility that he has been venereally infected by her.

11 **One . . . neck** refers either to the groans, which come thick and fast (*OED* neck 4; and Tilley, M1013, 'One misfortune comes on the neck of another'); or to the speaker and his mistress, who in embracing testify to his devotion. To 'fall on one's neck' is a biblical term for a loving embrace, as in Genesis, 33.4, 45.14; Acts, 20.37.

12 **my judgement's place** the place where my judgement resides, that is, my brain or consciousness. The conjunction in ll. 11–12 of *neck*, *witness*, *black* and 'the place of judgement' suggests an allusion to a condemned person being hanged, as in the proverb 'Wedding and hanging go by destiny', Tilley, W232; note also the possible sexual connotations of *place*, as in 6.3–4.

14 **this slander** the allegation, in ll. 5–6, that the woman's appearance makes her unlovable. One charge is disposed of, only to be replaced by a worse one.
as I think Booth (457) calls this phrase 'a single graceful razor stroke', especially since the speaker implies 'that she hasn't the moral sensitivity to notice that she has been cut apart'.

131

Thou art as tyrannous, so as thou art,
As those whose beauties proudly make them cruel;
For well thou knowst, to my dear doting heart
Thou art the fairest and most precious jewel.
Yet in good faith some say, that thee behold,   5
Thy face hath not the power to make love groan;
To say they err, I dare not be so bold,
Although I swear it to myself alone;
And to be sure that is not false, I swear
A thousand groans but thinking on thy face;   10
One on another's neck do witness bear
Thy black is fairest in my judgement's place.
   In nothing art thou black save in thy deeds,
   And thence this slander, as I think, proceeds.

4 jewel] Iewell   14 *not indented in Q*

132 Further elaborating the conceit of the mistress as both *black* and cruel, the speaker claims that her eyes mourn for her scorned lover.

1 **as** as if

2 **torment** probably infinitive, = (to) torment, forming an indirect statement after *Knowing*

3 **loving mourners** as in 127.10: further evidence that the reduplicated *eyes . . . eyes* in 127.9–10 is not an error, but an emphatic affirmation of the conceit of black eyes as mourners *suited* in black apparel

4 **pretty ruth** charming compassion

5 **morning** an obvious pun on 'mourning', made explicit in 9, which serves to suggest that this sun, like the eyes, is dark

6 **grey cheeks** the grey (perhaps cloudy) twilight of early dawn, seen as *cheeks* on either side of the face of the weakly shining sun: there seems little doubt that the praise here is ironical, for in no scale of beauty can human cheeks be praised for being *grey*. Like Miso and her daughter Mopsa in Sidney's *Arcadia*, the lady 'observe[s] decorum', having features which match each other in dinginess (*OA*, 30–1). Though Booth (457), perhaps trying to soften the sonnet's misogynistic taunts, claims that 'the sun gives colour to the gray clouds as it gives colour to the cheeks of a pallid person', both ll. 5–6 and 7–8 seem to sug-

gest dim light (eyes) which matches surrounding greyness rather than contrasting with it.

7 **that full star** the planet, generally Venus, though sometimes Mercury (cf. Sidney, *OA*, 71.7), which is the first visible star in the darkening sky: though *full*, this star sheds no light.

8 **sober** subdued in tone, neutral-tinted (*OED* 9a)

10–12 Building on his claim that the mistress's black eyes both betoken pity and look beautiful, the speaker pleads for her to extend her pity – equated with blackness – to all the rest of her body.

10 **beseem** more or less synonymous with 'become', = be fitting, be apt for: unusually, and perhaps to underline the unconventionality of what is being said, Shakespeare makes a new start after nine lines rather than the normal eight.

12 **suit** dress, adorn
   like alike, identically

13 **Then** if you pity me; by implication, acquiesce sexually

13–14 a somewhat swaggering assertion, especially since he has already made such a claim in 127: 'Respond to my advances, and I will use my poetic power to champion your blackness as the summation of beauty.' Cf, with the same *black/lack* rhyme, Berowne's ironic praise of 'black beauty', *LLL* 4.3.248–50.

132

Thine eyes I love, and they, as pitying me,
Knowing thy heart torment me with disdain,
Have put on black, and loving mourners be,
Looking with pretty ruth upon my pain;
And truly, not the morning sun of heaven   5
Better becomes the grey cheeks of the East,
Nor that full star that ushers in the even
Doth half that glory to the sober West
As those two mourning eyes become thy face:
O let it then as well beseem thy heart   10
To mourn for me, since mourning doth thee grace,
And suit thy pity like in every part:
    Then will I swear beauty herself is black,
    And all they foul that thy complexion lack.

2 torment] torments *Benson*   5 sun of heaven] Sun of Heauen   6 the East] th'East   7 star] Starre
even] Eauen   9 mourning] *Malone;* morning *Q*

133 The speaker rebukes the mistress for enslaving his *next self*, his friend, as well as himself, and tries to negotiate better terms by enclosing the friend's heart in his own bosom.

1 **Beshrew** evil befall, devil take: cf. *OED* 3b; *Oth* 4.3.78.
 makes . . . groan supposedly with adoration, as in 131.6, 10

2 **that . . . gives** primarily an application of the conventional conceit of male lovers' hearts wounded by darts from a lady's eyes, as in Sidney, *AS*, 2.2, 20.1, 48.12; but Booth (460) suggests an innuendo on the woman offering her sexual parts, sometimes described as a *wound*, as in *PP* 9.12–14, to both men.

4 **But** but that, without the consequence that
 slave to slavery tautology for 'enslaved to a tyrant', but also suggesting 'compelled to slavish drudgery (possibly sexual)'. The notion of a Petrarchan lover as a *slave* was conventional; cf. Sidney, *AS*, 29.14, 35.10, 53.5, 86.9.

5 **from myself** from my own nature

6 **my next self** the self nearest to me, i.e. my friend; cf. 36, 39.
 harder more severely, more cruelly

engrossed gathered up, gained a monopoly in (*OED* 4), with a further suggestion of 'gross' or greedy acquisitiveness

9 **Prison** imprison
 thy . . . ward the harshly unyielding prison cell of your bosom: for the notion of a 'bosom' as a tightly locked cell, cf. *MM* 5.1.11, 'To lock it in the wards of covert bosom'; for *ward*, cf. 48.4.

8 **crossed** thwarted, opposed

10 **bail** *OED* 1, 'To confine, *rare*', with this example: the reader may at first imagine that the speaker is offering his own heart as a pledge to the mistress on condition that she lets the friend out on 'bail', but the following lines indicate that *OED*'s gloss is correct.

11–12 Though the mistress may keep the speaker closely imprisoned, as in l. 9, so long as his heart in turn is permitted to be the *guard*, or jailer (or prisoner), of the friend's heart, she cannot torment him – *use rigour* – presumably because he will be so happy in the possession of his friend's heart.

13 **pent** imprisoned, enclosed

14 **all . . . me** i.e. the friend, enclosed in the speaker's bosom

133

Beshrew that heart that makes my heart to groan
For that deep wound it gives my friend and me;
Is't not enough to torture me alone,
But slave to slavery my sweet'st friend must be?
Me from myself thy cruel eye hath taken,   5
And my next self thou harder hast engrossed:
Of him, myself and thee I am forsaken,
A torment thrice threefold thus to be crossed.
Prison my heart in thy steel bosom's ward;
But then my friend's heart let my poor heart bail.   10
Whoe'er keeps me, let my heart be his guard;
Thou canst not then use rigour in my jail.
   And yet thou wilt, for I being pent in thee,
   Perforce am thine, and all that is in me.

3 enough] ynough   6 engrossed] ingrossed   8 threefold] three-fold   10 bail] bale   12 jail] Iaile

134 This sonnet continues from the preceding, with a further plea, couched in legal metaphors, for the mistress to release the friend from her keeping into his.

1   now now that

2   And and that

mortgaged pledged, legally bound
will desire, carnal appetite (cf. *MM* 2.4.164); sexual organ, as in the following sonnet. Booth (463–4) observes also that '*If* the speaker's friend is not a literary fabrication, and *if* his first name was William, *then* an informed reader would have heard "your William", "the William who is thine".'

3   so on condition that
that other mine that other 'self' I possess; cf. *PT* 36, 'Either was the other's mine'; in both cases with a secondary suggestion of a *mine* of precious metal

5   But however (despite the entreaty I have just made)

7 He discovered how to sign his name on my behalf only as a guarantor or proxy-wooer (*but surety-like*): the implication is that the friend became a *slave* to the woman (as in 133.4) only because he was *kind,* and was trying to help or liberate the speaker. It is tempting to take *write for me* as suggesting not merely a signature at the end of a legal agreement, but the composition of compromising letters or love poems on the speaker's behalf.

8   Under under the terms of; at the end of, at the bottom of (the document)
fast tightly, rigorously

9 'You will demand everything to which your beauty entitles you' (Booth, 465)

10 elaborating the notion of the woman as *covetous:* suggests that in her sexual voracity she is both miserly, like a *usurer* or money-lender, and overlavish, in 'putting forth', or exposing for sale or exhibiting (*OED* put 43b), *all* that she has for (sexual) use. Cf. 20.14; and contrast sonnet 4, in which the fair youth is a *Profitless usurer,* who has 'traffic with thyself alone'.

11   sue pursue (as if legally, for payment of a debt); sue to, woo
came (who) came

12   my unkind abuse either, 'the unkind mistreatment I have received (from the woman)'; or, 'my own injury to my friend (whom I have allowed to become embroiled on my behalf)'; or both

14   He . . . whole He pays the entire 'debt' to the *covetous* woman – that is, satisfies her sexually, as in the notion of the conjugal debt, the obligation to sustain sexual relations in marriage: cf. Chaucer, *Wife of Bath's* Prologue, 130, 153–5; St Paul, 1 Corinthians, 7.4.
free of debt, i.e. of sexual obligation or tie (RP)

134

So now I have confessed that he is thine,
And I myself am mortgaged to thy will,
Myself I'll forfeit, so that other mine
Thou wilt restore to be my comfort still;
But thou wilt not, nor he will not be free,   5
For thou art covetous, and he is kind;
He learned but surety-like to write for me,
Under that bond that him as fast doth bind.
The statute of thy beauty thou wilt take,
Thou usurer, that put'st forth all to use,   10
And sue a friend, came debtor for my sake:
So him I lose through my unkind abuse.
   Him have I lost; thou hast both him and me;
   He pays the whole, and yet am I not free.

---

1 confessed] confest   2 mortgaged] morgag'd   7 learned] learnd

135 This and the following elaborate the idea of the woman's sexual voracity by means of what Booth (466) calls 'festivals of verbal ingenuity', playing on *will* as a word for sexual desire, a male Christian name, and a word for sexual organs, male or female. Here the word occurs thirteen times (and *wilt* once), seven instances being italicized and capitalized in Q. Since there is probably a designed distinction between the two forms, capitalization has been retained.

1 suggests that while other women may enjoy or nourish mere 'wishes', the woman addressed possesses the more sexually defined and/or humanly individuated *Will*: 'While other women may have (mere) wishes, your sexual desires are fulfilled/you possess your William'. As in the preceding (see 134.14n.) there may be an allusion to Chaucer's Wife of Bath, whose *Tale* illustrates woman's desire for 'sovereynetee', along with the connected adage that 'Women will have their wills', Tilley, W723; cf. also Tilley, W715, 'Women must have their wills while they live because they make none when they die.'

2 **to boot** into the bargain, in addition (*OED* boot *sb.* 1). Q's spelling 'too' may perhaps reinforce the sense of excess.
   in overplus in addition, in excess

3 **More than enough** Playing with the concepts of one and many, the speaker seems to brag that he can serve the lady better than all her other lovers put together.
   am I probably quibbling on 'Will-I-am', as in 121.9
   vex harass, torment, in this case with repeated sexual approaches

4 by vexing you (as above) adding another *will* (sexual organ/man called

William) to your own *sweet* one

5 **whose . . . spacious** suggests, offensively, both that the addressee is generous in her desires, and that her vagina has been enlarged by promiscuity

6 **once** just this once; once and for all

7 **gracious** graceful, attractive

8 **in . . . shine** In, or with reference to, my desire will no prospect of favourable reception be manifest?

9 'The sea refuses no river (is never full)', Tilley, S181; and cf. Orsino's comments on his love, whose capacity 'Receiveth as the sea', *TN* 1.1.11, and in 2.4.101 is 'as hungry as the sea'.

11 **being . . . thy Will** being already rich in desire (your own and/or that of your lovers), and in a man or men called William, nevertheless (I bid you) add to the *Will* you already have: according to Booth (468), 'the slipperiness of the rhetorically calculated ellipsis results in a parody of the deviousness of an unscrupulous, unskillful, and unsuccessful would-be seducer'.

12 one desire (sexual organ) of mine, to enlarge your sexual capaciousness (cf. l. 5 and n.) yet further; there may be a further innuendo on tumescence: 'to make the (male) sexual organ, already enlarged by attraction to you, even bigger'.

13 possibly, 'Let no act of (uncharacteristic) unkindness (*unkind* as noun) frustrate any reasonable sexual entreaties'; or, if punctuated with a comma after '*no*, (*Let no, unkind . . .*) = 'Stop saying "no", unkind mistress, and killing *fair beseechers*'.

14 Regard all your *beseechers* – lovers – as a single one, and treat me as your only object of desire/man called William/ occupant of your sexual space.

135

Whoever hath her wish, thou hast thy Will,
And Will to boot, and Will in overplus;
More than enough am I, that vex thee still,
To thy sweet will making addition thus.
Wilt thou, whose will is large and spacious, 5
Not once vouchsafe to hide my will in thine?
Shall will in others seem right gracious,
And in my will no fair acceptance shine?
The sea, all water, yet receives rain still,
And in abundance addeth to his store; 10
So thou, being rich in Will, add to thy Will
One will of mine, to make thy large Will more:
    Let no unkind, no fair beseechers kill;
    Think all but one, and me in that one Will.

1, 2, 11, 12, 14 Will] *Will*   2 to] too   overplus] ouer-plus

136 This sonnet continues to elaborate puns on *will/Will* in support of the speaker's claim for sexual acceptance.

1 **soul** conscience; intuition
check reprove, rebuke
so near suggests sexual intimacy, as in *all too near*, 61.14

2 **thy blind soul** inherently blind, 'because it is shut up within the body and so cannot verify what is reported to it' (Booth, 470, summarizing T.G. Tucker); or blinded by passion
I . . . Will I was what you desired; your man called William

3 **admitted** allowed to enter; acknowledged as an entity
there refers both to the woman's *soul* and her genitals (RP)

4 **sweet** may apply to *love-suit*; or function as an address to the *sweet* woman; or, adverbially, suggest the sweetly pleasurable fulfilment of the *love-suit*

5 **Will will fulfil** 'William/sexual desire will gratify': the threefold *-ill* sound creates a comic or satiric effect, as well as hinting at the 'ill' or evil nature of what is proposed.
treasure associated with female sexual reward, as in 2.6, *Oth* 4.3.88; and with female pudenda, *Ham* 1.3.31, *MM* 2.4.97, *Cym* 2.2.42

6 **Ay . . . wills** opens up the word *fulfil* to bring out its literal application: Indeed, fill (your sexual organ) full to the brim with male sexual organs. Q's 'I' suggests also 'I, alone, can do this', resuming the sexual brag of 'More than enough am I' in l. 3 of the preceding sonnet. For puns on 'I/Ay', cf. *RJ* 3.2.45–50; *R2* 4.1.201.
my will one my sexual organ one among the crowd; my sexual organ unique, alone able to fill your treasury or satisfy your desire for *treasure*

7 **In . . . receipt** with reference to *things* (sexual organs; cf. *1H4* 3.3.20–4; *TGV* 3.1.342–6) of large capacity, able

to 'receive' or contain a great deal
with . . . prove we easily demonstrate (that)

8 Cf. Marlowe, *Hero and Leander*, 1.255–6: 'One is no number; maids are nothing then / Without the sweet society of men' (*Poems*, 17), a truism derived from Aristotle's *Metaphysics*, 1080a, becoming proverbial by this period; cf. Tilley, O54. *Reckoned* suggests both 'apprehended' and 'calculated'.

9 **in . . . untold** let me be included (embraced) in the *number* (of your lovers) uncounted, or unspoken of; cf. *tell* as 'count or calculate', as in 12.1.

10 **thy store's account** the list of goods you possess; the list of your ample (sexual) possessions: for *store* as 'ample possessions or provision', cf. 14.12, 64.8.

11 **hold . . . hold** plays on *hold* as 'embrace', as in 'to have and to hold' in the Prayer Book marriage vows (*BCP*, 292); and as 'esteem, evaluate', as in *Ham* 2.2.44–5: 'I hold my duty as I hold my soul / Both to my God and to my gracious King'.

12 **That nothing, me,** that nothing, thing of no worth, which is me
a . . . thee an object which is pleasurable, or lovable, or of value, in your estimation: echoes and redefines the ambivalent *sweet* of l. 4

13 **Make but** only make; make only

14 appears to clinch the case for the lady's assent by equating her self-evident love for *will* – her desire, sexual or otherwise – with the speaker's name: 'Your desire is your *will*, so *Will* must be what you love.' No doubt there is a suggestion both that 'my name is William' and 'my name is desire (will) – I am synonymous with what you want'; cf. *Ham* 1.2.146, 'Frailty, thy name is woman'.

136

If thy soul check thee that I come so near,
Swear to thy blind soul that I was thy Will,
And will, thy soul knows, is admitted there;
Thus far for love my love-suit sweet fulfil.
Will will fulfil the treasure of thy love,   5
Ay, fill it full with wills, and my will one;
In things of great receipt with ease we prove
Among a number one is reckoned none.
Then in the number let me pass untold,
Though in thy store's account I one must be.   10
For nothing hold me, so it please thee hold
That nothing, me, a something sweet to thee.
    Make but my name thy love, and love that still;
    And then thou lov'st me, for my name is Will.

2, 5, 14 Will] *Will*   6 Ay,] I   8 reckoned] reckon'd   12 something] some-thing   14 lov'st] louest

137 After eleven sonnets celebrating the erotic power of the 'dark lady', the speaker draws attention to his distorted vision: his eyes have construed the 'dark lady' as fair, leading his heart to believe, wrongly, that she is also virtuous; yet he continues to be governed by blind love.

1 **blind fool love** Cupid, traditionally represented as blind; cf. Tilley, L506, 'Love is blind.' Sidney called love a 'fool' in *AS*, 11.14.

2 **see . . . see** do not correctly interpret what they see; cf. the account of the heathen in Psalms, 115.5, 'eyes have they, but they see not'.

3 **where it lies** where (true) beauty resides; perhaps with a subsidiary sense of 'in what respect it is deceptive, lying'

4 **take** suppose, esteem (*OED* 47)

5 **corrupt . . . looks** whose judgement is distorted by looking with too much 'partiality', particular favour

6 **the . . . ride** the harbour (female body) where *all men* find sexual release: ships were normally described as 'riding' at anchor (*OED* ride 7a). For the sexual application of a ship coming in to harbour, cf. *Oth* 2.1.76–80: 'Great Jove, Othello guard, / And swell his sail with thine own powerful breath, / That he may bless this bay with his tall ship, / And swiftly come to Desdemona's arms'. Note also the more explicitly sexual elaboration of the metaphor in Thomas Carew's *A Rapture*, 85ff.: 'Yet my tall Pine, shall in the *Cyprian* straight / Ride safe at Anchor, and unlade her fraight'.

7 Still addressing love, the speaker asks 'Why have you fashioned (or falsely created) hooks out of the false judgement, or unreliability, of (my) eyes?' **forged** forgèd

8 **judgement . . . heart** inner judgement, love: the octave's sustained conceit depends on a strained distinction between *eyes* and *heart,* suggesting that, but for Cupid's mischievous manipulation, the speaker's eyes might have been deceived, leaving his heart nevertheless untouched.

9 **think** consider, believe
   a several plot a private, separate area, such as a walled or fenced garden-plot: see *OED* several 7a, 'of land, *esp.* of enclosed pasture'.

10 **the . . . place** the region where all people (at least, all male persons) go: a dry-land equivalent of 'the bay where all men ride' in l. 6

11 **Or mine eyes** or (why do) my eyes?
    this . . . this this fact, that the woman whose beauty I have praised is promiscuous

12 with the consequence that my eyes have projected sexual virtue, as well as beauty (*fair truth*), on to such an unattractive exterior: like many characters in Shakespeare's plays, the speaker has extrapolated from a *fair* appearance (though in this case, paradoxically, *foul,* but love is blind) a virtuous nature: cf. for instance *Cym* 5.5.62–6: 'Mine eyes / Were not in fault, for she was beautiful; / Mine ears that heard her flattery, nor my heart / That thought her like her seeming'.

13 **In** with regard to; cf. 136.7.

14 **this false plague** this 'affliction of distorted perceptions' (Booth, 476); this false woman, who is a *plague* to me. There is no doubt an additional suggestion that, because of her promiscuity, the woman is infected and infectious; cf. Lear's description of Goneril, *KL* 2.4.225–7, as 'a boil, / A plague-sore, or embossed carbuncle / In my corrupted blood'.
    transferred may be taken to suggest that the speaker formerly loved a *true* woman: the legal sense of 'transfer' as 'convey, make over' (*OED* 2) is partly applicable.

137

Thou blind fool love, what dost thou to mine eyes,
That they behold, and see not what they see?
They know what beauty is, see where it lies,
Yet what the best is, take the worst to be.
If eyes, corrupt by over-partial looks,   5
Be anchored in the bay where all men ride,
Why of eyes' falsehood hast thou forged hooks,
Whereto the judgement of my heart is tied?
Why should my heart think that a several plot
Which my heart knows the wide world's common
       place?   10
Or mine eyes, seeing this, say this is not,
To put fair truth upon so foul a face?
   In things right true my heart and eyes have erred,
   And to this false plague are they now transferred.

6 anchored] anchord   8 tied] tide

138 This sonnet analyses the system of mutually dependent self-deception by which the speaker pretends his mistress is chaste and she pretends he is young. This and 144 were included in *The Passionate Pilgrim* (1599); see Introduction, pp. 1–3.

1   **made of truth** composed of fidelity, perhaps with a pun on 'maid' = virgin

2   **lies** is lying; 'lies with' other men

3   **That** so that
    some untutored youth some young man inexperienced in love; cf. 'untutor'd churl', *2H6* 3.2.213; 'Untutor'd lad', *3H6* 5.5.32.

4   **Unlearned** unlearnèd: almost synonymous with *untutored* in the preceding line, yet elaborates the point: the speaker has neither been taught about the ways of the world, nor gained independent experience of them.
    the . . . subtleties the crafty and deceptive stratagems of the majority of humankind; cf. *OED* subtlety 3, 4; and *VA* 675, 'the fox which lives by subtlety'.

5   **vainly** wrongly, falsely; prompted by my own vanity, self-conceit

7, 8 **Simply, simple truth** Paradoxically, by pretending to be a 'simple-

ton' in behaving as if he believes the woman's flattering words, the speaker colludes with her in refusing to acknowledge the truth which is *simple* in the sense of self-evident, manifest.

9   **unjust** incorrect; inaccurate (cf. *OED* 3, 4, with an example from John Davies of Hereford's *Mirum in Modum* (1602), 1.2212): suggests a reference to the woman's untruthfulness in claiming to be *made of truth*, as in l. 1, i.e. faithful, constant; and in her consequent flattering of her lover as *young*

11 **best habit** the best adornment (garments); the best habitual demeanour or practice
    seeming trust in appearing to trust, or to be trustworthy, or both

12 **age in love** an old person when in love: for *age* as 'an aged person', cf. *WT* 4.4.750; also *PP* 12, 'Crabbed age and youth'.
    told recounted; enumerated

13 **lie with** collude in untruths with; have sex with: cf. Othello's confused railings, *Oth* 4.1.35–6: 'Lie with her? lie on her? We say lie on her when they belie her. Lie with her, zounds, that's fulsome!'

138

When my love swears that she is made of truth,
I do believe her, though I know she lies,
That she might think me some untutored youth
Unlearned in the world's false subtleties.
Thus vainly thinking that she thinks me young,   5
Although she knows my days are past the best,
Simply I credit her false-speaking tongue;
On both sides thus is simple truth suppressed.
But wherefore says she not she is unjust?
And wherefore say not I that I am old?   10
O love's best habit is in seeming trust,
And age in love loves not t' have years told:
    Therefore I lie with her, and she with me,
    And in our faults by lies we flattered be.

---

3 untutored] vntuterd   4 Unlearned] Vnskilfull *PP*   subtleties] subtilties *Q;* forgeries *PP, Benson*
6 she knows my days] I know my yeares *PP*   7 Simply I credite] I smiling, credite *PP*   false-
speaking] false speaking   8] Outfacing faults in Loue, with loues ill rest. *PP, Benson*   suppressed]
supprest   9 says . . . unjust] sayes my Loue that she is young *PP*   11 in seeming trust] a soothing
toung *PP, Benson*   13] Therfore I'll lye with Loue, and Loue with me, *PP, Benson*   14] Since that
our faults in Loue thus smother'd be. *PP, Benson*

139 The speaker elaborates the theme of the woman's lack of *truth* in an appeal to her to be less open in her wandering glances, however unfaithful she may be in actuality.

1 presumably alludes to the ingenious paradoxes of the two preceding sonnets, in which the speaker has expounded and to some extent 'justified' his devotion to a promiscuous woman

3 'Do not injure me by turning your eye elsewhere, but by speaking to me (of your other lovers).'

4 probably, 'deploy your power powerfully and/or overtly, and do not destroy me by means of oblique or subtle stratagems'.

5 **Tell . . . elsewhere** primarily, 'tell me that you love someone else'; but with a suggestion also of 'choose another, less public, place for telling me of your deviant affection'.

6 **Dear heart** a form of affectionate address to the woman, rather than an allusion to the speaker's own organ of emotion: cf. the application of the phrase to the fair youth in 95.13.

glance . . . aside make sidelong glances away from me – by implication, towards other lovers: for the metaphorical application of 'glance aside', cf. 76.3.

7 **cunning . . . might** *Cunning* and *might* correspond with the distinction between *art* and *power* in l. 4. The tone is probably sarcastic, for it seems

that the woman is being quite overt in making eyes at other men while she is with the speaker; but he supposedly implores her to be less subtle.

8 **my o'er-pressed defence** presumably, 'my already worn-down resistance (to the onslaught of your attractive looks)'

bide endure; withstand: cf. *RJ* 1.1.211, 'Nor bide th'encounter of assailing eyes'.

9 **Let . . . thee** Making a true *volta* in the sestet, the speaker attempts, after all, to justify, or *excuse*, the woman's wandering looks.

my love the woman

10–12 elaborates the Petrarchan conceit of the woman's eyes as 'killing' the lover: since they have thus injured the speaker, she supposedly spares him by turning their injurious force on others.

14 By turning her looks on him, rather than others, the woman can free him of pain by killing him *outright*: this suggests that the lady is like the basilisk, which could kill with its gaze (cf. *3H6* 3.2.187, *Cym* 2.4.107 and other examples), and may be read either as a plea for devoted affection, or as a satirical death-wish. Monarchs, too, were thought of as having killing looks, as in *R2* 3.2.165. Like the references to *groans* in 131 and 133, the speaker's elaboration of *looks* can be construed as savagely mocking rather than complimentary.

139

O call not me to justify the wrong
That thy unkindness lays upon my heart;
Wound me not with thine eye, but with thy tongue;
Use power with power, and slay me not by art.
Tell me thou lov'st elsewhere; but in my sight,   5
Dear heart, forbear to glance thine eye aside.
What need'st thou wound with cunning, when thy
        might
Is more than my o'er-pressed defence can bide?
Let me excuse thee: ah, my love well knows
Her pretty looks have been mine enemies,   10
And therefore from my face she turns my foes
That they elsewhere might dart their injuries.
   Yet do not so, but since I am near slain,
   Kill me outright with looks, and rid my pain.

4 art] Art   5, 12 elsewhere] else-where   8 o'er-pressed] ore-prest   14 outright] out-right

140 Building on the preceding sonnet, the speaker implores the woman at least to behave and speak as if she loves him, for fear of driving him mad and so provoking him to speak ill of her.

1 **press** subject to pressure, probably with reference to executing 'the punishment of *peine forte et dure* upon a person arraigned for felony who stood mute', *OED* press 1a, b. Shakespeare elsewhere associates unpleasant sexual dealings with a woman with 'pressing to death', as in *MM* 5.1.520; in *TC* 3.2.217–18 the image immediately precedes an allusion to 'tongue-tied maidens'.

2 **tongue-tied** Like Sidney's Astrophil, Shakespeare deploys the conceit of his own silence as a lover, despite the fact that the lover's voice alone is heard in his sonnets: cf. *AS*, 54.13.

4 **pity-wanting pain** 'pain caused by your lack of pity, and/or by my desire for you to pity me'

5 **wit** ingenuity, craftiness, perhaps with reference to the sexual knowingness that supposedly enables a woman to get or keep a man: cf. the Nurse's husband's remark to the toddler Juliet, 'Thou wilt fall backward when thou hast more wit', *RJ* 1.3.41.

5–6 'It would be better, though you are unable or unwilling to love me, at least to take pleasure (*to love*) in telling me that you do.'

7 **testy** short-tempered, peevish (*OED* 2a)

8 'Doctors give (peevish) dying men none but favourable bulletins, in order to avoid exciting their wrath.'

10 Though the speaker warns the woman that her cruel behaviour may provoke him to *speak ill* of her in the future, it could be argued, if the sonnets are read sequentially, that he has already spoken ill of her in the preceding sonnets, in which she is depicted as ugly and promiscuous. Seven sonnets further on, in 147, the speaker's prediction that he may *grow mad*, and consequently speak in a mad, disordered way, is explicitly fulfilled.

11 **Now** now that; now (it is the case) that
this ill-wresting world this world (of rumour and false speech) which is so apt to twist ('wrest') the truth, or to make the good seem bad

12 **mad ears** synecdoche for hearers, all those madmen who either 'wrest' the words they hear, or, conversely, fail to recognize them as slanderous
believed believèd

13 **belied** lied about; Q's 'be lyde' permits a suggestion also of 'be lain with', i.e. be spoken of as sleeping around; cf. *Oth* 4.1.35–6 (see 138. 13n.)

14 reverts to the more conventional allusion to a mistress's *eyes*, rather than *eye*: develops the Petrarchan and Sidneian conceit of her eyes shooting out beams of light like arrows from a (or Cupid's) bow: cf. Sidney, *AS*, 47.2, 66.11. She is implored to aim them at the speaker alone – *straight* – even though internally her *proud heart* carries her affections *wide* of the mark.

140

Be wise as thou art cruel, do not press
My tongue-tied patience with too much disdain,
Lest sorrow lend me words, and words express
The manner of my pity-wanting pain.
If I might teach thee wit, better it were,   5
Though not to love, yet love to tell me so,
As testy sick men, when their deaths be near,
No news but health from their physicians know:
For if I should despair, I should grow mad,
And in my madness might speak ill of thee;   10
Now this ill-wresting world is grown so bad,
Mad slanderers by mad ears believed be.
   That I may not be so, nor thou belied,
   Bear thine eyes straight, though thy proud heart go
      wide.

2 tongue-tied] toung tide   4 pity-wanting] pittie wanting   7 sick men] sick-men   8 physicians]
Phisitions   11 ill-wresting] ill wresting   13 belied] be lyde

141 Denying that he loves the woman with any of his five senses, the speaker claims somewhat sardonically to love her only with his heart, the site both of sin and of the suffering which is the penalty for sin.

1 **In faith** perhaps sarcastic; cf. *in good faith*, 131.5.
    eyes Cf. 137 on the corruption of both *eyes* and *heart*.

2 **errors** primarily, 'deviations from beauty, i.e. uglinesses'; but following allusions to the woman's promiscuity in the six preceding sonnets, there is doubtless some suggestion also of 'moral errors'.
    note notice; enumerate: cf. 99.14, and *Luc* 208.

3 **they** my eyes

4 **in . . . view** in spite of what my eyes see: probably with a pun on 'in despite of you'
    is . . . dote chooses to love excessively or foolishly (cf. 'please' as impersonal passive verb, *OED* 4b)

6 Nor is my own delicate sense of touch eager for *base touches*, i.e. low-grade or unpleasing sexual encounters: cf. the Duke's references to the 'abominable and beastly touches' which are the pimp's livelihood, *MM* 3.2.23. For *prone* as 'eager', cf. *Cym* 5.4.205.

7 **Nor taste** nor (do) taste

7–8 **desire . . . alone** The metaphor of sexual congress as a *sensual feast*, though found in Ficino and elsewhere, may here allude specifically to George Chapman's *Ovids Banquet of Sence* (1595), which explores Ovid's attraction to Corynna bathing through a celebration of each of the five senses, culminating in touch. The

final phrase makes the sexual application clear: while a literal *feast* would require the presence of many guests, this is a private banquet *with thee alone*.

9 **But my** but (neither) my
    five wits . . . senses Shakespeare consistently distinguishes the *five wits* from the *five senses*: cf. *RJ* 1.4.47, 3.4.78; *MA* 1.1.66; *KL* 3.4.58, 3.6.57. For a detailed analysis of the five senses and wits, cf. Sir John Davies, *Nosce Teipsum* (1599), 960–1171. But as Booth (487) observes, 'their juxtaposition is carefully calculated to confuse in the very act of distinguishing'.

10 **serving** rendering obedience to you as your lover, possibly with a subsidiary sense of 'mate with' – the second application normally referring to the copulation of animals (*OED* serve 8d, 52)

11 **unswayed** unwielded; uncontrolled (*OED*; and cf. *RJ* 4.4.470). Booth (487) paraphrases: 'the speaker's body is left unswayed – he is left a shell of a man – because his heart has left . . . to live in his lady's bosom as a slave'.

12 **slave . . . wretch** Cf. 57.1, where the speaker was the young man's *slave*, and 58.4, where he was his *vassal*.

13–14 Samuel Butler aptly glossed, 'I shall suffer less for my sin hereafter, for I get some of the punishment coincidentally with the offence' (quoted in Booth, 488). The *pain* the woman gives him may be either emotional – caused by her unkindness, her open promiscuity – or physical: if she infects him with venereal disease she punishes him directly for his sexual *sin*.

141

In faith, I do not love thee with mine eyes,
For they in thee a thousand errors note;
But 'tis my heart that loves what they despise,
Who in despite of view is pleased to dote.
Nor are mine ears with thy tongue's tune delighted,   5
Nor tender feeling to base touches prone,
Nor taste, nor smell, desire to be invited
To any sensual feast with thee alone:
But my five wits, nor my five senses, can
Dissuade one foolish heart from serving thee,   10
Who leaves unswayed the likeness of a man,
Thy proud heart's slave and vassal wretch to be:
    Only my plague thus far I count my gain,
    That she that makes me sin, awards me pain.

4 pleased] pleasd   11 unswayed] vnswai'd

397

142 Continuing from the end of the preceding sonnet, the speaker elaborates a chiastic conceit of his own sexual *sin* and the woman's sexual *virtue*, or scornful treatment of him.

1 The speaker sins in loving (wooing, or making love to) the woman, whereas she, in scorning him, appears to manifest virtue: *dear virtue* suggests 'the virtue you hold dear', but in context appears ironic.

2 suggests primarily that the woman hates the speaker's *sinful*, because lustful, *love* of her; however, in the light of the next eight lines it seems that the woman's *hate* is also 'grounded on sinful loving', i.e., derived from her own uncontrolled sexual desire; the pot calls the kettle black.

6 **profaned . . . ornaments** treats promiscuity as a form of sacrilege, in which the woman has dishonoured the holy redness of her lips by kissing too freely. Booth (491–2) suggests an allusion to 'scarlet vestments', and so, by association with cardinals, to the 'cardinal virtues'; but the following line invokes, rather, an association with red wax seals on legal documents, which might bear the impress of ecclesiastical or civic authority. Shakespeare nowhere else describes lips as *scarlet* (though Sidney does, identifying them with the scarlet robes of judges, *AS*, 73.11), and there may be an ironical inversion of the biblical associations of *scarlet* with sin in general and sinful women in particular: cf. Isaiah, 1.18; Revelation, 17.3; and cf. Spenser, *FQ*, 1.ii.13.2, 1.viii.29.2.

7 **sealed . . . love** bestowed kisses which have offered false assurances of commitment: Shakespeare often identifies kisses with seals, as in *VA* 511, *TGV* 2.2.7, *RJ* 5.3.114, *KJ* 2.1.20; closest analogy is offered by the song sung to Mariana, *MM* 4.1.5–6: 'But my kisses bring again, bring again; /Seals of love, but seal'd in vain, seal'd in vain'.

8 **others' . . . rents** The distinction between *rents* and *revenues* (pronounced revènues) is not a sharp one: the general sense is that 'you and I have both (often) deprived our lawful partners of their sexual due, bestowing sexual favours elsewhere'. Cf. Emilia's protest at straying husbands who 'pour our treasures into foreign laps', thus provoking their wives to do likewise, *Oth* 4.3.88.

9 **Be it** if it is
lawful allowable that I . . .

10 **Whom . . . woo** whom you pursue with amorous looks, as in 139 and 140
importune impòrtune

11 **Root** plant, establish

13 **what . . . hide** pity, here equated with sexual compliance: the notion seems to recall the citation of those 'That do not do the thing they most do show', 94.2: while those individuals are praised for moving others but being themselves unmoved, this addressee is implored, conversely, to release in herself the susceptibility to (sexual) feeling that she provokes in others.

14 **self-example** the example of yourself
denied denied (sexual favours)

142

Love is my sin, and thy dear virtue hate,
Hate of my sin, grounded on sinful loving;
O but with mine compare thou thine own state,
And thou shalt find it merits not reproving;
Or if it do, not from those lips of thine,   5
That have profaned their scarlet ornaments,
And sealed false bonds of love as oft as mine,
Robbed others' beds' revenues of their rents.
Be it lawful I love thee as thou lov'st those
Whom thine eyes woo, as mine importune thee,   10
Root pity in thy heart, that when it grows,
Thy pity may deserve to pitied be.
    If thou dost seek to have what thou dost hide,
    By self-example mayst thou be denied.

6 profaned] prophan'd   7 sealed] seald   8 Robbed] Robd

143 An unusually extended simile is set up in the first eight lines: the woman is compared to one who, in running after a strayed fowl, abandons her babe-in-arms, which pursues her. The *feathered creature* is presumably to be identified with the object or objects of the woman's amorous glances in 139–40 and 142.9–10, and the speaker, as becomes apparent in the last three lines, identifies himself with the *neglected child*. The sonnet plays on the traditional image of amorous pursuit as a hunt, but in a scaled-down, unchivalric, domestic arena – not a royal game forest, but a humble backyard. It also recalls and reverses the central thrust of *VA*: instead of showing a woman in hot sexual pursuit of a young boy who prefers hunting animals, Shakespeare here shows a child in desperate pursuit of a woman who prefers hunting for a chicken to caring for her infant.

1 **careful** conscientious, painstaking; full of cares or anxieties
housewife pronounced 'hussif': 'a woman who manages or directs the affairs of her household . . . a woman who manages her household with skill and thrift' (*OED* 1; and cf. *AYL* 1.2.33)

2 **feathered creatures** primarily denotes chickens or other domestic fowl, but there may also, as Booth (494–5) suggests, be a suggestion of 'the sort of dandified rivals – the "popinjays" – of which men in the speaker's situation are traditionally both jealous and scornful'. Also, since the woman gives priority to the *feathered creature* over her child, there may be a sidelong reference to the proverb 'Fair feathers make fair fowls', Tilley, F163.
broke away (which has) broken away (from the flock)

3 **dispatch** speed, haste (*OED* 6b)

4 **pursuit** stress on the first syllable

5 **holds . . . chase** chases after her, gives chase; with an ironical contrast between the child's 'holding chase' and the woman's failure to 'hold' the child

6 **to catch her** to capture her attention
bent directed, intent upon

7 **flies . . . face** exploits the coincidence in meaning between 'fly' and 'flee', both to suggest biblical images such as those of the ungodly who 'flee before' the face of God (Psalms, 68.1), or of Jacob, who 'fleddest from the face of Esau' (Genesis, 35.1), and to suggest that 'even as she is watching it, the bird takes to its wings'

8 **Not prizing** thinking nothing of, caring nothing for: see *OED* prize *v.* 3b, with this example; and *WT* 4.4.386.
discontent unhappiness, resentment; cf. *LC* 56.

10 **chase . . . behind** pursue you from a distant position to the rear: recalls two earlier unsuccessful lovers, Chaucer's Pandarus, who remarks 'I hoppe alwey byhynde' (*Troilus and Criseyde*, 2.1107), and Wyatt's persona in the sonnet 'Whoso list to hunt', who claims 'I am of them that farthest cometh behind' (Wyatt, 77)

11 **thy hope** that which you hope for: cf. Sidney's *OA*, 12, in which Pyrocles/Cleophila sings sapphics to Philoclea 'speaking as it were to her own hope'

12 **be kind** behave with natural affection, no doubt with a play on sexual 'kindness'

13 **thy Will** equated with *thy hope* in l. 11, as well as with 'that which all women wish for', as in 135–6. If both pursuer and pursued are named William, there is a redoubled suggestion that the speaker will pray for her to possess both.

14 **still** silence, pacify with kisses

143

Lo, as a careful housewife runs to catch
One of her feathered creatures broke away,
Sets down her babe, and makes all swift dispatch
In pursuit of the thing she would have stay;
Whilst her neglected child holds her in chase,   5
Cries to catch her whose busy care is bent
To follow that which flies before her face,
Not prizing her poor infant's discontent:
So run'st thou after that which flies from thee,
Whilst I, thy babe, chase thee afar behind.   10
But if thou catch thy hope, turn back to me,
And play the mother's part, kiss me, be kind:
   So will I pray that thou mayst have thy Will,
   If thou turn back and my loud crying still.

7 face,] face: 13 Will] *Will*

144 The speaker describes his *Two loves,*
apparently the 'fair youth' and 'dark
lady', and his fears that the latter has
inveigled the former into her sexual
space. He makes a sexual application
of the medieval concept of the psy-
chomachia, in which a good angel and
an evil one compete for possession of
a man's soul. The sonnet's number in
the sequence, 12 × 12, known as a
'gross', may be especially appropriate
to this enumeration of the speaker's
amorous possessions, which prove to
be 'gross' also in the sexual sense: cf.
Jonson, *Every Man in his Humour,*
3.1.81, where Lorenzo Junior pours
scorn on Stephen's supposed ability
to utter sonnets 'by the grosse'.

    With 138, this sonnet first
appeared in *The Passionate Pilgrim*
(1599) (see Introduction, pp. 1–6).
The *PP* text of 144 varies less radical-
ly from Q than does that of 138, and
in l. 6 offers a reading, *side* for Q's
'sight', which appears superior; see
below.

1 **Two loves** two objects of love
2 **spirits** incorporeal beings, often 'conceived as troublesome, terrifying, or
hostile to mankind' (*OED* spirit 3a): in
Marlowe's *Doctor Faustus,* for
instance, 'spirit' is used throughout to
denote specifically an evil spirit or
devil (Marlowe, *Doctor Faustus,* p. 10);
cf. also Lady Macbeth's invocation of
'you Spirits / That tend on mortal
thoughts', *Mac* 1.5.39–40.
    suggest insinuate (to evil), prompt (to
good or evil action) (*OED* 1a, b); cf.
MW 3.3.230, 'What spirit, what devil,
suggests this imagination?'
    still continually
3, 4 **The better angel . . . The worser
spirit** separates off *spirit,* with its predominantly negative associations,
from *angel,* with its predominantly
positive ones: cf. *Doctor Faustus* (B
text), where the first entry of the
Good and Bad Angels runs 'Enter the
Angel and *Spirit*'.
3 **right fair** As elsewhere, the *fair* youth
may not be so much literally blond in
complexion as *fair* because intensely

loved and lovable, as in the expression
'white boy', 'A favourite, pet or darling boy' (*OED* 1): cf. *A Yorkshire
Tragedy* (1608), Malone Society
(1973), 510–11.

4 **coloured ill** of an unpleasing or ugly
complexion; but like the 'fairness' of
the man, the bad colouring of the
woman may be as much emotional as
literal, especially given the sense of
coloured as 'specious' or 'falsely
glossed over' (*OED* 3a, b).

6 ***side** The *better angel* is identified
with the 'guardian angel' assigned to
each human being, whose normal
position would be at the *side* of the
person protected, as in depictions of
Tobias and the Angel; or cf. Herbert's
'The Pilgrimage', 16–18: 'Here I was
robb'd of all my gold, / Save one good
Angell, which a friend had ti'd / Close
to my side'. An even closer analogy is
Oth 5.2.207–10, Gratiano on Desdemona's father's death: 'did he live
now, / This sight would make him do
a desperate turn, / Yea, curse his better angel from his side, / And fall to
reprobation'. There seems little doubt
that *PP*'s *side,* rather than Q's *'sight',*
is correct.

8 **foul pride** pride and assurance which
she manifests despite her *foul* appearance; reprehensible ostentation, magnificence (for the latter, see *OED* pride
6a)

9–11 **fiend . . . friend** evidently an
acceptable rhyme in Elizabethan pronunciation; cf. *VA* 638, 640.

10 'I may be led to suspect, but cannot be
sure by means of direct proof or
sight': Shakespeare may be recalling
the words scratched on a window of
Woodstock Palace by the future
Elizabeth I when she was a prisoner
there: 'Much suspected by me /
Nothing proved can be', as well as the
proverb 'Suspicion is no proof'
(Tilley, S1019); and cf. *Oth* 1.3.106.

11 **being . . . friend** both are out of my
company and in that of each other,
and/or friendly towards each other:
for *from* as 'away from' cf. *OED* 5b,
and *Tim* 4.3.533, *H5* 1.2.272, *Ham*

144

Two loves I have, of comfort and despair,
Which, like two spirits, do suggest me still:
The better angel is a man right fair,
The worser spirit a woman coloured ill.
To win me soon to hell my female evil   5
Tempteth my better angel from my side,
And would corrupt my saint to be a devil,
Wooing his purity with her foul pride;
And whether that my angel be turned fiend
Suspect I may, yet not directly tell;   10
But being both from me both to each friend,
I guess one angel in another's hell.
    Yet this shall I ne'er know, but live in doubt,
    Till my bad angel fire my good one out.

1.2.168 and *passim*; for *to* as 'near to', 'Expressing contiguity or close proximity', see *OED* 5b. But *to each friend* suggests also 'friendly towards each other'. Like Booth (498–9), 'I retain the Q punctuation because it includes the idea that the alliance of the two beloveds occurred only because they were introduced by the mutual friend they have betrayed.'

12 **guess** conjecture
one . . . hell following the clear distinction between *better angel* and *wors-*

er spirit in ll. 3–4, the primary suggestion is that the *man right fair* sexually possesses the *woman coloured ill;* for the equation of the female genitals with *hell* cf. 129.14 and n., and *KL* 4.6.127–30. Booth's suggestion (499–500) that 'each is a punishment to the other' may be an attempt to mitigate the misogyny of the image by distributing culpability equally. Though many commentators have linked the phrase with the game of barley-break, played by three couples,

2 Which] That *PP*   suggest] sugiest   3, 4 The] My *PP*   4 coloured] collour'd *Q;* colour'd *PP*
6 side] *PP, Malone;* sight *Q*   8 foul] fowle *Q;* faire *PP*   9 turned fiend] turn'd finde *Q;* turnde feend
PP   11 from me] to me *PP*   13 Yet . . . know] The truth I shall not know *PP*

in which the middle ground, occupied by the middle couple, is called 'hell', the context no more specifically suggests an allusion to this than it does to the use of 'hell' to refer to the lower part of the stage in the theatre, or to part of the old lawcourts at Westminster, or to a debtors' prison (Chambers, *Stage*, 2.528; 3.30; *OED* hell 5, 6). J.Q.Adams suggested (Rollins, 1.370) that 144 influenced Epigram 15 in Samuel Rowlands's *The Letting of Humours Blood* [1600], the closest analogy being in the lines: 'How can he prove her for an Angell then? / That proves her selfe a Divell, tempting men, / And drawing many to the fierie pit, / Where they are burned for their ent'ring it.' But this, the present sonnet, and the *KL* passage may all draw on a shared traditional association of the female genitalia with a fiery 'hell'; cf., for instance, the obscene elaboration of the conceit in the satire 'News from Heaven and Hell' (see Peck, *passim*),

in which Leicester's lust is punished by perpetual congress with a female fiend: 'Thus was his paradice turned into his purgatory, his fine furred gape into a flaming trape, his place of pleasure into a gulfe of vengance, and his pricke of desier into a pillor of fier'.

13 **ne'er know** never know through observation, or as a fact (*OED* know 8, 10a)

14 until my good angel (the *man right fair*) is driven out by the evil one: see *OED* fire 8a, 'To drive (anyone) away from a place by fire', with examples from Marlowe's *Edward II* 3.2.127, and *KL* 5.3.22–3: 'He that parts us shall bring a brand from heaven, / And fire us hence like foxes'. In 144 there is presumably both an analogy with animals being smoked out of their holes or lairs and a suggestion that the man will sooner or later be venereally infected by the woman; cf. also the proverb 'One fire (heat) drives out another' (Tilley, F277).

144

Two loves I have, of comfort and despair,
Which, like two spirits, do suggest me still:
The better angel is a man right fair,
The worser spirit a woman coloured ill.
To win me soon to hell my female evil   5
Tempteth my better angel from my side,
And would corrupt my saint to be a devil,
Wooing his purity with her foul pride;
And whether that my angel be turned fiend
Suspect I may, yet not directly tell;   10
But being both from me both to each friend,
I guess one angel in another's hell.
    Yet this shall I ne'er know, but live in doubt,
    Till my bad angel fire my good one out.

145 This is a unique sonnet in octosyllabic lines: it describes a lover supposedly devastated by his mistress's declaration that she hates him, rescued only by the favourable completion of her utterance in the final line. Gurr has suggested that the sonnet is very early, belonging to the summer of 1582, when the 18–year-old Shakespeare was wooing Anne Hathaway: see l. 13n. Booth (500) calls it 'the slightest of sonnets', and Pooler (Ard¹) said 'Perhaps not Shakespeare's'.

1–5 make . . . Straight The fivefold iteration of similar sounds in *make . . . hate . . . sake . . . state . . . Straight*, in combination with short lines and a predominance of monosyllables, creates a childish, tripping movement which seems tonally to make light of the speaker's claim that the woman has the power of life and death over him; and note also *used, anew, who, threw* in ll. 7, 8, 12, 13.

1 love's own hand the hand of Cupid, or of Venus: cf. the fair youth's *woman's face,* painted with *nature's own hand,* 20.1.

2 This periphrastic way of indicating that the woman's lips uttered the phrase *I hate* suggests some play with the puffing aspirate at the beginning of *hate.*

3 languished . . . sake Cf. the octosyllabic charm in *MND* 2.2.26–8, when Oberon squeezes love-juice on Titania's

eyes: 'What thou seest when thou dost wake / Do it for thy true love take, / Love and languish for his sake'.

7 Was used was (wont to be) used, was habitually used
gentle doom merciful judgement

8 greet salute, offer words of address (*OED* 3a, b; and cf. *Tit* I. 1.1.90)

9–14 Malone aptly compares *Luc* 1534–40: ' "It cannot be," quoth she, "that so much guile," – / She would have said, – "can lurk in such a look." / But Tarquin's shape came in her mind the while, / And from her tongue "can lurk" from "cannot" took: / "It cannot be" she in that sense forsook, / And turn'd it thus: "It cannot be, I find, / But such a face should bear a wicked mind." '

10–11 as . . . night a tediously obvious analogy, as used in reverse form by Polonius to Laertes, *Ham* 1.3.79: 'it must follow as the night the day / Thou canst not then be false to any man'. The reminiscence of *gentle doom* (l. 7) also reinforces the idea that mercy is more natural to the woman than cruelty.
who refers primarily to *night,* but also suggests the woman's rapidly diminishing hatred

13 'hate' away Gurr suggests a pun on 'Hathaway'.

14 And Booth (501) suggests a play on 'Anne'.

145

Those lips that love's own hand did make
Breathed forth the sound that said 'I hate',
To me, that languished for her sake;
But when she saw my woeful state,
Straight in her heart did mercy come,   5
Chiding that tongue that, ever sweet,
Was used in giving gentle doom,
And taught it thus anew to greet:
'I hate' she altered with an end
That followed it as gentle day   10
Doth follow night, who like a fiend
From heaven to hell is flown away.
   'I hate' from 'hate' away she threw,
   And saved my life, saying 'not you'.

---

1 love's] Loues   2 Breathed] Breath'd   3 languished] languisht   7 used] vsde   doom] dome
9 altered] alterd   10 followed] follow'd   14 saved] sau'd

146 Addressing his *soul,* the speaker
questions the rich and expensive
adornments it bestows on the *earth,* or
body, in which it is housed, exhorting
it to prepare for death by consuming
spiritual riches and repudiating earthly ones. The sonnet has been very
extensively discussed, both because of
its status as Shakespeare's only explicitly religious poem, and because of the
unusually problematic textual crux in
l. 2: for some of the proposed emendations, see textual notes. As far as the
religious connotations go, the sonnet
is perhaps not quite so extraordinary
as has been claimed, but can be linked
with other sonnets on the speaker's
ageing and impending death, such as
63, 71, 73–4 and 81; however, the
absence of any explicit allusion to a
love-object is unusual. The problem
of ageing is here approached in an
individualistic way, posing the question of why an ageing body should be
expensively dressed or generously fed.

1 **centre . . . earth** The body, as a
microcosm of the world, has the soul
as its centre.

2 ***Feeding . . . array** The suggestion
is that the soul, of its essence a spiritual entity, has been captured by
greedy, fleshly forces, which *array,* or
deck splendidly, its external sur-
roundings (*OED* array 8a; there is
probably a play also on *OED* 1, to
draw up prepared for battle) and
require, like hungry troops, to be
'fed'. Maxwell points out that Daniel
used the phrase 'rebel powers' in
Cleopatra (1594), where it is applied to
her own 'False flesh and blood' which
threatens not to co-operate with her
mental determination to kill herself.
The similarity of application leaves
little doubt that this passage was
Shakespeare's source. The emendation *Feeding,* which completes a fourfold pattern of aural and semantic
play on 'feed', with *fading* in l. 6, *be fed*
in 12 and *feed . . . feeds* in l. 13, has
been adopted on the advice of Helen
Vendler. Presumably either eye-slip or
careless dictation led to the Q com-

positor's repetition of *My sinful earth.*

3 **pine** starve, lack food; waste away or
languish (*OED* 5a, b, c)

5 **cost** expense, expenditure; cf. 64.2
so . . . lease such a brief period of
legitimate residence: cf. 'leases of
short-numbered hours', 124.10.

6 **fading mansion** the ageing body,
seen as a decaying house within which
the soul's residence will be brief

8 **charge** expense, outlay (*OED* 10a)
Is . . . end Cf. 'Is this the promis'd
end?', *KL* 5.3.263: suggests both 'Is
this all that your richly adorned body
has come to?' and 'Is this the purpose
for which your body was destined, or
at which it aimed?' (cf. *OED* end 13a,
14a).

9 **thy servant's loss** the (impending)
loss of the body, which should properly be subordinate to the soul

10 **let . . . store** allow the body to languish or waste away (cf. l. 3) in order
to increase your own abundance of
possessions: for *aggravate* as 'increase,
strengthen', see *OED* 5.

11 **terms divine** suggests both legal
conditions or *terms* which are heavenly, hence durable, in contrast to
the 'short lease' of l. 5; and 'heavenly
periods of time' – times without limit,
eternity
hours of dross combines a notion of
wasted time and worthless material
possessions

12 **Within** inwardly
without externally

13 **feed . . . men** Cf. Psalms, 49, commenting on 'those that trust in their
wealth, and boast themselves in the
multitude of their riches', in particular verse 14: 'like sheep they are laid in
the grave; death shall feed on them;
and the upright shall have dominion
over them in the morning; and their
beauty shall consume in the grave
from their dwelling'.

14 The notion, though not the specific
wording, recalls several passages in
the Bible, such as Isaiah, 25.8, 'He will
swallow up death in victory; and the
Lord God will wipe away tears from
all faces'; or two sentences included in

146

Poor soul, the centre of my sinful earth,
Feeding these rebel powers that thee array,
Why dost thou pine within and suffer dearth,
Painting thy outward walls so costly gay?
Why so large cost, having so short a lease,   5
Dost thou upon thy fading mansion spend?
Shall worms, inheritors of this excess,
Eat up thy charge? Is this thy body's end?
Then soul, live thou upon thy servant's loss,
And let that pine to aggravate thy store;   10
Buy terms divine in selling hours of dross,
Within be fed, without be rich no more:
    So shalt thou feed on death, that feeds on men,
    And death once dead, there's no more dying then.

BCP, Burial of the Dead, 'The last enemy that shall be destroyed is death', and 'Death is swallowed up in victory' (1 Corinthians, 26.54). This last may have contributed to the image of 'feeding on' in the preceding line. The sonnet may in turn have contributed something to Donne's *Holy Sonnets*, 10.14, 'Death thou shalt die'.

2 Feeding] *this edn;* My sinfull earth *Q, Benson;* Fool'd by *Malone;* Foil'd by *IR;* [. . .] *Ard¹*

147 Identifying his passion for the woman as a disease, the speaker shows himself abandoned by reason and in the grip of love-madness, which has deranged his judgement. Gregor Sarrazin (Rollins, 1.379) aptly linked it with Sidney's *OA*, 41, an 'octave' in which the duchess Gynecia laments her unfulfilled and unfulfillable desires: 'Like those sick folks, in whome strange humors flowe, / Can taste no sweetes, the sower onely please: / So to my minde, while passions daylie growe, / Whose fyrie chaines, uppon his freedome seaze, / Joie's strangers seeme, I cannot bide their showe, / Nor brooke ought els but well acquainted woe. / Bitter griefe tastes me best, paine is my ease, / Sicke to the death, still loving my disease.'

1–2 longing . . . longer Placed in such close proximity, these words suggest that *longing still / For* contains also a sense of 'desiring to prolong'.

2 nurseth the disease cherishes and sustains the illness, rather than the individual who suffers from it

3 Feeding If the emendation *Feeding* is accepted in 146.2, the word links these two sonnets, which both present the speaker's helpless subjection to desire in terms of gluttony.

the ill the disease, sickness (*OED* ill *sb.* 6)

4 uncertain sickly appetite the waver-ing appetite (desire) of a sick man

5 My reason Perhaps it was 'reason's' voice that we heard in the preceding sonnet, imploring the pining soul to feed itself and not the body, or bodily appetites.

6 prescriptions 'doctor's orders', 'any course of hygiene ordered by a physician' (*OED* 2); limitations or restrictions (*OED* 3)

7 desperate in despair; desperately sick **approve** discover by experience (*OED* 9)

8 'that (sexual) desire to which medical advice took exception, or objected, is fatal or death-bringing': cf. *OED* except 4; and *R2* 1.1.72.

9 reverses the proverb 'Past cure, past care' (Tilley, C921): it is his lack of *care* – heedfulness to reason – that places him beyond hope of recovery – *cure*. Cf. *LLL* 5.2.28.

10 frantic mad frantically mad: see *OED* frantic 4, with this as the first example

11 discourse speech

12 At random haphazardly, aimlessly: see *OED* random 3a; cf. also *1H6* 5.3.84, 'He talks at random (*F*: randon): sure the man is mad'. Q's spelling, 'randon', is correct in the period, deriving from Old Fr. *randon,* force, rapid movement.

13 I . . . fair as in sonnets 127 and 130

14 as black as hell proverbial: cf. Tilley, H397, and *LLL* 4.3.254.

147

My love is as a fever, longing still
For that which longer nurseth the disease,
Feeding on that which doth preserve the ill,
Th'uncertain sickly appetite to please:
My reason, the physician to my love,   5
Angry that his prescriptions are not kept,
Hath left me, and I, desperate, now approve
Desire is death, which physic did except.
Past cure I am, now reason is past care,
And frantic mad with ever more unrest;   10
My thoughts and my discourse as madmen's are,
At random from the truth vainly expressed:
    For I have sworn thee fair, and thought thee bright,
    Who art as black as hell, as dark as night.

---

5 physician] Phisition 8 physic] Phisick 9 reason] Reason 10 ever more] euer-more
12 random] *Malone;* randon *Q* expressed] exprest

148 This sonnet continues from the end of the preceding, elaborating the theme of the speaker's love-madness and distorted judgement.

1 love Whereas in line 147.1 *love* seemed to denote the emotion felt by the speaker, it seems here to be displaced into an external force, implicitly equated with Cupid.

4 censures ... aright explores the possibility that the error is not in his eyes, but in his capacity to judge or appraise correctly what his eyes see, *censures* here having no sense of 'judge adversely': cf. *OED* censure 1, and *JC* 3.2.16, 'Censure me in your wisdom'.

5 both affirms and denies the validity of his appraisal of the love-object, by first raising the possibility that this object is indeed – according to external criteria – *fair*, yet describing the eyes that view her adoringly as *false*. For *dote* cf. 141.4 and n.

6 the world people in general, general opinion (*OED* 15); and cf. 107.2

7–8 love ... men's 'The love (I have) indicates clearly that the vision of those in love is not as accurate as that of everyone else': a circuitous way of arriving at the truism that 'Love is

blind' (Tilley, L506). For *denote* as 'indicate (outwardly)', cf. *OED* 3 and *RJ* 3.3.110.

8–9 Love's eye ... love's eye seems to conflate Cupid's eyes – which are, of course, blind – with the wearied eyes of the speaker, perhaps with a play on 'love's I'

10 vexed afflicted, troubled with pain or distress (*OED* vex 2, 3a).
watching staying awake at night, keeping watch; cf. 61.13 and n.

11 No marvel It is not surprising, or cause for amazement: cf. *VA* 390, 'Therefore no marvel though thy horse be gone'.

12 The sun, as in 18.5, is treated as 'the eye of heaven', which here cannot see (the earth) until the intervening *heaven* is free of clouds.

13 cunning skilful, ingenious; artful, sly (*OED* 2,5)
love seems here to conflate *love* = Cupid with *love* = the woman loved: both keep the speaker blind with tears so that the *foul faults* (l. 14) of both are obscured. However, *foul faults* seems more aptly to apply to the woman, as in 138.14.

14 eyes well seeing eyes which see truly

148

O me! What eyes hath love put in my head,
Which have no correspondence with true sight?
Or if they have, where is my judgement fled,
That censures falsely what they see aright?
If that be fair whereon my false eyes dote,   5
What means the world to say it is not so?
If it be not, then love doth well denote,
Love's eye is not so true as all men's: no,
How can it? O how can love's eye be true,
That is so vexed with watching and with tears?   10
No marvel then though I mistake my view:
The sun itself sees not, till heaven clears.
    O cunning love, with tears thou keep'st me blind,
    Lest eyes well seeing thy foul faults should find.

---

10 vexed] vext

149 The speaker is so acquiescent to his mistress's desires that he loves and hates those whom she loves and hates, even if that means hating himself.

2 **partake** take sides: *OED* 5, with this example. Sidney uses 'partakers' in the sense of 'supporters' in *The Lady of May* (*Prose*, 21).

4 *****all . . . sake** Malone's insertion of commas on either side of *all tyrant* has been adopted. The address to the mistress as *cruel*, combined with the Petrarchan convention of identifying the mistress as a *tyrant* (cf. Sidney, *AS*, 5.85; Spenser, *Amoretti*, 10.5), support his interpretation: 'that is, for the sake of thee, thou tyrant'. However, if *tyrant* is not so marked off, the phrase may with some difficulty be read as suggesting 'Entirely for your sake, I am prepared to be a tyrant to anyone or everyone (including myself)', *all* being either the object of *tyrant* – 'to all' – or an adverb modifying it – 'entirely' – or both.

5 **Who** who is there who?

7 **lour'st** look on me angrily, scowl: cf. *VA* 75, 'still he lours and frets'.
spend mete out; employ (*OED* 1, 8) but as Booth (523) observes, ' "to spend revenge" is most unidiomatic', and 'This line is strange and strained generally'.

8 **present moan** immediate grief, or expression of grief

9 **respect** esteem, regard as valuable: see *OED* 4b; and cf. *TGV* 1.2.134.

10 'That is so proud as to despise being your servant' (Booth, 523)

11 **all my best** all that is best in me, as distinct from those parts that are *so proud*, as above
worship thy defect adores your faults, possibly with a bawdy allusion to that which women lack, as distinct from the anatomical *addition* (20.11) which identifies the male; there may also be a sardonic echo of the *BCP* marriage service, 'with my body I thee worship' (293).

12 **motion** movement; ?persuasive force (*OED* 1a, 7b)

13–14 Booth (524) calls the couplet 'a sudden and arbitrary recurrence to the topic of sonnet 148 and an implied and not at all witty contradiction of 148.13–14'; yet, in so far as all the sonnets in the group 147–50 exemplify the speaker's love-blindness and love-madness, as well as analysing it, an arbitrary-seeming resolution is apt: we should not expect the speaker to be other than confused.

13 **hate on** persist in hating me.

149

Canst thou, O cruel, say I love thee not,
When I against myself with thee partake?
Do I not think on thee, when I forgot
Am of myself, all, tyrant, for thy sake?
Who hateth thee, that I do call my friend? 5
On whom frown'st thou, that I do fawn upon?
Nay, if thou lour'st on me, do I not spend
Revenge upon myself with present moan?
What merit do I in myself respect
That is so proud thy service to despise, 10
When all my best doth worship thy defect,
Commanded by the motion of thine eyes?
    But, love, hate on; for now I know thy mind:
    Those that can see thou lov'st, and I am blind.

---

4 all, tyrant,] *this edn.;* all tyrant, *Malone;* all tirant *Q*   7 lour'st] lowrst

150 The speaker ponders further on the woman's power to move him, through her very weaknesses, to praise her for beauties that his rational self knows her to lack. The sonnet bears some resemblance to Shakespeare's presentation of Cleopatra, praised by Antony even when she is quarrelsome (*AC* 1.1.48–51), and of whom Enobarbus says 'vilest things / Become themselves in her' (2.3.238–9).

1 **from what power** suggests the operation of an external, or supernatural, power, which gives the woman strength in weakness, as well as or instead of her own inner ability or capacity

2 **to move my heart** (to love you), or alter its direction, by means of inadequacy, incapacity: see *OED* insufficiency 2, 1a; and cf. *MND* 2.2.128, where Helena applies the word to her own supposed lack of beauty.

3 **give . . . sight** tell my eyesight, which sees correctly, that it does not

4 **brightness . . . day** suggests a denial of the propositions that *brightness* is what defines day, distinguishing it from night, and that bright sunshine, rather than clouds or shadow, are what *grace* an individual day, making it pleasing

5 **this . . . ill** this capacity to improve bad things, to make them appear pleasing; or to 'become' them by association with them. The first application is elliptical and unusual; the

second supported by *OED* become 9c; and cf. its paradoxical application in *TS* 1.2.252–3.

5–7 The *ill/skill* rhyme here, combined with the picture of a blinded and enslaved lover, recalls the couplet of 57: 'So true a fool is love, that in your will, / Though you do any thing, he thinks no ill'.

6 **refuse** that which is cast aside as worthless (*OED* 8. 1)

7 **warrantise** guarantee, surety

11 **what . . . abhor** that which others, who are not so blinded, have a conventional distaste for (i.e. *things ill*)

12 **With others** along with others, aligning yourself with the world in general **abhor my state** hate or despise the condition I am in: recalls the speaker's *outcast state* in 29.2. The iteration of *abhor* in ll. 11 and 12 suggests a play on 'whore': cf. Desdemona's 'I cannot say "whore": / It does abhor me now I speak the word' (*Oth* 4.2.160–2), where 'abhor' suggests 'compromise myself by appearing to name myself "whore"'; cf. also the executioner 'Abhorson' (a 'whoreson' character) in *MM*.

13–14 As Booth observes (525), this implies not only that 'my unselfish generosity has earned your love in return', but also that 'since you are unworthy and I find unworthiness lovable, I am a fitting person for you to love'. When the following sonnet has been read an innuendo may be discovered in *raised*.

150

O from what power hast thou this powerful might,
With insufficiency my heart to sway,
To make me give the lie to my true sight,
And swear that brightness doth not grace the day?
Whence hast thou this becoming of things ill,   5
That in the very refuse of thy deeds
There is such strength and warrantise of skill
That in my mind thy worst all best exceeds?
Who taught thee how to make me love thee more,
The more I hear and see just cause of hate?   10
O, though I love what others do abhor,
With others thou shouldst not abhor my state:
   If thy unworthiness raised love in me,
   More worthy I to be beloved of thee.

13 raised] raisd   14 beloved] belou'd

151 This sonnet resumes (from 146) the conflict between soul and body, but with the body now unashamedly victorious. The iteration of *conscience* in ll. 1, 2 and 13 suggests a concealed pun on the prick of conscience and the prick which has no conscience, as in the proverb *Penis erectus non habet conscientiam* (Booth cites Archer Taylor, *The Proverbs* [Cambridge, Mass., 1931], 171).

1   **Love** here equated with the child Cupid
    conscience consciousness of right and wrong; moral sense (*OED* II): Booth (526) claims that 'here, and in lines 2, 11 and 13, "con-"' alludes to 'the commonest name for the female sex organ'.

2   Though the *who knows not . . . ?* formula implies that the proposition is proverbial or familiar, it does not appear to be so: indeed, the surprisingness of a connection between erotic love and conscience is indicated in Falstaff's remark (*MW* 5.5.28–9) 'Why, now is Cupid a child of conscience: he makes restitution'. But there may be a saucily misapplied suggestion that conscience, or the inward prompting of a moral sense, is a product of the love of God.

3   **gentle cheater** an oxymoron in which the moral condemnation of *cheater* is mitigated by the affectionate epithet *gentle*; cf. *tender churl*, 1.12.
    urge not do not charge me strongly with, or press a strong claim for: see *OED* urge 3c, 9a.

4   **prove** turn out to be

5   **thou betraying me** when, because, or since, you betray me

6   **My nobler part** the soul, as in l. 7; and cf. 'nobler parts', *KJ* 3.1.217, and 'nobler reason', *Tem* 5.1.26.
    my . . . treason the treason of my body, which is *gross* – overfed and/or vicious: cf. the *rebel powers* of the body in 146.2.

7   **may** primarily, 'has permission to',

but perhaps also suggesting 'it is possible that he will'

8   **Triumph** triùmph: 'to prevail, gain the mastery' (*OED* 2)
    flesh an unusual application of the word, often associated with female flesh as a sexual commodity, to the male member
    stays waits for, awaits (*OED* 19); cf. *MND* 2.1.235, *VA* 894.
    no further reason no additional cause or pretext; no longer (waits for) the guidance of reason

9   **point out** show, direct attention to (*OED* 10)

10 **proud . . . pride** an apparent tautology; but there may be an allusion to animals who are 'in pride', or sexually excited; cf. 'As salt as wolves in pride', *Oth* 3.3.410, and *OED* pride 11. The speaker's *flesh* exults in, or brags of, *this* tumescence.

12 **stand** a common pun on the military and sexual applications of the word: cf. *RJ* 1.1.27–8, Sampson's obscene threat to the maids, 'Me they shall feel while I am able to stand, and 'tis known I am a pretty piece of flesh'. For the military application, 'to take up an offensive position against an enemy', see *OED* 10.
    fall . . . side continues the metaphor of sexual congress as a military engagement, suggesting both 'endure defeat while fighting on your behalf' and 'detumesce in proximity to you'

13 **No . . . it** Do not reckon it to be a defect of *conscience*: cf. 'For nothing hold me', 136.11 and n.

14 **rise and fall** suggests, in addition to tumescence and detumescence, a blasphemous play on the Resurrection, as in Donne's 'The Canonization', 26–7: 'We die and rise the same, and prove / Mysterious by this love'. In the light of the two final sonnets, the reader may discover also an implication that the speaker has 'fallen' sexually through infection; cf. *OED* fall 14a, and *1H4* 3.3.1–3.

151

Love is too young to know what conscience is:
Yet who knows not conscience is born of love?
Then, gentle cheater, urge not my amiss,
Lest guilty of my faults thy sweet self prove;
For, thou betraying me, I do betray   5
My nobler part to my gross body's treason;
My soul doth tell my body that he may
Triumph in love; flesh stays no further reason,
But rising at thy name doth point out thee
As his triumphant prize, proud of this pride: 10
He is contented thy poor drudge to be,
To stand in thy affairs, fall by thy side.
   No want of conscience hold it that I call
   Her 'love', for whose dear love I rise and fall.

2 born] borne

152 This sonnet describes sexual and artistic betrayal. The blunt allusions to double adultery grieved early commentators, such as George Ross, who claimed that Shakespeare's 'spirit was delicate and loved purity, yet it is obvious that it did not hinder him from lapsing into an unchaste life' (quoted in Rollins, 1.389). However, the poet's self-betrayal through false language is treated as worse even than sexual betrayal.

1 I am forsworn I have broken an oath or told a lie: may refer to the fact that the speaker, like Shakespeare, is married; or to his claims in 1–126 of exclusive devotion to the fair youth; or to the breach of some other oath not apparent to the reader.

2 twice . . . swearing In your swearing love to me you break two oaths (thus behaving twice as badly as me): the present participle effectively leaves open the question of whether she swears love to the speaker now, or has done so in the past.

3 In act in the act of sexual congress: elsewhere more fully defined, as in 'act of sport' or 'act of shame' (*Oth* 2.1.226, 5.2.212). In *TC* 3.2.81–2 it is used alone, as here: 'the desire is boundless, and the act a slave to limit'.

3–4 new . . . bearing may be read as suggesting that the woman (unlike Shakespeare, married back in 1582) is recently married, and already expressing *new hate* for her husband, in favour of love for the speaker; or that she has betrayed both her husband and the speaker in favour of some third party, either, as in 133–4, the speaker's *friend,* or yet another

7 to misuse thee to treat you badly, by deception or otherwise; to exploit you sexually; to lie about you, misrepresent you: for the first two senses of *misuse,* cf. *OED* 2 and 2b; the third is discovered in retrospect when ll. 9–12 have been read.

8 initially suggests, 'all my amorous trust of you is betrayed'; but the next six lines indicate a more thorough-going compromise of the speaker's *honest faith,* in which he has told endless lies with reference to the woman.

9 deep oaths . . . kindness *Deep oaths,* or solemn, heartfelt, oaths, are conventional: cf. *LLL* 1.1.23; or 'deep-sworn', *KJ* 3.1.231. The definition of *oaths,* in ll. 9–10, as oaths *of* – i.e. 'concerning' – subtly shifts the issue from one of fidelity to another person to fidelity to truth itself. The repetition of *deep* may introduce an innuendo on *deep kindness* as 'unlimited sexual receptivity'.

11 to enlighten thee to illuminate you, or make you lighter in appearance (*OED* 2)

gave . . . blindness initially suggests a reference to blind Cupid: cf. Sidney, *NA,* 5, 'Hath not she thrown reason upon our desires and, as it were, given eyes unto Cupid?' However, the couplet makes it clear that the *eyes* are those of the speaker, who has given (over) his eyes to blindness, in claiming to see merit and beauty in the woman.

12 swear against give contrary evidence to; set up in opposition to

the thing possibly with some play on the use of *thing* for 'genitals'; cf. *1H4* 3.3.114–18, and *Son* 136.7, 11–12.

13 sworn thee fair sworn that you are beautiful; attempted to make you beautiful by swearing that you are

eye often, since Malone, emended to 'I'; yet *eye* continues logically from l. 12, in which *eyes* are the subject of *swear,* while readily yielding an aural pun on 'I'; the word also yokes 152 to the last line of 153.

14 foul plays paradoxically on the 'foulness' of a false claim for the woman's 'fairness'; and cf. the proverbial 'Fair without but foul within' (Tilley, F28).

152

In loving thee thou knowst I am forsworn;
But thou art twice forsworn to me love swearing,
In act thy bed-vow broke and new faith torn,
In vowing new hate after new love bearing.
But why of two oaths' breach do I accuse thee,   5
When I break twenty? I am perjured most,
For all my vows are oaths but to misuse thee,
And all my honest faith in thee is lost:
For I have sworn deep oaths of thy deep kindness,
Oaths of thy love, thy truth, thy constancy,   10
And to enlighten thee gave eyes to blindness,
Or made them swear against the thing they see:
    For I have sworn thee fair: more perjured eye,
    To swear against the truth so foul a lie.

6 perjured] periur'd 13 perjured] periurde eye] I *Malone*

153–4 Both sonnets play on a conceit deriving from a six-line epigram by Marianus Scholasticus, a sixth-century Byzantine poet (cf. Cameron, 70–2), in the *Greek Anthology* 4.19.35, literally translated: 'Here beneath these plane trees, exhausted Love was sleeping softly. He had entrusted his torch to the Nymphs. But the Nymphs said to one another, "Come on, why are we waiting? Let's put out the torch and with it quench the fire in human hearts." But the torch set light even to the waters, and the Nymphs of Love have filled the bath with hot water ever since.' Or, in modern verse: 'Beneath these plane trees Love lay fast asleep; / His torch was given to the Nymphs to keep. / "Why wait?" they said, "Let's put out Cupid's brand, / And quench the fire that burns the heart of man." / But it inflamed the water, burnt the lot: / The baths the Nymphs of Love take now are hot.' (Both versions by Emily Wilson, 1996). For a detailed discussion of possible sources, see Hutton. Ben Jonson owned a copy of the first Latin translation of the *Greek Anthology*, that of Lubinus, 1603 (Jonson, 11.598; Hutton, 385n.; see also McPherson). A possible route by which the epigram reached Shakespeare might be an English version of the epigram by Jonson himself, now lost, perhaps part of his projected Book II of *Epigrammes*. If this conjecture is right, the sonnets cannot have been written before 1603. Such a source would suit the competitive, exaggeratedly amplified rhetoric of 153–4. Although there were many other Latin and vernacular adaptations of the epigram from the early sixteenth century onwards (and cf. Giles Fletcher's *Licia* (1593), 27, deriving from Angeriano's 1512 epigram), Shakespeare's sonnets seem closer to the Greek original than to any of the Latin or vernacular adaptations of it. Whether through Jonson or some other English intermediary, Shakespeare must have had access to a close rendering, such as that of Lubinus. Epigrams were often structured as pairs, with two different renderings of the same motif; indeed, Marianus's epigram which is Shakespeare's model is itself the second of a pair on baths with special properties, the preceding epigram being on one called 'Eros' made fragrant by being being bathed in by Venus.

In both sonnets Cupid's *brand* is given a bawdy application, and both draw on the twofold association of hot baths with the treatment of sexually transmitted disease and with sexual encounters which may cause such disease, a double association which goes back to antiquity (cf. Martial, *Epigrams*, 11.80). The suggestion initiated by George Steevens and seconded by some later commentators, such as E.H. Plumptre, Gregor Sarrazin and E.I. Fripp (Rollins, 1.391–2), that the sonnets allude specifically to Bath, Buxton or some continental spa seems unnecessary, since in both sonnets it is *my mistress* who is defined as the physical location for hot water, therapy and disease.

153.1 laid . . . brand put aside his torch: a hymeneal torch, rather than a bow and arrows, was the more ancient attribute of Cupid: cf. *Cym* 2.4.91.

2 a maid of Dian's either, if the scene is consistently mythological, one of the virgin nymphs who attended the chaste goddess Diana; or, by extension, any virgin

4 cold valley-fountain suggests both one of the cool springs associated with the goddess Diana, and the female genitals in which the hot male member seeks to be cooled or quenched: cf. Venus' erotic invitation to Adonis: 'Graze on my lips, and if those hills be dry, / Stray lower, where the pleasant fountains lie' (*VA* 233–4). Cf. also Thomas Heywood's *Oenone and Paris* (1594), 458, 'Bathe in this fountaine here a while to sport thee' (Heywood, 28).

153

Cupid laid by his brand, and fell asleep;
A maid of Dian's this advantage found,
And his love-kindling fire did quickly steep
In a cold valley-fountain of that ground,
Which borrowed from this holy fire of love   5
A dateless lively heat still to endure,
And grew a seething bath, which yet men prove
Against strange maladies a sovereign cure:
But at my mistress' eye love's brand new fired,
The boy for trial needs would touch my breast;   10
I, sick withal, the help of bath desired,
And thither hied, a sad distempered guest,
    But found no cure; the bath for my help lies
    Where Cupid got new fire: my mistress' eye.

---

5   **this . . . love** the *holy fire* of Cupid's torch, whose 'holiness' seems here rather suspect: it may hint, spooneristically, at a 'fiery hole' (RP).

6   The tautology of this line matches the tautology of the paired sonnets: the water's heat remains without 'date' or terminus (cf. *dateless night*, 30.6, and 'dateless bargain', *RJ* 5.3.115), and has the capacity to remain so continually – *still*.

7   **grew** was transformed into
    a seething bath warm water in which bathers are 'seethed', or stewed: see *OED* seethe 1.

    prove discover to be: the allusion may be not so much to a specific therapeutic spring as to a therapeutic principle – 'Men find hot baths an effective remedy.'

8   **strange maladies** suggests 'exotic' maladies, diseases possibly contracted through contact with *strange*, or foreign, women. Syphilis, 'pox', or *morbus gallicus*, was always viewed as an exotic disease, whether brought to

1 Cupid] *CVpid*   2 Dian's] *Dyans*   5 borrowed] borrowd   12 distempered] distemperd   guest,] guest.   14 Cupid] *Cupid*   eye] eyes *Benson*

Italy or England from France, or to Europe from the New World, or even the other way round: cf. Fracastoro, 12–14.

sovereign efficacious, potent: see *OED* 3.

9 **new fired** was ignited afresh: develops the Petrarchan conceit of the mistress's eyes as darting forth fiery beams, as in the 'flamie glistering lights' of Stella's eyes in Sidney's *AS*, 76.10, a particularly erotically-charged sonnet.

10 **for trial** to test (whether his torch was still alight)

touch with a suggestion of 'infect, taint' (*OED* 7); and cf. *KJ* 5.8.2, 'It is too late, the life of all his blood / Is touch'd corruptibly'.

11 **withal** from contact with Cupid's brand

help . . . desired sought for therapy of the warm and supposedly curative waters: sweating tubs were used in the treatment of venereal disease, as in

Timon's verbal onslaught on the courtesan Timandra: 'Make use of thy salt hours; season the slaves / For tubs and baths; bring down rose-cheek'd youth / To the tub-fast and the diet' (*Tim* 4.3.86–8).

12 **hied** hastened, betook myself speedily; see *OED* hie 2b.

14 **distempered** disordered, diseased; insane (*OED* 3.4)

my mistress' eye Q's singular 'eye' has been retained, despite its imperfect rhyme with *lies*, for the following reasons: (1) it matches the *perjured eye* of 152.13; (2) it repeats the phrase in identical form from l. 9; (3) in its singular form only, it suggests an allusion to what Chaucer called the 'nether ye' (*Miller's Tale*, 3852; and cf. *OED* eye 20, 'A hole or aperture'); (4) the imperfection of the rhyme matches the poem's theme of disappointment and disillusion: in seeking to cure himself, the speaker reinfects himself.

153

Cupid laid by his brand, and fell asleep;
A maid of Dian's this advantage found,
And his love-kindling fire did quickly steep
In a cold valley-fountain of that ground,
Which borrowed from this holy fire of love   5
A dateless lively heat still to endure,
And grew a seething bath, which yet men prove
Against strange maladies a sovereign cure:
But at my mistress' eye love's brand new fired,
The boy for trial needs would touch my breast;   10
I, sick withal, the help of bath desired,
And thither hied, a sad distempered guest,
   But found no cure; the bath for my help lies
   Where Cupid got new fire: my mistress' eye.

154 See 153 headnote.

2 **Laid . . . side** conflates *laid* from the preceding sonnet with 'fall by thy side' from 151.12, thus suggesting the brand's phallic character, and explaining the apparent absurdity pointed out by Hutton (401) in ll. 1–2, which 'makes the love-god in his sleep perform the act of laying aside his brand': the laying-by may correspond with involuntary detumescence.

5 **The fairest votary** the most beautiful devotee (of chastity and/or Diana); refines on the more random-sounding *maid of Dian's* in 153.2, allowing for a possibility that Cupid's assailant is Diana herself: see *OED* votary 1 a, b.

6 **legions** multitudes, large numbers (*OED* 3a): in its allusion to Roman legions, supports the classical character of the anecdote, as well as the military image in the next line

7 **general . . . desire** As Booth (536) observes, this phrase can be read almost simultaneously as defining Cupid as the *general*, or supreme commander (*OED* 7a), of *hot desire*, and, when taken in conjunction with the following lines, as describing him as *disarmed*, or deprived, of the *hot desire* (*brand*) which was formerly his defining attribute. For the erotic application of *general*, cf. 'Our general's wife is now the general', *Oth* 2.3.305–6.

8 Cf. *Ham* 1.5.74–5: 'Thus was I, sleeping, by a brother's hand/Of life, of crown, of queen, at once dispatch'd' (RP).

9 **quenched** quenchèd
   a . . . by The *cool well* which is *by*, = nearby (*OED* by *adv.* 1a), the fair votary probably carries an innuendo on the female organ in which the hot desire of the male is quenched: cf.

153.4n. and quotations.

11 **Growing** becoming, developing into: see *OED* grow 4.
   a bath a warm bath, a therapeutic spring

12 **my mistress' thrall** The enslavement of the speaker to his mistress is perhaps distinguished from the more general allegiance of 'legions of true hearts' in l. 6.

13 **Came** with a play on 'reach orgasm': although *OED*'s earliest example (17) is from 1650, Partridge (89) identifies the sense in *MA* 5.2.20–2 and *TN* 3.4.29–30; to these could possibly be added *AC* 5.2.286.
   this . . . prove The following is what I discover by means of that experience.

14 **Love's fire heats water** The point that Cupid's brand has the capacity to transform a cool spring into a hot one is by now rather obvious, but there is probably also an allusion to the burning *water*, or urine, which is a common symptom of venereal disease. Cf. Song of Solomon, 8.7, 'Many waters cannot drown love'; however, the pervasive bawdy innuendo suggests a more brutal implication that neither venereal disase nor the treatment of it abates the sex-drive. Like *LC*, the sonnets end with an affirmation of the persistence of desire: see Introduction, p. 95.

FINIS. As well as marking the end of the sonnet sequence, the 'FINIS' may hint at an allusion to the miraculous draught of fishes in St John's Gospel, 21.11, 'an hundred and fiftie and three: and for all there were so many, yet was not the net broken', at least if the non-sonnet 126 is left out of the reckoning: see Introduction, p. 98.

154

The little love-god lying once asleep,
Laid by his side his heart-inflaming brand,
Whilst many nymphs, that vowed chaste life to keep,
Came tripping by; but in her maiden hand
The fairest votary took up that fire   5
Which many legions of true hearts had warmed;
And so the general of hot desire
Was, sleeping, by a virgin hand disarmed.
This brand she quenched in a cool well by,
Which from love's fire took heat perpetual,   10
Growing a bath and healthful remedy
For men diseased; but I, my mistress' thrall,
    Came there for cure, and this by that I prove:
    Love's fire heats water, water cools not love.

FINIS.

1 love-god] Loue-God   3 nymphs] Nymphes   vowed] vou'd   6 legions] Legions   warmed] warm'd   7 general] Generall   8 virgin] Virgin   disarmed] disarm'd   9 well] Well   12 diseased] diseasd   mistress'] Mistrisse

A LOVER'S
COMPLAINT

A LOVER'S COMPLAINT

From off a hill whose concave womb reworded
A plaintful story from a sist'ring vale,
My spirits t'attend this double voice accorded,
And down I laid to list the sad-tuned tale;
Ere long espied a fickle maid full pale,   5
Tearing of papers, breaking rings a-twain,
Storming her world with sorrow's wind and rain.

A LOVER'S COMPLAINT This is a complex example of the female-voiced 'complaint', in rime royal, often added to sonnet sequences from Daniel's *Complaint of Rosamund*, appended to *Delia* (1592), onwards; cf. also Thomas Lodge's *Complaint of Elstred*, which follows *Phillis* (1593); Michael Drayton's *Matilda the faire*, following *Ideas Mirrour* (1594); and Richard Barnfield's *Cassandra*, following *The Affectionate Shepherd* (1595). Uniquely, however, Shakespeare's *fickle maid* (l. 5) is unnamed, as are the three other characters, the *reverend man* (52), once a courtier, who acts as her confessor; her youthful seducer; and the *nun* (232) who tried to seduce him. The opening ten stanzas, in the voice of an *I* who is also unidentified, set the scene; in the next fifteen, ll. 71–175, the maid describes her attraction to the young man; his wooing speeches are reported in a further fifteen stanzas, 176–280; and in the final seven stanzas, 281–329, the maid exclaims at the irresistibly beguiling power of the youth's words and tears, to which she would willingly submit once more.

TITLE The title will naturally be read initially as denoting 'a complaint *by* a lover'. The application of the word to a woman, though uncommon, was not unknown in this period. *OED* (2a) offers the example of Crispinus's song in Jonson's *Poetaster*, 2.2.163–5: 'If I freely may discover / What would please me in my lover: / I would have

her faire, and wittie'; cf. also *AYL* 5.2.74–5. But by the time the poem is read to the end, the title can be glossed also as 'a complaint *concerning* a lover'. It might be tempting also to read it as 'the disease of a lover', since the speaker has been disordered by the *infected moisture* (l. 323) of the youth's eye, but *OED* (6) does not record this sense of *complaint* before 1705.

1–7 The opening stanza strongly recalls the folk-song: 'Early one morning, just as the day was dawning, / I heard a maid sing in the valley below: / O, don't deceive me, O, never leave me, / How could you use a poor maiden so?'

1 **From off** off from, resounding from **concave womb** a hollow cave: the use of the word *womb* in the opening line immediately suggests the feminine complementarity of *LC* to the male-voiced sonnets which precede it, especially sonnets 151, with its play on male *flesh*, and 153–4, on Cupid's phallic *brand*.

reworded resonated, reiterated: cf. *Ham* 3.4.144–5, 'Bring me to the test, / And I the matter will re-word'.

2 **plaintful** mournful; in the form of a complaint

sist'ring 'having a relationship comparable in some way to that of a sister or sisters' (*OED*); and note *OED*'s quotation from William Drummond, 'The Roman was almost naked from the Waste upwards, discovering the sistering Apples of her Breast.'

7 **her world** the 'little world of (wo)man', her body as a microcosm

A LOVER'S COMPLAINT] A Louers complaint. *BY* WILLIAM SHAKE-SPEARE.   4 sad-tuned] *Oxf;* sad tun'd *Q*   6 a-twain] *Malone;* a twaine *Q*   7 sorrow's] sorrowes,

Upon her head a plaited hive of straw,
Which fortified her visage from the sun,
Whereon the thought might think sometime it saw   10
The carcass of a beauty spent and done;
Time had not scythed all that youth begun,
Nor youth all quit, but spite of heaven's fell rage
Some beauty peeped through lattice of seared age.

Oft did she heave her napkin to her eyne,   15
Which on it had conceited characters,
Laund'ring the silken figures in the brine
That seasoned woe had pelleted in tears,
And often reading what contents it bears;
As often shrieking undistinguished woe,   20
In clamours of all size, both high and low.

---

8 **hive** a high-crowned straw hat: Linthicum (231) claims that 'The straw hat does not seem to have been worn by any except country folk during Shakespeare's age', and Sir John Harington's epigram 4.91, 'In commendation of a straw, written at the request of a great Lady, that ware a straw Hat at the Court' (Harington, 285), seems to confirm this; yet a straw hat survives at Hatfield House allegedly worn by Elizabeth when a prisoner there.

10 **the thought** the thought or mind (of an onlooker)

11 **carcass** the dead body, or surviving relics, of her former beauty

12 **scythed** scythèd: cut away with his scythe

13 **heaven's fell rage** Cf. *time's fell hand*, 64.1.

14 **lattice** often applied figuratively to the face, or to eyes gazing out of the face's *lattice*: *OED* cites Donne's *Second Anniversarie*, 296–7: 'Thou shalt not peep through lattices of eyes, / Nor hear through labyrinths of ears'.

seared withered, blighted (*Glossary*)

16 **conceited characters** witty or inventive letters (synecdoche for 'words'): the epithet was often applied to Shakespeare's own writings, as in Thomas Edwards's *Narcissus* (1595); and cf. *RJ* (First Quarto), entitled *An excellent conceited Tragedy*; or *TC* (Quarto), unrevised title-page, . . . *with the conceited wooing of Pandarus Prince of Licia*.

17 **silken figures** suggests emblematic images, as well as words, embroidered on the *napkin*; cf. *Glossary*, 'figure', 6.

18 **seasoned** established, of long duration (*OED* 7), perhaps with a play on 'flavoured, spiced' (*OED* 2)
pelleted formed into pellets or small globular shapes, and/or discharged like gunshot

19 **contents** contènts

20 **undistinguished** indistinguishable, indefinable; cf. *KL* 4.6.271, 'O indistinguished space of woman's will!'

21 **both . . . low** Cf. l. 3 of the song 'O mistress mine', *TN* 2.3: 'That can

8 plaited] plattid   9 sun] Sunne   14 peeped] peept   lattice] lettice   seared] sear'd   15 napkin] Napkin   20 undistinguished] vndistinguisht

432

Sometimes her levelled eyes their carriage ride,
As they did batt'ry to the spheres intend;
Sometime, diverted, their poor balls are tied
To th'orbed earth; sometimes they do extend   25
Their view right on; anon their gazes lend
To every place at once, and nowhere fixed,
The mind and sight distractedly commixed.

Her hair, nor loose, nor tied in formal plait,
Proclaimed in her a careless hand of pride;   30
For some untucked descended her sheaved hat,
Hanging her pale and pined cheek beside;
Some in her threaden fillet still did bide,
And, true to bondage, would not break from thence,
Though slackly braided in loose negligence.   35

sing both high and low'. The line as a whole suggests some mockery or burlesque; whether of the *fickle maid*, or of the conventions of oxymoronic rhetoric, is hard to judge.

22 **levelled . . . ride** The image is of warfare, with the maid's *eyes* as movable cannon aimed, or *levelled* (*OED* level 7a), and wheeled into position ready for discharge (*OED* carriage 27).

23 **As** as if
   batt'ry assault, continuing the metaphor of cannon-fire

24 **balls** eyeballs, neatly reducing the image of eyes as guns firing balls to one of sockets in which the balls are tied down: for 'balls' as 'eyeballs', cf. *MV* 3.2.118, *AC* 2.5.64.

25 **th'orbed** th'orbèd: the image of the earth as an 'orb', or sphere, continues the imagery of spherical objects, from *pelleted* tears in l. 18, heavens as *spheres* in 23, and eyes as *balls* in 24.

26 **right on** straight ahead

28 **anon** next
   commixed mingled

29–35 Cf. Sidney's decription of the disguised Pyrocles in *NA* (68): 'Well might he perceive the hanging of her hair in fairest quantity, in locks, some curled and some as it were forgotten, with such a careless care and an art so hiding art that she seemed she would lay them for a pattern, whether nature simply, or nature helped by cunning, be the more excellent; the rest whereof was drawn into a coronet of gold'.

30 **careless . . . pride** presumably, 'a hand neglectful, or heedless, of pride'

31 **sheaved** composed of sheaves (of straw); nonce word

32 **pined** pinèd.

33 **threaden fillet** a 'little long band or narowe ribben wherewith women doe wreathe or bind theire haire' (John Baret, *An Alvearie or Quadruple Dictionarie* (1580), quoted in Linthicum, 236): in this case made of threads, possibly gold, rather than ribbon

22 levelled] leueld   24 tied] tide   27 fixed] fixt   28 commixed] commxit   29 tied] ti'd
30 Proclaimed] Proclaimd   31 untucked] vntuck'd   sheaved] sheu'd

A thousand favours from a maund she drew,
Of amber, crystal and of beaded jet,
Which, one by one, she in a river threw,
Upon whose weeping margent she was set,
Like usury, applying wet to wet,   40
Or monarch's hands, that lets not bounty fall
Where want cries 'Some!', but where excess begs, 'All!'

Of folded schedules had she many a one,
Which she perused, sighed, tore and gave the flood;
Cracked many a ring of posied gold and bone,   45
Bidding them find their sepulchres in mud;
Found yet moe letters, sadly penned in blood,
With sleided silk, feat and affectedly
Enswathed and sealed to curious secrecy.

These often bathed she in her fluxive eyes,   50
And often kissed, and often gave to tear;

36 **favours** love tokens, in this instance made of semi-precious minerals: see *OED* favour 7a, b; and cf. *LLL* 5.2.130–2.
maund wicker basket with a handle
37 **beaded** presumably, 'formed into beads'; another nonce word
39 **margent** edge, bank
40 The maid's barren *usury*, in which she adds coin-like tears to the stream which already has water in abundance, may be contrasted with the reproductive *usury* recommended to the youth in 6.5.
41–2 **lets . . . 'All!'** For the unusual use of 'let fall' as 'bestow (blessings or bounty)', cf. *Tem* 4.1.18; with the notion of giving to those who already have too much, rather than to the needy, cf. *Son* 135.9–10; also Donne's 'The Will', in which the speaker promises to give 'To women or the sea, my tears', having been taught by love to 'give to

none, but such, as had too much before' (*Songs and Sonnets*, 54).
43 **schedules** pieces of paper, short notes (*OED* 1)
44 **gave** gave (to)
45 **posied** inscribed with posies or mottoes; nonce word in the period
48 **sleided** apparently for 'sleaved', = separated into loose threads: cf. *Per* 4 Prol. 21.
feat and affectedly neatly, becomingly (*OED* feat 6b); earnestly or affectionately (*OED* affectedly 1): the association of *affectedly* with falsity or posing is not recorded before 1656.
49 wrapped up (in frayed silk) and sealed to achieve elaborate secrecy, or against those who are *curious* to penetrate their secrets
50 **fluxive** flowing, fluid
51 **gave to tear** gave herself up to tearing: see *OED* give 64d.

37 beaded jet] *Ard¹;* bedded Iet *Q*   41 monarch's] Monarches   44 perused] perus'd   sighed] sighd
45 Cracked] Crackt   posied] Posied   46 sepulchres] sepulchers   47 moe] *Ard¹, Riv;* mo *Q;* more
Malone   penned] pend   49 Enswathed] Enswath'd   sealed] seald   50 bathed] bath'd   51 kissed] kist

Cried, 'O false blood, thou register of lies,
What unapproved witness dost thou bear!
Ink would have seemed more black and damned here.'
This said, in top of rage the lines she rents,   55
Big discontent so breaking their contents.

A reverend man, that grazed his cattle nigh,
Sometime a blusterer, that the ruffle knew
Of court, of city, and had let go by
The swiftest hours observed as they flew,   60
Towards this afflicted fancy fastly drew,
And, privileged by age, desires to know
In brief the grounds and motives of her woe.

52 **register of lies** chronicle or record of lies: cf. Lucrece's complaint against night as 'Dim register and notary of shame', *Luc* 765.
53 **unapproved** unapprovèd: = unconfirmed by trial, unproved (*Glossary*)
54 Black ink, manifestly sinister, would have been more honest than seemingly heartfelt blood.
   damned damnèd
55 **rents** rends, tears
56 **contents** contènts
57 **reverend** dignified, aged, with some religious associations which make him an apt confessor-figure (*OED* 1, 2); however, the stress on the man's *age* in 62 and 70 make this the primary connotation. The witnessing *I* of the opening stanzas is presumably different; see Introduction, p. 92.
58 **blusterer** 'boaster, braggart' (*OED*, with this as the first example)
   ruffle ostentatious bustle, display (*OED* 3, with this as the first exam-

ple); the word was also associated with quarrels and skirmishes; cf. Robert Naunton, *Fragmenta Regalia* (1641), 33, on Lord Hunsdon, patron of the Lord Chamberlain's Men, 'as he lived in a Roughling time, so he loved sword and Buckler men, and such as our Fathers were wont to call men of their hands'.
60 **observed** observèd. In his 'blustering' days we might suppose, rather, that the man would have passed his hours 'unobserved'; but presumably the suggestion is that even in his youth he was unusually reflective.
61 **afflicted fancy** unhappy apparition (*OED* fancy 2), or victim of delusion (ibid. 3)
   fastly firmly; speedily (*OED* 2, 4)
63 **grounds and motives** causes and inward promptings or desires (*OED* motive 2a, 4a; and cf. Kerrigan, *Motives*, vi).

54 seemed] seem'd   57 grazed] graz'd   59 court] Court   city] Cittie   62 privileged] priuiledg'd

435

So slides he down upon his grained bat,
And comely distant sits he by her side,   65
When he again desires her, being sat,
Her grievance with his hearing to divide:
If that from him there may be aught applied
Which may her suffering ecstasy assuage,
'Tis promised in the charity of age.   70

'Father,' she says, 'though in me ye behold
The injury of many a blasting hour,
Let it not tell your judgement I am old:
Not age, but sorrow, over me hath power.
I might as yet have been a spreading flower,   75
Fresh to myself, if I had self-applied
Love to myself, and to no love beside.

'But woe is me! Too early I attended
A youthful suit; it was to gain my grace;
O, one by nature's outwards so commended   80

---

64 **grained bat** the object may be akin to Aufidius's 'grained ash', *Cor* 4.5.109, apparently a stout wooden lance or cudgel. A 'bat' is normally a wooden walking stick (*OED* 1): cf. Spenser, *Mother Hubberds Tale* (1591), 215–18, in which the ape pretends to be an old soldier: 'But neither sword nor dagger did he beare . . . / In stead of them a handsome bat he held, / On which he leaned, as one farre in elde' (*Shorter Poems*, 342). **grained** grainèd
65 **comely distant** becomingly distant, at a discreet distance
67 **divide** share (*OED* 8b)
68 **applied** offered as a remedy
72 **blasting** blighting (*OED* 1): cf. *TGV* 1.1.45–9: 'as the most forward bud / Is eaten by the canker ere it blow, /

Even so by Love the young and tender wit / Is turn'd to folly, blasting in the bud, / Losing his verdure, even in the prime'.
76 **Fresh to myself** Cf. 94. 9–10.
77 The maid has suffered for doing what the youth is implored to do in sonnets 1–17: contrast especially sonnet 4.
78 **attended** initially suggests that, like the *reverend man* when young, the maid *attended* at court; but the next line indicates that it was to the *youthful suit* that she paid heed (*OED* attend 7, 2).
79 **A youthful suit** the request of a youthful suitor
80 **outwards** exterior, outward appearance: see *OED* outward B2; and cf. *TC* 3.2.169; *Cym* 1.1.23.

---

70 promised] promist   73 judgement] Iudgement   76 self-applied] selfe applyed   77 love] Loue
79 suit it (*Ard¹* suit; it)

That maidens' eyes stuck over all his face;
Love lacked a dwelling, and made him her place;
And when in his fair parts she did abide
She was new-lodged and newly deified.

'His browny locks did hang in crooked curls,   85
And every light occasion of the wind
Upon his lips their silken parcels hurls;
What's sweet to do, to do will aptly find;
Each eye that saw him did enchant the mind:
For on his visage was in little drawn   90
What largeness thinks in paradise was sawn.

'Small show of man was yet upon his chin;
His phoenix down began but to appear,
Like unshorn velvet, on that termless skin,

81 Cf. the suggestions in sonnets 3 and 16 of numbers of young women longing to be made pregnant by the youth; and cf. 'the eyes of all that were in the synagogue were fastened on him', Luke, 4.20.

82–4 **her . . . deified** The female pronoun indicates that *Love* is here equated with the goddess Venus.

85–98 This passage seems to amalgamate Sidney's descriptions of the two princes Musidorus and Pyrocles (*OA*, 376–7): 'His fair auburn hair (which he ware in great length, and gave at that time a delightful show with being stirred up and down with the breath of a gentle wind) . . . his face, now beginning to have some tokens of a beard, was composed to a kind of manlike beauty; his colour was of a well pleasing brownness . . . Pyrocles of a pure complexion, and of such a cheerful favour as might seem either a woman's face on a boy or an excellent boy's face in a woman'.

85 **browny** inclining to brown (*OED*)

87 **parcels** parts, portions

90–1 His face had depicted on it a miniature of that which, in amplified form, (a beholder) might imagine to have been cut out, or carved, in Paradise (*OED* sawn 1): though we may also construe *sawn* as a clumsy form of 'seen', there is no analogy to this, and 'sawing' offers not merely a better rhyme, but a better semantic analogy, to 'draw' (n.). Cf. Sidney's description of Amphialus (*NA*, 195) as 'such a right manlike man as nature, often erring, yet shows she would fain make'.

93 **phoenix down** facial hair resembling the glorious plumage of the Phoenix; perhaps also hair which, like the Phoenix, dies (when the youth shaves) and is self-renewed: for the association of the Phoenix with bright plumage, cf. *Tim* 2.1.31.

94 **unshorn velvet** velvet which has not been trimmed, or shaved
termless inexpressible, beyond description (*OED* 2); cf. *phraseless*, l. 225.

82 lacked] lackt   84 new-lodged] *Oxf;* new lodg'd *Q*   deified] *Malone;* Deified *Q*

437

Whose bare out-bragged the web it seemed to wear;   95
Yet showed his visage by that cost more dear,
And nice affections wavering stood in doubt
If best were as it was, or best without.

'His qualities were beauteous as his form:
For maiden-tongued he was, and thereof free;   100
Yet if men moved him, was he such a storm
As oft 'twixt May and April is to see,
When winds breathe sweet, unruly though they be.
His rudeness so with his authorized youth
Did livery falseness in a pride of truth.   105

'Well could he ride, and often men would say,
"That horse his mettle from his rider takes,
Proud of subjection, noble by the sway,

95 whose bareness was more triumphantly beautiful than the (rich)
fabric it *seemed to wear*: the Sidneian
conceit of some of the face being
bare, some hairy, recalls the description of the maid's hair, some loose,
some tied up, in ll. 29–35; *out-bragged*
recalls both *outbraves*, 94.12, and 'nor
shall death brag', 18.11.
96 **cost** expensive ornament (*OED* 4); cf.
64.2.
97–8 Cf. the passage from Sidney (*NA*,
68) quoted above, ll. 29–35n.
97 **nice** fastidious, discriminating (*OED*
12a, b)
98 **If best were** whether (the youth's
chin) were best
100 **maiden-tongued** with a soft, gentle
voice, like that of a maiden
free generous, liberal (*OED* 21a, b)
101 **moved** provoked to anger: cf.
Brutus' description of Martius
(Coriolanus), *Cor* 1.1.255: 'Being
mov'd, he will not spare to gird the
gods'.

101–3 **was . . . be** His anger was at once
violent and sensuous, like the *Rough
winds* which 'shake the darling buds of
May' in 18.3.
104 **rudeness . . . youth** continues oxymoronic conceit: the young man's
harshness (*rudeness*) combined with
the youth which legitimated (*authorized*) it to veil (his) deception behind
a splendid appearance (*pride*) of sincerity
106–12 Cf. Pamela's praise of Dorus's
riding (Sidney, *NA*, 153): 'he ever
going so just, either forthright or
turning, that it seemed as he borrowed the horse's body, so he lent the
horse his mind . . . sometimes making
him turn close to the ground like a cat
when scratchingly she wheels about
after a mouse, sometimes with a little
more rising before, now like a raven,
leaping from ridge to ridge'.
108 **noble . . . sway** ennobled by the
youth's sovereignty over him

95 out-bragged] out-brag'd seemed] seem'd wear] were   100 maiden-tongued] maiden tongu'd
101 moved] mou'd   103 breathe] breath   104 authorized] authoriz'd

What rounds, what bounds, what course, what stop he
    makes!"
And controversy hence a question takes,   110
Whether the horse by him became his deed,
Or he his manage, by th' well-doing steed.

'But quickly on this side the verdict went:
His real habitude gave life and grace
To appertainings and to ornament,   115
Accomplished in himself, not in his case;
All aids, themselves made fairer by their place,
Came for additions; yet their purposed trim
Pieced not his grace, but were all graced by him.

'So on the tip of his subduing tongue   120
All kind of arguments and question deep,
All replication prompt, and reason strong,
For his advantage still did wake and sleep,
To make the weeper laugh, the laugher weep:
He had the dialect and different skill,   125
Catching all passions in his craft of will.

110 **controversy** còntrovèrsy: disputation on a matter of opinion (between
opponents) (*OED* 1b)
112 **manage** trained movements (of a
horse) (*OED* 2); cf. *AYL* 1.1.13.
114 **real habitude** true character or disposition (*OED* habitude, with this
example)
115 **appertainings** 'belongings, appurtenances' (*OED*, this example only)
116 **case** container, outward clothing
118 **trim** adornment, trappings
119 **Pieced not** did not add to or aug-
ment; cf. *H5* Prol. 23, 'Piece out our
imperfections with your thoughts';
also *TC* 3.1.51.

122 **All replication prompt** all quick
replies
125 **dialect** (effective) manner of speaking (*OED* 1); cf. *MM* 1.2.172–3, 'in
her youth / There is a prone and
speechless dialect / Such as move
men'.
126 The image of the youth *Catching* the
passions of his hearers through his
versatile rhetoric recalls the image of
Hercules drawing people along with
chains from his mouth, which appears
in Andrea Alciati's *Emblemata* (1531),
E6, as well as in many other emblem
books.

112 manage] mannad'g, by th' well-doing steed] by'th wel doing Steed 116 Accomplished]
Accomplisht himself] him-selfe 117 themselves] them-selves 118 Came]*Ard¹;* Can purposed]
purpos'd 119 Pieced] Peec'd graced] grac'd

'That he did in the general bosom reign
Of young, of old, and sexes both enchanted
To dwell with him in thoughts, or to remain
In personal duty, following where he haunted;   130
Consent's bewitched, ere he desire have granted,
And dialogued for him what he would say,
Asked their own wills, and made their wills obey.

'Many there were that did his picture get
To serve their eyes, and in it put their mind,   135
Like fools, that in th'imagination set
The goodly objects which abroad they find,
Of lands and mansions, theirs in thought assigned,
And labouring in moe pleasures to bestow them
Than the true gouty landlord which doth owe them.   140

'So many have, that never touched his hand,
Sweetly supposed them mistress of his heart:
My woeful self that did in freedom stand,
And was my own fee-simple, not in part,
What with his art in youth, and youth in art,   145
Threw my affections in his charmed power,
Reserved the stalk and gave him all my flower.

127 **That** so that
  the general bosom Cf. 31.1.
130 **haunted** spent his time, habitually
  resorted
131 'The loving consent (of those who
  encountered him) was won by
  enchantment before he had even
  acknowledged his desires.'
132 **dialogued** expressed in dialogue
  form (*OED* 3, with this example)
134 **get** procure, obtain
136–40 'Like fools who imagine themselves owners of fine lands and hous-
  es they have only seen, and bestow
  more labour (in imagination) in

improving their amenity than does the
true and decrepit owner' (RP).
139 **bestow** confer (pleasures on) (*OED* 6)
140 **owe** own, possess
144 **my own fee-simple** my absolute
  possession, owned without limitation
  (*OED* fee-simple a): continues, from
  ll. 136–40, the metaphor of land
  tenure
146 **charmed** charmèd
147 **stalk . . . flower** plays on the association of a *flower* with virginity, as in
  the description of Marina, *Per*
  4.6.32–40, as a 'rose', one 'which
  grows to the stalk; never pluck'd yet'

131 bewitched] bewitcht   132 dialogued] dialogu'd   133 Asked] Askt   138 assigned] assign'd
140 landlord] Land-lord   141 touched] toucht   142 supposed] suppos'd   144 fee-simple, not in
part,] fee simple (not in part)   147 Reserved] Reserv'd

'Yet did I not, as some, my equals, did,
Demand of him; nor, being desired, yielded,
Finding myself in honour so forbid: 150
With safest distance I mine honour shielded.
Experience for me many bulwarks builded
Of proofs new-bleeding, which remained the foil
Of this false jewel and his amorous spoil.

'But ah! Who ever shunned by precedent   155
The destined ill she must herself assay,
Or forced examples 'gainst her own content,
To put the by-passed perils in her way?
Counsel may stop a while what will not stay:
For when we rage, advice is often seen   160
By blunting us to make our wits more keen.

'Nor gives it satisfaction to our blood
That we must curb it upon others' proof,
To be forebode the sweets that seems so good,
For fear of harms that preach in our behoof: 165
O appetite, from judgement stand aloof!
The one a palate hath that needs will taste,
Though reason weep and cry, "It is thy last!"'

---

149 **desired** desirèd: requested (sexual)
favour
153 **proofs new-bleeding** elliptical for
'instances of newly wounded (perhaps
= deflowered) girls who had been less
careful to protect themselves'
foil the dull metal which set off the
young man's jewel-like splendour; the
evidence of his ability to *foil*, or over-
come, many women
155–6 Cf. Spenser, *FQ*, 3.xxvii.1–2: 'But
ah, who can deceive his destiny, / Or
weene by warning to auoyd his fate?',
which is applied to the warning

to Marinell to avoid 'The love of
women'. *Assay* = test out by experience (*OED* 1a).
157 **forced** attached importance to, cared
for (*OED* 14)
159 **Counsel** sage advice
162 **blood** fleshly nature, sexual appetite
(*OED* 6, with this example): cf. l. 184.
164 **forebode** forbidden
sweets sexual delights: cf. 'saucy
sweetness', *MM* 2.4.45
165 **in our behoof** on our behalf, in
defence of our own moral welfare

151 shielded.] sheelded,   153 new-bleeding] new bleeding   remained] remaind   154 jewel] Iewell
155 shunned] shun'd   156 destined] destin'd   157 forced] forc'd   158 by-passed] by-past
164 forebode] forbod

'For further, I could say, "This man's untrue",
And knew the patterns of his foul beguiling;   170
Heard where his plants in others' orchards grew;
Saw how deceits were gilded in his smiling;
Knew vows were ever brokers to defiling;
Thought characters and words merely but art,
And bastards of his foul adulterate heart.   175

'And long upon these terms I held my city,
Till thus he 'gan besiege me: "Gentle maid,
Have of my suffering youth some feeling pity
And be not of my holy vows afraid:
That's to ye sworn to none was ever said,   180
For feasts of love I have been called unto,
Till now, did ne'er invite, nor never woo.

' "All my offences that abroad you see
Are errors of the blood, none of the mind:
Love made them not; with acture they may be   185

171 **his . . . grew** implies that the youth
had made women pregnant: cf. the
'many maiden gardens, yet unset' of
16.6–7. The use of *orchards*, rather
than 'gardens', activates also a suggestion of forbidden fruit, both stolen
and planted.
173 **vows . . . defiling** (his) oaths were
always agents of sexual/moral corruption: cf. 'men's vows are women's
traitors', *Cym* 3.4.54.
174 **characters and words** words and
letters: cf. the embroidered *conceited
characters* of l. 16.
   merely but art no more than artifice,
guile (*OED* art 14); cf. l. 295.
176 **city** virginity, chastity: cf. 'this blem-
ish'd fort', *Luc* 1175.
179 **holy vows** sacred (seeming) oaths:
suggests that the youth is well aware

that the maid has observed his deception of other women. There may also
be a sexual innuendo in *holy* – cf.
153.5 and *AW* 1.3.30 – in addition to
a suggestion of 'holey', or leaky, unreliable vows.
180 What is (now) sworn to you was
never said (previously) to anyone.
181 **feasts of love** like the *sensual feast* of
141.8, may recall the commanding
metaphor of Chapman's *Ovids Banquet of Sence* (1595)
184 **blood** Cf. l. 162 and n.
185 **acture** the process of acting; action
(*OED*, this example only): the word
sounds quasi-legal, but is not easy to
explain in its context. Perhaps the suggestion is that 'acts of sex may be
engaged in (readily) in situations where
neither party is faithful or loving'.

171 orchards] Orchards   174 characters] Characters   176 city] Citty   181 called] call'd   182 woo]
Capell; vow *Q*, *Riv*

Where neither party is nor true nor kind;
They sought their shame that so their shame did find,
And so much less of shame in me remains,
By how much of me their reproach contains.

' "Among the many that mine eyes have seen,   190
Not one whose flame my heart so much as warmed,
Or my affection put to th' smallest teen,
Or any of my leisures ever charmed:
Harm have I done to them, but ne'er was harmed;
Kept hearts in liveries, but my own was free,   195
And reigned commanding in his monarchy.

' "Look here what tributes wounded fancies sent me,
Of pallid pearls and rubies red as blood,
Figuring that they their passions likewise lent me
Of grief and blushes, aptly understood,   200

187–9 The youth, as reported, seems to have befuddled the maid with quasi-legal quibbling on the word *shame* as, in its first occurrence, 'disgrace' (*OED* 3a); in its second, '(act of) shame' (*OED* 3b); and in its third 'modesty, shamefastness' (*OED* 2). The contorted reasoning of 188–9 appears to be that, since his cast-off mistresses are as guilty as he is, the more they reproach him, the more he is exonerated.
191 **Not one** (there was) not one
192 **teen** injury, damage (*OED* 1)
194 **harmed** heartbroken, or injured emotionally: cf. *MA* 2.3.26–30, where Benedick boasts of his heart-whole-ness: 'One woman is fair, yet I am well; another wise, yet I am well; another virtuous, yet I am well; but till all graces be in one woman, one woman shall not come in my grace'.
195 **in liveries** in service, as retainer; cf.

OED livery 3b, 'under livery'.
197 **wounded fancies** ellipsis for 'women wounded in their fancy': cf. the description of the *fickle maid* as an *afflicted fancy* (l. 61 and n.)
199–203 The pearl and ruby jewels, resembling the *conceited* and *posied* love tokens of ll. 16 and 45, yield a complex conceit of conflicting emotions, with the pale pearls suggesting pain and chastity, the blood-red rubies shame and rage (*mood* = anger, as in *OED* 2b); and the conflict between the two serving as external token of the opposing armies *Encamped* within the girls' bosoms. Cf. Sidney's description of Amphialus visiting the girl with whom he is painfully in love (*NA*, 321): 'About his neck, he wore a broad and gorgeous collar, whereof, the pieces interchangeably answering, the one was of diamonds and pearl set

186 party] Party   192 th'] th,   193 charmed] Charmed   196 reigned] raignd   197 here] heare
198 pallid] palyd

In bloodless white and the encrimsoned mood,
Effects of terror and dear modesty,
Encamped in hearts, but fighting outwardly.

' "And lo! Behold these talons of their hair,
With twisted metal amorously empleached,   205
I have received from many a several fair,
Their kind acceptance weepingly beseeched,
With th'annexions of fair gems enriched,
And deep-brained sonnets, that did amplify
Each stone's dear nature, worth and quality.   210

' "The diamond? Why, 'twas beautiful and hard,
Whereto his invised properties did tend:
The deep green emerald, in whose fresh regard

with a white enamel . . . and the other piece, being of rubies and opals, had a fiery glistering – which he thought pictured the two passions of fear and desire, wherein he was enchained'.

204 **talons** Though Q's 'talents' has been previously glossed as 'coins', as in the Parable of the Talents (Matthew, 25.14–30), this is the regular Elizabethan spelling of *talons* = claws: cf. *LLL* 4.2.64, 'If a talent be a claw, look how he claws him with a talent'. The reference is probably to claw-shaped brooches or pendants woven with hair interlaced with gold or silver wire. Weaving hair and *twisted metal* (205) around a coin would pose practical problems, as well as masking the coin's value; additionally, claw-shaped jewels suggest the amorously predatory aspirations of the givers.

205 **empleached** interwoven, intertwined, from 'pleach' (*OED* 1a, b), most often applied to the twisting or

interlacing of branches or vine-stems; cf. *MA* 3.1.7, 'pleached bower'.

208 **annexions** adjuncts, additions (*OED*'s earliest example, under sense 2)

209 **deep-brained sonnets** profoundly pondered, equipped with thought: cf. the odd use of 'brain' in *Cym* 5.4.147, 'Such stuff as madmen tongue and brain not'.

210 **dear** precious; inherent

212 **his** its

invised nonce word, presumably denoting 'unseen' (*OED*); however, Q's 'inuis'd' could possibly be a compositorial misreading of 'invi'd' or 'invied', = envied, admired.

213–14 **emerald . . . amend** Cf. Philemon Holland, trans., Pliny, *The Historie of the Worlde* (1601), Book 37, chapter 5: 'True it is, that we take great delight to behold greene hearbes and leaves of trees, but this is nothing to the pleasure wee have in looking upon the Emeraud, for compare it

201 encrimsoned] encrimson'd   203 Encamped] Encampt   204 lo!] Lo   talons] tallents   hair] heir
205 metal . . . empleached] mettle . . . empleacht   206 received] receau'd   207 beseeched] beseecht
208 enriched] inricht   209 deep-brained] deepe brain'd   210 nature] Nature   211 diamond]
Diamond   212 invised] *Oxf*; inuis'd *Q*   213 emerald] Emrald

Weak sights their sickly radiance do amend;
The heaven-hued sapphire and the opal blend   215
With objects manifold; each several stone
With wit well-blazoned smiled, or made some moan.

' "Lo, all these trophies of affections hot,
Of pensived and subdued desires the tender,
Nature hath charged me that I hoard them not,   220
But yield them up where I myself must render,
That is, to you, my origin and ender:
For these of force must your oblations be;
Since I their altar, you empatron me.

with other things, be they never so greene, it surpasseth them all in pleasant verdure . . . Nay, if the sight hath beene wearied and dimmed by intentive poring upon any thing else, the beholding of this stone doth refresh and restore it againe, which lapidaries well know, that cut and engrave fine stones; for they have not a better means to refresh their eyes than the Emeraud, the mild greene that it hath doth so comfort and revive their wearines and lassitude'.

215–16 **The . . . manifold** Perhaps in contrast to the single powerful properties attributed to the diamond and the emerald, the sapphire and opal are linked with many other elements – *objects manifold* – to yield a variety of symbolism.

217 The *deep-brained sonnets* accompanying them, skilfully enumerating the jewels' attributes, caused them either to smile (attractively) or complain (imploringly).

219 **pensived** probably, rendered pensive or sad, saddened (*OED*, this example only)
 tender offering, token; cf. 83.4, 'The barren tender of a poet's debt'.

220–1 Strongly echoes sonnet 1, with its account of the addressee as *niggarding*, as well as 126, with its anticipation of the time when nature must *render* the youth up to death; but what is disconcertingly different here is that instead of making a gift of his inherent gifts – youth, beauty, rank – the speaker is applying the argument against *niggarding* to gifts bestowed on him by others.

222 **origin and ender** takes the deification of the mistress to the unusual extreme of identifying her with God himself, as 'Alpha and Omega, the beginning and the ending' (Revelation, 1.8)

223 **oblations** offerings: another word with strong biblical associations; cf. Leviticus, 7.38.

224 **Since I** since I am
 empatron patronize; stand in the relation of patron to (*OED*, this example only): the somewhat strained argument seems to be that the maid is to the young man as an *altar*, or subject of devotion, equivalent to what he is for all the other women, so the love-gifts previously offered to him are now all due to her.

215 heaven-hued] *Ard'*; heauen hewd *Q* sapphire] Saphir opal] Opall 217 well-blazoned smiled] well blazond smil'd 219 pensived] *Oxf*; pensiu'd subdued] subdew'd 220 charged] chargd 224 altar] Aulter empatron] enpatrone

' "O then advance of yours that phraseless hand,   225
Whose white weighs down the airy scale of praise;
Take all these similes to your own command,
Hallowed with sighs that burning lungs did raise:
What me, your minister for you, obeys,
Works under you; and to your audit comes   230
Their distract parcels in combined sums.

' "Lo, this device was sent me from a nun,
Or sister sanctified, of holiest note,
Which late her noble suit in court did shun,
Whose rarest havings made the blossoms dote;   235
For she was sought by spirits of richest coat,
But kept cold distance, and did thence remove
To spend her living in eternal love.

225 **phraseless** beyond description; cf. *termless*, l. 94.

226 an elaborate way of saying that her hand's whiteness is beyond praise: with his words on one side of the balance, and its whiteness on the other, the words will fly up as inadequately lightweight.

227 **these similes** the similes used to and about the young man by his previous mistresses in their love-gifts and sonnets

228 *****Hallowed** another word with strong religious associations (cf. l. 222 and n.), as in 'hallowed be thy name' in the Lord's Prayer (*BCP*)

229–30 **What . . . you** another contorted argument (cf. 187–9 and n.): presumably, 'Since I act as a mediator on your behalf, that which is subject to my control, or under obedience to you, is now under yours.'

230–1 **to . . . sums** The separate portions (*parcels*) of love offered to the young man are now transferred collectively to your own reckoning of accounts; the literal sense of *audit* as 'hearing' may have some bearing here.

231 **combined** combinèd

232–3 **nun . . . sanctified** The rhetorical correction of *nun* to *sister sanctified* suggests that the woman described (in this post-Reformation poem) may be not technically a member of a religious order, merely a woman who has made a nun-like decision to devote herself to chastity.

234 **noble suit** amorous address made to her by a nobleman, or noblemen

235 **havings** possessions; behaviour (*OED* 2, 3)
     blossoms perhaps suggests the 'flower' of young men at court; cf. also Venus' address to Adonis as 'the field's chief flower', *VA* 8.

236 **richest coat** most splendid coat of arms (cf. *OED* coat 4, with this example), therefore of the most ancient nobility

238 **living** the rest of her life
     eternal love love of God, as distinct from the transitory love between human beings: cf. Sidney, *CS*, 32, which begins 'Leave me, O Love, which reachest but to dust', and ends 'Eternall Love maintaine thy life in me'.

225 of yours] (of yours)   228 Hallowed] *Malone;* Hollowed *Q*   232 nun] Nun   233 sister] Sister

' "But O, my sweet, what labour is't to leave
The thing we have not, mast'ring what not strives,   240
Planing the place which did no form receive,
Playing patient sports in unconstrained gyves;
She that her fame so to herself contrives
The scars of battle 'scapeth by the flight,
And makes her absence valiant, not her might.   245

' "O pardon me, in that my boast is true;
The accident which brought me to her eye
Upon the moment did her force subdue,
And now she would the caged cloister fly,
Religious love put out religion's eye;   250
Not to be tempted would she be immured,
And now to tempt all liberty procured.

239–40 **what . . . not** How difficult it is to relinquish (desire for) the thing we do not have: presumably this applies to the *sister sanctified*, who finds it hard to sustain her negative vow to forswear earthly love.
what not strives that which does not resist
241 ***Planing** Capell's emendation of Q's 'Playing' has been adopted, on the presumption that the copy MS read 'Playning' or 'Plaÿing'. The suggestion presumably is that a surface already smooth, or paper empty of signs, is pointlessly 'planed', or smoothed over (cf. *OED* plane *v.* 1a, b, c): the *sister*, already chaste, seeks to reinforce her chastity further.
242 playing at being patient in fetters voluntarily adopted, not enforced by others
243–5 A reputation for chastity based on the avoidance of temptation is nega-

tive, not positive: images perhaps picked up by Milton in 'I cannot praise a fugitive and cloister'd vertue, unexercis'd & unbreath'd, that never sallies out and sees her adversary' (*Areopagitica*, in Milton, *Prose Works*, 2.515).
246 **my boast** the boast I am about to make
247 **accident** chance
248 **subdue** brought it into (emotional) subjection: see *OED* 2a, and cf. the association of the word with erotic enchantment in *Oth* 1.3.112, 2.3.331, 3.4.57.
249 **caged** cagèd
250 'Quasi-religious erotic devotion quenched her (previous) spiritual vision.'
251 **would she be** she wished to be
252 **to . . . procured** obtained full freedom in order to tempt (me)

241 Planing] *Capell;* Playing *Q*   place] Place   242 unconstrained] vnconstraind   251 immured] *Oxf;* enur'd   252 procured] procure

447

' "How mighty then you are, O hear me tell!
The broken bosoms that to me belong
Have emptied all their fountains in my well,   255
And mine I pour your ocean all among:
I strong o'er them, and you o'er me being strong,
Must for your victory us all congest,
As compound love, to physic your cold breast.

' "My parts had power to charm a sacred nun,   260
Who, disciplined, I dieted in grace,
Believed her eyes, when they t'assail begun,
All vows and consecrations giving place.
O most potential love! Vow, bond, nor space,
In thee hath neither sting, knot, nor confine,   265
For thou art all and all things else are thine.

' "When thou impressest, what are precepts worth
Of stale example? When thou wilt inflame,

255 **fountains** For the association of
'fountains' with female genitalia, cf.
VA 234, and Nashe's 'The Choise of
Valentines', 112 (Nashe, 3.408).
256 **mine** my (sexual) gifts donated by
the other women
258 **congest** gather together, collect as a
mass (*OED* 1): the maid is to win the
collective amorous submissions of his
previous mistresses to the young man,
as well as those of the young man
himself.
259 plays on the sense of *compound* as a
compounded drug, medicine (*OED*
2a; and cf. *Luc* 531, *Cym* 1.1.58),
which will heal, or mollify, the maid's
amorous coldness
260 **parts** talents, attractions; cf. 17.4
and n.
261 continues medical metaphor: though
the *nun* had *disciplined* herself to
remain chaste, the young man *dieted*

her, or 'regulated her food for the
benefit of her health' (*OED* diet 2a),
by offering a favourable response to
her love.
263 **giving place** yielding, giving
ground to (*OED* give 47a, d)
264 **potential** powerful, commanding
(*OED* 1); cf. *Oth* 1.2.13.
264–5 **Vow . . . confine** a slightly clumsy
use of *correlatio*, in which the three
components *vow, bond, space* are defined
as correspondingly transcending the
restrictions of *sting, knot* or *confine* (here
a noun = limit or boundary: cf. *KL*
2.4.150): the whole is an elaborate way
of saying that 'Love overcomes all'
(Tilley, L527). 'Sting' does not apply
well to 'vow', however; conceivably the
word here should be 'strength' (RP).
267 **impressest** enforce, urge; imprint
idea (of love) on the mind (*OED*
impress *v.* 3)

256 ocean] Ocean   260 nun] *Capell;* Sunne *Q*   261 Who, disciplined,] Who disciplin'd
262 Believed] Beleeu'd

How coldly those impediments stand forth,
Of wealth, of filial fear, law, kindred, fame?   270
Love's arms are peace, 'gainst rule, 'gainst sense, 'gainst
    shame,
And sweetens in the suff'ring pangs it bears
The aloes of all forces, shocks and fears.

' "Now all these hearts that do on mine depend,
Feeling it break, with bleeding groans they pine,   275
And supplicant their sighs to you extend,
To leave the batt'ry that you make 'gainst mine,
Lending soft audience to my sweet design
And credent soul to that strong-bonded oath
That shall prefer and undertake my troth."   280

'This said, his wat'ry eyes he did dismount,
Whose sights till then were levelled on my face;
Each cheek a river running from a fount

269 **impediments** Cf. 116.2.
271 **Love's . . . peace** Love's weapons are, paradoxically, those of peace: implies that love achieves instant conquest and consent.
271–3 **rule . . . fears** Though again deploying threefold elements (cf. 264–5 and n.), this time there is no correspondence between the two groups of three nouns: they simply produce an effect of rhetorical battery, corresponding with the military allusions in the image of love's powerful conquest.
273 **aloes** literally, a purgative drug with a bitter taste, 'procured from the inspissated juice of plants of the genus *Aloe*'; figuratively, bitter experiences, trials (*OED* 3, 4)
277 **leave** desist from
    batt'ry bombardment or succession of blows to a besieged fortress (OED 3a): the young man's suggestion that

the maid is besieging him, instead of his besieging her (as in 176–8), is particularly neat.
278 **audience** (favourable) hearing, attention (*OED* 1)
279 **credent** trustful, credulous (*OED* 1); cf. *Ham* 1.3.30.
280 **prefer and undertake** assist and act as surety for (*OED* prefer 2; undertake 4g, with this example)
    troth truth, or promise of faithfulness: a word strongly associated with the promise made in the marriage service, 'And thereto I plight thee my troth' (*BCP*, 292).
281 **dismount** Like the maid's eyes in ll. 22–5, the young man's eyes are seen as guns mounted on a gun carriage, which are now lowered (cf. *OED* dismount 6, 8).
282 **levelled on** aimed at; cf. *her levelled eyes*, l. 22.

273 aloes] *Alloes*   279 strong-bonded] strong bonded   282 levelled] leaueld

With brinish current downward flowed apace.
O how the channel to the stream gave grace,   285
Who glazed with crystal gate the glowing roses
That flame through water which their hue encloses!

'O father, what a hell of witchcraft lies
In the small orb of one particular tear!
But with the inundation of the eyes   290
What rocky heart to water will not wear?
What breast so cold that is not warmed here?
O cleft effect! Cold modesty, hot wrath,
Both fire from hence and chill extincture hath.

'For lo, his passion, but an art of craft,   295
Even there resolved my reason into tears;
There my white stole of chastity I daffed,
Shook off my sober guards and civil fears,
Appeared to him as he to me appears,

285–7 a mannered conceit of the youth's tears as 'glazing', or glassing over, forming a *crystal gate* over, the *roses* of his cheeks, seen also as a *flame* shining through water

290–1 **But . . . wear?** The reasoning is that if even one tear is irresistibly powerful, containing a *hell of witchcraft* (cf. the erotic witchcraft of Katherine's lips, *H5* 5.2.301), no heart can fail to be melted by an *inundation* of tears.

292 **warmed** warmèd

293–4 Developing the oxymoronic conceit of *flame through water* from l. 287, the maid now expounds the *cleft*, or divided, *effect* of the young man's tears: from the same source (*hence*), her *modesty* receives *fire*, and her *hot wrath* – presumably anger with the

youth for his persistence – is coldly extinguished. *Extincture*, for 'extinction', is yet another nonce word, and perhaps carries with it a sense of 'tincture' in the sense of 'stain' or 'taint' (*OED* 3a, 5a), anticipating the 'poisoning' of l. 301.

295 **art of craft** (the product of) an art of crafty deception

296 **resolved** dissolved; transformed; cf. *Ham* 1.2.130; *Tim* 4.3.442.

297 **white . . . chastity** The image suggests an imaginative conflation of the *maid* with the *nun* of 232ff.
daffed took off, disrobed myself of; cf. *AC* 4.4.13.

298 **sober guards** suggests both metaphorical *guards*, and sober clothes which had appeared to protect her

284 downward] downe-ward 286 glazed] glaz'd crystal] Christall roses] Roses 288 witchcraft] witch-craft 293 O] *Malone;* Or *Q* 296 resolved] resolu'd 297 daffed] *Oxf;* daft *Q* 299 Appeared] *this edn.;* Appeare *Q*

All melting, though our drops this diff'rence bore: 300
His poisoned me, and mine did him restore.

'In him a plenitude of subtle matter,
Applied to cautels, all strange forms receives,
Of burning blushes, or of weeping water,
Or swooning paleness; and he takes and leaves 305
In either's, aptness, as it best deceives,
To blush at speeches rank, to weep at woes,
Or to turn white and swoon at tragic shows.

'That not a heart which in his level came
Could 'scape the hail of his all-hurting aim, 310
Showing fair nature is both kind and tame;
And veiled in them, did win whom he would maim.
Against the thing he sought he would exclaim;
When he most burned in heart-wished luxury
He preached pure maid, and praised cold chastity. 315

300 **melting** primarily, 'dissolving with tears'; but the word also has strong erotic associations, as in Song 10 of Sidney's *AS*: 'My life melts with too much thinking', where 'melt' suggests 'experience orgasm'; cf. also Partridge, 153.

301 **poisoned** If the sexual application of *melting*, in the preceding line, is pursued, there is a suggestion of venereal infection as well as moral corruption.

302 **subtle matter** delicate, malleable, deceptive material (that of the human body)

303 **cautels** wiles, deceptions; cf. *Ham* 1.3.15.

306 **either's, aptness** in either of these moods, (he assumes and provokes) an

appropriate measure (of emotion): the young man sounds like both the ideally responsive auditor, and a consummately versatile actor, whose body, like that of the First Player in *Ham* 2.2., can generate tears and physical manifestations of passion at command.

309 **level** range (of his aim), reverting to the military imagery of 281–2

312 **veiled in them** presumably, in a *fair* appearance of natural kindness and gentleness

314 **heart-wished luxury** lechery which he desired in his heart

315 **preached pure maid** preached as if he were a pure maid; preached a doctrine of maidenliness

300 diff'rence] diffrence 301 poisoned] poison'd 303 cautels] Cautills 305 swooning] *Malone;* sounding *Q;* swounding *Capell* 306 either's, aptness,] eithers aptnesse 308 swoon] *Malone;* sound *Q* 310 all-hurting] *Malone;* all hurting *Q* 311 nature] Nature 312 veiled] vaild 314 burned] burnt heart-wished] hart-wisht 315 preached] preacht praised] praisd

'Thus, merely with the garment of a grace,
The naked and concealed fiend he covered,
That th'unexperient gave the tempter place
Which, like a cherubin, above them hovered.
Who, young and simple, would not be so lovered?   320
Ay me, I fell, and yet do question make
What I should do again for such a sake.

'O, that infected moisture of his eye!
O, that false fire which in his cheek so glowed!
O, that forced thunder from his heart did fly!   325
O, that sad breath his spongy lungs bestowed!
O, all that borrowed motion, seeming owed,
Would yet again betray the fore-betrayed,
And new pervert a reconciled maid.'

316 **garment of a grace** outward appearance of an angel
317 **concealed** concealèd
318 **unexperient** person(s) without experience: nonce word
318–19 **tempter . . . cherubin** The Devil (often referred to in Tyndale's Bible as 'the tempter') is imagined as hovering over the pair, disguised as a *cherubin* (the normal Elizabethan word for 'cherub').
320 **lovered** provided with a lover: nonce word. This line makes explicit the gradually implied reversal of the meaning of the title, from 'complaint *by* a lover' to 'complaint *about* a lover'.
323–9 What initially seems to be a succession of disjointed exclamations turns out to assemble, rather as the love-gifts to the young man were assembled, a collective rhetoric which betrays the maid even as she re-invokes it in her attempt at self-

purgation.
326 **spongy** soft, absorbent: presumably here suggesting a treacherous capacity to generate false breath, or words; cf. Fulke Greville, *Alaham* (1633), II.iii, 'The spungie hearts of men / Their hollowes gladly fill with women's love'; and *Ham* 4.2.12–14.
327 **seeming** apparently
owed possessed, inherent
329 **pervert . . . maid** Following the *tempter/cherubin* images in the preceding stanza, this suggests that the maid, transiently repentant, or *reconciled* to God, is ready to be once again 'perverted' by the recollection of his false body-language.
reconciled reconcilèd: for the religious and ecclesiastical application of the word, especially with reference to the Church of Rome, cf. *OED* reconcile 5a, b; 2.

317 covered] couerd   319 cherubin] Cherubin   hovered] houerd   320 lovered] louerd   324 glowed] glowd   325 forced] forc'd   329 maid] Maide.

A P P E N D I X
M A N U S C R I P T   T E X T S

The history of the manuscript transmission of individual sonnets belongs, almost certainly, with 'Reception', not 'Text'. That is, it tells us something about which sonnets were most admired by collectors of verse, but provides no textual evidence independent of Q. None of the twenty-five extant texts[1] antedates 1609, and there is no good reason to believe that any of them derives, directly or indirectly, from independent authorial versions, such as those 'sugred sonnets' to which Francis Meres referred in 1598 (see Introduction, p. 1). Gary Taylor has defended the 'authenticity' of some of the variant readings in the eleven manuscript versions of sonnet 2 ('When forty winters . . . '), claiming that these are 'characteristic both of Shakespeare's early style and of the themes and imagery of the relevant sonnets themselves'[2]. It is odd, if so, that the wide circulation of this sonnet occurred only in the 1620s and 1630s, more than a decade after the appearance of Q, and that it is found largely in the company of late Jacobean and Caroline verse, not with other pre-1609 poems. Indeed, in its context in the miscellanies, alongside poems by Carew, Strode, Corbett and Herrick, Shakespeare's speaker's plea for fruition and procreation – implicitly, and sometimes explicitly, addressed to a young girl – comes across as in effect an honorary 'Cavalier' seduction lyric. Given Shakespeare's commanding reputation, and the uninvited publicity given to his non-dramatic verse by Meres and William Jaggard, there must have been many collectors of lyric poetry before 1609 who would have loved to get hold of individual sonnets. Yet no pre-1609 manuscript

---

1 For a full list, see Beal, 2.449–63. Beal's system of reference, ShW + number, is used.
2 *TxC*, 444.

texts survive, nor do any literary manuscripts by Shakespeare, and it is rather hard to imagine from what source, other than Q, the seventeenth-century texts could derive.

Taylor gave especial praise to the version of 2 in ShW18, George Morley's commonplace book.[1] He suggested that it might be relatively early, though it is not clear whether he inspected the manuscript personally.[2] Not only does this item appear soon after Morley's own poem 'On the death of King James' – whose subject-matter places it in 1625 or later – it seems to have been added to the commonplace book some time later than the material surrounding it. The much more open, sprawling version of Morley's hand in which the sonnet is written suggests that it may have been a matter of many years later. On folios 48^v-49^r a batch of five poems, including the elegy on King James, has been written in a neat and careful hand, the last of them a horribly misogynistic epigram 'On an olde woeman'. The much-circulated version of sonnet 2, under the title 'To one *that* would dye a maid', which occurs also in three other manuscripts (ShW12, ShW13, ShW19), occupies a space on the lower part of folio 49^r, and presents every appearance of late addition. We may speculate about whether Morley inserted Shakespeare's sonnet (here unattributed) at this point merely because the half-page left blank was the right size for a sonnet, or because he felt that there was a thematic connection between the 'toothless Scilla' of the epigram and the addressee of sonnet 2, here to be presumed female, whose 'hollow suncken eyes' are foreseen. The poem immediately following, from folio 49^v onwards, the much-circulated 'The parliament fart', also looks as if it was transcribed by Morley at an earlier date than sonnet 2. Though the embarrassingly public emission celebrated in John Hoskyns's poem originally occurred in 1607, the poem's widest circulation, in a much adapted and expanded version, as here, occurred after

1 Westminster Abbey MS 41, fol. 49^r.
2 Taylor, 'Some MSS', 220.

1628.[1] The suggestion transmitted by both Taylor and Kerrigan that the version of 2 in ShW18 could be as early as 1619[2] is most unlikely to be correct. George Morley's commonplace book takes its place alongside the ten other manuscripts in which a text of 2 appears as an interesting and varied miscellany of the Caroline period, with no special or independent links with pre-1609 sources.

Taylor has also made much of the 'Shakespearian' deftness of the title '*Spes Altera*', which is applied to sonnet 2 in four manuscripts (ShW8, ShW9, ShW10, ShW14).[3] He traces it to its source in Virgil's *Aeneid*, 12.168, where it refers to Aeneas' son Ascanius, 'second hope of great Rome'. Yet the deployment of a Latin title seems most uncharacteristic of Shakespeare, and much more typical of the university and Inns of Court environment to which so many of the Jacobean and Caroline miscellanies belong.[4] Also, by labelling the seventeenth-century collectors of 2 'copyists' Taylor suggests that they were unthinking and unlearned scribes, who might accidentally and unconsciously transmit an early variant version of a Shakespeare sonnet derived from a text produced several decades before. Yet many of the compilers of these miscellanies can be identified as individuals who had enjoyed considerably more formal education and social advantages than Shakespeare had done. George Morley, for instance, was educated at Westminster and Christ Church, and was to end his life as Bishop of Winchester. Horatio Carey, shown by Taylor to be the compiler of ShW26,[5] was a great-grandson of Shakespeare's patron the first Lord Hunsdon. Margaret Bellasys, owner of the manuscript containing ShW8,[6] seems to have been the daughter of Thomas Bellasys (1577-1653), who was created Baron Fauconberg by Charles I

1   Whitlock, 283–95.
2   Kerrigan, 441.
3   Taylor, 'Some MSS', 233–6.
4   For a general survey of these, see Marotti, 31–7.
5   Rosenbach MS 1083/17, fols 132ᵛ–133.
6   BL MS 10309, fol. 143.

in 1627. Collectors of poems in this period frequently introduced readings which could in some sense be called improvements, and may have taken a pride in doing so. The variant readings in the manuscript versions of sonnet 2 which Taylor has defended as 'Shakespearian' were more probably arrived at through such a process of later intervention. Though Taylor claims that 'the transcriber of a sonnet in the 1620s should not have introduced a tissue of reminiscences of poems and plays which Shakespeare wrote three decades earlier'[1], the significant point here is not so much the date when the poems and plays were written as the time when they became generally accessible. After the appearance of the First Folio in 1623 bookish men and women, such as were the compilers of the Caroline manuscript miscellanies, were likely to have studied Shakespeare's work in some detail.

I am not myself convinced that any of the variants in the manuscript versions of sonnet 2 seem particularly 'Shakespearian'; but if they were, a response to Shakespeare's published works would be the likeliest explanation. To the present editor, however, this version appears dilute and conventional, lacking many of the rich complexities of the Q text. For instance, in Q, lines 1-2 sustain a consistent military metaphor, in which 'forty winters' will 'besiege' the young man's beauty – synecdochically represented by his 'brow' – by digging 'deep trenches' in it. The manuscript versions' 'trench deep furrows', for Q's 'digge deep trenches', substitutes a clod-hopping metaphor of ploughing furrows in a field. Not only does this deviate from the image of siege warfare; it introduces associations with seed-sowing and eventual harvest which are wholly inappropriate, since the dynamic of the sonnet depends upon an absolute contrast between the invasive threat posed to the youth's beauty by 'forty winters' if he fails to marry, and the fruitful alternative if he does. Likewise, in line 6, the substitution for Q's

1 Taylor 'Some MSS', 236.

> Where all the treasure of thy lusty daies

of

> Where all the lustre of thy youthful days

is weak and shallow. The Q version alludes specifically to the young man's reproductive capacity, with his semen ('treasure') diminishing unused if he lets his 'lusty' – sexually vigorous – time go by. The manuscript version – implicitly, and in some texts explicitly, addressed to a woman – makes only a superficial and bowdlerized allusion to the loss of beauty, 'lustre' looking suspiciously like a memorial conflation of 'lusty' and 'treasure' by someone who had tried to learn the poem by heart, or was copying inattentively. A text of the manuscript version of sonnet 2 is included here so that readers can judge for themselves.

Eleven further sonnets, or part-sonnets, are found in manuscript versions. Some, like ShW6, ShW22 and ShW27, are extremely late – *circa* 1660 – and self-evidently derivative.[1] Only one sonnet, 106 ('When in the chronicle of wasted time'), achieves repeat circulation, in ShW25 and ShW26. Both manuscripts belong to 1630 or later, and the latter heterosexualizes the sonnet by adding the title 'On his M*ist*ris Beauty'. ShW 20[2] has a text of sonnet 8 which resembles the '*Spes Altera*' versions of 2 in having a Latin title added, '*In laudem Musice et opprobrium Contemptorii eiusdem*' ('In praise of music, and in contempt of its despiser'). The title gives the sonnet the air of belonging to an academic debate, as do some other poems in this manuscript, such as the pair of poems with which it opens, the first claiming that love is water, the second that it is fire. The text of sonnet 8 is on the same leaf as two epitaphs on Prince Henry (1612), but other nearby material, such as R. Moore's translation of Musaeus (folios 16ᵛ-22ʳ), dated 11 November 1630, suggests a much later date. The variants in 8 may reflect some concern to

---

1 All in Folger MS V.a.148, Part 1, fols 22–7.
2 BL MS Add. 15226, fol. 4ᵛ.

457

14a Early transcription of sonnet 128. From Bodleian MS Rawl. poet 152, fol. 34ʳ

make the musical metaphors technically more correct, at the
price of making them poetically less expressive, as in the reading
at line 8, 'a parte, *w*hich thou shouldst bere', for Q's 'the parts
that thou should'st bear'. Though a single musician may indeed
perform only one 'part', the manuscript version eliminates Q's
allusion to the young man's 'parts' in the sense of 'talents, attain-
ments', as in 17.4, 37.7, 69.1 and *LC* 260. But because of its
unique status a transcript is included below.

Two further texts which merit discussion – and are included
here – also have a musical dimension. ShW28[1] presents a version

1   New York Public Library, Drexel MS 4257, no. 33; reproduced in Cam³, 27.

458

14 b Transcription on same ms of William Browne, 'Love's Labyrinth', and Sonnet II in Francis Davison's *A Poetical Rhapsody*. From Bodleian MS Rawl. poet 152, fol. 34^v

of sonnet 116 ('Let me not to the marriage of true mindes') adapted into three six-line stanzas and set to music by Henry Lawes. The added lines develop a sectarian religious metaphor, with their allusions to 'Selfe blinded error', 'hereticks' and the 'flameing Martyr'. Great interest attaches to this because of its links with William Herbert, Earl of Pembroke. Not only did Pembroke quote a phrase from the same sonnet, 'love is not love', in one of his own poems (see Introduction, pp. 68–9); it was from

1 Cf. Hobbs, 112–13.

Henry Lawes that John Donne the younger acquired many of the texts of Pembroke's poems that he published in 1660.[1] The Shakespeare–Pembroke–Lawes connection might well reward further investigation. The song also forges a link with Milton, for whose *Arcades* and *Comus* Lawes composed music. However, it is not significant textually. Though Blakemore Evans called it 'near-contemporary', this adaptation and setting probably belong to the 1630s, Lawes's most active period as a song-composer.[1]

ShW29[2] offers a text of sonnet 128 ('How oft when thou my musike musike playst'), one of only two 'dark lady' sonnets to achieve representation in manuscript. Like sonnet 8, it has a musical theme, and it may have been transcribed by someone who recognized Shakespeare's use of the word 'jacks' in lines 5 and 13 as technically incorrect – while failing to see its richness in innuendo – and for that reason altered it to 'kies' (keys). The substitution of 'tuched' for 'tikled' in line 9 may also reflect some concern with musical exactitude. This, rather than ShW18, is probably the earliest surviving transcription of any of Shakespeare's sonnets. It appears as the second poem of four,[3] all crowded rather inelegantly on to a single small leaf of paper (15 × 15 cm.), and written in an unlearned-seeming hand apt to use phonetic spellings (Figures 14 a and b). It is unlikely to derive from an independent manuscript text, for all three of the accompanying poems (two of them not previously identified) appear to be drawn from printed sources. The first item is the opening stanza of Song XII from John Dowland's *First Booke of Songes or Ayres*, printed in 1597 and again in 1600, 1606 and 1613. Following the version of 128 comes William Browne's poem 'Love's Labyrinth', which appeared in the first book of *Britannia's Pastorals* (1613), 61. Though this poem achieved

1 Cam³, 289; cf. Evans, 'Lawes'; also the entry on Lawes in *New Grove Dictionary of Music*.
2 Bodleian MS Rawl. poet 152, fol. 34ʳ.
3 Perhaps misled by a line drawn across the page in the Dowland stanza, Robbins claimed that there are 'five pieces of verse'.

some manuscript circulation elsewhere,[1] the source is most probably the printed text. Likewise, the fourth and final poem, 'I bend my wits and beate my werye breene', derives from a printed source, being Francis Davison's Sonnet II in Davison's *A Poetical Rhapsody*, published in 1602, 1608 and 1611. It seems, then, that this writer was collecting love lyrics from printed sources, and transcribing them, rather inaccurately, some time in or after 1613. Some readings are nonsensical, such as 'of loues despight' for 'of my delight' in line 3 of the Dowland poem. Others are clumsy or careless, such as the non-rhyming 'reped' for 'reape' in 128.7, or 'to imprinsen' for 'T"imprison' in the Davison sonnet. One reading points to a faithful but unintelligent response to the printed original, suggesting that these texts derive directly, and not through a manuscript intermediary, from their printed sources. William Browne's 'Love's Labyrinth' is presented emblematically in the printed text as an inscription on a continuous interlaced ribbon, with shading to indicate depth at points where the ribbon crosses over. The nonsensical manuscript reading 'in a rounde shuts up all quaringe' reflects its writer's failure to notice a partly shaded initial 's', the correct word being, of course, 'squaring'. In the light of this contextual evidence, Taylor's suggestion that ShW29 'may represent an earlier draft of the poem'[2] can be rejected, as can his and Beal's proposed dating, *circa* 1625–40s. A more plausible date would be 1613–20.

What is remarkable about this manuscript is not its status as an independent witness to the text of a Shakespeare sonnet – it is simplified and inaccurate – but its testimony to some interest in and appreciation of *Shakespeare's Sonnets* in the years immediately after 1609. While the location of sonnet 2 among lyrics by Carew, Suckling and Herrick, combined, usually, with the omission of Shakespeare's name, gives the manuscript version of

1   Cf. Bodleian MS Rawl. poet 160, fol. 102ᵛ.
2   *TxC*, 446.

'When forty winters . . . ' an anachronistically 'Cavalier' status, this manuscript, much more aptly, associates 'How oft when thou my musike . . . ' with songs, sonnets and pattern poems of the period 1597-1613. It may even have been transcribed during Shakespeare's lifetime, with the three accompanying poems offering some reflection of the cultural context in which *Shakespeare's Sonnets* was first read. For an uninformed reader of *The Passionate Pilgrim* Shakespeare had been associated with Dowland in the sonnet attributed to him, though actually by Barnfield, 'If music and sweet poetry agree', which includes the lines

> Dowland to thee is dear, whose heavenly touch
> Upon the lute doth ravish human sense . . .

In all of its editions, Dowland's *First Booke of Songs* was dedicated to Sir George Carey, Lord Hunsdon, who succeeded his father as Lord Chamberlain, and therefore as patron of Shakespeare's company, in March 1597. The conjunction of Shakespeare's sonnet with one by Francis Davison is also thought-provoking, in the light of Davison's dedication of *A Poetical Rhapsody* to William Herbert, Earl of Pembroke (see Introduction, p. 64). William Browne, too, was to be closely associated with the Herbert family, dedicating the two-book version of *Britannia's Pastorals* to Pembroke in 1616. None of the other manuscripts seems to be so early or to shed so much light on the early reception of *Shakespeare's Sonnets*. For this reason, despite its clumsiness, the manuscript is reproduced in full (Figs 14 a and b).

In the following transcripts, contractions have been expanded, and the expanded portions italicized; the style and spacing of stanza numbers have been regularized.

[2]

Spes Altera

When thre score winters shall beseige thy brow
And trench deepe furrowes in *tha*t louely feild
Thy youths faire Liu'rie soe accounted now
Shall be like rotten weeds, of no worth held.
Then being ask'd where all thy beautie lies   5
Where's all *tha*t Lustre of thy youthfull dayes
To saye w*i*thin these hollow-suncken eies,
Were an all-eaten truth, & worthlesse praise.
O how much better were thy beauties vse
If thou couldst say, this pretty childe of mine   10
Saues my account, & makes my old excuse
Making his beautie by succession thine.
   This were to be new borne, when *tho*u art old
   And see thy bloode warme, when *tho*u feelst it cold.

From BL MS Add. 10309, fol. 143^r (Margaret Bellasys's commonplace book,
c. 1630).

1 thre score] fortie *Q*   2 trench deepe furrowes] digge deep trenches *Q*   3 faire] proud
Q   accounted] gaz'd on *Q*   4 Shall] Wil *Q*   like rotten weeds,] a totter'd weed *Q*   no]
small *Q*   6 Where's] Where *Q*   *tha*t] the *Q*   Lustre] treasure *Q*   youthfull] lusty *Q*
7 these hollow-suncken] thine owne deepe sunken *Q*   8 all-eaten truth] all-eating shame
Q   worthlesse] thriftlesse *Q*   9 O how much better were] How much more praise deseru'd
Q   10 say] answere *Q*   pretty] faire *Q*   11 Saues my account] Shall sum my count *Q*
makes] make *Q*   12 Making] Proouing *Q*   13 borne] made *Q*

[8]

In laudem Musice et opprobrium Contemptorii eiusdem

1

Musicke to heare, why hearest thou Musicke sadly
Sweete with sweetes warre not, Joy delightes in Joy
Why louest *tho*u that which thou receauest not gladly
or else receauest with pleasure thine annoy

2

If the true Concord of well tuned Soundes   5
By Vnions maried doe offend thy eare
They doe but sweetlie chide thee, whoe confoundes
In singlenes a parte, which thou shouldst beare

3

Marke howe one stringe, sweet husband to another
Strikes each on each, by mutuall orderinge   10
Resemblinge Childe, & Syer, and happy Mother
Which all in one, this single note doth singe
    whose speechlesse songe beeinge many seeming one
    Singes this to thee, Thou single, shalt pro*u*e none

W. Shakspeare.

From BL MS Add. 15226, fol. 4ᵛ (*c.* 1630–50).

1 hearest] hear'st *Q*   2 Sweete] Sweets *Q*   3 louest] lou'st *Q*   4 receauest] reaceau'st *Q*
6 thy] thine *Q*   8 a parte] the parts *Q*   which] that *Q*   10 on] in *Q*   11 Childe, & Syer]
sier, and child *Q*   12 Which] Who *Q*   this single] one pleasing *Q*   doth] do *Q*   14 shalt]
wilt *Q*

[Adapted and expanded version of **116**]

Selfe blinding error seazeth all those mindes;
who with falce Appellations call that loue
w*hi*ch alters when it alteration findes
or with the mouer hath a power to moue
not much unlike *th*e heretickes p*r*etence   5
that scites trew scriptures but p*r*eventes ther sence:

Henry Lawes

2

Oh no Loue is an euer fixed marke
That lookes on tempestes but is neuer shaken
It is the starr to euery wandring barke
Whose worth's unknowne although his height be taken   10
Noe mowntebanke with eie-deludeing flashes
But flameing Martyr in his holly ashes

3

Loue's not tymes foole though Rosie lippes & Cheekes
Within his bynding Circle compas rownd
Loue alters not with his briefe howers & weekes   15
But holdes it out euen to the edge of doome
If this be errour & not truth approu'd
Cupids noe god nor Man nere lou'd

From MS Drexel 4257, No. 33 (New York Public Library, Music Division) (*c.* 1630–50).

Lines 3-4, 7-10, 13-14, correspond to lines 3-4, 5-8, 9-14 of Q.

[128]

how ouft when thow, deere deerest musick plaiest,
vpon that blessed wood whose mocions sounds,
with thy sweet fingers when thow gen\t/ly swaies,
the wiry concord that myne eare consoun\d/es,
o how I enuy those kies that nimble leapes,   5
to kisse the tender inward of thy hand,
whilst my poore lippes wich should that haruest reped,
at the wood bouldnes by thee blushinge stand,
to bee so tuched the faine would change there state,
and situacion with those dancinge chippes,   10
ouer whome youre fingers walke with gentle gate,
makeing deed wood more blest then liuing lipes,
Since then those keyes soe happy are in this,
giue them youre fingers mee youre lipes to kisse.

From Bodleian MS Rawl. poet 152, fol. 34ᵛ. (A single leaf, *c.* 1613–20.)

1 deere deerest] my musike *Q*   2 mocions] motion *Q*   3 swaies] swayst *Q*   4 consoun\d/es]
confounds *Q*   5 o how] Do *Q*   kies] Iackes *Q*   leapes] leape *Q*   7 reped] reape *Q*   8 wood]
woods *Q*   9 tuched] tikled *Q*   the faine] they *Q*   11 ouer] Ore *Q*   youre] their *Q*   13 then
those keyes] sausie Iackes *Q*   14 youre fingers] their fingers *Q*   youre lipes] thy lips *Q*

ABBREVIATIONS AND REFERENCES

Unless otherwise specified, the edition of Shakespeare used for references and quotations from works other than *Sonnets* is Arden 2. The Bible used for scriptural references and quotations is A.W.Pollard's edition (Oxford, 1911) of the Authorized Version. All quotations and translations from classical authors are taken from the Loeb Classical Library, unless another source is indicated. In all references, the place of publication is London unless otherwise stated.

ABBREVIATIONS

ABBREVIATIONS USED IN THE NOTES

*	precedes commentary notes involving readings altered from the early edition on which this edition is based
this edn	a reading adopted for the first time in this edition

WORKS BY AND PARTLY BY SHAKESPEARE

AC	*Antony and Cleopatra*
AW	*All's Well That Ends Well*
AYL	*As You Like It*
CE	*The Comedy of Errors*
Cor	*Coriolanus*
Cym	*Cymbeline*
Ham	*Hamlet*
1H4	*Henry IV, Part 1*
2H4	*Henry IV, Part 2*
H5	*Henry V*
1H6	*Henry VI, Part 1*
2H6	*Henry VI, Part 2*
3H6	*Henry VI, Part 3*
H8	*Henry VIII*
JC	*Julius Caesar*
KJ	*King John*

KL	*King Lear*
LC	*A Lover's Complaint*
LLL	*Love's Labour's Lost*
Luc	*The Rape of Lucrece*
MA	*Much Ado About Nothing*
Mac	*Macbeth*
MM	*Measure for Measure*
MND	*A Midsummer Night's Dream*
MV	*The Merchant of Venice*
MW	*The Merry Wives of Windsor*
Oth	*Othello*
Per	*Pericles*
PP	*The Passionate Pilgrim*
PT	*The Phoenix and the Turtle*
R2	*Richard II*
R3	*Richard III*
RJ	*Romeo and Juliet*
Son	*Shakespeare's Sonnets*
TC	*Troilus and Cressida*
Tem	*The Tempest*
TGV	*The Two Gentlemen of Verona*
Tim	*Timon of Athens*
Tit	*Titus Andronicus*
TN	*Twelfth Night*
TNK	*The Two Noble Kinsmen*
TS	*The Taming of the Shrew*
VA	*Venus and Adonis*
WT	*The Winter's Tale*

REFERENCES

EDITIONS OF SHAKESPEARE COLLATED

Ard[1]	C.Knox Pooler, ed., *The Works of Shakespeare: Sonnets*, The Arden Shakespeare (1918)
Benson	*Poems: Written by Wil. Shake-speare. Gent*, published by John Benson (1640)
Booth	Stephen Booth, ed., *Shakespeare's Sonnets* (New Haven, Conn., and London 1977)
Cam[2]	J.Dover Wilson, ed., *Sonnets* (Cambridge, 1966)
Cam[3]	G.Blakemore Evans, ed., *The Sonnets* (Cambridge, 1996)
Capell	Edward Capell, marked-up copy of *Sonnets* published by Bernard Lintott (1711), in the library of Trinity College, Cambridge
IR	W.G.Ingram and Theodore Redpath, eds, *Shakespeare's Sonnets* (1964, 1978)
Kerrigan	John Kerrigan, ed., *The Sonnets and A Lover's Complaint*, The New Penguin Shakespeare (Harmondsworth, 1986)
Malone	Edmond Malone, *Supplement to the Edition of Shakespeare's Plays published in 1778* (1780)
Oxf	Stanley Wells & Gary Taylor, eds, *Complete Works* (1986)
PP	*The Passionate Pilgrime. By W.Shakespeare.* (1599), Huntington Library Copy, reproduced in J.M.Osborn, Louis L.Martz & Eugene M.Waith, eds, *Shakespeare's Poems: A Facsimile of the Earliest Editions* (New Haven and London, 1964)
Q	*Shake-speare's Sonnets. Neuer before Imprinted*, published by Thomas Thorpe (1609); facsimile ed. J.M.Osborn (New Haven, Conn., 1964), and also included in Booth
Riv	*Works*, gen. ed. G.Blakemore Evans, Riverside Shakespeare (Boston, Mass., 1974)

OTHER WORKS CITED

The list comprises edited texts and works of scholarship later than 1850. Unedited manuscripts and early printed books are not itemized here, and are referred to by their original, old-spelling titles.

Abbott	E.A.Abbott, *A Shakespearian Grammar*, 2nd edn (1870)
Armada	Richard Ormond *et al.*, *Armada* (1988)
Baldwin	T.W.Baldwin, *On the Literary Genetics of Shakespeare's Poems and Sonnets* (Urbana, Ill., 1950)
Barroll	J.Leeds Barroll, *Politics, Plague, and Shakespeare's Theatre* (Ithaca and London, 1991)
Barton	Anne Barton, *Ben Jonson, Dramatist* (1984)

BCP	John E.Booty, ed., *The Book of Common Prayer 1559: The Elizabethan Prayer Book* (Charlottesville, Va., 1976)
Beal	Peter Beal, *Index of Literary Manuscripts 1450-1625*, 2 vols (New York, 1980)
Bearman	Robert Bearman, *Shakespeare in the Stratford Records* (1994)
Bentley	G.E.Bentley, *The Jacobean and Caroline Stage*, 7 vols (1968)
BL MS	British Library Manuscript
Bloom	Harold Bloom, ed., *Critical Interpretations: Shakespeare's Sonnets* (New York, 1987)
Bradbrook	M.C.Bradbrook, *The School of Night* (1936)
Brennan	Michael Brennan, *Literary Patronage in the English Renaissance* (1988)
Brown & Feavor	Ivor Brown & G.Feavor, *Amazing Monument* (1939)
Burrow	J.A.W.Burrow, *The Ages of Man* (1986)
Cameron	Alan Cameron, *The Greek Anthology from Meleager to Planudes* (1993)
Castiglione	Baldassare Castiglione, *The Booke of the Courtier*, trans. Sir Thomas Hoby (1561), The Tudor Translations, 23 (1900)
Chambers, *Shakespeare*	E.K.Chambers, *William Shakespeare: A Study of Facts and Problems*, 2 vols (Oxford, 1930)
Chambers, *Stage*	E.K.Chambers, *The Elizabethan Stage*, 4 vols (1923)
Chaucer	*The Riverside Chaucer*, ed. F.N.Robinson, rev. L.D.Benson (1987)
Chedgzoy	Kate Chedgzoy, *Shakespeare's Queer Children: Sexual Politics and Contemporary Culture* (Manchester and New York, 1995)
Cheney	C.R.Cheney, *Handbook of Dates for Students of English History* (1970)
Coleridge	T.M.Raysor, ed., *Coleridge's Shakespearean Criticism* (1930)
Colie	Rosalie Colie, *Shakespeare's Living Art* (1974)
Colie, *Resources*	Rosalie Colie, *The Resources of Kind: Genre-Theory in the Renaissance* (Los Angeles and London, 1973)
CSP	*Calendars of State Papers*
Davies	Robert Krueger, ed., *Poems of Sir John Davies* (1975)
DNB	Sir Leslie Stephen & Sir Sidney Lee, eds, *Dictionary of National Biography* (1885-1901)
Dobson	Eric Dobson, *English Pronunciation 1500-1700*, 2 vols (1968)
Donne	A.J.Smith, ed., *The Complete English Poems of John Donne* (1971)
Drayton	J.W.Hebel, Kathleen Tillotson, Bernard Newdigate *et al.*, eds, *The Works of Michael Drayton*, 6 vols (1961)
Dubrow	Heather Dubrow, *Captive Victors: Shakespeare's Narrative Poems and Sonnets* (1987)

Duncan-Jones, 'Canker blooms'	Katherine Duncan-Jones, 'Deep-dyed canker blooms: botanical reference in Sonnet 54', *RES,* n.s. 46:184 (1995), 521–5
Duncan-Jones, 'Modernizing'	Katherine Duncan-Jones, 'Filling the unforgiving minute: modernizing SHAKE-SPEARES SONNETS (1609)', *EC,* 45:3 (1995), 199–207
Duncan-Jones, 'Nashe'	Katherine Duncan-Jones, 'Nashe in Newgate', *TLS,* 22 March 1996, 15
Duncan-Jones, 'Red and white'	Katherine Duncan-Jones, 'Much ado with red and white: the earliest readers of Shakespeare's *Venus and Adonis* (1593)', *RES,* n.s. 44:176 (1993), 479–501
Duncan-Jones, *Sidney*	Katherine Duncan-Jones, *Sir Philip Sidney: Courtier Poet* (1991)
Duncan-Jones, 'Sonnets called?'	Katherine Duncan-Jones, 'What are Shakespeare's sonnets called?', *EC,* 47.1 (1997), 1–12
Duncan-Jones, *'Sonnets* unauthorized?'	Katherine Duncan-Jones, 'Was the 1609 *Shake-speares Sonnets* really unauthorized?', *RES,* 34 (1983), 151–71
Duncan-Jones, *'Syren* teares'	Katherine Duncan-Jones, '"*Syren* teares": infection or enchantment in Shakespeare's Sonnet 119', *RES,* ns. 48.189 (1997), 56–60
EC	*Essays in Criticism*
Edward III	C.F.Tucker Brooke, ed., in *The Shakespeare Apocrypha,* 1908
E.E.D.-J	Mrs. E.E.Duncan-Jones, private communication
ELR	*English Literary Renaissance*
Empson	William Empson, *Seven Types of Ambiguity* (1935; rev. edn, 1953)
Evans, 'Lawes'	Willa McClung Evans, 'Lawes' version of Shakespeare's Sonnet CXVI', *PMLA,* 51 (1936), 120–2
Everett, 'Greening'	Barbara Everett, 'Shakespeare's greening', *TLS,* 8 July 1994, 11–13
Everett, 'Mrs. Shakespeare'	Barbara Everett, 'Mrs. Shakespeare', *LRB,* 8 (19 December 1986), 7–10
Farmer	Norman K.Farmer, 'Holograph revisions in two poems by Fulke Greville', *ELR,* 4 (1974), 98–110
Ferry	Anne Ferry, *All in War with Time: Love Poetry of Shakespeare, Donne, Jonson, Marvell* (1975)
Fettiplace	Hilary Spurling, ed., *Elinor Fettiplace's Receipt Book* (1986)
Foster	Donald Foster, 'Master W.H., R.I.P.', *PMLA,* 102 (1987), 42–54
Fowler	Alastair Fowler, *Triumphal Forms* (1970)
Fracastoro	Geoffrey Eastough, ed., *Fracastoro's 'Syphilis'* (Liverpool, 1984)

Fraunce   Abraham Fraunce, *The Arcadian Rhetorike* (1588), ed. Ethel Seaton (1950)

Garber   Marjorie Garber, *Vice Versa: Bisexuality and the Eroticism of Everyday Life* (1995)

Gascoigne   J.W.Cunliffe, ed., *The Works of George Gascoigne*, 2 vols (1907)

Glossary   C.T.Onions, *A Shakespeare Glossary*, rev. Robert D. Eagleson (Oxford, 1986)

Graziani   René Graziani, 'The numbering of Shakespeare's Sonnets 12, 60 and 126', *Shakespeare Quarterly*, 35 (1984), 79–82

Gurr   Andrew Gurr, 'Shakespeare's first poem: Sonnet 145', *EC*, 21 (1971), 221–6

Hanks & Hodges   P.Hanks & F.Hodges, *A Dictionary of Surnames* (1988)

Harington   N.E.McClure, ed., *The Letters and Epigrams of Sir John Harington* (1930)

Harris   Frank Harris, *The Man Shakespeare and his Tragic Story* (1909)

Henslowe Papers   R.A.Foakes, ed., *The Henslowe Papers*, 2 vols (1977)

Herbert   F.E.Hutchinson, ed., *The Works of George Herbert* (1941)

Heywood   Thomas Heywood, *Oenone and Paris* (1594), ed. J.Q.Adams (1943)

Hieatt, '*LC, Cym* and *Son*'   A.K.Hieatt, T.G.Bishop & E.A.Nicholson, ' "Lover's Complaint", *Cymbeline* and *Sonnets*', *N&Q*, 232 (1987), 219–24

Hieatt, 'When?'   A.K.Hieatt, Charles W.Hieatt & Anne Lake Prescott, 'When did Shakespeare write *Sonnets* 1609?', *SP*, 88:1 (Winter 1991), 69–109

HMC   Historical Manuscripts Commission, *Reports on Manuscripts*

Hobbs   Mary Hobbs, 'Shakespeare's Sonnet II: a "sugred sonnet"?', *N&Q*, 224 (1979), 112–13

Honigmann   E.A.J.Honigmann, 'There is a world elsewhere: William Shakespeare, businessman', in W.Habicht, D.J.Palmer & R.Pringle, eds, *Images of Shakespeare* (1988), 40–6

Hopper   Vincent F.Hopper, *Medieval Number Symbolism: Its Sources, Meaning and Influence* (New York, 1935; repr. 1969)

Hotson   Leslie Hotson, *'Shakespeare's Sonnets Dated' and Other Essays* (1949)

Hutton   James Hutton, 'Analogues of Shakespeare's Sonnets 153–4: contributions to the history of a theme', *Modern Philology*, 38 (1940–1), 385–403

Hyde, *Other Love*   H.Montgomery Hyde, *The Other Love: An Historical and Contemporary Survey of Homosexuality in Britain* (1975)

Hyde, *Trials*   H.Montgomery Hyde, *The Trials of Oscar Wilde* (New York, 1962)

Jackson, *'Complaint'*	MacD.P.Jackson, 'Shakespeare's *A Lover's Complaint:* its date and authenticity', *University of Auckland Bulletin*, 72, English Series, 13 (Auckland, 1965)
Jackson, 'Compositors'	MacD.P.Jackson, 'Punctuation and the compositors of Shakespeare's *Sonnets* (1609)', *The Library*, 5th series, 30 (1975), 9–10
Jones	Emrys Jones, ed., *The New Oxford Book of Sixteenth Century Verse* (Oxford, 1991)
Jonson	C.H.Herford & Percy Simpson, eds, *Ben Jonson*, 11 vols (Oxford, 1925–52)
Kerrigan, *Motives*	John Kerrigan, ed., *Motives of Woe: Shakespeare and 'Female Complaint': A Critical Anthology* (1991)
Knight	G.Wilson Knight, *The Mutual Flame: On Shakespeare's Sonnets and 'The Phoenix and the Turtle'* (1955)
Lacey	Robert Lacey, *Robert Earl of Essex: An Elizabethan Icarus* (1971)
Lee	Sidney Lee, *A Life of William Shakespeare* (1904)
Leishman	J.B.Leishman, *Themes and Variations in Shakespeare's Sonnets* (1961)
Lennard	John Lennard, *'But I Digress': The Exploitation of Parentheses in English Printed Verse* (1991)
Lindley	David Lindley, *The Trials of Frances Howard: Fact and Fiction at the Court of King James* (1993)
Linthicum	M.Channing Linthicum, *Costume in the Drama of Shakespeare and his Contemporaries* (1936)
LRB	*The London Review of Books*
McKerrow	R.B.McKerrow, *Introduction to Bibliography for Literary Students* (1927)
McPherson	David McPherson, 'Ben Jonson's library and marginalia', *SP*, 71 (1974), 46–7
Mahood	Molly Mahood, *Shakespeare's Wordplay* (1957)
Marlowe, *Dr Faustus*	Christopher Marlowe, *Doctor Faustus*, ed. J.D.Jump (1962)
Marlowe, *Poems*	Millar MacLure, ed., *Christopher Marlowe: The Poems* (1988)
Marotti	Arthur F.Marotti, *Manuscript, Print, and the English Renaissance* (Ithaca and London, 1995)
Martin	Peter Martin, *Edmond Malone, Shakespearean Scholar* (1995)
Marvell	H.M.Margoliouth, P.Legouis & E.E.Duncan-Jones, eds, *The Poems and Letters of Andrew Marvell* (1971)
Maxwell	J.C.Maxwell, '"Rebel Powers": Shakespeare and Daniel', *N&Q*, 212 (1967), 139
Milton, *Poems*	John Carey and Alastair Fowler, eds, *The Poems of John Milton* (New York and London, 1968)

Milton, *Prose Works*	Douglas Bush *et al.*, eds, *Complete Prose Works of John Milton*, 8 vols (New Haven and London, 1953–82)
Morgan	Paul Morgan, ' "Our Will Shakespeare" and Lope de Vega: an unrecorded contemporary document', *Shakespeare Survey*, 16 (1963), 118–20
Moryson	Fynes Moryson, *An Itinerary* (1617; Glasgow, 1907)
Muir	Kenneth Muir, *Shakespeare as Collaborator* (1960)
Murray	Peter B.Murray, 'The authorship of *The Revenger's Tragedy*', *Papers of the Bibliographical Society of America*, 56 (1962), 195–218
N&Q	*Notes and Queries*
Nashe	R.B.McKerrow, ed., *The Works of Thomas Nashe*, 5 vols, 2nd edn, ed., F.P.Wilson (1958)
Nosworthy	J.M.Nosworthy, 'All too short a date: internal evidence in Shakespeare's Sonnets', *EC*, 2 (1952), 311–24
Nowottny	Winifred Nowottny, *The Language Poets Use* (1962)
ODQ	*The Oxford Dictionary of Quotations*, 3rd edn (Oxford, 1979)
OED	*The Oxford English Dictionary*, 2nd edn (Oxford, 1989)
Ovid, *Met.*	Ovid, *Metamorphoses*
Partridge, *Bawdy*	Eric Partridge, *Shakespeare's Bawdy: A Literary and Psychological Essay and a Comprehensive Glossary*, rev. edn (1955)
Partridge, *Grammar*	A.C.Partridge, *A Substantive Grammar of Shakespeare's Nondramatic Texts* (Virginia, 1976)
Partridge, *Orthography*	A.C.Partridge, *Orthography in Shakespeare and Elizabethan Drama* (1964)
Peck	D.C.Peck, ' "News from Heaven and Hell": a defamatory narrative of the Earl of Leicester', *ELR*, 8 (1978), 141–58
Pequigney	Joseph Pequigney, *Such Is My Love: A Study of Shakespeare's Sonnets* (Chicago and London, 1985)
PMLA	*Publications of the Modern Language Association of America*
Proudfoot	Richard Proudfoot, 'The Reign of King Edward the Third (1596) and Shakespeare', *Proceedings of the British Academy*, 71 (1985), 159–85
Race	Sidney Race, 'J.P.Collier and the Dulwich Papers (cxv.33)', *N&Q*, 195 (1950), 112–47
Ralegh	A.M.C.Latham, ed., *The Poems of Sir Walter Ralegh* (1951)
RES	*Review of English Studies*
Robbins	R.H.Robbins, 'A seventeenth-century manuscript of Shakespeare's Sonnet 128', *N&Q*, 212 (1967), 137–8
Roche	T.P.Roche, *Petrarch and the English Sonnet Sequences* (New York, 1989)
Rollins	H.E.Rollins, ed., *A New Variorum Edition of Shakespeare: The Sonnets*, 2 vols (Philadelphia and London, 1944)

Rowse	A.L.Rowse, *Shakespeare's Sonnets: the Problems Solved* (1973)
RP	Richard Proudfoot, private communication
Schaar	Claes Schaar, *Elizabethan Sonnet Themes and the Dating of Shakespeare's Sonnets,* Lund Studies in English, 32 (1962)
Schmidgall	Gary Schmidgall, *Shakespeare and the Poet's Life* (Kentucky, 1990)
Schoenbaum, *Life*	Samuel Schoenbaum, *William Shakespeare: A Documentary Life* (Oxford, 1975)
Schoenbaum, *Lives*	Samuel Schoenbaum, *Shakespeare's Lives,* rev. edn (Oxford, 1991)
Schoenbaum, *Records*	Samuel Schoenbaum, *William Shakespeare: Records and Images* (Oxford, 1981)
Sedgwick	Eve Kosovsky Sedgwick, *Between Men* (New York, 1985)
Sidney, *AS*	Sir Philip Sidney, *Astrophil and Stella,* in W.A.Ringler ed., *The Poems of Sir Philip Sidney* (Oxford, 1962)
Sidney, *CS*	Sir Philip Sidney, *Certain Sonnets,* in W.A.Ringler, ed., *The Poems of Sir Philip Sidney* (Oxford, 1962)
Sidney, *NA*	V.J.Skretkowicz, ed., *The Countess of Pembroke's Arcadia (The New Arcadia)* (Oxford, 1987)
Sidney, *OA*	Jean Robertson, ed., *The Countess of Pembroke's Arcadia (The Old Arcadia)* (Oxford, 1973)
Sidney, *Poems*	W.A.Ringler, ed., *The Poems of Sir Philip Sidney* (Oxford, 1962)
Sidney, *Prose*	Katherine Duncan-Jones & J.van Dorsten, eds, *Miscellaneous Prose of Sir Philip Sidney* (Oxford, 1973)
Robert Sidney, *Poems*	P.J.Croft, ed., *Poems of Sir Robert Sidney* (1984)
Sisson	C.J.Sisson, *New Readings in Shakespeare,* 2 vols (1956)
Slater	Eliot Slater, 'Shakespeare: word links between poems and plays', *N&Q,* 220 (1975), 157–63
SP	*Studies in Philology*
Spenser, *FQ*	Edmund Spenser, *The Faerie Queene,* ed. A.C.Hamilton, rev. edn (1977)
Spenser, *Prose Works*	Rudolf Gottfried, ed., *Spenser's Prose Works* (Baltimore, 1949)
Spenser, *Shorter Poems*	W.A.Oram, ed., *The Shorter Poems of Edmund Spenser* (New Haven, 1989)
STC	A.W.Pollard & G.R.Redgrave, *A Short-title Catalogue of Books printed in England, Scotland and Ireland 1475-1640,* rev. W.A.Jackson and F.S.Ferguson, completed by Katharine F.Pantzer, 3 vols (1989–91)
Stone	Donald Stone, *Ronsard's Sonnet Cycles: A Study in Tone and Vision* (New Haven and London, 1966)
Suckling, *Plays*	L.A.Beaurline, ed., *The Works of Sir John Suckling: The Plays* (1971)

Taylor, 'Some *MSS*'	Gary Taylor, 'Some manuscripts of Shakespeare's Sonnets', *Bulletin of the John Rylands Library*, 68 (1985–6), 210–46
Tennyson	Christopher Ricks, ed., *The Poems of Tennyson*, 2nd edn (Harlow, 1987)
Tilley	Morris Palmer Tilley, *A Dictionary of the Proverbs in England in the Sixteenth and Seventeenth Centuries* (Ann Arbor, 1950)
TLS	*The Times Literary Supplement*
TxC	Stanley Wells & Gary Taylor, with John Jowett & William Montgomery, *William Shakespeare: A Textual Companion* (Oxford, 1987)
Ungerer	Gustav Ungerer, *A Spaniard in Elizabethan England: The Correspondence of Antonio Perez's Exile*, 2 vols (1975)
Vendler	Helen Vendler, 'Reading stage by stage: Shakespeare's Sonnets', in Russ McDonald, ed., *Shakespeare Reread: The Texts in New Contexts* (Ithaca and London, 1994), 23–41
Weever	John Weever, *Epigrammes* (1599), ed. E.A.J.Honigmann, in *John Weever* (1987)
Whitlock	Baird W.Whitlock, *John Hoskyns, Serjeant-at-Law* (Washington, 1982)
Wilde, *Letters*	Rupert Hart-Davis, ed., *The Letters of Oscar Wilde* (1962)
Wilde, 'W.H.'	Oscar Wilde, 'The Portrait of Master W.H.', *Blackwood's Edinburgh Magazine*, July 1889
Wiles	David Wiles, *Shakespeare's Almanac: 'A Midsummer Night's Dream', Marriage and the Elizabethan Calendar* (1993)
Wilson	F.P.Wilson, *The Plague in Shakespeare's London* (1927)
Wyatt	R.A.Rebholz, ed., *Poems of Sir Thomas Wyatt* (1978)

INDEX

477

FIRST LINE INDEX